Cathedral of St. Peter

Rockford, Illinois

Dear Cathedral of St. Peter Parishioners:

"THOU ART PETER, AND UPON THIS ROCK I WILL BUILD MY CHURCH." These words, which greet all who enter the Cathedral, were spoken by Jesus to His friend Peter nearly 2000 years ago. Today we are the beneficiaries of Peter's faith and Jesus' grace and mercy. Our faith has been passed on to us through centuries of human history thanks to the love and sacrifices of those who have gone before us.

This year the Rockford Diocese marks an incredible milestone in its history thanks to the dedication and faithfulness of so many: 100 years as a Diocese. This centennial history book is one component of the celebration which will hopefully help us to appreciate the goodness of God poured out on our Diocese, our Parishes and our families.

In this centennial year we are especially privileged to be members of the Cathedral Parish. We have a rich history of our own to celebrate and we continue to play a central role in the Diocese as the future unfolds before us; today becoming tomorrow's history.

May we always thank God for His blessings and continue to ask His guidance and protection in all that the future holds. As the Cathedral of St. Peter Parish family we are grateful for our past and filled with hope for our future. May God bless you all!

Yours in Christ,

Fr. Kenneth P. Wasilewski, S.T.L., Rector

History of the Diocese of

Rockford

Acknowledgements

This history of the first 100 years of the Rockford Diocese is only possible because of the many parishes
and individuals who have contributed their stories, photographs and other historical material.
It would be a futile effort to try and list every contribution,
for certainly someone would unintentionally be forgotten.
For those who have helped in so many ways, thank you very much.

AUTHORS
Msgr. David Kagan
Diocesan history

Laurine M. Easton
William F. Easton
Parish histories

EDITORS
Dr. Michael Cieslak
Penny Wiegert

RESEARCH
Coni Schwandt
Head researcher
Anne Hayes
Assistant

PHOTO RESTORATION
Dr. Michael Cieslak
Coni Schwandt

COVER DESIGN
Dan Lauder

PUBLISHER
Éditions du Signe
B.P. 94 – 67038 Strasbourg – Cedex 2 – France
Tel (+33) 388 789 191
Fax (+33) 388 789 199
info@editionsdusigne.fr

PUBLISHING DIRECTOR
Christian Riehl

DIRECTOR OF PUBLICATION
Joëlle Bernhard

PUBLISHING ASSISTANT
Marc de Jong

DESIGN AND LAYOUT
Juliette Roussel

PHOTOGRAPHY
John Glover
Dr. Michael Cieslak

Photoengraving
Atelier du Signe - 107207

© Éditions du Signe 2007
ISBN 13: 978-2-7468-1816-3

◆ FRONT COVER: The Circular window depicting the Holy Spirit was in the private chapel of Bishop Muldoon at his residence, 1704 National Avenue, Rockford. Though the chapel of Rockford's first Bishop has long been disassembled, the stained glass window still exists today in the house.
◆ BACK COVER: St. Peter Cathedral, two views from the choir loft. The stained glass window depicts the fifth Glorious Mystery of the Rosary, the coronation of the Blessed Virgin Mary in heaven.

Table of Contents

Foreword

On the occasion of the Golden Jubilee of the Diocese of Rockford, The Most Reverend Loras T. Lane, sixth Bishop of Rockford, wrote of the Diocese then, and set it on its future course. He said: "The historical account of this area of God's vineyard gives clear evidence that the clergy and people, in cooperation with their Bishops, have endeavored to give to Christ His rightful place in all things."

No matter what the age of mankind, the living history of the Catholic Church has as its *modus operandi* the faithful striving to always give to Christ the Lord His "rightful place in all things." This history is no abstract idea. It is written by the living faith, hope and charity of each and every person who belongs to Christ in His Church.

As such, there cannot be written a complete or final history of the Church. What we can and must do here is record for ourselves and those who will come after us this wonderful narration of what has been bequeathed to us — the growth and flowering of this one hundred year old portion of the vineyard of the Lord. This is a priceless gift which has been appreciated and used continuously by the faith and good works of the bishops, priests, religious and laity of the Diocese of Rockford for a century.

This volume very clearly demonstrates that the living and lived faith of our predecessors has borne much good fruit. The continued vitality of our Diocesan Church throughout these one hundred years is attested to by the steady increase in the numbers of Catholic institutions of service. However wonderful all of this has been and, we pray, will continue to be, the greatest measure of the vitality of our Diocese in these one hundred years has been and is the constant devotion to Almighty God and His Church by our laity, religious and clergy.

All of us are grateful to the authors of this next history of the Diocese of Rockford. They have offered us an inspiring look back at our Catholic roots and have provided us with a glimpse of what faith in action always accomplishes with God's grace.

Laudetur Iesus Christus!
(Praised be Jesus Christ!)

+ Thomas G. Doran

Bishop of Rockford

The Catholic Church

in the United States

Several well written histories of the United States of America include references to the presence of Roman Catholics from the earliest days of colonization. Catholics were certainly well represented in the Continental Army of the American Revolution, as well as in the membership of those whom we have come to know as the Founding Fathers. In particular, Charles Carroll and his cousin, the Reverend John Carroll, played prominent roles in the days of the Revolution and thereafter as our government was taking shape.

In 1784 Father John Carroll was named by the Holy See to be the superior of the American Catholic missions which had about 25 priests distributed over the former colonies. Just five short years later, Pope Pius VI erected the first diocese in the United States at Baltimore, Maryland, and named the Reverend John Carroll, its first bishop. Carroll was consecrated early in 1790 in England and then returned to begin what would be a fruitful but

◆ **The 1896-97 class of St. James School, Rockford.**

difficult episcopacy. In 1793, the Holy See erected the Diocese of Louisiana and the Two Floridas, which had not yet been entirely incorporated into the territory of the United States.

◆ **The original St. James Church, 1853, the first Catholic Church in the city of Rockford.**

As further evidence of the rapid growth of Catholicism in the United States, Pope Pius VII on April 8, 1808, divided the nation's original Diocese of Baltimore and erected four new suffragan sees of Boston, New York, Philadelphia, and the only diocese west of the Allegheny Mountains at Bardstown, Kentucky.

It is the Diocese of Bardstown (later Louisville) which is of particular interest since several dioceses later erected by the Holy See, including Rockford, can trace their origins to this important Catholic community on what was considered to be the "frontier," so word about Bardstown and its bishop is useful. Benedict Joseph Flaget (1763-1850), a French-born Sulpician priest, was appointed Bardstown's first bishop. Bishop Flaget, having immigrated to the United States in 1792, was consecrated as Bishop of Bardstown by Archbishop John Carroll on November 4, 1810. However, since Bishop Flaget was literally penniless, he was not able to set out from Baltimore until May 11, 1811. Bishop Flaget left Baltimore with three priests, three seminarians and three servants. They traveled overland to Pittsburgh where, on May 22, they chartered a flat-boat for the journey on the Ohio River, arriving 13 days later on June 4 at Louisville. Again, Bishop Flaget and his entourage traveled overland to Bardstown, arriving there on June 9 that year to be met by his Vicar General, Father Badin and most of his Catholic people. When he arrived at Bardstown, there was no church.

Before returning to the Diocese of Bardstown, we should consider now one of the great missionaries to the United States of America and his zealous work in the territory that would eventually become the Rockford Diocese.

The Reverend Samuel C. Mazzuchelli, O.P. (1806-1864), born in Milan, Italy, came to the United States in 1828 and was sent by his superior from St. Louis into what had been a large tract of federal land called the Northwest Territory. Father Mazzuchelli's zeal for souls was matched by his tireless efforts to not only bring the faith to the region,

◆ **The young Father Samuel C. Mazzuchelli.**

but to root it firmly in the territory. For almost 40 years he labored with great effectiveness in Illinois, Iowa and Wisconsin, establishing parishes and missions, founding a teaching order of Dominican Sisters at Sinsinawa Mound, and building a bishop's residence in Dubuque and designing the first capitol at Iowa City. He served as the chaplain to the first territorial legislature of Wisconsin. Of note for the Rockford Diocese is that Father Mazzuchelli founded St. Michael Parish, Galena, and had a hand in the design of the parish church as well as the Galena courthouse. His influence in that part of Illinois and this diocese is still evident to this day.

The Northwest Territory and its most important western section, included New France from which Illinois would be carved and where the Diocese of Chicago would be erected and encompass the entire state. The territory was obtained by the United States in 1779 as a result of George Rogers Clark capturing it during the American Revolution. The Northwest Ordinance of 1787 provided for the creation of as many as five states in a territory originally planned by Thomas

Jefferson in 1784. The territory was east of the Mississippi River and between the Ohio River and the Great Lakes. The Northwest Ordinance established the boundaries of the proposed states, excluded slavery and required that there be 6,900 "stable" residents before statehood. In time, the states of Ohio, Indiana, Illinois, Michigan and Wisconsin were organized within the limits of the Northwest Territory.

Illinois was admitted to the Union as the 21st State on December 3, 1818.

As growth both in the territories and in the Catholic populations continued, it became necessary for Pope Gregory XVI to erect the Diocese of Vincennes, Indiana in 1834. This new diocese was created from the Diocese of Bardstown which, within seven years, would be transferred to the much larger City of Louisville, Kentucky in 1841. The new Diocese of Vincennes encompassed the entire State of Indiana and a large eastern portion of the State of Illinois.

◆ **1856 view of Galena, Illinois.**

A non-religious development at this time had one of the most significant impacts on both the future of the Church in the Midwest as well as on the development of the United States and its economy. This development was the invention of the "self-polishing" plow by a transplanted Vermonter by the name of John Deere. A blacksmith by trade, Deere set up his homestead and shop in the small Rock River settlement of Grand Detour, Illinois, in 1836. He has been referred to as an enterprising and innovative individual and proved that by coming to the aid of the farmers of his era. Farmers had complained to him of their great difficulties in plowing and cultivating the rich but very thick and sticky soil. Deere, experimenting with a used saw blade, forged a new plow that was durable, "self-polishing" and would easily shed the thick Midwestern soil. In 1837, his "self-polishing" plow worked and quickly grew in popularity and use. This, perhaps more than any other technological advance, opened the Midwestern prairie and plains to development and greater opportunities so alluring to immigrants, many of whom were Roman Catholics of European origin.

The State of Illinois

and the Diocese of Chicago

In the decade of the 1840's approximately 700,000 Catholic immigrants arrived in the United States, most entering at New York or Boston, but also many at New Orleans. Not all settled in the more developed eastern states. The rapidly developing states of the Midwest drew many thousands to work on farms, the canals and railroads.

On November 28, 1843, the portion of the Diocese of Vincennes in eastern Illinois was erected as the new Diocese of Chicago, also taking territory from the Diocese of St. Louis. In effect, the Diocese of Chicago encompassed the entire State of Illinois, some 55, 947 square miles. The second bishop of Chicago, James O. Van de Velde, S.J., (1795-1855) noted in a letter to the Vatican to the Propaganda Fide in December 1849, that he had toured the entire Diocese, i.e., the State, and that there were approximately 80,000 Catholics being served by 57 priests.

Bishop Van de Velde noted that his dilemma was trying to provide sufficient priests, churches and schools to meet the steadily increasing Catholic immigrant population since, in the main, they were very poor. Most Catholic historians state that this situation was typical of most dioceses in the Midwest at this time.

Within ten years of the establishment of the Diocese of Chicago, a second diocese was erected in the State of Illinois. Pope Pius IX established the Diocese of Springfield on July 29, 1853. The two ecclesiastical territories tended to the spiritual and temporal welfare of the Catholic people of Illinois. Both dioceses, although mainly rural and agricultural and largely immigrant, were still affected by the beginnings of industry and the changes it brought with it. The development of river shipping, the building of a canal system, and the coming of the railroads, along with coal and lead mining, would do much to increase the population of these two dioceses and require tremendous efforts by the bishops, priests and religious in providing for their people's spiritual, educational and temporal well-being.

The outbreak of hostilities between the North and the South was *the* preoccupation of all Americans for the first half of the decade of the 1860's. However, with peace restored the growth and development of the United States was paralleled by an even more dramatic growth and development in the Catholic Church in the United States, especially in Illinois.

Rt. Rev. J. O. Van De Velde, D.D.
Second Bishop 1849-1853

◆ **Bishop James O. Van de Velde, second bishop of Chicago.**

◆ **St. Vincent Orphanage, Freeport, 1896.**

A matter of some note, at this time was the elevation of the Diocese of Chicago to the status of an Archdiocese on September 10, 1880, and the creation of the Province of Chicago, with The Most Reverend Patrick A. Feehan, the first Archbishop and Metropolitan.

In the 12 years following the surrender at Appomattox, the Catholic population in the Dioceses of Chicago and Springfield grew to such an extent that Pope Pius IX erected the Diocese of Peoria on May 1, 1877, taking territory from the two existing dioceses in Illinois. A brief nine and one-half years later, Pope Leo XIII erected the Diocese of Belleville on January 7, 1887, which encompassed the entire southern portion of the State of Illinois.

With the rapid growth and expansion taking place across the United States in the three and one-half decades between the end of the American Civil War and the dawn of the Twentieth Century, an unprecedented wave of immigration from southern and eastern Europe began. By far, the majority of these immigrants were Catholics either of the Latin Rite or one of the Eastern Rites in union with the Holy See. Where those newer immigrants settled is of importance to us since they were more inclined to live and seek work in the cities. The two cities most notably settled by this influx of immigrants were New York and Chicago, making them the largest and second largest cities in the United States at the turn of the century.

◆ **St. Mary, Elgin, 1902 First Communion.**

The Dawn

of the 20ᵗʰ Century

While increased numbers of Catholics alone are not a gauge of the Church's progress, they are an indicator of it and a definite consideration in the creation of new dioceses and new parishes. At the beginning of the 20ᵗʰ Century the best estimate of the Catholic population for the United States was 12,041,000. This was a remarkable phenomenon considering that there were, at most, 35,000 Catholics in the United States in 1789, the year the Diocese of Baltimore was established and Father John Carroll named its first bishop.

The territory within the Archdiocese of Chicago, which would become the fifth diocese erected in the State of Illinois, that is, Rockford, was witnessing the evident increase in Catholic population characteristic of the United States as a whole.

A date not well known to Catholics in the United States but one of great importance, and one which marks a watershed for the Catholic Church in the United States was June 29, 1908. It was on this date that Pope Pius X issued the apostolic constitution *Sapienti consilio,* declaring that the Church in the United States had been removed from the jurisdiction of the Sacred Congregation *de Propaganda Fide* and had been placed on a basis of equality with other churches such as France, Spain, Italy and Germany. By this act, the United States was no longer considered by the Holy See to be a mission land or territory. The Catholic Church in the United States of America had come of age!

◆ **Locations of diocesan parishes and missions on September 23, 1908. Kendall County was originally part of the Rockford Diocese but was given to the newly founded Joliet Diocese in 1948.**

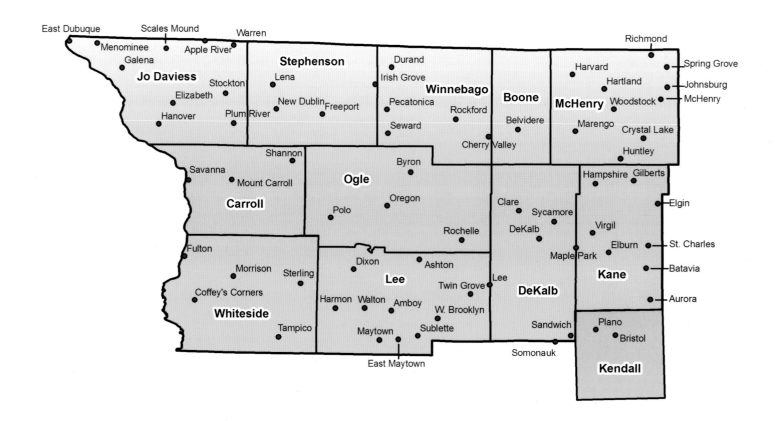

The Diocese of Rockford

On September 23, 1908, Pope Pius X (a future saint) erected the Diocese of Rockford, Illinois, placing it under the patronage of the Immaculate Conception. The territory of the fifth diocese in the State of Illinois and the Province of Chicago was comprised of 12 counties in the Northwestern part of the State. Those counties were: McHenry, Kane, Kendall, DeKalb, Boone, Winnebago, Ogle, Stephenson, Lee, Jo Davies, Carroll and Whiteside. The western boundary of the new diocese was the Mississippi River, the northern boundary the Illinois-Wisconsin state line, the eastern boundary was the remaining counties of the Archdiocese of Chicago, and the southern boundary the northernmost counties of the Diocese of Peoria. The Diocese of Rockford encompassed 6,867 square miles. According to the 2006 Catholic Directory, the Diocese of Rockford was the first diocese erected in the United States of America after Pope St. Pius X issued the apostolic constitution *Sapienti consilio*.

The City of Rockford was established by Rome as the See City of the new Diocese and St. James Parish, the older of the two parishes in the City of Rockford, was designated by the Holy See as the Pro-Cathedral for the new Diocese.

Five days after the creation of the Diocese, on September 28, 1908, Pope Pius X, named The Most Reverend Peter James Muldoon, D.D., the first Bishop of the Diocese of Rockford. Born on October 10, 1862, in Columbia, California, Bishop Muldoon had been serving the Archdiocese of Chicago since his ordination to the priesthood on December 18, 1886. In November 1888, the then Father Muldoon was appointed the Chancellor of the Archdiocese of Chicago and Secretary to Archbishop Feehan (1880-1902). In 1895 he was named the first Pastor of St. Charles Borromeo Parish, Chicago, and on July 25, 1901, Father Muldoon was appointed Auxiliary Bishop of Chicago and Vicar General to Archbishop Feehan.

Bishop Muldoon was installed at the Pro-Cathedral of St. James, Rockford, on December 15, 1908, by the Archbishop of Chicago, James E. Quigley, D.D. Bishop Muldoon assumed his responsibilities and was ably assisted and supported by all of his priests. In particular, Bishop Muldoon appointed the Right Reverend Monsignor James J. Bennett, Pastor of St. Mary Parish, Sterling, Illinois, the first Vicar General of the Diocese of

◆ **Bishop Peter J. Muldoon outside the Coliseum in Chicago, 1908.**

Rockford, and appointed The Reverend Thomas Finn, Rector of the Pro-Cathedral, the first Chancellor of the Diocese of Rockford as well as his personal secretary.

At the time of the establishment of the Diocese of Rockford, the Catholic population stood at about 50,000 souls with 64 diocesan priests serving them in 12 counties in a total of 61 parishes (having a resident priest) and another seventeen missions (church with no priest in residence) and nine stations (no church and no resident priest, but Catholics were served from a neighboring parish). Of special note and indicative of the deep roots of Catholicism in the new Diocese is the fact that 22 of the 61 parishes and three of the 17 missions were settled and active prior to the American Civil War.

◆ **Father Thomas Finn, the first Chancellor of the Rockford Diocese.**

The Muldoon Years

1908-1927

It is a fact that the 19 years of Bishop Muldoon's episcopate were full and active from start to finish. What Bishop Muldoon either initiated or further developed in the areas of Catholic education, Catholic social and charitable action, the creation of new parishes, the expansion of existing parishes, Catholic health care and the support and furtherance of Catholic life in general, set the standard for all of his successors. Bishop Muldoon gave his full attention and energy to every aspect of his diocese and its further increase and development as the Catholic Church of Northwestern Illinois.

Much more will be said in another section of this history about each of the parishes and missions of the Diocese, but it is noteworthy that Bishop Muldoon was responsible for the establishment of 20 parishes and missions during his years as bishop. The parishes and missions were established in almost every sector of the Diocese of Rockford, in response to the continued growth of the Catholic population and the advance of the Catholic faith. Bishop Muldoon established three more parishes in the City of Aurora, one parish at Cary, one parish in Dundee and a mission in Erie. He erected two more parishes in the City of Freeport, one parish each in Geneva, Genoa, Hanover, Prophetstown, Sandwich and South Beloit. In the City of Rockford, Bishop Muldoon created five more parishes and a mission in Davis Junction served by a Rockford parish during his episcopate.

An element in the Catholic life of any diocese is the provision for the burial of Catholics in their own Catholic cemeteries. As is the usual case, many parishes maintain their own cemeteries for the Catholic people of that parish; however, since not all parishes had a cemetery, diocesan cemeteries were also needed for the burial of Catholics. Prior to the erection of the Diocese of Rockford, there were three diocesan cemeteries in the territory which would become the Diocese. These cemeteries are still in use today: Mount Olivet in Aurora, Mount Hope in Elgin and St. Mary-St. James in Rockford. In time, two more diocesan cemeteries would be created to accommodate the steadily growing Catholic population of the diocese.

In addition to the creation of parishes and the initiation of other apostolates, the need for a sufficient number of priests to serve in the new diocese was apparent. In these first years it was Bishop Muldoon himself who promoted vocations and sought the assistance of other bishops willing to release priests to serve in the Diocese of Rockford. Charles F. Conley was the first priest to be ordained for the new Diocese of

◆ **Bishop Peter J. Muldoon, founding bishop of the Rockford Diocese. Motto: For God and for country.**

◆ **Father Charles F. Conley, first priest ordained for the Rockford Diocese.**

Rockford. He studied in Rome and was ordained there on April 10, 1909, taking up his first assignment as assistant at St. Mary Parish, Elgin, in 1909.

As Auxiliary Bishop of Chicago, Bishop Muldoon had ordained some of the priests who later became priests of Rockford. However, the first priests ordained for the new diocese by Bishop Muldoon as the first Bishop of Rockford were Benno A. Hildebrand and Joseph M. Lonergan on June 27, 1909, Father Lonergan being the first native son of the new diocese to be ordained. Father Charles Schnueckel, Pastor of St. Nicholas Parish, Aurora, since 1880, was the first priest of the Diocese of Rockford to die on October 14, 1908. Among the many reasons Bishop Muldoon was loved and respected by the priests of the Diocese was his solicitude for their spiritual welfare. The summer of 1910 marked the first of the annual priest retreats arranged by Bishop Muldoon which he attended. The retreats were held for many years at St. Bede's Benedictine Abbey in Peru, Illinois.

CATHOLIC EDUCATION

Bishop Muldoon's concern for the Catholic education of the faithful was manifested consistently during his entire episcopate. As early as September 1910, Bishop Muldoon saw to it that first year Catholic high school education began in the See City in a make-shift set of classrooms in the hall of St. James parochial school. According to Father Cornelius J. Kirkfleet, O.Praem. (first diocesan historian), classes began with twenty pupils and were taught by three Sinsinawa Dominican Sisters, who were staffing the parochial school, and Father John J. Flanagan, Vice-Chancellor and Bishop's Secretary. By the following September, 50 pupils were enrolled in the first two years of what was then

◆ **Aurora Area priests, circa 1908: Fathers Charles Schnueckel (St. Nicholas pastor), Leon M. Linden (OLGC pastor), and Alfred A. Heinzler (St. Nicholas assistant).**

referred to as the Central Catholic High School of Rockford. Two courses of study were taught: a four-year classical course, and a two-year commercial course; in June 1912, five young women graduated from the latter course of studies. So popular was this Catholic school that Bishop Muldoon was able to purchase from the Board of Education of the City of Rockford the Ellis School property at the corner of West State and Stanley Streets.

As purchased, this former public grade school was not large enough to accommodate the ever-growing number of Catholic children being enrolled. Construction to enlarge and double the school's size was begun in June 1912, as thus, the third year began again at St. James with 87 pupils. The new high school opened with great anticipation and was dedicated as St. Thomas High School on November 9, 1912. By September 1913, 90 pupils were enrolled. Each successive year the enrollment continued a steady increase with 150 students registered by September 1918.

Bishop Muldoon's foresight in the area of Catholic education was not limited to his firm support for parish grade schools (almost every parish he established had a parochial school attached), as is attested by St. Thomas High School. In September 1921, he dedicated the St. Thomas Business "College" to augment the excellent education offered at the high school. Thus, all enrolled in the commercial course of studies attended the newly purchased and renovated Coliseum next to the high school and the high school was able to be used exclusively for the four-year classical course of studies.

The year 1923 also proved to be a very productive time for Bishop Muldoon and his plan to develop Catholic secondary education. Three more Catholic high schools were opened under his direct encouragement and supervision and the plans for a fourth high school were put in motion. Based on the success of St. Thomas High School in Rockford, Bishop Muldoon met with the pastors and trustees of the Freeport parishes in July 1923, to organize what would be called The Catholic Community High School of Freeport, eventually known as Aquin High School. On September 1, 1923, the new Catholic high school opened with 35 pupils under the tutelage of the Dominican Sisters of Sinsinawa, Wisconsin. St. Mary Parish, Sterling, and St. Mary Parish, Woodstock, with the firm encouragement and support of Bishop Muldoon, opened high schools in the Autumn of 1923 to serve the growing numbers of Catholic pupils graduating from the parish grade schools.

◆ **At the 1910 priest retreat, Bishop Muldoon with diocesan priests and the retreat master, dressed in white.**

◆ **The first graduating class in 1914 of the coeducational St. Thomas High School, Rockford.**

In October 1923, Bishop Muldoon met with the pastors of the Aurora parishes for the purpose of establishing a Catholic high school. By June 9, 1924, all plans had been finalized, and work was begun at the Lake Street site and the School Sisters of St. Francis, Milwaukee, were engaged by Bishop Muldoon to administer the new school which would be named Aurora Community High School. Due to a change in the original plans of Bishop Muldoon and the Aurora pastors, separate high schools for boys and girls were constructed and opened in 1926 and 1927 - Madonna High School for girls in 1926 and The Fox River Valley Catholic High School for boys in 1927. Madonna was administered by the

◆ **Sewing class at Madonna High School, Aurora, in the 1920s.**

School Sisters of St. Francis and the boys school was administered by the Augustinian Fathers.

Perhaps less well-known to the Catholics of this age but very well-known and esteemed in the earliest days of the Rockford Diocese was Mt. St. Mary Academy in St. Charles, Illinois. When the Farnsworth estate located in St. Charles and owned by the Caldwell family became available in 1907, the Pastor of St. Patrick Parish contacted the Mother General of the Sisters of St. Dominic of Adrian, Michigan. The property was found to be ideal for

their purposes, and was purchased for $15,000, The Sisters took possession of it on August 15, 1907, and one month later, opened it as an all girls academy for boarders as well as a parochial day school. The day school was discontinued in 1910 but the academy quickly expanded both in physical facilities and in the numbers of young ladies enrolled. Bishop Muldoon approved several more expansions for Mt. St. Mary Academy which had consistent enrollments of more than 200 pupils for many years.

CATHOLIC ACTION

What might be termed today as "social service," was referred to as "Catholic action" in Bishop Muldoon's day but was something every Catholic would understand. It meant that the Catholic Church offered charity to the poor and less fortunate in a physical manner, such as orphanages, the distribution of clothing, monetary assistance to widows and children, providing for the care of the aged and providing the means for immigrants to settle in the United States.

Bishop Muldoon came to his new diocese with a wealth of experience in this area of the Church's apostolate. He was well-known and well-regarded for his active organization and care for the poor, the sick and the immigrant, during his years as priest

◆ **Mount St. Mary Academy, St. Charles.**

◆ St. Elizabeth Community Center, Rockford, current building and former building, used until the 1970s.

and Auxiliary Bishop in Chicago. Bishop Muldoon continued and increased his efforts in this fertile field of the apostolate as Bishop of Rockford. In fact a separate volume could be devoted to just this one aspect of Bishop Muldoon's episcopate in the Diocese of Rockford. It is hoped that his legacy will inspire the interested reader to take a closer look at the charitable institutions and organizations he created or expanded.

In the City of Rockford Bishop Muldoon formed a group of devoted Catholic women to assist him in the service of the poor and immigrants continuing to settle here. The Catholic Woman's League was the first Catholic lay organization Bishop Muldoon initiated, which soon afterward, established a social center in Rockford in September 1911. From its humble beginnings this center quickly grew to serve the many physical and educational needs of a large and varied group of people. By the end of 1912, the center moved to its current and permanent location on South Main Street and was formally dedicated as St. Elizabeth Social Center. The services of St. Elizabeth continued and in September 1921, the administration of St. Elizabeth's was handed on to the religious community of women called the Missionary Servants of the Most Blessed Trinity.

On May 15, 1911, Bishop Muldoon purchased St. Vincent's Orphan Asylum in Freeport, from the Franciscan Sisters of the Sacred Heart. The Pastor of St. Joseph Parish, the Reverend Monsignor Clemens Kalvelage, was most influential in the establishment of the Catholic institution, which opened on March 15, 1896. Bishop Muldoon greatly developed the Catholic apostolate and enhanced the physical facility by transferring it to its present location and building a new asylum which was dedicated on October 2, 1912. With the new building now used exclusively for orphans, the older buildings were devoted to the care of the aged and infirm.

Of special note in the diocese's history is the establishment of Mooseheart on July 22, 1913, on 1,000 acres of land approximately five miles north of the City of Aurora near the Fox River. It was developed as a residential vocational school and home for dependent children of the Loyal Order of the Moose, and their mothers. From the earliest days there was a Catholic element to the Mooseheart population as the children and their mothers used a special trolley car to attend Mass at Holy Angels Parish, Aurora. Bishop Muldoon had such an interest in Mooseheart that he named a resident chaplain for the facility. Father John J. Laffey took this post on April 28, 1919.

CATHOLIC HOSPITALS

Several Catholic hospitals in the Diocese of Rockford pre-dated the establishment of the Diocese itself and introduced to the Catholic people and the new Diocese different religious orders of women who have made tremendous contributions to Catholic healthcare ever since. Several Catholic hospitals grew and expanded during Bishop Muldoon's time and a few more Catholic hospitals opened during his episcopacy.

St. Anthony Hospital in Rockford, founded in 1899, by the Sisters of the Third Order of St. Francis (Peoria) and the institution experienced significant growth under Bishop Muldoon with his active encouragement. The very same occurred in Aurora when St. Charles Hospital, opened in February 1900, under the administration of the Franciscan Sisters of the Sacred Heart. Bishop Muldoon, as Auxiliary Bishop of Chicago, dedicated this hospital in the latter part of 1902. The hospital was enlarged in 1914; a separate maternity hospital was built in 1923 as well as a nursing school.

A second Catholic hospital opened in Aurora in March 1911, under the care of the Sisters of Mercy and was dedicated to St. Joseph. It quickly expanded with Bishop Muldoon's permission and support first, in 1912, and again in 1919 when a separate sanitarium was developed and became the well-known and well-regarded Mercyville Sanitarium. The same Sisters of Mercy were entrusted with the staffing of St. Mary Hospital, DeKalb, which was dedicated by Bishop Muldoon on October 19, 1922. Unlike the aforementioned hospitals, St. Mary's was a further development of the parish of the same name and patronage.

Like several of the other Catholic hospitals in the Diocese of Rockford, St. Joseph Hospital in Belvidere was established on March 19, 1900, by the Sisters of St. Joseph from Concordia, Kansas. That same year two of the sisters went to Elgin and asked permission of the Pastor of St. Joseph Parish to solicit funds for a Belvidere hospital. This led to the sisters purchasing property in Elgin but, due to various obstacles, the Sisters of St. Joseph transferred their Elgin holdings in early 1902, to the Franciscan Sisters of Joliet who opened St. Joseph Hospital in Elgin on March 31, 1902.

St. Francis Hospital in Freeport had been established seven years before the St. Vincent Orphan Asylum by the same far-sighted Monsignor Kalvelage. The hospital was founded in 1889 and dedicated on February 12, 1890. Two days later the first patient was admitted. This hospital was under the administration of the Franciscan Sisters of the Sacred Heart.

◆ **St. Anthony Hospital, Rockford, 1903.**

◆ **St. Francis Hospital, Freeport, circa 1921.**

Religious Communities

Several communities of women religious were present and active in the Diocese of Rockford prior to and at the time of its creation in September 1908. These religious women served in hospitals and schools with great devotion and success. Bishop Muldoon gave them his support and encouraged them to expand their good works. Besides those orders of religious women already mentioned, several other communities were also at work in the territory of the new Diocese of Rockford.

The School Sisters of Notre Dame were at St. Mary School, Galena since 1866; the Dominican Sisters of Sinsinawa were at St. Mary School, Freeport, since 1871; the School Sisters of St. Francis had been at Annunciation School, Aurora, since 1879; the Franciscan Sisters of the Holy Family were at Nativity of the Blessed Virgin Mary School, Menominee, from 1881-1923; the Congregation of the Third Order of St. Francis of Mary Immaculate were at St. Joseph School, Freeport, since 1883; the Sisters of Providence were at St. Mary School, Aurora, from 1902; and the Sisters of St. Francis of Assisi were at St. John the Baptist School, Johnsburg, since 1903.

Realizing the great task which lay ahead for him and for all the Catholic people of the new Diocese of Rockford, Bishop Muldoon desired to have a community of contemplatives who would sustain, with their prayers and penances, all of the works and the welfare of the Church in this territory of Rockford.

◆ **Sister Oswina (Anna Artman) of St. Mary, Elizabeth, circa 1890.**

◆ **Father F.X. Chouinard, C.S.V., pastor of Sacred Heart Parish, Aurora, circa 1880.**

All of his efforts bore good fruit when Mother Mary Theresa, Abbess of the Poor Clares of Cleveland, Ohio, sent five nuns to Rockford in March 1916 to begin what is now a 91-year blessing for the Diocese of Rockford. In April 1916, the small Poor Clare community bought a house on Avon Street in Rockford, making certain changes to accommodate the cloister. On the feast of St. Clare in August 1916, Bishop Muldoon blessed and dedicated the home under the title of Corpus Christi Monastery.

Evidence of the blessings bestowed on the Diocese through the prayers and penances of the Poor Clares are catalogued throughout this work. God's blessings were bestowed on them as well through increased vocations. By the winter of 1919-1920, the Poor Clares had outgrown their first monastery. Through the diligent efforts of Bishop Muldoon and other friends of the nuns, when the Broughton Sanitarium came up for sale, the Poor Clares were able to purchase the 12-acre site on South Main Street. On March 1, 1920, the community moved to its new and current location, and Bishop Muldoon dedicated the second Corpus Christi Monastery and its basement chapel that same year. A further indication of Bishop Muldoon's solicitude for the Poor Clares, and an indicator of their own great benefit to the entire Diocese was the appointment of Father William A. O'Rourke, the Pastor of St. Mary Parish, Polo, as the first permanent Chaplain for Corpus Christi Monastery on May 8, 1921.

◆ **Broughton Sanitarium, circa 1920, used by the Poor Clares as their first monastery on the South Main Street site.**

◆ **Sinsinawa Dominicans, circa 1942.**

Bishop Muldoon continued his staunch support of the Catholic school system by inviting more religious orders of women to the Rockford Diocese to staff the schools of the many parishes he was establishing.

The Italian Missionary Franciscan Sisters of the Immaculate Conception were invited to the Diocese of Rockford in 1910 to staff the school at St. Anthony of Padua Parish, Rockford, which had been erected as an Italian national parish. The Dominican Sisters of Springfield in Illinois were asked by Bishop Muldoon to take charge of Holy Angels Parish School in Aurora in 1911, and they also began teaching at the parish schools in Cary and Crystal Lake in 1927.

The Sisters of Loretto at the Foot of the Cross from Denver, Colorado, were invited to staff St. Mary Parish School, Sterling, in 1912, and in 1915 they also took charge of the Catholic Community High School in Sterling. In 1922 they were asked to staff the newly opened St. Peter Parish School in Rockford. In 1917, the Holy Cross Sisters from Notre Dame, Indiana, were invited to staff the newly built St. Mary Parish School in Woodstock.

One religious order of men entered the Diocese of Rockford during the episcopate of Bishop

Muldoon. In 1923, Father J. Dicks, M.S.C., sought and was given permission to establish "a foundation in the Diocese of Rockford for the training of young men in the United States for home and foreign mission work." In mid-1924 the Missionaries of the Sacred Heart purchased property in Aurora for their headquarters and, at the urging of Bishop Muldoon, they also purchased a farm of some 40 acres south of the Village of Geneva. The first Mass was offered there on December 8, 1925, and shortly thereafter the first three seminarians arrived. The solemn dedication of the seminary took place on the Feast of the Sacred Heart, May 31, 1926. Thanks to Bishop Muldoon's interest in the Church's universal mission, the work of the Missionaries of the Sacred Heart in the Diocese of Rockford continues today.

THE FIRST SYNOD OF THE DIOCESE OF ROCKFORD

One of the many challenges which Bishop Muldoon faced so ably was the governing of a new and rapidly growing diocese without a codified system of Church laws. It would not be until 1917 that Pope Benedict XV, would promulgate for the Universal Church the first Code of Canon Law.

◆ **Joan Hamas at her First Communion, St. Patrick, Dixon, 1958.**

In order to better organize and systematize the many aspects of Church life and discipline, Bishop Muldoon called the First Synod of the Diocese of Rockford in 1916. The Synod was opened April 4, 1916, at St. James Pro-Cathedral, with the celebration of a Pontifical High Mass in honor of The Most Holy Ghost, in accord with the prescriptions of the Roman Pontifical. Father Kirkfleet, O. Praem. names the officers as: "The Rt. Rev. Peter J. Muldoon, D.D., Celebrant; the Very Rev. James J. Bennett, V.G., Presbyter assistant; the Revs. Clemens Kalvelage and Thomas F. Leydon, Deacons of Honor; the Rev. Thomas J. Kearney, Deacon; the Rev. Anthony J. Vollman, Sub-deacon. Ninety priests were present and 18 absent."

The First Synod's legislation was placed into two major sections: the edification of the faithful, and the sanctification of the clergy. The former concerned and included a very careful and proper presentation on the correct administration of each of the seven sacraments; preaching; the administration of schools; and the management of parishes. The latter section created "precepts and

◆ **The First Diocesan Synod, 1916.**

◆ **Monsignor James J. Bennett, the first Vicar General, a position he retained until his death in January 1922.**

admonitions to the priests for the regulation of their own lives, for the practice of virtue and the avoidance of vice." (Kirkfleet) The Diocese itself was given a more formal structure. Seven parishes were made irremovable; the Diocese was divided into four sectors for the inspection of the schools, with four inspectors in each; the number of diocesan consultors was set at six and the number of synodal examiners was set at five.

The division of the Diocese into four sectors is of particular note since, it was from those four sectors that three districts were created to better organize the administration of the Diocese. These three districts were: Eastern (McHenry, Kane, Kendall, and DeKalb counties), Central (Boone, Winnebago, Lee and Ogle counties), and Western (Jo Daviess, Carroll, Stephenson and Whiteside counties). The three districts formed the basis for the eventual division of the Diocese of Rockford into the current seven deaneries. The first Dean of the Eastern district was Father Henry Bangen, Pastor of Annunciation Parish,

Aurora, the first Dean of the Central district was Father Michael J. Foley, Pastor of St. Patrick Parish, Dixon, and the first Dean of the Western district was Father Francis J. Antl, Pastor of St. John the Baptist Parish, Savanna.

THE DIOCESE OF MONTEREY AND LOS ANGELES

One of the signs of the great affection with which Bishop Muldoon was held by his priests as well as by the Catholic people of the Diocese of Rockford was recorded in 1917. An Associated Press dispatch from Rome dated March 22, 1917, announced that Bishop Muldoon had been named and transferred to be the Bishop of Monterey and Los Angeles in California. However, the bishop himself had no notice of this appointment by the Holy Father, Pope Benedict XV.

◆ **Father Henry Bangen, the first dean of the eastern district of the Rockford Diocese.**

Priests of the Diocese sent an immediate and fervent appeal to the Pope begging him not to transfer Bishop Muldoon. The Holy Father granted this request and revoked Bishop Muldoon's transfer. He received this revocation on June 8, 1917, the day after he had received the bulls of appointment to California which were returned at once to the Holy See.

It was around this same time that Bishop Muldoon purchased property on the near West Side of Rockford for a new, permanent Bishop's residence. Those plans were cancelled in March 1917. However in September of that year, a home was purchased in the same general vicinity for this purpose at 1704 National Avenue. The purchase price was $22,000, and according to Father Kirkfleet's history, "the funds needed for the

◆ **Bishop Muldoon's residence, located at 1704 National Avenue, Rockford, was a gift from diocesan priests.**

purchase of the present Bishop's home were a voluntary offering from the priests of the Rockford Diocese."

WORLD WAR I AND THE N.C.W.C.

Bishop Muldoon, as the United States entered World War I, took the lead in the Diocese in support of the nation and its troops. The U.S. Government had selected Rockford as the site of one of its training camps. It was named Camp Grant, and began training draftees in September 1917. The Knights of Columbus in Rockford and throughout the Diocese, as well as members of the Catholic Woman's League, responded to their Bishop's call for assistance and cooperated with the priests of the Diocese to provide spiritual and material support to the Camp Grant trainees.

At this time Bishop Muldoon's efforts in the Rockford Diocese were complemented by the fact that he had been chosen to be the chairman of the administrative committee of the National Catholic War Council (N.C.W.C.). Virtually all of his time was spent either promoting Catholic support for America's War effort in his Diocese or traveling around the country helping other bishops and Catholic organizations do the same in a coordinated

◆ **Bishop Muldoon speaking at a Flag Day celebration in 1917.**

and organized manner. The N.C.W.C. at its establishment in August 1917 consisted of 68 dioceses, and 27 other national Catholic societies.

By the time of the armistice in November 1918, the N.C.W.C. had distinguished itself in its activities of spiritual and corporal charity. As Bishop Muldoon reported to Pope Benedict XV in the Autumn of 1920, on the occasion of his *ad limina* visit, the N.C.W.C. had collected and expended some $40 million for all of the welfare work accomplished by the Catholic Church in the United States during the war. At war's end Bishop Muldoon, along with several other bishops on his administrative committee, became convinced that a form of permanent organization should be continued as a coordinating agency for Catholic affairs in the United States. Cardinal Gibbons agreed and at the first general meeting of the Catholic hierarchy (since 1884) in September 1919, the bishops voted by a wide margin to establish such an organization. Its first name was the National Catholic Welfare Council and had an administrative committee of five prelates in charge and answerable to the general hierarchy.

Before any further action could be taken, the bishops needed the approval of the Holy See. After various interventions by Rome and the bishops, and a change of the word "Council" to "Conference" in order to avoid any confusion or ambiguity, Roman approval was granted by Pope Pius XI on July 2, 1922.

The original structure of the National Catholic Welfare Conference as organized in February 1920, had five departments – Education, Lay Activities, Press, Social Action, and Missions. Even though the conference has undergone more than one major reorganization, those five departments still form the foundation for this ground-breaking organization of the Catholic hierarchy in the United States.

THE POST-WAR DIOCESE OF ROCKFORD

Significant changes occurred not only in the United States, but in the Diocese as well. Father Thomas Finn, one of Bishop Muldoon's close and original assistants, died October 5, 1920 at the age of 64. He was the first Chancellor of the Diocese, first Bishop's Secretary and Rector of the Pro-Cathedral. Since Bishop Muldoon was making his *ad limina* visit, Father John J. Flanagan, Vice-Chancellor and Administrator in the Bishop's absence celebrated a solemn high Funeral Mass for the beloved Father Finn on October 7, 1920. Shortly after his return from Rome, Bishop Muldoon appointed the Reverend Frederick F. Connor to be the second Chancellor of the Diocese of Rockford on January 15, 1921, and he also served as the Bishop's Secretary. On that same date, the Reverend John J. Flanagan was appointed Rector of the Pro-Cathedral.

In early 1921 and in anticipation of the Holy See's final approval of the N.C.W.C., Bishop Muldoon convoked a general meeting of the diocesan priests. The purpose was to explain the need for parallel structures for the Diocese and for each parish to the N.C.W.C. The intent would be to involve as many clergy and laity in the works of the N.C.W.C.

This meeting resulted in the formation of the Diocesan Catholic Welfare Council. It was Bishop Muldoon's plan for every parish to have a similar council. He outlined his plan in a March 1921, letter to the priests and in another letter to them the next month, he wrote in part: ". . . organizing of parish councils . . . will be of incalculable value to the country and to the Church." The Bishop's focus for these local councils was to support mostly the social action efforts of the N.C.W.C., but it certainly seems to have been prophetic in urging greater cooperation between clergy and laity and greater participation by the laity in the apostolate.

◆ **Bishop Muldoon and Father Frederick Connor, the second chancellor of the Rockford Diocese, 1921.**

In January 1922, the Rt. Rev. Monsignor James J. Bennett, first Vicar General of the Diocese and Pastor of St. Mary Parish, Aurora, died at the age 77. The Rt. Rev. Monsignor Clemens Kalvelage was appointed the second Vicar General on March 2, 1922, while remaining Pastor of St. Joseph Parish, Freeport. Father Connor was officially appointed the Pastor of St. Peter Parish, Rockford, in October 1922, and took up residence there the following June. At that time he relinquished his position as Secretary to the Bishop but remained as Chancellor of the Diocese. A young Father Laurence C. Prendergast, ordained by Bishop Muldoon on January 1, 1921, was appointed the Bishop's Secretary on June 29, 1923, and took up residence with the Bishop on National Avenue.

During the early and mid 1920's Bishop Muldoon's schedule was quite full and demanding. Due to his prominent role in overseeing the National Catholic War Council and then his pivotal role in the formation of its successor organization, the National Catholic Welfare Conference, he traveled widely in the United States on its business. However, he always made the Diocese his first priority and actively participated in its activities.

◆ **Bishop Muldoon with priests from Lee County on the occasion of his first trip to Amboy, circa 1910.**

The Holy Year of 1925 celebrated throughout the Universal Church as well as in the Diocese of Rockford, saw the ordination of five men to the Sacred Priesthood. They were: Fathers John L. Daleiden, Ladislaus A. Jasinski, Arthur M. Kreckel, Henry M. Schmitz and Joseph J. Tully.

The pace of Bishop Muldoon's daily routine began to take its toll on his physical health. Nonetheless, he continued to keep his schedule of appointments and events in the diocese, and kept his commitments to the N.C.W.C. One of those commitments was to attend and participate in the International Eucharistic Congress held in the Archdiocese of Chicago on the grounds of St. Mary of the Lake Seminary in Mundelein in the summer of 1926. Though not feeling well and against the advice of friends and his doctor, Bishop Muldoon did attend and, it is said, caught a terrible cold due to the inclement weather. This, combined with a ruptured appendix in June, rendered him so seriously ill that his recovery was much in doubt.

Bishop Muldoon remained hospitalized in St. Louis from June 1926 to early in the next year since that is where he was traveling when he suffered the ruptured appendix. He was not able to return to Rockford until late March 1927 but the affairs of the Diocese were administered by Father Connor, his Chancellor, as his health was in serious decline. Nonetheless and by all accounts, Bishop Muldoon remained as fully engaged in the life of the Diocese as his health allowed.

On Saturday, October 8, 1927, Peter James Muldoon, D.D., the first Bishop of Rockford, died. At his side were his sister, his nurse, his housekeeper and his secretary, Father Prendergast. The Metropolitan Archbishop of Chicago, George Cardinal Mundelein, officiated at Bishop Muldoon's Funeral Mass on October 12, 1927, at St. James Pro-Cathedral. Bishop Muldoon was buried in St. Mary-St. James Cemetery in Rockford.

Standing out among the many and well-deserved tributes to Bishop Muldoon at the time of

◆ **Bishop Muldoon at the Eucharistic Congress in Chicago, June 1926.**

With the death of Bishop Muldoon on October 8, 1927, the Chancellor of the Diocese, Father Frederick Connor, was made Administrator of the Diocese of Rockford. When a See becomes vacant for whatever reason, the office of Chancellor is one of only a few positions in a Diocese which does not lapse. Father Connor capably managed the ordinary affairs of the Diocese in what was a relatively brief vacancy. It was announced on February 10, 1928, that His Holiness, Pope Pius XI had appointed The Most Reverend Edward Francis Hoban, D.D., Auxiliary Bishop of Chicago, to be the second Bishop of the Diocese of Rockford.

his death, is probably the one offered by his fellow Bishops and enshrined today at the headquarters of the Bishops' Conference. It is most indicative of the esteem in which he was held by so many and captures the sentiments of a very grateful Diocese, then and now. It was a most fitting tribute, to the man and his life as a servant of God and the Church.

◆ **Plaque in honor of Bishop Muldoon at the National Conference of Catholic Bishop headquarters, Washington, D. C.**

◆ **Mourners outside St. James Pro-Cathedral during Bishop Muldoon's funeral, October 12, 1927.**

The Hoban Years

Bishop Hoban was not unfamiliar with the Rockford Diocese nor was the Diocese and its clergy unfamiliar with him. His ecclesiastical life prior to his appointment as Bishop of Rockford on February 10, 1928, by Pope Pius XI was, in many respects, very similar to that of Bishop Muldoon.

Edward Francis Hoban was a native Chicagoan born on June 27, 1878, the son of William and Bridget O'Malley Hoban. His education was completed in Catholic schools, first at the parish grade school of St. Columbkille and then at St. Ignatius High School in Chicago. Edward Hoban then completed his philosophical and theological training at St. Mary Seminary,

Baltimore, Maryland, and was ordained to the sacred priesthood at Holy Name Cathedral, Chicago, on July 11, 1903, by The Most Reverend James E. Quigley, D.D., Archbishop of Chicago.

Father Hoban's first assignment for a brief time was as the Assistant Priest at St. Agnes Parish, Chicago. He was then assigned to studies in Rome, Italy, at the Pontifical Gregorian University where by 1906 he obtained doctoral degrees in both Philosophy and Theology. Upon his return to the Archdiocese he was named the Assistant Chancellor to Monsignor Edmund Dunne, the Chancellor. That same year Father Hoban was appointed a professor at Quigley Preparatory Seminary. When Monsignor Dunne was named the Bishop of the Diocese of Peoria, Father Hoban was named Chancellor for the Archdiocese of Chicago in 1910.

When Archbishop George Mundelein succeeded Archbishop Quigley in 1916, Father Hoban was reappointed Chancellor that same year and then in November 1916, Pope Benedict XV named him a Papal Chamberlain with the title of Very Reverend Monsignor. It was during Monsignor Hoban's tenure as Chancellor for the Archdiocese of Chicago that he supervised the establishment of what was then named the Associated Catholic Charities of Chicago.

Five years after Edward Hoban had been named a Papal Chamberlain, Pope Benedict XV elevated him to the rank of Auxiliary Bishop of the Archdiocese of Chicago on November 21, 1921. He was consecrated by Archbishop Mundelein at

◆ **Bishop Edward F. Hoban, second bishop of the Rockford Diocese. Motto: Come, Light of Hearts.**

◆ **Dignitaries accompany Bishop Hoban on the day of his installation, May 15, 1928.**

Holy Name Cathedral on December 21, 1921. For the next six-plus years Bishop Hoban served the Archdiocese faithfully in several administrative posts, including its Vicar General in 1924, and as the president of the International Eucharistic Congress in 1926. It has been noted that the acknowledged success of this Congress was due, in large part, to Bishop Hoban's administrative skill and his manifest ability to marshal and organize the efforts of clergy, religious and laity. The Congress was the first-ever held outside of Italy and Europe, and attracted more than one million pilgrims.

Bishop Hoban was installed on May 15, 1928, by His Eminence, George Cardinal Mundelein at St. James Pro-Cathedral in Rockford. Twenty-eight other archbishops and bishops attended his installation.

As Bishop Hoban assumed his many duties in the relatively new but steadily growing and developing Diocese, he did so with the same zeal and competence that had been characteristic of his time as priest and Auxiliary Bishop in Chicago. All that had been either initiated or further developed by Bishop Muldoon was continued and enhanced by Bishop Hoban. He was responsible for initiating two new apostolates in the Diocese of Rockford which have been mainstays – *The Observer*, the Diocese's official newspaper, and Catholic Charities.

PROGRESS AND CHANGE FOR THE DIOCESE

Whenever a transfer of leadership occurs in a diocese, or even in a parish, both progress and change soon become apparent. Progress occurs based on what has been accomplished already, and change follows by making even more effective those accomplishments.

◆ **Bishop Hoban's installation dinner at the Nelson Hotel, Rockford, May 15, 1928.**

Father Frederick Connor, who served as Chancellor and Administrator of the Diocese after the death of Bishop Muldoon was reappointed Chancellor by Bishop Hoban and served until 1929 when it was necessary for him to devote all of his time to his growing parish of St. Peter in Rockford. In 1928, Father Laurence Prendergast, the Bishop's Secretary, was appointed to the City of Elgin to see to the establishment of a third parish. The parish of St. Laurence was formally erected there in 1929.

Father Leo W. Binz, a native son of Holy Cross Parish, Stockton (and future Bishop and Archbishop), was appointed to replace Father Prendergast in 1928 and to replace Father Connor in 1929. He served as Chancellor until 1932 when he was appointed as Pastor of St. Peter Parish, Rockford. Bishop Hoban then appointed Father Francis J. Conron as Chancellor on February 1, 1932.

The Diocese had grown so rapidly since 1917 when the first chancery and rectory were purchased it became necessary for Bishop Hoban to construct a much larger Chancery and, in the process, a new residence for the Bishop of the Diocese.

◆ **Bishop Hoban outside St. Peter Church, Rockford, circa 1935.**

Property was purchased on North Court Street near to St. Peter Parish Church and construction of the new Chancery Office and Bishop's residence was undertaken and completed in 1929. A note of interest about this building is that it is actually two buildings joined to each other and then covered by exterior stone, giving the impression of one uniformly constructed building. The north end was newly built and the south end was a large home to which the new part was attached.

The year 1929 marked the beginning of a decade of rapid development of new initiatives in Catholic education, the creation and expansion of parishes, Catholic action, Catholic press promotion and the completion of Bishop Muldoon's initiative in establishing the Diocesan Welfare Council. This, in fact, was developed by Bishop Hoban as Catholic Charities. In 1929 Bishop Hoban restructured the Diocese into four deaneries: Aurora (Kane, Kendall and DeKalb counties); Freeport (Jo Daviess, Stephenson and Carroll counties); Rockford (Winnebago, Boone and McHenry counties); and Sterling (Ogle, Lee and Whiteside counties).

Not only was Bishop Hoban working tirelessly in his Diocese but for most of the decade of the 1930's, he served as an assistant bishop on the

◆ **The new Chancery building on North Court Street was completed in 1929, just as the Great Depression was starting.**

◆ **Marmion Academy, Aurora.**

Administrative Board of the National Catholic Welfare Conference. Most notable was his service for eight years as the Assistant Episcopal Chairman of the Press Department of the N.C.W.C.

CATHOLIC EDUCATION

Due to the great success of St. Thomas High School in Rockford, Bishop Hoban took a dramatic step in developing Bishop Muldoon's concept of Catholic secondary education. In 1929, Bishop Hoban divided the co-educational school into two schools with an all-boys school newly built on Mulberry Street, keeping the name St. Thomas. He then built a larger, all-girls school on Stanley Street naming it Bishop Muldoon High School. Both schools were opened for classes for the 1930 school year. The Sinsinawa Dominican Sisters continued to administer Bishop Muldoon High School until 1933. The Christian Brothers were given charge of the new St. Thomas High School and they, too, remained there until 1933.

In 1933, more significant changes in Catholic high school education were effected by Bishop Hoban. When Fox Valley High School opened in 1927 the Augustinian Fathers were given charge of it. Bishop Hoban asked them to relinquish this as well as the administration of St. Rita of Cascia Parish, Aurora, and move to Rockford to assume the administration of St. Thomas High School, as well as St. Mary Parish, Rockford's second oldest parish.

Another important move came that year when the Benedictine Monks of Jasper, Indiana, assumed the administration of the Fox Valley High School in Aurora and changed its name to Marmion Military Academy. Nine monks made up the faculty for the school as well as the first Benedictine establishment in the Diocese of Rockford. The growth of Marmion was rapid and almost all of the surrounding property was also purchased and developed by the monks for the use of the Academy as well as for their own priory.

It was also in 1933 that Bishop Hoban transferred the administration of Bishop Muldoon High School from the Sinsinawa Dominican Sisters to the Adrian Dominican Sisters.

◆ **The 1931 dedication of Muldoon High School, Rockford. This all-girls school was administered by the Sinsinawa Dominican Sisters until 1933, when control was given to the Adrian Dominican Sisters.**

◆ The Poor Clares Chapel was built in 1925 alongside the former Broughton Mansion. The elegant mansion did not fit into the simple lifestyle of the Poor Clares, and was demolished in 1931.

Eight years later, with the firm support of Bishop Hoban, the pastors of the three parishes in Elgin, joined together to establish a Catholic high school for that City's growing Catholic population. A former public school building was purchased and renovated in 1941 and opened for classes in September 1942. Bishop Hoban dedicated the new Catholic high school on October 12, 1942, and it was named St. Edward in his honor.

A second religious order of men, the Servite Fathers, established a seminary in the Diocese of Rockford near St. Charles, for the education to the priesthood of boys of Italian descent. Bishop Hoban dedicated the minor seminary on August 14, 1938. Later, a new Sacred Heart Seminary was dedicated by Bishop Hoban at Geneva on May 31, 1942.

The growth of the Poor Clares continued during the Hoban years. He authorized the purchase of more property adjoining the Monastery on South Main Street in Rockford and in 1931, he gave permission for a brick wall to be built to enclose most of the property. Then, in 1934, he authorized the addition of a new wing to be built onto the original Monastery.

PARISH LIFE

One cannot forget that during the episcopate of Bishop Hoban there was even more historic upheaval than during Bishop Muldoon's episcopacy. In October 1929, the Stock Market crashed and thus began what has been called the Great Depression. This event has had an enduring impact on the United States and its citizens, and the Catholic people of the Diocese were not exempt from the economic pressures of those years. In fact, almost the entire time of Bishop Hoban's episcopacy in Rockford was directly influenced by the Great Depression and its widespread effects.

In December 1941, the United States of America was attacked by Japan and thus began America's total involvement in World War II. In both instances, Bishop Hoban's firm and unflagging faith and his administrative skill helped the Diocese of

◆ **The investiture of Monsignor Andrew Burns as Protonotary Apostolic on July 10, 1938.**

Rockford to weather these storms and emerge stronger and more vibrant in promoting the Gospel at all levels of diocesan life.

Between 1928 and 1942, Bishop Hoban erected new parishes in the Diocese and he changed the status of a mission to that of a parish. Bishop Hoban erected St. Peter Parish in Aurora; St. Anne Parish in Dixon; St. Laurence Parish in Elgin; and St. Edward Parish in Rockford. He changed the status of St. Rita of Cascia Parish, Cherry Valley, from a mission of the Pro-Cathedral to that of a full territorial parish. As did his predecessor, Bishop Hoban gave full and enthusiastic support to these new parishes and to the establishment in each of a Catholic grade school. At this same time, several other parishes embarked upon major renovation projects in order to expand the capacity of the parish church building or the parish school.

Bishop Hoban created the fourth diocesan cemetery on February 4, 1939, for the Rockford area on property due west of the city limits and it was named Calvary Cemetery.

◆ **Stanley Ywanauskas, altar boy at SS. Peter & Paul, Rockford, circa 1935.**

CATHOLIC ACTION

Bishop Hoban continued the Diocese's full support for St. Elizabeth Community Center and its many efforts to assist the poor as well as new immigrants to the United States. Moreover, he launched a renovation and expansion of the Diocese's care for orphans and the aged. According to its records, nine separate buildings were either renovated or newly constructed in 1931 at St. Vincent Orphanage and St. Joseph Home for the aged in Freeport.

The continuing growth and success of Catholic hospitals in the Diocese of Rockford was evidenced by the building of two new institutions in Aurora between 1930 and 1932 — St. Joseph Mercy and St. Charles hospitals respectively. In the City of Rockford, the Sisters of the Third Order of St. Francis built a large addition to their St. Anthony Hospital in 1930, almost doubling its capacity. Bishop Hoban actively supported all of these good works of Catholic action, and regularly encouraged the clergy, religious and laity to do the same.

MORE DIOCESAN CHANGES

The mid 1930's also marked some further changes for priests of the Diocese. In addition to the ordinations, assignments and transfers of priests, two priests of the Diocese received special appointments. In September 1935, Father Francis J. Miller was appointed Vice-Chancellor having completed his studies in Rome. In 1936 Monsignor Leo Binz, Pastor of St. James Parish, Belvidere since 1933, was appointed secretary for the Apostolic Delegate to the United States, Archbishop Amleto Cicognani. He left the parish and the Diocese to take up his new duties in Washington, D.C. in August 1936. In June 1937, Bishop Hoban appointed Father Louis J. Franey whom he had ordained a priest five years earlier, to the office of Vice-Chancellor of the Diocese and this began Father Franey's 51 years of dedicated and capable service to the entire Diocese.

NEW DIOCESAN APOSTOLATES

Some early diocesan records indicate there was a Catholic publication circulated at least in the City of Rockford in the earliest days of the Diocese by the name of the *Catholic Monthly*. However, this is all the information available and it is probable that this was not a creation of Bishop Muldoon. This changed dramatically in 1935 and, no doubt, was owing to Bishop Hoban's work for the N.C.W.C.'s Press Department.

Late in 1935 Bishop Hoban established the Diocese's first official newspaper and he named it *The Observer*. He named Monsignor Charles Conley, Pastor of St. Mary Parish, Freeport, its first editor. November 28, 1935, the First Sunday of Advent that year, marked the first issue of *The Observer* as the official organ of communication between the Bishop and the Catholic people of the Diocese of Rockford. The history of the development and the changes which *The Observer* has undergone over the last 70-plus years is a study in itself and cannot be done justice in this present work.

Nonetheless, Bishop Hoban's establishment of *The Observer* proved to be a lasting contribution to Catholic journalism. What must be recorded here are a few of the front page citations from that first issue. The top right hand side of the first edition featured a quote from Pope Pius XI: "You are my voice. I do not say that you make my voice

◆ **St. Vincent Orphanage, Freeport.**

◆ **Home of *The Observer* at St. Mary Church, Freeport.**

heard, but that you are really my voice itself; for few indeed would be the number of children of our common Father who could learn my wishes and thoughts without the aid of the Catholic press." At the top left hand side of the first issue was a statement of the purpose of a Catholic newspaper. "A Catholic paper stimulates piety, a love of Catholic ideals, and an interest in the activities of the Church of Christ. It makes for a great advance in the knowledge and love of religion."

In his letter of introduction of *The Observer* to all the Catholics of the Diocese, Bishop Hoban gave voice to the specific purpose of the publication and what we still consider as its mission today. He wrote: "The truths of our religion as revealed by our Divine Master teach us of eternal life and the means to attain it. To keep alive our precious gift of faith, and to stimulate the practice of our holy religion we must study the revealed truths of Christ, presented to us by His Church, commissioned to teach them . . . We must have recourse to the press, which is today an important, if not necessary, auxiliary to the pastors of souls in the spread

of Catholic doctrine... Our new Catholic weekly will present to us the various truths of our faith, properly edited and interpreted according to the mind of the Church, whose mission is to carry on Christ's work and to spread His Kingdom."

Monsignor Charles F. Conley very ably guided *The Observer* for its first three years and ensured its firm establishment. He asked to be relieved of this duty due to the press of his parish responsibilities and Bishop Hoban appointed Father Philip L. Kennedy, the Superintendent of St. Vincent Orphanage and St. Joseph Home for the Aged, Freeport, the second editor of *The Observer* in 1938.

In the meantime Bishop Hoban had observed that the Diocese needed to centralize and better coordinate its many and growing charitable activities and services. To this end, in September 1937, he organized and formally established the Catholic Charities Agency of the Diocese of Rockford, naming Father Francis P. McNally its first director. In less than one year Father McNally organized a board of directors for Catholic Charities in Rockford which began to meet regularly in May 1938, and in November of that year it was admitted as a member of the Rockford Community Chest.

Father McNally, at the direction of Bishop Hoban, organized a diocesan board for Catholic Charities since its works were quickly developing in other areas of the Diocese. This led to the establishment of a second board of directors for Catholic Charities' activities in Aurora in 1942.

◆ **The first issue of *The Observer*, debuted on November 28, 1935.**

From its formal establishment in 1937, Catholic Charities organized collections of food, clothing and other necessities throughout the Diocese for distribution to the poor. The pervasive effects of the Great Depression were still being felt by virtually every citizen and Catholic Charities proved to be a most valuable Catholic relief agency. It very ably assisted in the care of our troops stationed in the Diocese during World War II, and it extended its services to the continuing influx of immigrants. The agency's hallmark has always been its ability to adapt its activities according to the changing needs of the times, while maintaining its distinctive Catholic character as the official charitable arm of the Rockford Diocese.

WAR AND CHANGE

The Diocese, as the nation, was still in the throes of the Depression while the specter of another war loomed on the horizon as the decade of the 1940's opened. The United States government reactivated Camp Grant since the military draft had been resumed. Bishop Hoban dedicated a Catholic chapel there in September 1941, and within three months the United States was at war. The life of the Church continued in spite of these hardships and Bishop Hoban continued a very busy schedule, made even more so by the demands of the war on the N.C.W.C.

The Diocese of Rockford experienced honor and sadness at the promotion of Bishop Hoban as Coadjutor Bishop of Cleveland with the right of succession. His Holiness, Pope Pius XII appointed him to that office on November 16, 1942. Archbishop Joseph Schrembs remained in office until his death on November 2, 1945, at which time Bishop Hoban became the Bishop of Cleveland. In July 1951, Pope Pius XII elevated Bishop Hoban to the rank of personal Archbishop.

◆ **Catholic Charities' offices in the 100 block of North Church Street, Rockford, circa 1940.**

◆ **Father Leon Linden, pastor of Our Lady of Good Counsel, Aurora, 1941.**

◆ **Monsignor Leo Binz, center, and Fathers Arthur O'Neill and Joseph Healey on a Holy Land pilgrimage, 1950.**

The zeal for souls and the welfare of the Church with which Bishop Hoban shepherded the Diocese of Rockford for almost 15 years, continued unabated in Cleveland until his death on September 22, 1966, at the age of 88. He spent 63 years as a priest and almost 45 years as a bishop. Edward F. Hoban, second Bishop of the Diocese of Rockford, and Archbishop-Bishop of the Diocese of Cleveland, was buried in the Cathedral of St. John the Evangelist, Cleveland, Ohio.

◆ **Bishop Edward F. Hoban at St. Patrick, Dixon, circa 1930.**

THE VACANT SEE

Monsignor Francis J. Conron assumed the duties of Administrator for the Diocese of Rockford until its third Bishop would be installed in early 1943. During this brief vacancy of the Diocesan See, a great honor came to one of the Diocese's own, Monsignor Leo Binz, was named by Pope Pius XII on November 21, 1942, to be the Coadjutor Bishop and Apostolic Administrator for the Diocese of Winona. Monsignor Binz was consecrated at St. James Pro-Cathedral, Rockford, on December 21, 1942, by the Apostolic Delegate, Archbishop Amleto Cicognani. Co-consecrators were Bishop Edward F. Hoban and Bishop Henry P. Rohlman, Bishop of Davenport, Iowa.

Bishop Binz served in the Diocese of Winona until October 1949, when he was named the Coadjutor Bishop with the right of succession to Archbishop Henry P. Rohlman of Dubuque; Bishop Binz succeeded to the See of Dubuque on December 2, 1954, obtaining the rank of Archbishop. On December 16, 1961, Archbishop Binz was appointed the Archbishop of St. Paul and Minneapolis where he served with great distinction until his retirement on May 21, 1975. Archbishop Binz died on October 9, 1979.

The Boylan Years

On November 21, 1942, the same day the appointment of Monsignor Binz was announced, Monsignor John J. Boylan, President of Dowling College in Des Moines, Iowa, was named by His Holiness, Pope Pius XII, to be the third Bishop of the Diocese of Rockford and the first Rockford Bishop not from the Archdiocese of Chicago.

John Joseph Boylan was born in New York City on October 7, 1889, the son of Lawrence and Bridget Morrissey Boylan. At a young age his family moved to Rhode Island where he attended Catholic grade and high schools. He completed his college classical studies at Mt. St. Mary College, Emmitsburg, Maryland. John Boylan studied philosophy and theology at St. Bernard Seminary, Rochester, New York from 1910 to 1915, and was ordained to the sacred priesthood at Providence,

Rhode Island, by The Most Reverend Thomas F. Doran, Auxiliary Bishop of Providence on July 28, 1915. Father Boylan was ordained for the Diocese of Des Moines, Iowa.

Father Boylan's first assignment was as Assistant at St. Francis Parish, in Council Bluffs, Iowa, but this was to be a brief assignment. Soon he was assigned to complete further studies at The Catholic University of America in Washington, D.C., and then on to the Pontifical Atheneum in Rome, Italy where he obtained a doctorate in Sacred Theology. In September 1918, Father Boylan was appointed to the faculty of Des Moines College by the first Bishop of Des Moines, Austin Dowling (this College would be renamed in his honor and Bishop Dowling would become the Archbishop of St. Paul). During his years on the faculty, Father Boylan did further studies at both Iowa State University and at Harvard University earning, in time, a Ph.D.

In 1923, Father John J. Boylan was named President of Dowling College and remained in that post for the next 20 years. In 1933, he was named a Right Reverend Monsignor by Pope Pius XI, and in 1934, Bishop Gerald T. Bergan, named him Vicar General of the Diocese of Des Moines in addition to his duties as Dowling College's President. Pope Pius XII named Monsignor Boylan a Protonotary Apostolic in 1941, citing him for his exemplary work in the field of Catholic education.

John J. Boylan was consecrated a bishop on February 17, 1943, at St. Ambrose Cathedral, Des Moines, Iowa, by The Most Reverend Gerald T. Bergan, Bishop of Des Moines, and the co-consecrators

◆ **Bishop John J. Boylan, third bishop of the Rockford Diocese. Motto: Peace be with you.**

were Bishop Henry P. Rohlman of Davenport, Iowa, and Bishop Edmund Heelan of Sioux City, Iowa.

The Most Reverend John J. Boylan was installed as the third Bishop of the Diocese of Rockford by the Archbishop of Chicago, Samuel A. Stritch, at St. James Pro-Cathedral, Rockford, on February 24, 1943. The ten plus years of Bishop Boylan's episcopacy were years of continued growth in the diocesan Catholic population. It was also a time of further development and refinement of the Diocese's growing Catholic educational system, and the realization of the necessity to create more parishes and to expand the Church's charitable apostolates. These needs had to be met by Bishop Boylan while, at the same time, he devoted himself to retiring the Diocese's debt accrued from continuous expansion and development. This was made all the more difficult since World War II would not end until 1945 and the United States would experience an economic slow-down in the years immediately following the war's end. However, none of this deterred Bishop Boylan. In fact, his total dedication to the Diocese bore good fruit as Catholic schools grew, vocations to the priesthood and religious life increased, the work of Catholic Charities expanded and organizations for Catholic youth were fostered.

◆ **In November 1948 the Rockford Diocese officially celebrated its 40th anniversary with a Pontifical High Mass and rededication of the recently-renovated Pro-Cathedral. Dignitaries present included: Bishop John P. Cody, Auxiliary of St. Louis; Bishop Boylan; Samuel Cardinal Stritch, Archbishop of Chicago; Bishop Russell J. McVinney, Providence, Rhode Island; and Bishop Albert R. Zuroweste, Belleville.**

CATHOLIC EDUCATION

While Bishop Boylan did not establish any new Catholic high schools, what he did to further develop and enhance the quality of Catholic education across the diocese would be most important. Since most of Bishop Boylan's priesthood was devoted to Catholic education, he applied his considerable knowledge, skill and experience as teacher and administrator to the schools of the Diocese.

One of the first official acts of Bishop Boylan was to establish set institute days for all teachers in the diocesan schools. These were days meant to further their own educational advancement in their fields of study as well as to increase their understanding of the Catholic faith and its practices. Another effort Bishop Boylan initiated was to arrange his busy schedule in order to be present and speak at the graduation ceremonies in each of the Catholic high schools in the diocese. It was an

◆ **St. Thomas High School campus, Rockford.**

opportunity for him to promote two very important matters — the necessity of a Catholic education for children and young people, and the opportunity to promote vocations to the priesthood and religious life. Because Bishop Boylan had an abiding interest in the spiritual and temporal welfare of young people, he promoted vigorously the establishment of Catholic Youth Organizations (CYO) in parishes.

PARISH LIFE

Even though Bishop Boylan was working systematically to reduce the Diocese's overall indebtedness, when the need arose, he did not hesitate to establish new parishes with schools to better serve the needs of the steadily growing Catholic population. In his 10 years as third Bishop of Rockford, Bishop Boylan established St Bridget of Erin Parish, Loves Park (1946); Christ the King Parish, Wonder Lake (1947); and St. Andrew Parish, Rock Falls (1950).

In addition to the establishment of these new parishes, Holy Angels Parish in Aurora, completed construction on a new church and it was dedicated by Bishop Boylan on February 3, 1952. The new St. Patrick Church in Rockford was completed and dedicated on May 20, 1952. Two parishes built new

schools in this same year of 1952, St. Patrick Parish, McHenry, and St. Andrew Parish, Rock Falls, which used the school's auditorium as a temporary church.

DIOCESAN PRIESTS

As mentioned, Bishop Boylan actively promoted vocations to the priesthood and with the able cooperation of his priests, the numbers of young men studying for the priesthood for the Diocese increased. Within one month of his installation Bishop Boylan ordained his first class of diocesan priests. These men were: Father Leo H. Ambre, Father John J. Kilduff, Father James F. McGuire, and Father Arthur J. O'Neill (a future successor to Bishop Boylan as seventh Bishop of Rockford). An important appointment made by Bishop Boylan which would have a long and good effect on the Diocese was that of Father Louis J. Franey as Chancellor of the Diocese, Secretary to the Bishop and Officialis of the Matrimonial Curia, which was done on October 18, 1943. Father Franey faithfully served in these offices for the next 14 years until September 10, 1957.

◆ Father James Vanderpool, left, and Father Anthony Becker with Wonder Lake Catholics in the summer of 1947. A building fund had just been created for a new parish, Christ the King.

◆ Bishop Boylan and Father Arthur O'Neill at a Muldoon High School ring ceremony in the early 1950s.

◆ **St. Patrick Church and rectory, Rockford, nearing completion, 1952.**

CATHOLIC ACTION

In 1950, the Catholic Men's Club of Rockford (a Catholic counterpart to the Catholic Woman's League) purchased the Talcott home at 839 North Main Street. This property was donated to Bishop Boylan for the use of the Diocese. Given Bishop Boylan's great interest in Catholic young people, he gave it over to the management and direction of Catholic Charities to be used as a Catholic Youth Center. With this added service to the already growing number of services provided by Catholic Charities, Bishop Boylan appointed Father Michael Shanahan to be the second Diocesan Director of Catholic Charities. Father Shanahan succeeded Father Francis P. McNally who was appointed Pastor of St. Patrick Parish, Rockford, in 1950. Father McNally immediately made plans to move the parish to a new site on School Street in response to its rapid growth.

The Catholic Youth Center in Rockford closed as a separate entity in 1953 but its services were continued by Catholic Charities through several of its other programs. In August 1953, Catholic Charities moved its offices into the closed Youth Center.

By 1945, there were three Diocesan Catholic Charities boards — Rockford, Aurora and Elgin. In October 1945, Bishop Boylan merged all three boards into one truly diocesan board increasing its effectiveness and involving a far greater cross section of Catholics within the diocese.

RELIGIOUS COMMUNITIES

It was 1945 when the Order of Friars Minor Conventual received permission from Bishop Boylan to open St. Mary Minor Seminary in Crystal Lake. Bishop Boylan dedicated this new institution for the training of young men for the priesthood on September 5, 1945. The seminary continued until 1969 when the Franciscan Fathers made the hard decision to close the seminary due to declining enrollment.

Father Ignatius Esser, received word from the Holy See on March 21, 1947, that Pope Pius XII had raised Marmion Priory and its military academy to the rank of Abbey, thus making it an independent foundation of Pontifical Right. It was officially named the Abbey of St. Augustine of Canterbury. Father Gerald Benkert, Marmion's headmaster from

◆ **Marmion Academy, Aurora, 1958.**

1938 to 1940, was named Marmion's first Abbot. He was installed on May 22, 1947.

The continued success of Marmion Military Academy made expansion and relocation of its site necessary. In 1950, the Benedictines broke ground on a new 230-acre site just north of the City of Aurora. The new Marmion Abbey and Academy opened in 1952 and were dedicated by Bishop Boylan in June 1953.

The orders of religious women already at work in the Diocese continued to offer children and young people an excellent Catholic education, as well as operating their hospital, orphanage and nursing home apostolates. Some of these religious communities took on additional teaching missions. For instance, the Holy Cross Sisters who had been staffing St. Mary Parish grade school in Woodstock, increased their numbers and took over the parish high school in 1951. The Sisters of the Presentation, already teaching at St. Mary Parish School in Oregon, received permission from the Holy See to establish their Motherhouse in Oregon in 1946, for the Staten Island Presentation Sisters. Along with this permission the sisters were allowed to establish a novitiate and begin accepting young women as candidates for vows.

THE YEAR OF 1948

The year of 1948 marked two important events in the Diocese's history over which Bishop Boylan presided, and one of those events has yet to be repeated.

In September of that year, the diocese marked its 40th Anniversary. Father Joseph T. Healey, Administrator of St. James Pro-Cathedral, had undertaken a major renovation of the Cathedral Church and, with the work completed, Bishop Boylan celebrated a Pontifical High Mass in November 1948, as the official anniversary celebration for the Diocese. On this happy occasion, Samuel Cardinal Stritch preached the sermon of the Mass. The Pro-Cathedral's three altars were consecrated by three attending bishops: the main altar by Bishop John P. Cody, Auxiliary of St. Louis (classmate of Father Healey's and future Cardinal Archbishop of Chicago); the Blessed Mother altar by Bishop Russell J. McVinney of Providence, Rhode Island; and the St. Joseph altar by Bishop Albert R. Zuroweste of Belleville.

Another historic event occurred on December 11, 1948 when Pope Pius XII, erected a sixth Diocese in the State of Illinois and the Province of Chicago at Joliet. The new diocese was comprised of seven

◆ **The 1945 graduating class, St. Mary, Aurora. The priest is Father John Dolan, assistant pastor.**

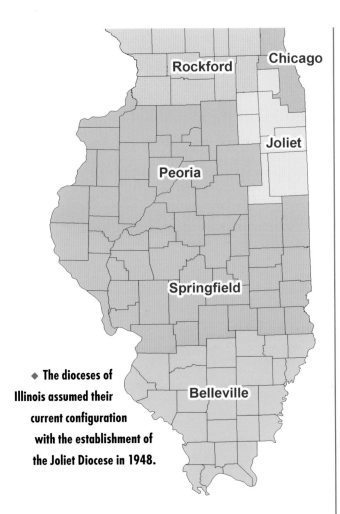

◆ The dioceses of Illinois assumed their current configuration with the establishment of the Joliet Diocese in 1948.

counties, one of which was Kendall County and thus Bishop Boylan and the Diocese of Rockford contributed one priest, one parish and one mission to the Diocese of Joliet: Father John C. Then, Pastor of St. Mary Parish, Plano, and its mission of St. Patrick Parish in Bristol. Joliet's first bishop was The Most Reverend Martin D. McNamara who would later come to the assistance of the Rockford Diocese.

◆ An early photograph of St. Mary Church, Plano. This parish was transferred from the Rockford Diocese to the new Joliet Diocese in 1948.

With the erection of the Diocese of Joliet 40 years after that of the Diocese of Rockford, the make up of the Catholic Church of the Province of Chicago was set and, to date, has not changed. The Archdiocese of Chicago is composed of two counties and a total of 1,411 square miles. The Diocese of Springfield is composed of 28 counties with a total of 15,139 square miles. The Diocese of Peoria is composed of 26 counties with a total of 16,933 square miles. The Diocese of Belleville is composed of 28 counties with a total of 11,678 square miles. The Diocese of Rockford is now composed of 11 counties and a total of 6,457 square miles. The Diocese of Joliet is composed of seven counties with a total of 4,218 square miles.

THE UNIVERSAL CHURCH AND THE DIOCESE

The year of 1950 was a Holy Year to be celebrated throughout the Universal Church. That year, four men were ordained to the diocesan priesthood. They were: Fathers Charles W. McNamee, James A. Molloy, J. Philip Reilly and Raymond G. Stewart. A moment of the greatest importance to the Diocese of Rockford occurred at the Vatican on the Solemnity of All Saints, November 1, 1950 when Pope Pius XII, proclaimed as infallible the dogma of the Assumption of the Blessed Virgin Mary. Bishop Boylan directed that every parish of the Diocese of Rockford would celebrate in an especially solemn fashion, the first holy day of obligation for the Assumption of the Blessed Virgin Mary on August 15, 1951.

In January 1953, Pope Pius XII modified the sacramental discipline of the Church in order to encourage more Catholics to a greater practice of their faith, to a more frequent Mass attendance and reception of holy Communion. The Pope allowed for the celebration of evening Masses, and he relaxed the regulations for the Eucharistic fast. According to records extant from this period, pastors reported to Bishop Boylan that Mass attendance had indeed increased along with an increase in the numbers of Catholics receiving the sacraments.

THE DEATH OF BISHOP BOYLAN

The priests, religious and laity of the diocese were stunned and grieved to learn that Bishop Boylan had died while on a visit to his family in Rhode Island, July 19, 1953. Most were aware that he had undergone successful major surgery in December 1952. He seemed to have recovered and had returned to Rockford and his duties the next February. Still, the serious nature of Bishop Boylan's condition was not widely known, and his death was a shock even to his closest collaborators in the diocese.

Samuel Cardinal Stritch, Archbishop of Chicago, officiated at Bishop Boylan's Funeral Mass, at St. James Pro-Cathedral, July 24, 1953. Bishop Boylan's friend and mentor, Archbishop Gerald T. Bergan of Omaha (formerly Bishop of

◆ **First Communion at Our Lady of the Good Counsel, Aurora, 1942.**

Des Moines), and principal consecrator at Bishop Boylan's installation only 10 years earlier, preached the funeral sermon.

Though his death was a great loss, Bishop Boylan had made a lasting impression on the Catholic faithful of the Diocese of Rockford.

THE VACANT SEE

With the death of Bishop Boylan, Monsignor Louis J. Franey, P.A., administered the Diocese's daily affairs. This vacancy of the Episcopal See lasted for approximately six months. The announcement of the appointment of the fourth Bishop of the Diocese of Rockford would not come until November 1953, and the Diocese's new Bishop would not be installed until January of the next year.

◆ **The baseball team of St. Mary, McHenry.**

◆ **St. Mary/St. James Cemetery, Rockford. The graves of Bishops Boylan and Muldoon are the first two graves on the right.**

The Hillinger Years

Pope Pius XII, named a Chicago priest, Raymond Peter Hillinger, to be the fourth Bishop of the Diocese of Rockford on November 3, 1953. He was consecrated Bishop on December 29, 1953, at Holy Name Cathedral, Chicago, by Samuel Cardinal Stritch, with Bishop Martin D. McNamara of Joliet and Bishop William A. O'Connor of Springfield as co-consecrators. On January 14, 1954, The Most Reverend Raymond P. Hillinger was installed as the fourth Bishop of the Diocese of Rockford, at St. James Pro-Cathedral, Rockford, by Cardinal Stritch.

Raymond Peter Hillinger was born in Chicago on May 2, 1904, the son of Philip and Magdalene Neuses Hillinger. He attended Catholic grade schools at St. Henry Parish, Chicago, and St. Joseph Parish in Wilmette, and attended New Trier High School in Winnetka. Bishop Hillinger pursued studies for the priesthood first, at Quigley Preparatory Seminary in Chicago, and then completed them at St. Mary of the Lake Seminary at Mundelein.

He was ordained to the sacred priesthood on April 2, 1932, in the Chapel of St. Mary of the Lake Seminary, by George Cardinal Mundelein, Archbishop of Chicago. His first priestly assignment was as assistant at St. Aloysius Parish, Chicago, where he served for three years. In 1935, Father Hillinger, a most gifted preacher and speaker, joined the Chicago Archdiocesan Mission Band and served in that position for 15 years. On June 2, 1950, he was appointed the Rector of Angel Guardian Orphanage in Chicago and was serving in this assignment when he was appointed Bishop of Rockford. Raymond Hillinger had been named a Monsignor by Pope Pius XII only one week before he was appointed as Rockford's Bishop.

DIOCESAN STRUCTURE

When Bishop Hillinger began his active but all too brief episcopate, the Diocese of Rockford had again grown steadily in population and in the numbers of priests and religious, as well as parishes, schools and other charitable institutions. In 1954 the number of Catholics in the Diocese had grown to more than 80,000. The number of parishes had increased to 89 and there were 250 diocesan and religious priests working in the Diocese. One of Bishop Hillinger's first official acts as Diocesan Bishop was to create the Diocese's fifth deanery. He established the McHenry County Deanery in March 1954, and the

◆ **Bishop Raymond P. Hillinger, fourth bishop of the Rockford Diocese. Motto: To serve God first.**

◆ **Bishop Hillinger shares bulls (his episcopal appointment) with Monsignor Louis Franey in January 1954.**

Right Reverend Monsignor Charles F. Nix, Pastor of St. Mary Parish, McHenry, was named its first Dean.

PARISH LIFE AND DEVELOPMENT

Recall that Pope Pius XII had allowed for evening Masses and had modified the rules for the Eucharistic fast in January 1953. Bishop Hillinger celebrated the first evening Mass in diocesan history on September 15, 1954, at St. James Pro-Cathedral. Records from that time indicate that as many as 1,000 Catholics crowded into the Pro-Cathedral for the historic Mass.

The year of 1954 was a special year for Our Blessed Mother. Marian Year Masses were celebrated in all of the dioceses of the United States, which is dedicated to Our Blessed Mother under her title of the Immaculate Conception. That year was the 100th Anniversary of the proclamation of the infallible dogma by Pope Pius IX. Bishop Hillinger oversaw the year-long celebration of this Marian

Year in the Diocese, with the main event taking place at the Sterling High School stadium on September 19, 1954.

This event included a group recitation of the Rosary by the more than 6,000 participants. Bishop Hillinger preached a beautiful and stirring sermon at the Holy Hour which followed the Rosary and Archbishop Leo Binz celebrated Benediction of the Most Blessed Sacrament at the close of the holy our. Bishop Hillinger closed the Marian Year by directing that every parish in the diocese observe a triduum ending on December 8, 1954. He officially closed the Marian Year with a Pontifical High Mass on December 8, 1954, at 8:00 P.M. at St. James Pro-Cathedral.

As the number of Catholics continued to expand, Bishop Hillinger recognized the need to erect another parish in the newly established McHenry County Deanery. St. Margaret Mary Parish in Algonquin was formally established on June 1, 1954.

◆ **Monsignor Charles S. Nix, the first dean of the McHenry Deanery.**

◆ **Bishop Hillinger with Fathers Emmett Murphy and James Murphy at St. Edward Church, Rockford, in the mid-1950s. The older Father Murphy was the uncle of the younger Father Murphy, who ended up succeeding him as pastor at St. Edward.**

A second Romanian Catholic parish was reconciled to the Roman Catholic Church in the City of Aurora. This formal reconciliation of St. George Parish was solemnly confirmed at a ceremony there on April 7, 1955. Because of Bishop Hillinger's poor health, the Chancellor, Monsignor Louis J. Franey, represented him at this ceremony.

A near tragedy occurred on Memorial Day, 1955, when the diocese's oldest parish experienced a major fire in its church building. St. Michael Parish in Galena almost lost its church when a fire destroyed the sanctuary and gutted nearly the entire nave of the church building. The structure was able to be saved and under the able direction of its Pastor, Father Vincent L. Cottam, the parishioners restored and rebuilt the church which was dedicated on May 30, 1956.

CLERGY, RELIGIOUS AND LAITY

Monsignor Franey, who had been Chancellor of the Diocese under Bishop Boylan and the Administrator of the Diocese after Bishop Boylan had died, was confirmed by Bishop Hillinger as Chancellor and Officialis. Also, Bishop Hillinger named Father Arthur J. O'Neill to succeed Father Philip L. Kennedy as the

managing editor of the diocesan newspaper The Observer on April 7, 1954. It was with the appointment of Father O'Neill that The Observer offices were moved from Freeport to Rockford. The new offices were located on the second floor of the Catholic Charities office building at 839 North Main Street.

In 1954, Bishop Hillinger ordained nine men as diocesan priests. It was the single largest ordination class to that date. In addition, Bishop Hillinger ordained two Benedictine monks as priests that same year. Again, due to his serious health problems, these ordinations would be the only ones Bishop Hillinger would be able to administer.

On July 1, 1954, with the full approval and support of Bishop Hillinger, the priests of the Diocese formed what was named The Clergy Relief Society. Two of the priests who took the lead in organizing this voluntary association for the care of sick and disabled diocesan priests were Father Joseph M. Egan, Pastor of St. Mary Parish, Woodstock, and Father Peter A. Watgen, Pastor of St. Wendelin Parish, Shannon, who served as its first Secretary-Treasurer.

◆ **The future Monsignor Charles McNamee, attended his first scout camp in 1937 as a young teen.**

In September, 1954, Bishop Hillinger named Father Charles W. McNamee to be the diocesan Scout Chaplain. With the appointment of Father McNamee, Catholic Scouting for boys and girls experienced an unparalleled growth and development throughout the parishes of the Diocese. The promotion of Catholic Scouting by Bishop Hillinger and his successors did much to advance the goals of Bishop Boylan in seeing to the welfare of Catholic youth.

In March 1955, Bishop Hillinger established the Diocesan Council of Catholic Women (DCCW). Each parish was represented at its first meeting that month and Monsignor Frederick J. Connor, Pastor of Holy Angels Parish, Aurora, was named the first diocesan moderator, and Mrs. Charles Thomas of Rockford was elected its first president.

Upon the invitation of Bishop Hillinger, a novitiate for the Holy Heart of Mary Sisters was established in Batavia in August 1955 and opened in September 1956. The Sisters continue to maintain this as their canonical novitiate.

With the restoration of solemn vows to orders of women devoted to the contemplative life by Pope Pius XII, the Poor Clares professed their solemn vows as well as a fourth vow of enclosure on June 9, 1955, before one of the priest-friars of St. Anthony Parish, Rockford, a delegate of Bishop Hillinger.

DIOCESAN ADMINISTRATION

Bishop Hillinger's decline in health became more serious during the course of the year of 1955 to the extent that the Auxiliary Bishop of the Lithuanian Diocese of Kaunas, Bishop Brizgys, celebrated the Holy Thursday ceremonies at St. James Pro-Cathedral that year and the next year of 1956, when the revised Ritual of Holy Week Services was able to be used. Bishop Martin McNamara of Joliet willingly celebrated and administered the Sacrament of Holy Orders by ordaining priests for the Diocese of Rockford in 1955 and again in 1956.

◆ **Monsignor Andrew J. Burns, Vicar General, was named Administrator of the Diocese in 1955, when Bishop Hillinger's health deteriorated.**

◆ **Monsignor Frederick F. Connor, first diocesan moderator of the DCCW in 1955.**

Cardinal Stritch, as Metropolitan for the Province of Chicago, announced in November 1955, that the Vicar General, Monsignor Andrew J. Burns, Pastor of St. Mary Parish, Sterling, would be the Administrator of the Diocese of Rockford, such was the state of health of our Bishop Hillinger. Monsignor Burns administered diocesan affairs until Bishop Hillinger was named an Auxiliary Bishop of Chicago on June 27, 1956, resigning as the fourth Bishop of Rockford. Bishop Hillinger was also appointed the Pastor of St. Mel-Holy Ghost Parish where he remained until his retirement in 1968.

In his retirement, Bishop Hillinger's health never improved and, in fact, worsened and after a protracted illness, he died on Saturday, November 13, 1971, at the age of 67. He was buried in All Saints Cemetery, Des Plaines, Illinois. Though his episcopate in Rockford was brief in numbers of days, Bishop Hillinger remains fondly remembered by clergy and laity alike as a holy and kindly bishop, always concerned for the spiritual and temporal welfare of his people.

THE VACANT SEE

June 27, 1956, marked the appointment of Monsignor Donald M. Carroll as the fifth Bishop of the Diocese of Rockford by His Holiness, Pope Pius XII. Since the See of Rockford was without a bishop as of that date, Monsignor Burns, Bishop Hillinger's Administrator for the Diocese also ceased in that office. He called a meeting of the College of Consultors who proceeded to elect Monsignor Louis J. Franey Diocesan Administrator for a second time.

Donald Martin Carroll

Bishop-elect of Rockford

Donald Martin Carroll was born on November 25, 1909, in Chicago, the son of John and Margaret Boland Carroll. He received a Catholic education first at Blessed Sacrament Parish school, then at Quigley Preparatory Seminary, Chicago, and finally at St. Mary of the Lake Seminary, Mundelein, Illinois. Donald Carroll was ordained to the Sacred Priesthood by George Cardinal Mundelein on April 7, 1934, at St. Mary of the Lake Seminary.

The newly ordained Father Carroll was assigned to pursue post-graduate studies in Canon Law at the Pontifical Gregorian University in Rome where he obtained a doctorate in Canon Law in 1937. Upon his return to the United States, Father Carroll was appointed to serve in the Archdiocesan Matrimonial Tribunal and he was appointed at the same time the Assistant for Visitation Parish in Chicago. Father Carroll faithfully and ably fulfilled the responsibilities of both assignments for the next five years.

In 1942, he was appointed to be a secretary at the Apostolic Delegation in Washington, D.C., and while serving in this post, he also served as a chaplain at St. Ann's Infant Home in Washington, D.C. His appointment by Pope Pius XII to be the fifth bishop of the Diocese of Rockford was announced in Washington, D.C. and in Rockford on June 27, 1956.

Bishop-elect Donald M. Carroll's consecration had been scheduled for August 30, 1956, but due to his illness was delayed. The nature of Monsignor Carroll's illness made it necessary for him to resign the See of Rockford on September 25, 1956. Monsignor Carroll was appointed Pastor of St. Edmund Parish, Oak Park, Illinois, where he served until January 1967, when he was appointed the Chaplain for Columbus Hospital in Chicago where he remained until his retirement.

◆ **Bishop-elect Donald M. Carroll, fifth bishop of the Rockford Diocese. Motto: Let us put on Jesus.**

◆ **Bishop-elect Donald Carroll at St. Ann's Infant Home, Washington, D.C., 1956.**

The Right Reverend Monsignor Donald M. Carroll, Bishop-elect as the fifth Bishop of the Diocese of Rockford, died on Thursday, January 3, 2002, at age 92. Francis Cardinal George, OMI, Archbishop of Chicago, celebrated his funeral Mass on Wednesday, January 9, 2002, at St. Timothy Parish, Chicago, with several auxiliary bishops of Chicago concelebrating.

On behalf of the Rockford Diocese, Monsignor David D. Kagan, Vicar General, sent a letter of condolences to Cardinal George upon receiving the news of Monsignor Carroll's death. He wrote, in part, "Monsignor Carroll will always have a special place in the affections of the Catholic people of this Diocese since he had been appointed to be our Bishop. The Holy Sacrifice of the Mass will be offered here for Monsignor Carroll's eternal rest and peace. We shall keep you and all the Catholic faithful of the Archdiocese in our prayers."

THE VACANT SEE

With the resignation from the See of Rockford by Bishop-elect Carroll on September 25, 1956, the Diocesan vacancy continued for only 16 days longer. His Holiness, Pope Pius XII, appointed The Most Reverend Loras T. Lane, Auxiliary Bishop of the Archdiocese of Dubuque, and President of Loras College to be the sixth Bishop of the Diocese of Rockford.

◆ Camp Fire Girls who were the first winners of the Marion Award in 1963, St. Patrick, Rochelle.

◆ Choir practice at the Newman Center, DeKalb, in the late 1950s.

The Lane Years

Loras Thomas Lane was born in Cascade, Iowa, on October 19, 1910, to Thomas and Josephine Barrett Lane. Loras Lane attended parochial grade and high schools at St. Martin Parish, Cascade, Iowa. He attended the University of Notre Dame, obtained a Bachelor of Arts degree in Business Administration in 1932 and then attended Loras College, Dubuque, where he completed his studies in philosophy in 1933. He was then assigned to The Pontifical North American College and the Pontifical Gregorian University in Rome for his priestly formation and theological studies and training.

Loras Thomas Lane was ordained to the Sacred Priesthood on March 19, 1937, in Rome by His Eminence, Cardinal Marchetti-Selvagianni. His first priestly assignment was as the Assistant for Nativity Parish in Dubuque where he served for three years. In 1940, Father Lane was appointed to the faculty of Loras College where he taught until 1944 when he was appointed the secretary to Archbishop Henry P. Rohlman. At this time the Archbishop assigned Father Lane to post-graduate studies in Canon Law at The Catholic University of America in Washington, D.C., and he obtained his doctorate there in 1947. Upon Father Lane's return to the Archdiocese he was appointed the Vice-Chancellor and two years later in 1949, Pope Pius XII named him a Domestic Prelate with the title of Right Reverend Monsignor.

Loras Thomas Lane was named Auxiliary Bishop of the Archdiocese of Dubuque by Pope Pius XII on May 29, 1951; on June 15, 1951, he was appointed President of Loras College and on August 20, 1951, The Most Reverend Leo Binz, Archbishop of Dubuque consecrated Loras Thomas Lane at St. Raphael Cathedral, Dubuque. The co-consecrators were The Most Reverend Joseph C.

◆ **Monsignor Franey meets Bishop Lane at the Illinois Central Train Station, Rockford, on November 19, 1956, and welcomes him to the Rockford Diocese.**

◆ **Bishop Loras T. Lane, sixth bishop of the Rockford Diocese.**
Motto: The way of Truth.

Willging of Pueblo, Colorado, and The Most Reverend Edward J. Fitzgerald of Winona, Minnesota. At the time of his consecration as a bishop, Loras Lane, 40, was the youngest bishop in the United States. Bishop Lane served the Archdiocese of Dubuque as its Auxiliary Bishop and as President of Loras College for the next five years until his appointment as Bishop of Rockford.

After his installation as Bishop of Rockford on November 20, 1956, at St. James Pro-Cathedral, by Samuel Cardinal Stritch, Metropolitan Archbishop of Chicago, Bishop Lane initiated a 12-year period of growth and renewed activity in the Diocese. Bishop Lane devoted himself to every aspect of Church life and activity and reinvigorated them all.

BISHOP LANE'S FIRST YEAR

DIOCESAN ADMINISTRATION

As required by the law of the Church, Bishop Lane reappointed Monsignor Andrew J. Burns, P.A., Pastor of St. Mary Parish, Sterling, to be Vicar General of the Diocese. Monsignor Burns had served as Vicar General for Bishops Hoban, Boylan and Hillinger; he had been named the Administrator for the Diocese by Cardinal Stritch when Bishop Hillinger's health had worsened. This faithful priest, servant of the Church and one of the original priests of the Diocese of Rockford died on March 28, 1957. His funeral Mass and burial were celebrated by Bishop Lane on April 1, 1957 at St. Mary Parish, Sterling. Monsignor Andrew J. Burns was 86 years of age when he died.

Bishop Lane made two important diocesan appointments which would have a very beneficial and long-term effect on virtually every aspect of Church life. On September 10, 1957, Bishop Lane appointed Monsignor Louis J. Franey, P.A., the Chancellor, Officialis and Secretary to the Bishop, to be the Vicar General of the Diocese of Rockford. Monsignor Franey would serve in that office for the next 30 years.

That same day, Bishop Lane appointed Father Raymond J. Wahl, J.C.D., to be the Chancellor and Officialis for the Diocese as well as the Diocesan Director of Education. This began a long tenure of

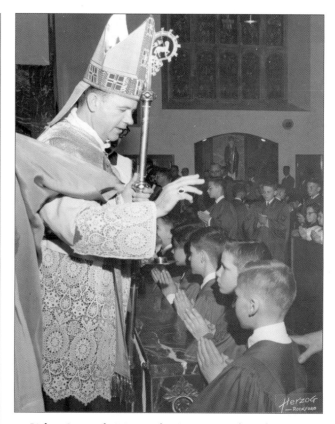

◆ **Bishop Lane administers the Sacrament of Confirmation at St. Patrick Church, Rockford.**

diocesan administrative service, as well as a fruitful pastoral service, for the future Monsignor Wahl who would be appointed to be the pastor of seven different parishes over the next 40-plus years. Father Donald L. Schuler was appointed to succeed Monsignor Franey as Secretary to the Bishop on September 10, 1957. A little over a month later on October 26, 1957, Father Schuler and Father Francis

P. McNally (first Diocesan Director of Catholic Charities and the then Pastor of St. Patrick Parish, Rockford) were killed in a light plane crash returning from a Notre Dame football game when they encountered an early, freakish snowstorm. Father J. Francis Moroney was appointed to take Father Schuler's place as Secretary to the Bishop and Father John F. Regan was appointed Pastor of St. Patrick Parish, Rockford, to succeed Father McNally.

Diocesan Activities

Bishop Lane truly energized the entire Diocese with his own enthusiasm for the life of the Church and the advance of the Gospel. In the first year alone, Bishop Lane visited 78 parishes to administer the Sacrament of Confirmation. Bishop Lane also took those occasions to make a canonical visit to the parish to examine all of its activities.

In May 1957, The Rockford Serra Club received its charter, bringing the number of chartered clubs in the diocese to four — Aurora, McHenry, Rockford and the Rock River Valley. The four Serra Clubs sponsored the televising of Bishop Lane's first priesthood ordinations of five men on May 25, 1957.

The autumn of 1957 was an especially busy and productive time during Bishop Lane's first year as bishop. In October, Bishop Lane erected two parishes – St. Bernadette Parish, Rockford, with Father Daniel B. Geoghegan appointed as its first Pastor, and St. Monica Parish, Carpentersville, where Father Edmund P. Petit was appointed the first pastor. Bishop Lane gave Father Hubert V. McGinn permission to build a Catholic Center with a chapel for the Newman Club at Northern Illinois University in DeKalb. The success of this venture would lead to Bishop Lane's alteration of the Center to the status of a non-territorial parish in 1966.

Two related activities which would have far-reaching effects on parish and family life also occurred in 1957. Bishop Lane established the Family Life Bureau for the Diocese of Rockford and gave it the responsibility for fostering programs throughout the Diocese which would support and promote greater strength of married and family life. The Pre-Cana and Cana conferences and the Christian Family Movement (CFM) were early and very popular programs promoted by this office.

◆ **Bishop Lane with the trustees of St. Bernadette Parish, Rockford, circa 1960.**

◆ **Bishop Lane at one of his many appearances at events in the Diocese.**

Another activity of 1957 occurred on October 6, when the first convention of the Diocesan Council of Catholic Women was held in Rockford. Bishop Lane offered the opening Mass of the convention at St. James Pro-Cathedral. At the close of the convention's business and activities, Bishop Lane spoke to the assembled women and offered them three tasks to take home to their parishes and families: first, to have at least one member of each of their families attend daily Mass; second, to foster and increase prayers for vocations; and third, to encourage participation in the programs of the new Diocesan Bureau of Family Life. Monsignor Frederick J. Connor, Pastor of Holy Angels Parish, Aurora, and first Diocesan Moderator of D.C.C.W., continued in this position until Bishop Lane appointed Monsignor Louis J. Franey the second Diocesan Moderator of D.C.C.W. in June 1959.

Plans had been made for the celebration of the Diocese's Golden Anniversary since shortly after Bishop Lane's installation. Father Francis McNally had been named the general chairman of the Diocese's Jubilee and with his untimely death in October 1957, Bishop Lane entrusted this important task to Monsignor Louis J. Franey, Vicar General.

THE GOLDEN JUBILEE OF 1958

The Jubilee Year of the Diocese of Rockford was opened in every church and chapel on December 31, 1957, with a Holy Hour of Exposition and Benediction of the Most Blessed Sacrament. Bishop Lane, in his letter announcing the Golden Jubilee Year to the Catholic faithful set the tone for the entire year. In part, he wrote: "The Jubilee Year, therefore, should be primarily one of thanksgiving... Our gratitude should be demonstrated not only by thanking God for His gifts and graces, but also by an increase in our love for Him by the deepening of our religious spirit, and by our zealous efforts to advance the work of the Church for the salvation of men." The anniversary year would find Bishop Lane, the priests, religious and laity, actively involved in celebrating the abundant blessings of the first 50 years, as well as continuing to advance and develop the spiritual and temporal life of the Diocese for the future.

Bishop Lane, like his predecessor Bishop Boylan, had a keen interest in Catholic secondary education, as well as Catholic higher education. Beginning in the Diocese's Golden Jubilee Year and continuing virtually until his death 10 years later, Bishop Lane created and reorganized the system of Catholic high school secondary education in the Diocese which resulted in the establishment of the central Catholic high school system. He also promoted the establishment of single-gender Catholic high schools as well as a Catholic college for women.

◆ **Marian Jubilee Year Rally at Sterling, May 25, 1958.**

◆ **Newman Central Catholic High School, Sterling.**

In January 1958, Bishop Lane announced plans to erect a new central Catholic high school in Sterling, and that more than $1.4 million had already been raised for that effort. The new high school would serve the entire Sterling Deanery; it was to be named Newman Central Catholic High School. It would replace the former Community High School approved by Bishop Muldoon and renamed in honor of Cardinal Newman in 1952 with the approval of Bishop Boylan.

On Sunday, February 9, 1958, Bishop Lane awarded to Boy Scouts from across the Diocese, the *Ad Altare Dei* medal in a ceremony at St. James Pro-Cathedral. The following Wednesday, February 12, the first Educational Convention for the Diocese was held in Rockford at the Faust Hotel. This gathering of our Catholic school teachers was organized and hosted by Father Raymond J. Wahl, Diocesan Director of Education. Monsignor William J. Donovan, the former and first Director of Education and then Pastor of Holy Cross Parish, Batavia, was the keynote speaker. The topic of his address was "Fifty Years of Educational Progress in the Diocese of Rockford."

Forty-two years after Bishop Muldoon convoked the First Synod of the Diocese of Rockford in 1916, Bishop Lane convoked the Second Synod of the Diocese of Rockford on March 11, 1958. After announcing the Synod on July 19, 1957, the intervening time was devoted to its preparation.

The Second Synod was held at St. James Pro-Cathedral with a Solemn Pontifical Mass of the Holy Spirit offered by Bishop Lane, with Monsignor Franey, the Promoter of the Synod preaching the sermon of the Mass. Bishop Lane addressed the assembled clergy and explained the Synod's procedures. They proceeded to elect Synodal Judges, Parish Priest Consultors and Synodal Examiners. The new particular laws for the Diocese of Rockford were approved by the assemblage. Bishop Lane set the effective date of the Synod laws to be September 23, 1958—50 years to the day of the establishment of the diocese.

In March 1958, Bishop Lane appointed Father Raymond J. Wahl, the Diocesan Director of Education (as well as Chancellor and Officialis), to also be the Director of the Confraternity of Christian Doctrine. The first organized presentations of the

◆ **Boy Scout Sunday at St. James Pro-Cathedral, February 9, 1958.**

◆ Adult choirs from across the diocese are honored at St. Anthony of Padua, Rockford, April 13, 1958.

Pre-Cana and Cana Conferences in four areas of the Diocese — Aurora, Crystal Lake, Rockford and Sterling, were held in March. More conferences were then held in other areas of the Diocese as time went on.

Bishop Lane authorized a novena for vocations from March 2 to 9 throughout the Diocese and he turned over the promotion of this novena to the four chartered Serra Clubs in the Diocese. On March 21, 1958, a joint announcement was made by Bishop Lane and Mother Mary Corona, O.S.F., that Rome had granted permission to the School Sisters of St. Francis of Milwaukee to establish a new Province with its motherhouse in the Rockford Diocese. Property was purchased on the east side of the City of Rockford and the project to build a Provincialate began to take shape. This new Province would include all of Illinois outside of the Archdiocese of Chicago, plus the states of Indiana and Missouri.

In April 1958, a Jubilee Mass was offered by Bishop Lane at St. Anthony of Padua Parish, Rockford. It was to honor the many adult choirs from across the diocese and 700 members of those choirs participated in this televised Mass. April 20 marked the observance of Christian Rural Life Day at St. Charles Borromeo Parish, Hampshire. Father Clement P. Petit, Pastor of the parish, hosted the

many Catholics from the mostly rural and agricultural areas of the Diocese. Bishop Lane offered a Pontifical High Mass and afterwards blessed the seed, the soil and the farm equipment as was the custom each spring. At the end of April, Bishop Lane announced the construction of another central Catholic high school in the McHenry Deanery. It would be named Marian Central Catholic High School and would be located in Woodstock. The new central high school would replace St. Mary Parish High School, and would be staffed by the Sisters of the Holy Cross who had charge of the Parish High School.

◆ The first diocesan convention of the Catholic Family Movement was held at St. Patrick, Rockford, May 4, 1958.

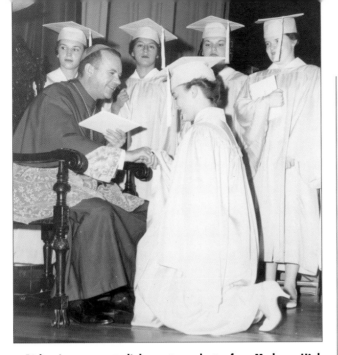

◆ **Bishop Lane presents diplomas to graduates from Madonna High School, Aurora**

The first diocesan convention of the Catholic Family Movement (CFM) was held at St. Patrick Parish, Rockford, on May 4, 1958. A Diocesan Catholic Youth Congress for all high school pupils was held in Rockford on May 9-10, 1958. A dinner for all the participants was scheduled for that Friday evening at the Faust Hotel. Bishop Lane offered Mass for the group on Saturday morning at St. Patrick Parish and a music festival was held that afternoon at the Rockford Armory where 600 young people combined their considerable talents. The Illinois Catholic Veterans were welcomed to the Diocese by Bishop Lane for their three-day convention in Rockford from May 16-18, 1958. Bishop Lane ordained five men to the priesthood for the Diocese at the end of May 1958, and two other men studying at the American College in Louvain, Belgium were ordained for the Diocese in June 1958, for a total of seven newly ordained priests.

The Marian Rally held in Sterling on May 25, 1958, had a double significance since it was not only a part of the Diocesan Jubilee Year, but it marked the centennial of the apparitions of Our Lady at Lourdes under her title of the Immaculate Conception. Mary is also the patroness of the Rockford Diocese under this beautiful title. Eighteen thousand Catholics from across the Diocese participated in the ceremonies which were concluded by Bishop Lane who lead all in

the Jubilee prayer and solemn celebration of Benediction of the Most Blessed Sacrament. Amidst the joy of the Jubilee Year, the Diocese paused to mourn the death of Cardinal Stritch on May 27, 1958. He had been named the Pro-Prefect of the Sacred Congregation for the Propagation of the Faith and had only recently departed Chicago for Rome when he died.

The advent of the summer season did not slow down Diocesan or Jubilee activities. In June 1958, the Sisters of St. Joseph in Belvidere, announced plans to build a new, 100-bed hospital there on a recently purchased 20-acre site. The cost of the project was estimated to be $2 million. At the end of June, Bishop Lane established the Rockford Diocesan Curia of the Legion of Mary and appointed Father Sylvester J. Eye its first Diocesan Director.

Father Joseph T. Healey, Pastor of St. Joseph Parish, Harvard, was named the coordinator and spiritual director for the Jubilee Pilgrimage to Lourdes and Rome. Thirty-eight Catholics from the Diocese made the pilgrimage which set sail on the *Ile de France* from New York City on June 12, 1958, after Mass at St. Patrick Cathedral. The diocesan pilgrims were met at Lourdes by Bishop Lane who offered Mass for them at the Basilica of Lourdes. He continued on to Rome with the group where he offered Mass for them at the tomb of St. Peter as well as in the other major basilicas. The high point of the Rome portion of the pilgrimage was an audience with Pope Pius XII, who imparted his apostolic blessing to all in the Diocese.

◆ **Father Philip L. Kennedy, first dean of the Elgin Deanery.**

On July 18, 1958, Bishop Lane announced the establishment of a sixth deanery in the Diocese of Rockford. The Elgin Deanery was created from 10 parishes and one mission parish, and Father Philip L. Kennedy, Pastor of St. Laurence Parish, Elgin, was named the first dean. The new deanery was comprised of the three parishes in

Elgin, and the parishes in Carpentersville, Hampshire, Genoa, St. Charles, Sycamore, Virgil, Dundee and its mission in Gilberts.

The last four months of the Golden Jubilee Year were marked with great enthusiasm for the Catholic apostolates, solemn liturgical celebrations and the passing of a beloved Pontiff and the election of his successor, a future saint. With the resumption of classes in the Diocesan parochial and high schools, Father Wahl announced that there were 22,758 pupils enrolled. On September 14, 1958, Bishop Lane celebrated a Jubilee Mass for the City of Elgin on the athletic field of St. Edward High School.

◆ **Diocesan 50th anniversary Mass celebrated by Archbishop Edward F. Hoban, 1958.**

The anniversary day of the Diocese, September 23, 1958, was celebrated with a Solemn Pontifical Mass at St. James Pro-Cathedral. With Bishop Lane presiding in the sanctuary, Mass was offered by Archbishop Edward F. Hoban, the Archbishop-Bishop of Cleveland and second Bishop of Rockford. Archbishop Leo Binz, native son and the Archbishop of Dubuque preached the Jubilee sermon. Eighteen members of the hierarchy were also present, along with the clergy, religious and laity of the Diocese and many invited dignitaries, including 18 Mothers General. A formal banquet followed at the Faust Hotel to bring this great day to a fitting close. Five days later on September 28, Bishop Lane celebrated a Pontifical field Mass in Aurora to mark the Silver Anniversary of the Benedictine Fathers and Brothers at Marmion Academy.

On October 5, 1958, the second convention of the Diocesan Council of Catholic Women opened with a Solemn Pontifical Mass at St. James Pro-Cathedral offered by Bishop Lane. The Catholic faithful of the Diocese grieved with the rest of the Catholic Church and the world at the news of the death of Pope Pius XII on October 9, 1958. Bishop Lane authorized all the churches in the Diocese to be draped in black during the nine-day period of mourning. He offered a Solemn Pontifical Requiem Mass the evening of the Pope's death and another at the close of the mourning period, both at the Pro-Cathedral. Three weeks later on October 28, 1958, the Patriarch of Venice, Angelo Giuseppe Cardinal Roncalli, was elected Supreme Pontiff, taking for himself the name of John XXIII.

The Diocese's official newspaper, *The Observer*, hosted the Midwest Regional Catholic Press Convention October 16-17, 1958 in Rockford.

Bishop Lane offered a Solemn Pontifical Mass of the Coronation on November 4, 1958, at St. James Pro-Cathedral to mark the election of Pope John XXIII and the official beginning of his Pontificate. On November 7, 1958, Bishop Lane announced that the Sisters of the Third Order of St. Francis had purchased property to build a new

◆ **Bishop Lane and his mother, Josephine, with Pope John XXIII, October 1959.**

St. Anthony Hospital. The new location was on the far east side of Rockford on State Street, east of Alpine Road. The new hospital would provide for 225 beds and be expandable to 350 beds.

The final month of the Golden Jubilee Year was highlighted by two events. On Sunday, December 14, 1958, Bishop Lane, along with four visiting bishops, administered the Sacrament of Confirmation to 1,250 adult converts from across the Diocese. The ceremony was held at the Illinois National Guard Armory in Rockford and was significant not only for the Diocese but gained national attention as well. The Most Reverend George Biskup, Auxiliary Bishop of Dubuque, Iowa, The Most Reverend Vincent Brizgys, Auxiliary Bishop of Kaunas, Lithuania in exile, The Most Reverend James Casey, Bishop of Lincoln, Nebraska, and The Most Reverend Frederick Freking, Bishop of Salina, Kansas, assisted Bishop Lane at that historic ceremony.

The Golden Jubilee Year had opened with holy hours celebrated in all the churches and chapels of the Diocese, and closed in the same manner on December 31, 1958.

◆ **Jubilee Year Confirmation at the National Guard Armory, Rockford, December 1958.**

THE NEXT TEN YEARS

The Diocese, along with the Universal Church, received with joy the announcement of Pope John XXIII's intention to convoke the Second Ecumenical Council of the Vatican and the 21st Ecumenical Council of the Church. The announcement was made on January 25, 1959, and began an intense four-year period of preparation which would involve directly Bishop Lane.

Locally, in the 10 years following the Diocese's Golden Jubilee, Bishop Lane established three more parishes, the Central Catholic High School system, expanded the facilities of several of the Catholic high schools, approved the establishment of two all-girls Catholic high schools and another all boys Catholic high school, dedicated a Catholic college for women, and continued to promote vocations to the priesthood and the religious life. Bishop Lane also dedicated a significant amount of time and resources to the further development of the spiritual welfare of the Catholic laity and their own continued education in the Catholic faith and its practice.

PARISH LIFE AND DEVELOPMENT

Bishop Lane erected St. Thomas More Parish in Elgin on March 23, 1959, and appointed Father Walter C. Roberts as its first pastor. With the establishment of this new parish, the Elgin Deanery now was comprised of 11 parishes and one mission parish. In April 1962, Bishop Lane erected a new parish on the northeast side of the City of Rockford. It was his intent that this parish be the new Cathedral Parish for the Diocese. Plans were formulated and a new school and gymnasium were the first two buildings erected and in use by the spring of 1964, the gymnasium serving as a temporary church. Bishop Lane appointed Monsignor Herman A. Meilinger the first Pastor of the parish. The plans for this to be the new Cathedral Parish did not come to fruition and thus, the new parish was named Holy Family. St. Mary Hospital in DeKalb which developed as an adjunct of St. Mary Parish, itself, closed in 1965 due to demographic and financial factors.

◆ Valentine's Day for the missions at Bishop Lane's residence, 1961.

◆ Groundbreaking ceremonies for the new Cathedral Parish, Rockford, 1963. Later this parish was renamed Holy Family.

In October 1960, Bishop Lane had dedicated the newly completed chapel at the Newman Center in DeKalb. On December 11, 1966, Bishop Lane altered the status of the Newman Center and established it as a university and non-territorial parish. He appointed Father Hubert V. McGinn, Newman Center Chaplain, the first Pastor of Christ the Teacher University Parish, DeKalb. Its status was unique for Newman Centers.

Bishop Lane established a fifth diocesan cemetery on January 26, 1962, in the fast growing area of Kane County near the towns of Batavia, Geneva and St. Charles, naming this new Catholic cemetery Resurrection Cemetery.

CATHOLIC SCHOOLS

Ground was broken in Rockford on July 21, 1959, by Bishop Lane for a new central Catholic high school. In February 1960, this new school was named in honor of John J. Boylan, third Bishop of the Diocese of Rockford. The new Boylan Central Catholic High School opened for classes in September 1960. As a result of this new co-educational school, St. Thomas High School (an all boys Catholic school) tried to continue as a college preparatory school but eventually closed in 1962, with most of its remaining pupils transferring to Boylan.

◆ **Boylan Central Catholic High School, Rockford, in the early 1960s.**

In 1959, Bishop Lane designated Aquin High School in Freeport a central Catholic high school and broke ground for a new addition to it that same year. On March 19, 1961, Bishop Lane returned to Freeport to dedicate the new addition.

In August 1961, Bishop Lane announced plans to construct two new high schools in Aurora, and he broke ground for them in July 1962. An all boy's school to be named Roncalli High School would be staffed by the Christian Brothers, and Rosary High School for girls would be staffed by the Springfield Dominican Sisters. Until separate buildings could be completed both schools opened for classes in September 1963, in the old Holy Angels Parish grade school. Separate schools were ready for classes in 1964. Roncalli closed in June 1968, but Rosary continues to provide a quality Catholic education for the Aurora area.

Bishop Lane announced in 1963 that the Adrian Dominican Sisters would add to their already considerable apostolate of Catholic education in the Diocese, by opening St. Dominic College in St. Charles. It was the first four year Catholic college to be established in the Diocese of Rockford. On April 27, 1964, the Archbishop of Chicago, Albert Cardinal Meyer, and Bishop Lane dedicated the Catholic institution for women. In June 1964, Bishop Lane dedicated a new addition to St. Edward Central Catholic High School which he had

◆ **Aquin Central Catholic High School's new library, in the early 1960s.**

designated a central Catholic high school the prior year.

In September 1965, Notre Dame High School for girls opened for classes in DeKalb and was dedicated by Bishop Lane on June 3, 1966. The School Sisters of Notre Dame were in charge of this new Catholic high school in the Diocese. On March 8, 1968, Bishop Lane announced plans for another reorganization of Catholic secondary education in the City of Aurora. A new Central Catholic High School would be created from the merger of Roncalli High School for boys and Madonna High School for girls. Aurora Central Catholic high school opened for classes in September 1968.

HOUSES OF RELIGIOUS

Bishop Lane and Mother M. Calestine, O.S.F., broke ground for the new motherhouse for the Rockford Province of the School Sisters of St. Francis on October 22, 1961. On December 3, 1961, Bishop

◆ **Bishop Lane and his secretary, Father Francis Moroney, leave for Rome to attend one of the sessions of the Second Vatican Council. Also shown are Monsignors Raymond Wahl and Louis Franey.**

Lane blessed and laid the cornerstone for an addition to the Poor Clares Monastery of Corpus Christi in Rockford. In November 1961, Bishop Lane blessed and laid the cornerstone for the new St. Anthony Hospital and Sisters' Convent; the hospital would be ready for occupancy in April 1963. The Servite Fathers' St. Joseph Seminary in St. Charles was closed in 1966 due to a decline in enrollment and the rising costs of operations. In March 1959, the Resurrection Fathers purchased property in Woodstock in order to build a novitiate and in May 1960, Bishop Lane consecrated the altars for the new St. Joseph Novitiate.

THE SECOND VATICAN COUNCIL 1962-1965

In October 1961, Pope John XXIII appointed Bishop Lane a member of the Preparatory Commission for Seminary Education, and in December 1961, he traveled to Rome to attend a series of meetings of that commission. Bishop Lane was elected by the Council Fathers in December 1963, to a similar commission created by Pope Paul VI.

While the years of the Second Vatican Council required a great deal of Bishop Lane's time and energy, he devoted himself to his diocesan responsibilities with the same zeal and vigor as always. The year 1962 was significant not only for what Bishop Lane continued to do for the Diocese, but it was also the year of his Silver Anniversary of ordination to the Priesthood. Having been ordained a priest on March 19, 1937, he deferred the celebration to September 23, the 54th anniversary of the Diocese. After celebrating a Pontifical Mass of Thanksgiving, Bishop Lane invited all of the priests of the Diocese and their parents to a special dinner. His remarks at this dinner revealed his keen interest in promoting vocations and his appreciation for the role parents play in fostering them. He said: "I especially wanted to invite the mothers and fathers of our priests to come to this observance, and I am delighted that so many found it possible to

◆ **Bishop Lane in Rome during the Second Vatican Council.**

In the midst of the great enthusiasm and anticipation generated by the Second Vatican Council, the whole Church and indeed, the world mourned the death of Pope John XXIII on June 3, 1963. His successor, Giovanni Battista Cardinal Montini, Archbishop of Milan, was elected on June 21, 1963, and took to himself the name Paul VI. With the death of Pope John XXIII the Council ceased and Pope Paul VI reconvoked the Council after his election and it continued to its conclusion.

DIOCESAN LIFE

Even though Bishop Lane was busy with the work of the Council, when he was in the Diocese he made great efforts to keep priests and laity informed of its workings and progress. In the summer of 1963, Bishop Lane established a new program for seminarians ordained as deacons in anticipation of ordination to the priesthood. That program has become the usual method for the first grade of the Sacrament of Holy Orders. Men ordained deacons would spend at least the summer before priesthood ordination working in parishes to obtain some experience of parish life and the daily life and duties of a parish priest.

attend. It is largely due to you that we have such wonderful priests today. It is you who brought them into the world. You trained them, nourished them with the divine truth and taught them the Christian way of life. It was your good example that helped them along the road to the priesthood. I am deeply grateful to you, and I am sure everyone in the Diocese shares my gratitude."

Not three weeks later, on October 11, 1962, Bishop Lane attended the opening session of the Second Vatican Council in the Basilica of St. Peter in the Vatican. The zeal for the good of souls of his Diocese was displayed by Bishop Lane for the whole Church by his faithful and capable attendance at all four sessions of the Council which closed on December 8, 1965.

◆ **Bishop Lane surveys the damage after fire destroyed the interior of St. Mary Church, Rockford, February 12, 1962.**

The first document issued by the Fathers of the Second Vatican Council and approved by the Pope was the Decree on the Sacred Liturgy. Bishop Lane took steps immediately to begin to educate the clergy and laity alike in the particulars of this decree. In 1964, he was one of the first bishops in the United States to initiate and promote the "Neighborhood Mass" or the "Home Mass," observing the specific requirements for this celebration of the Mass. This quickly became a very popular practice and, as intended, it increased the appreciation of all for the Mass itself. It was in 1964

◆ **Bishop Lane ordained the future Father Robert Willhite a Subdeacon in the Chancery Chapel, 1962. Father Willhite has served in Spanish-speaking ministry from 1970 to the present.**

◆ **Father William P. Knott, first director of the Post Conciliar Center, in its bookstore in 1967.**

that some English began to be used along with Latin in parts of the Mass. In the next few years, churches began to have altars turned so that Mass was offered facing the congregation rather than the priest continuing to offer Mass turned away from the congregation. In each and every instance Bishop Lane took great care to inform all of the change and its purpose.

On January 23, 1966, the first televised Mass for Shut-in's was aired in Rockford on WREX-TV and continues to this day. In fact, to further provide resources for parishes and individuals to educate themselves in what the Second Vatican Council called for and to provide assistance in implementing its changes, Bishop Lane created the Post-Conciliar Center in Rockford within a year of the Council's close. In August 1966, Father William P. Knott was named the director, and the vacant St. Thomas High School was opened for this purpose.

Another emphasis of the Council was the universality of the Church and reiteration of the

Church's mission to evangelize. In 1966, Bishop Lane entered into an agreement with Bishop McNabb of the Diocese of Chulucanas, Peru, to send two diocesan priests to work for a five year period of time in parishes of that Diocese. The first two priests to be sent to learn Spanish and then to take up that mission were Fathers J. Philip Reilly and John W. Jones in July 1966.

The Council Fathers emphasized in several documents that every Catholic receives from the Sacrament of Baptism a universal call to holiness no matter what a person's particular vocation from God may be. On October 22, 1966, Bishop Lane dedicated the Diocese's new Retreat House. It was the realization of his desire to provide for the spiritual nourishment of all the Catholic faithful of the Diocese, as well as to offer to all a place of respite and prayer. Shortly after Bishop Lane's death and at the urging of the priests of the Diocese, it was renamed officially "Bishop Lane Retreat House".

With the Second Vatican Council's giving consideration to the changing circumstances in different parts of the world and how they influenced Catholics, the suggestion of the usefulness of national bishops' conferences gained momentum. The bishops of Rockford had been in the fore since the creation of the National Catholic War Council, it seemed only fitting that in November 1966, the National Conference of Catholic Bishops (formerly the National Catholic Welfare Conference) emerged, and Bishop Lane was elected one of the 30 bishops to serve on its new Administrative Committee. In fact, Bishop Lane would be elected the chairman of the Bishop's Committee on Priestly Formation.

During this time Bishop Lane made some administrative changes made necessary by the increased activity in the Diocese's parishes and schools. In 1962, Bishop Lane appointed the newly named Monsignor Wahl to be Director of Vocations for the Diocese and to be Pastor of St. Rita of Cascia Parish in Rockford. [A note of interest — in August 1963, the number of seminarians studying for the priesthood for the Diocese of Rockford over the

◆ **Bishop Lane Retreat Center, today and in the mid-1960s, when it was undeveloped land.**

span of the twelve year seminary program was 120] In August 1965, Bishop Lane appointed Father Thomas G. Doran to be his Secretary. On August 9, 1966, Father Thomas C. Brady, the Superintendent of Boylan Central Catholic High School since August 15, 1963, was appointed to also be the Diocesan Director of Adult Education.

Another influential development emerging from the work of the Second Vatican Council was the establishment of a senate or council of diocesan priests. This would have an enduring influence on the life of priests, their relationship with their bishops and on the pastoral life of their dioceses. In 1967, in accord with the intent of the Council Fathers, Bishop Lane established the Priests' Senate of the Diocese of Rockford. This body is an advisory

group to the diocesan Bishop in pastoral matters affecting both clergy and laity. The first officers of the Diocese's Priests' Senate were: Father Francis J. Bonnike, President; Father Andrew J. Plesa, Vice-President; Father William P. Knott, Secretary; and Father Norbert M. Richter, Treasurer. One of its first recommendations to Bishop Lane was to create a priest personnel board to advise the Bishop regarding the appointment of priests to various assignments. On May 10, 1968, Bishop Lane established the first priest personnel board.

After the close of the Second Vatican Council, in addition to his continued, active administration of Diocesan business Bishop Lane received another responsibility from Pope Paul VI. In March 1968, Bishop Lane was named a member of the Sacred Congregation for Catholic Education. It was not long after this appointment was announced that Bishop Lane finalized plans with the School Sisters of St. Francis to open a school in Freeport for trainable mentally handicapped children. This special Catholic institution was named St. Francis School for Exceptional Children.

THE DEATH OF BISHOP LANE

Bishop Lane's health began to fail noticeably about one year before his death. While he kept to his busy schedule, the long-standing kidney ailment with which he had been afflicted was taking its toll. In July 1968, Bishop Lane had to be hospitalized at Michael Reese Hospital in Chicago, and on July 22, 1968, Bishop Lane died at the age of 57.

Bishop Lane's solemn Requiem Mass was offered by John Cardinal Cody, Metropolitan Archbishop of Chicago at St. James Pro-Cathedral. Archbishop Leo Binz, Archbishop of St. Paul and Minneapolis, preached the funeral sermon for Bishop Lane. It was he who had consecrated Loras Lane a bishop of the Church 17 years earlier in Dubuque. Even though it was increasingly evident to clergy and laity alike that Bishop Lane was very

◆ **Archbishop Leo Binz preaches at Bishop Lane's funeral, July 1968.**

seriously ill, his death was deeply felt and mourned by all in the Diocese. Cardinal Cody expressed perhaps best the sentiments of affection and respect for Bishop Lane held by all: "Bishop Lane gave a life of dedicated service to the Church and to his people ... Ever willing to serve the Church, his Diocese, his clergy, and his people, he was ready to sacrifice his life in their interest." Bishop Lane was buried at Calvary Cemetery, west of Rockford, in the section reserved for priests.

THE VACANT SEE

With Bishop Lane's death on July 22, and as required by Church law, the College of Consultors for the Diocese of Rockford met to elect an Administrator for the Diocese. Monsignor Louis J. Franey, P.A., Vicar General, was elected. This was the third and final time Monsignor Franey would be called upon by his peers to see to the ordinary affairs of the Diocesan Church while awaiting the appointment of a new bishop. That appointment of the seventh Bishop for Rockford was made by His Holiness, Pope Paul VI on August 19, 1968.

The O'Neill Years

1968~1994

The Apostolic Delegate to the United States, Archbishop Luigi Raimondi, announced the appointment of Monsignor Arthur Joseph O'Neill, Pastor of St. Peter Parish, Rockford, as the seventh Bishop of the Diocese of Rockford, on August 21, 1968. The Bishop-elect's consecration and installation were scheduled for October 11, 1968. Bishop-elect Arthur J. O'Neill was the first native son of the Diocese of Rockford to be elevated to the office of its Bishop.

Arthur Joseph O'Neill was born in East Dubuque, Illinois, on December 14, 1917, the son of Leslie and Clara Runde O'Neill. He attended St. Mary Parish grade school and then attended Columbia Academy, Dubuque, Iowa, for his high school education. He continued his classical education for two years at Columbia College (Loras), Dubuque, and then completed his philosophical and theological studies at St. Mary Seminary, Baltimore, Maryland, from 1937 to 1943. Arthur Joseph O'Neill was ordained to the Sacred Priesthood by The Most Reverend John J. Boylan at St. James Pro-Cathedral, Rockford, on March 27, 1943.

Father O'Neill's first assignment was as the Assistant at the Pro-Cathedral Parish in Rockford where he served under three Rectors: Monsignor John P. McGuire, Father Joseph T. Healey

◆ **Father O'Neill's ordination portrait, 1943.**

(Administrator) and Monsignor Leo M. Keenan.

In April 1954, in addition to his parochial duties, Father O'Neill was appointed the editor of the diocesan newspaper, *The Observer*. On October 4, 1954, he was appointed Administrator for St. Thomas Aquinas Parish, Freeport and became the Pastor there in 1957. Father O'Neill served his parish and the Diocese from Freeport for the next 10 years. Pope John XXIII named him a Papal Chamberlain with the title Very Reverend Monsignor on January 5, 1963. On January 9, 1967, Bishop Lane appointed Monsignor O'Neill Pastor of St. Peter Parish, Rockford, and he continued to serve as the editor of *The Observer*. It was while serving in these assignments that Monsignor Arthur J. O'Neill was appointed the seventh Bishop of the Diocese of Rockford.

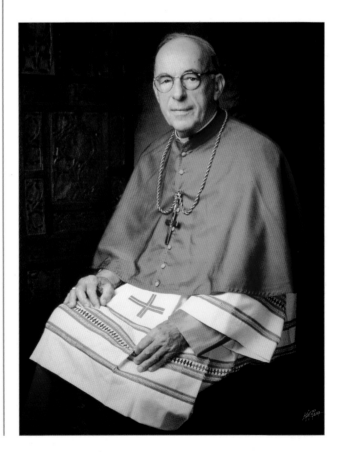

◆ **Bishop Arthur J. O'Neill, seventh bishop of the Rockford Diocese.**
Motto: That all may be one.

◆ **Bishop O'Neill was installed as the seventh bishop of Rockford, October 11, 1968 by Archbishop Luigi Raimondi.**

Pope Paul VI had authorized and approved a revised rite for the ordination of bishops on June 18, 1968. The word "ordination" was now used rather than the former term "consecration" to better express the essential relation between the three grades of orders of the Sacrament of Holy Orders: deacon, priest, and bishop. Thus, The Most Reverend Arthur J. O'Neill was ordained and installed as the seventh Bishop of the Diocese of Rockford on October 11, 1968, at St. Peter Church, Rockford. The Apostolic Delegate to the United States, Archbishop Luigi Raimondi, was the principal celebrant and consecrator, with Archbishop Leo Binz of St. Paul and Minneapolis, and Archbishop James J. Byrne of Dubuque, as the senior concelebrants and co-consecrators. John Cardinal Cody, Metropolitan Archbishop of Chicago was present and presided in the sanctuary.

Bishop O'Neill's episcopacy is, to date, the longest in the history of the Diocese of Rockford. From the date of his ordination and installation to the date of the acceptance of his resignation as bishop in accord with Church law, he served the local Church for 25 years, six months and eight days. It would be a work in itself to catalog all that transpired and all that Bishop O'Neill initiated and advanced during that quarter century and will, perhaps, be done at some future time. From what follows, it will be evident immediately that Bishop O'Neill continued and expanded what all of his predecessors had done to strengthen and spread the Catholic faith, to deepen the spiritual and liturgical life of the Catholic faithful, to expand and refine the Church's apostolate of Catholic education, to increase the means and methods of communicating with the people of the Diocese, to promote vocations, to foster Catholic social action and services to the poor, to assist the increasing numbers of new migrants and immigrants as they arrived in the Diocese, and to find a more creative means for clergy and laity alike to support their parishes and their Diocese with their time, talent and treasure.

FROM 1968 TO 1970

The first two and one-half years of Bishop O'Neill's episcopacy were not only busy years but they set the tone for the rest of his time as the Bishop of Rockford. About one month prior to his ordination and installation as Bishop, the newly created Aurora Central Catholic High School opened for classes. Within days of his installation, Bishop O'Neill named Mr. Ben Lingis as the managing editor of *The Observer*. In November 1968, Bishop O'Neill broke ground for the new St. Joseph Mercy Hospital in Aurora.

The year of 1969 was no less busy for Bishop O'Neill. The month of January marked some significant diocesan appointments by Bishop O'Neill. Monsignor Wahl was appointed for a second time the Officialis of the Diocesan Tribunal. Father Thomas C. Brady was appointed the Diocesan Director of Education, succeeding Monsignor Wahl in that post. Father Thomas G. Doran, Secretary to the Bishop, was appointed the Chancellor of the Diocese, succeeding Monsignor Wahl in this office.

May 1969, marked the first priesthood ordinations for Bishop O'Neill. Five men were ordained to the Sacred Priesthood in their home parishes during this month. They were: Fathers Donald D. DeSalvo, Daniel J. Hermes, Joseph B.

◆ **Father Robert Miller, author of "That All May be One", presents Bishop O'Neill with a copy of the last diocesan history, 1976.**

Linster, Robert R. Miller, and Robert J. Sweeney. It should be noted that Father Miller was the author of the last history of the Diocese completed in 1976. Father Miller died suddenly on August 2, 1995, while serving as the Pastor of St. Thomas More Parish, Elgin.

During the summer of 1969 and as a result of the work of the Fathers of the Second Vatican Council, Saturday evening Mass was allowed to be celebrated as the anticipated Mass for Sunday, fulfilling the Sunday obligation for Catholics. During that summer St. Mary Minor Seminary in Crystal Lake closed due to a lack of enrollment and rising costs. September 1969, marked the closing of St. Peter Mission in Davis Junction and the Catholics of the area were then affiliated with St. Mary Parish, Byron. It was during the autumn of this year that Bishop O'Neill traveled to the Diocese's mission in Chulucanas, Peru, for a pastoral visit. While on this visit, he dedicated a new social center at the mission which the priests and people would use for most of their educational and social programs, and it served as the base from which the priests would travel to the more remote sections of the mission's territory.

With the end of the school year in 1970, Muldoon High School for girls in Rockford closed its doors. The Adrian Dominican Sisters who staffed this school and most of its remaining pupils transferred to the faculty and student body of Boylan Central Catholic High School. At this time as well, St. Dominic College in St. Charles closed its doors for much the same reasons – falling enrollment and rising costs. St. Joseph Novitiate of the Resurrection Fathers in Woodstock also closed in 1970. In June 1970, Father Thomas J. Monahan was appointed by Bishop O'Neill to be the executive

◆ **Bishop O'Neill celebrates Mass at the dedication of the social center at the mission in the Diocese of Chulucanas, Peru, 1969. The mission church built by the Rockford Diocese, shown in 2006, is now the center of life in the village of Montero.**

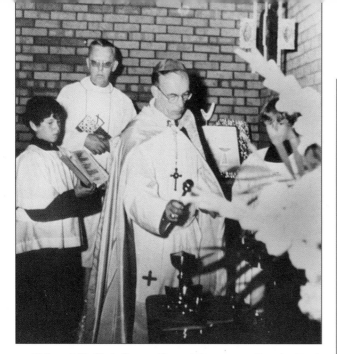

◆ Bishop O'Neill dedicates Blessed Sacrament Church, North Aurora, 1975. Behind Bishop O'Neill is the first pastor, Father Edward Wright, who went on to serve the parish for 34 years.

◆ Officers of the diocesan Priests' Senate with Bishop O'Neill in the early 1970s. Shown, left to right, are: Father Edward Wright, Father Thomas Dzielak, Bishop O'Neill, Father Robert Miller, and Father Philip O'Neil.

editor of *The Observer* and Ben Lingis continued on as its manager of advertising.

October 1970, was a most important period of time in the Diocese's history. On October 4, 1970, Bishop O'Neill erected a new parish in North Aurora and it was dedicated as Blessed Sacrament Parish. The Pastor of St. Mary Parish, Byron, Father Edward S. Wright was appointed its first and founding pastor. The following week on October 11, 1970, Bishop O'Neill formally announced that St. Peter Church, Rockford, had been designated the Cathedral for the Diocese of Rockford, sixty-two years after St. James had been designated the new diocese's Pro-Cathedral.

With the establishment of Blessed Sacrament Parish in North Aurora, the Aurora Deanery was now comprised of 13 parishes with Father Sylvester J. Eye as the Dean since 1967. At that time, due to the increased growth of the Catholic population in that area of the Diocese, Bishop O'Neill established a seventh and, to date, the last deanery in the Diocese — the DeKalb Deanery. Recall that these parishes of the new DeKalb Deanery had been originally part of the Aurora Deanery when the original four deaneries were created in the 1920's.

The DeKalb Deanery was comprised of 12 parishes: two in DeKalb, and one each in Elburn, Genoa, Hampshire, Lee, Maple Park, Rochelle, Sandwich, Somonauk, Sycamore and Virgil. Father Harold L. Nilges, the Pastor of St. Mary Parish, DeKalb, was named the first Dean of the DeKalb Deanery in November 1970.

The year of 1970 ended with a first, not only for the Diocese of Rockford, but for the Catholic Church in the United States. In December, Bishop O'Neill celebrated the newly approved Rite for the Communal Anointing of the Sick at the Elgin State Hospital for approximately 500 patients. On December 31, 1970, the Jesuits' Bellarmine School of Theology in Aurora closed.

1971 TO 1980

Groundbreaking for a new St. Joseph Hospital in Elgin took place in February 1971; and it was this same month when Bishop O'Neill formed the Diocese's Vocations Commission to promote vocations to the priesthood and the religious life, as well as to support those men already affiliated with the diocese as seminarians.

In May of 1971 the first ordinations took place in the recently designated Cathedral of St. Peter in Rockford. In June 1971, Notre Dame High School for girls in DeKalb closed after only six years of operation due to declining enrollment and rapidly rising costs. St. Charles Hospital in Aurora, serving that community since 1900, closed its doors in anticipation of a merger with the newly constructed St. Joseph Mercy Hospital which Bishop O'Neill dedicated in September 1971. September also marked the establishment of the Diocese's Spanish Speaking Apostolate with Father John W. Jones being appointed its first Director.

◆ **Father J. Philip Reilly, diocesan director of the Spanish Speaking Apostolate from 1973 until 1984.**

Early in the new year of 1972, and in response to a request for more formal Church recognition and supervision, Bishop O'Neill created the Community of the Holy Spirit in February. It was a non-territorial parish for all Catholics involved in the charismatic movement in the Diocese of Rockford.

In June 1972, Mt. St. Mary Academy in St. Charles closed after 65 years of service to Catholic young women. Also, Sacred Heart Seminary in Geneva, operated by the Missionaries of the Sacred Heart since 1925, closed its doors.

Bishop O'Neill appointed Father J. Philip Reilly to be second Diocesan Director of the Spanish Speaking Apostolate in January 1973. The office was moved from Rockford to Aurora to the St. Nicholas Parish convent in order to be more accessible to the larger number of Hispanic Catholics in the Diocese. In March 1973, Bishop O'Neill formed the first Board of Mediation and Arbitration for the Catholic faithful and employees of the Diocese. Its purpose was to assist persons in resolving certain disputes that may arise in the course of Church life and to do so in a spirit of charity and cooperation. March also marked the 30th anniversary of Bishop O'Neill's ordination to the priesthood. St. Anthony Hospital in Rockford opened its Special Care Pavillion in June when Bishop O'Neill presided at its dedication.

In August 1973, with Bishop O'Neill presiding, the opening and dedication of the new St. Joseph Hospital in Elgin took place. The Franciscan Friars of Assumption Province from Pulaski, Wisconsin, were entrusted with the administration of St. Elizabeth Social Center in Rockford by Bishop O'Neill. In this same month, Bishop O'Neill named Father Richard R. Kramer the full-time Diocesan Director of Communications. In September 1973, three parish grades schools in the City of Rockford consolidated to form St. Francis Consolidated school, using two sites at St. Anthony and St. Stanislaus Parishes (the third school was SS. Peter & Paul). Bishop O'Neill marked his fifth anniversary as the seventh Bishop of the Diocese of Rockford on October 11, 1973.

The next year of 1974 was a busy and productive time for the Diocese and for Bishop

◆ **Bishop O'Neill administers the Sacrament of the Sick at a communal anointing at the Elgin State Hospital, 1970.**

◆ **Bishop O'Neill and Father William Collins at the dedication of Martin House, Rockford, 1975.**

O'Neill. Much of this year was devoted to preparing for his first *ad limina* visit to Rome in the autumn of that year. In the summer of 1974, Bishop O'Neill created the Office of Divine Worship and named Father John A. Slampak its Director. In September 1974, St. Vincent's Residential School opened on the campus of St. Vincent-St. Joseph Home in Freeport.

In October 1974, Bishop O'Neill traveled to Rome on his first *ad limina* visit and it would be the first of his five official visits to Rome to report to the Holy Father on the status of the Diocese of Rockford. On October 23, 1974, Bishop O'Neill had his private audience with Pope Paul VI, 53 years to the day after Bishop Muldoon, on his first *ad limina* visit, met with Pope Benedict XV.

Upon his return from Rome, Bishop O'Neill began preparations for the celebration of the Holy Year of 1975 proclaimed by Pope Paul VI. He celebrated a special Holy Year Mass in each of the Diocese's seven deaneries during special one-day conferences leading up to the formal opening of the Holy Year on December 24, 1974. On December 3, 1974, Bishop O'Neill announced plans for a Pastoral Synod. Fathers J. Philip Reilly and James M. Weber had been named the co-chairmen of the Synod process. The next two years would involve the study and discussion of each of the documents of

the Second Vatican Council and then the formulation of specific diocesan documents with guidelines for implementation of the Council's teachings.

The Holy Year of 1975 was just as active for the Diocese as the prior year. In January, Bishop O'Neill dedicated the Martin House in Rockford as a center for Inner City ministry. March 1975, marked the unveiling of a new and expanded format for *The Observer* in reporting more Catholic Church news to the faithful. In April 1975, after a wide consultation, Bishop O'Neill announced a different and broader based method for funding diocesan apostolates and programs. Thus, the Diocesan Services Program (DSP) for the Diocese of Rockford was born. On May 17, 1975, the first class of permanent deacons was ordained at the Cathedral of St. Peter. On Sunday, May 18, 1975, Pentecost Sunday, the liturgical convocation for the Diocesan Pastoral Synod took place at a concelebrated Mass at the Cathedral of St. Peter, Rockford.

◆ **Bishop O'Neill inaugurates the annual Diocesan Services Program appeal, April 1975.**

◆ **Sister James Marie O'Connor, S.S.N.D., Vicaress of Women Religious since 1975.**

June 14, 1975, marked the Holy Year ordinations to the Sacred Priesthood of three men. They were Fathers Thomas E. Brantman, David D. Kagan and Michael F. Simonini. On July 1, 1975, Mr. Robert Dylak was named by Bishop O'Neill to be the managing editor of *The Observer*. In the same month, Bishop O'Neill appointed Father Thomas C. Brady the Diocesan Director of Priest Personnel, and Father Robert N. Sherry the Director of Vocations for the Diocese of Rockford. In July 1975, Bishop O'Neill gave official approval to the Rockford Curriculum Guide for Religious Education and promulgated its use in the Diocese. It was also in the summer of 1975 that Bishop O'Neill asked Sister James Marie O'Connor, S.S.N.D., to come to the Diocese and assume the newly created position of his representative for Women Religious (Vicaress). Sister James Marie continues to serve the Diocese in this office now some 32 years later.

In September 1975, Bishop O'Neill attended a special seminar for bishops held in Rome and was able to be present for the canonization of Mother Seton by Pope Paul VI. Later that same month Bishop O'Neill dedicated the newly constructed Knights Community Complex of the Muldoon Council 470 in Rockford. In October, Bishop O'Neill renamed the Post-Conciliar Center in Rockford, Seton Center, in honor of St. Elizabeth Ann Seton. This was the former St. Thomas High School which now housed several diocesan offices and agencies. In December 1975, Bishop O'Neill was elected to a three-year term to the United States Catholic Conference Committee on Communications.

The Bicentennial year of 1976 began with an important appointment for a newly created diocesan

◆ **A Pro-Life march on the northwest side of Rockford.**

◆ **Seton Center, Rockford, was home to many diocesan offices and apostolates.**

office. In January, Bishop O'Neill appointed Father Francis X. Lawlor, O.S.A., the Diocesan Director for Pro-Life Activities. Father Lawlor, an Augustinian priest living in residence at St. Mary Parish, Rockford, entrusted to the care of the Augustinian Fathers since Bishop Hoban's time, was to coordinate all diocesan programs seeking to educate Catholics concerning the Supreme Court's *Roe v. Wade* decision in January 1973 which legalized abortion. This significant diocesan effort has continued to the present with the office now under the able direction of Mrs. Patricia Bainbridge. January 5, 1976, marked another significant appointment. Father Thomas G. Doran

was appointed the Officialis of the Diocesan Tribunal in addition to his duties as the Chancellor, succeeding Monsignor Raymond J. Wahl.

In February 1976, it was announced that Bishop O'Neill had been named a member of the National Advisory Committee for the NCCB/USCC. The former novitiate building of the Resurrection Fathers in Woodstock reopened in June 1976, as Resurrection House of Prayer, used for individual days of prayer as well as for retreats. Much of the activity of the Diocese during this entire year involved meetings of the clergy, religious and laity in their various study groups preparing for the Pastoral Synod.

The year of 1977 was highlighted by two events — the establishment of a second parish in St. Charles, east of the Fox River, and the solemn closing of the Third Pastoral Synod for the Diocese of Rockford.

June 12, 1977, the Solemnity of Corpus Christi, marked the promulgation of the results of more than two years of study, discussion and cooperation among the clergy, religious and laity of the Diocese. Nine Synod papers, each with recommendations for future action, were approved and promulgated by Bishop O'Neill. In his letter of promulgation Bishop O'Neill said, in part: "Specific areas of Catholic life and concern were selected for the consultations. Through the work of the several committees there was developed a better understanding of our strengths and weaknesses. The Pastoral Synod Papers provide a basis for updating programs and directives in the future ... We pray to The Holy Spirit that the Diocesan Synod will truly renew us in faith, hope and love."

The very next month of July 1977, Bishop O'Neill erected a new and second parish for the rapidly growing Catholic population in the City of St. Charles. The parish was dedicated in honor of the newly canonized St. John Neumann, Bishop of Philadelphia. Bishop O'Neill appointed Father Daniel J. Hermes to be the first and founding Pastor of this parish. The Elgin Deanery was now comprised of 10 parishes.

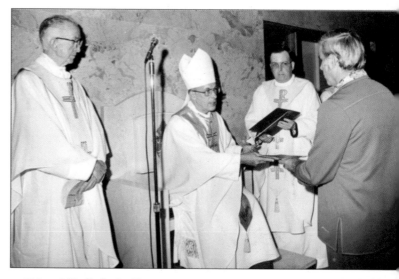

◆ **Bishop O'Neill, flanked by Monsignor Louis Franey and Father Thomas Doran, presents participants of the 1977 Pastoral Synod with the final Synod papers, July 12, 1977.**

The year of 1978 proved to be another busy and productive year for the Diocese and for Bishop O'Neill. On February 22, 1978, ground was broken for a new retirement facility for diocesan priests. It would be attached to the north end of the Bishop Lane Retreat House and would be able to accommodate six priests living in private, self-contained apartments, but would also have a common area and chapel. Bishop O'Neill dedicated this home as Vianney Oaks in honor of St. John Vianney, patron of parish priests. In March, Bishop O'Neill celebrated his 35th anniversary of ordination to the Sacred Priesthood and in October he observed his 10th anniversary as Bishop of Rockford.

◆ **The future site of St. John Neumann, St. Charles, 1978.**

◆ **Father Joseph Kulak, pastor of St. Elizabeth Ann Seton, Crystal Lake, at the groundbreaking of the parish complex, 1981.**

In the last quarter of 1978, Bishop O'Neill erected two new parishes in the Fox Valley and the McHenry County Deanery. Resurrection Parish in Woodstock was established in October and Father Michael Mas, CR was appointed its first Pastor. In December, St. Elizabeth Ann Seton Parish in Crystal Lake was established and Father Joseph F. Kulak was appointed its first and founding Pastor. In November 1978, Bishop O'Neill traveled to Rome, making his second *ad limina* visit. On November 9, 1978, he met in audience, Pope John Paul II, newly elected as Supreme Pontiff on October 16, 1978.

In 1980, Bishop O'Neill, in consultation with the Priests' Senate and the Diocesan Planning Committee, embarked upon a diocesan self-assessment process. The purpose was to carefully examine various aspects of diocesan life and its administration in order to achieve better long-range planning, new parish development and to improve the Diocese's evangelization apostolates. The firm of Norman Shawchuck and Associates was retained to coordinate and conduct this process. The process also included a comprehensive demographic study of the entire Diocese by The Catholic Open Research Project. The self-assessment portion of this effort was begun in August 1980 and completed on August 3, 1981; the demographic study was begun in March 1981 and finalized in January 1982.

Due to steady growth in northern Winnebago County especially in the Roscoe and Rockton areas, Bishop O'Neill erected a mission parish in Roscoe in 1980. The Church of the Holy Spirit Parish was attached to St. Peter Parish, South Beloit and placed under the pastoral care and administration of the Pastor of the South Beloit Parish. In the summer of 1980, Bishop O'Neill approved what would be a first for the Diocese of Rockford, as well as

◆ **Sister Audrey Straub, S.S.N.D., was the Secretary and Director of Tribunal Services when she retired in 2005.**

one of the first such efforts in the United States. The Diocesan Tribunal hired two religious women to work as advocates in its large file of marriage cases. Sister Audrey Straub, S.S.N.D., and Sister Muriel Glodosky, S.S.N.D., began this full time service to the Diocese. Sister Audrey Straub would continue with this work for the next 25 years. This began a very fruitful relationship between the Diocese of Rockford and various religious communities of women serving capably in the Tribunal, as so many religious women have and continue to serve the Diocese in other areas of the apostolate.

1981 TO 1990

One of the most significant administrative decisions made by Bishop O'Neill became effective on July 1, 1981. After careful consideration and wide consultation, Bishop O'Neill created the Diocesan Investment and Loan program, commonly referred to as DIAL. This internal, self-financing effort proved to be a great service to parishes, diocesan agencies, diocesan high schools and the Diocese itself. The program allowed the necessary expansion of parish and diocesan physical facilities, as well as diocesan programs to meet the demands of a

♦ **Harry Koplin shows the papal blessing he received from Pope John Paul II. Mr. Koplin was instrumental in creating DIAL.**

growing Diocese without paying high interest rates on commercial loans and borrowing.

After consulting the Priests' Senate and with both the Shawchuck Report and the demographic study of the Diocese having been completed (August 1981, and January 1982, respectively), Bishop O'Neill reorganized the administrative structure of the Diocese. On May 1, 1982, Bishop O'Neill established the Episcopal Vicar system, dividing all of diocesan life into five vicariates or areas of Catholic activity. Bishop O'Neill appointed five diocesan priests to be his Episcopal Vicars and assigned each to one of the five vicariates. These priests and their vicariates were:

Father Leo H. Ambre,
  Episcopal Vicar for Finance & Administration;
Father David E. Beauvais,
  Episcopal Vicar for Social Concerns;
Father Thomas C. Brady,
  Episcopal Vicar for Lay Spiritual Formation;
Father Thomas G. Doran,
  Episcopal Vicar for Catholic Education;
Father Robert B. Hoffman,
  Episcopal Vicar for Clergy & Religious.

♦ **Bishop O'Neill, Bishop Maurice Dingman, Diocese of Des Moines, and Archbishop Pio Laghi, Apostolic Delegate to the U.S., at the 75ᵗʰ anniversary celebration of the Rockford Diocese in 1983.**

During the latter part of 1982, Bishop O'Neill appointed a committee to make the preparations for a celebration of the 75th anniversary of the founding of the Diocese of Rockford. Fathers Leo H. Ambre and Michael A. Binsfeld were named the co-chairmen of the Anniversary Committee. This celebration would be one of the major diocesan events in the next year. On November 18, 1982, Bishop O'Neill appointed Father David D. Kagan, Vice-Officialis of the Diocesan Tribunal to be also the Director of the Office of Communications for the Diocese. He served in that post until October 31, 1986.

Indeed, the year of 1983 was one of thanksgiving and celebration as the 75th Anniversary of the Diocese of Rockford was observed. A solemn, concelebrated Mass of Thanksgiving was celebrated by Bishop O'Neill and many visiting bishops, with priests (diocesan and religious) of the diocese, as well as from outside the diocese. The numbers of clergy, religious and laity participating was so large that the Metro Center in downtown Rockford was chosen as the site of this solemn observance. The actual date for the Diamond Jubilee was Sunday, October 9, 1983. Archbishop Pio Laghi, Apostolic Delegate to the United States of America was the homilist of the Mass; 24 other bishops were in attendance and concelebrated. The total number of participants at the anniversary Mass was estimated to be more than 3,000, representing all parishes, diocesan agencies and ministries and religious orders of men and

women working in the diocese. Father Robert A. Balog was the Master of Ceremonies and the two deacons of the Mass were The Reverend Mr. Eric R. Barr and The Reverend Mr. Joseph F. Jarmoluk. Along with the diocesan anniversary, this Mass marked the 40th anniversary of priestly ordination for Bishop O'Neill and his 15th anniversary as Bishop of Rockford.

In addition to the planning for the Diocese's 75th Anniversary, Bishop O'Neill authorized the planning for the introduction to the Diocese of a parish-based program for spiritual renewal and formation called RENEW. The planning committee spent the year training parishioners to be leaders for RENEW, assisting their parish priests to implement its principles in parish life. In August, Bob Dylak, editor of *The Observer* since July 1975, left the Diocese to assume the position of editor for the Newark Archdiocesan newspaper. Bishop O'Neill named Owen Phelps, Jr. the new editor of *The Observer*. He held this position and very capably managed the newspaper for the next 19 years. In November 1983, Bishop O'Neill left for Rome in order to make his *ad limina* visit, the third such official visit of his episcopacy.

◆ **Sister Ann Regina Baker, O.P. and Father Karl Ganss directed RENEW in the Diocese. They are shown here with members of their staff**

The plans which had been being formulated to build a Catholic nursing facility in Rockford were finalized by mid-1984. Bishop O'Neill announced to the Diocese that St. Anne Nursing Center would be built on land adjacent to Holy Family Parish. This period of time was spent in making all the immediate preparations for construction.

Bishop O'Neill made some important priest appointments in July 1984. He appointed Father Thomas G. Doran to be the Rector for the Cathedral of St. Peter, while remaining the Chancellor. Father Doran succeeded Father Thomas C. Brady who was appointed the Director of Bishop Lane Retreat

◆ **Archbishop Pio Laghi preaches at the Diamond Jubilee Mass at the Metro Center, Rockford, October 9, 1983.**

◆ **Bishop O'Neill and Father Raymond Gordon at the dedication of St. Anne Center, Rockford, 1986.**

House. However, Bishop O'Neill appointed Monsignor Raymond J. Wahl, then Pastor of St. Michael Parish, Galena, the Officialis of the Diocesan Tribunal, relieving Father Doran of that responsibility. This marked the third time Monsignor Wahl had been given charge of the Diocesan Tribunal. Also, at the end of July 1984, Bishop O'Neill named Monsignor Wahl the Diocesan Director of the Propagation of the Faith.

Sunday, October 7, 1984, marked the opening of the first season of RENEW. Bishop O'Neill had gathered the clergy, religious and parish teams at the Cathedral on Sunday, September 30, 1984, for the solemn liturgy opening RENEW in the Diocese. Bishop O'Neill urged the Catholic faithful to participate in this three-year process. In part, he said: "As the diocesan bishop, I place great hope in the religious influence that RENEW will have in the Diocese. I am grateful for the opportunity the Lord is offering us to grow in a spirit of prayer, faith and service. I ask your prayers, commitment and cooperation for the RENEW program." Over the course of the three years five renewal themes would be followed: The Lord's Call, Our Response to the Lord's Call, Empowerment by the Spirit, Discipleship, and Evangelization. In November 1984, Bishop O'Neill appointed Father William R. Schuessler the Episcopal Vicar for Hispanic Ministry.

In 1985, the 12-year experiment with consolidated Catholic grade school education in the city of Rockford ended with the closing of St. Francis Consolidated School in May. May 18, 1985, marked the groundbreaking for St. Anne Center in Rockford, a Catholic nursing facility under the administration of the Sisters of the Holy Heart of Mary. The facility opened in October 1986. In June 1985, Bishop O'Neill appointed Father David D. Kagan Officialis of the Diocesan Tribunal, succeeding Monsignor Raymond J. Wahl, and appointed Father Robert J. Verstynen the Episcopal Vicar for Catholic Education.

The year 1986 brought a Papal appointment to one of the priests of the Diocese and a distinct honor for the Diocese itself. It was announced in June that Father Thomas G. Doran, Rector for the Cathedral of St. Peter, had been appointed a Judge Auditor of the Roman Rota by Pope John Paul II. On July 1, 1986, Bishop O'Neill established a new diocesan agency — the Office of Ministry Formation. By 2006 more than 1,000 Catholic men and women from across the Diocese had been trained to serve in a variety of parish and deanery ministries. It was in July that Bishop O'Neill appointed Father David E. Beauvais the Episcopal Vicar for Finance and Administration, and Father Leo J. Bartel, Pastor of St. Mary Parish, Morrison, to be the next Episcopal Vicar for Social Ministries.

◆ **In its early days the Ministry Formation program was guided by an advisory board. Four members of the 1988 board were Jim Falco, Mike Nachman, Mi Loran, and Loretta Reif.**

With the departure of Father Doran for Rome, Bishop O'Neill appointed Father Charles W. McNamee the Chancellor of the Diocese of Rockford on October 1, 1986.

HESED HOUSE

In April 1986, Hesed House was dedicated in Aurora with the support of Bishop O'Neill and many Aurora parishes. This interfaith center derives its name from the Hebrew word "hesed," which means "God's unconditional and everlasting love that seeks justice on behalf of the least of God's people." Hesed House comprises several ministries that feed, clothe and shelter the truly poor in the Aurora area. Since its founding, Hesed House has received considerable encouragement and publicity from the Rockford Diocese as well as the participation of thousands of Catholic volunteers from parishes in the Aurora area.

◆ **Sister Rose Marie Lorentzen, BVM, retired as executive director of Hesed House in 2004, after serving in that position for 19 years.**

In 1987, Bishop O'Neill made another significant financial decision for the Diocese and its many parishes and other institutions. After much discussion and planning, on June 30, 1987, The Catholic Foundation for the People of the Diocese of Rockford was officially and legally incorporated and its first account was opened in October 1987. By 2006, the Foundation included almost 300 accounts which totaled more $75 million.

A singular achievement was reached on August 3, 1987, with the retirement of the Right Reverend Monsignor Louis J. Franey, P.A. He had served the Diocese for 50 years in the Chancery and each of the Diocese's bishops except for its first, Bishop Muldoon. Monsignor Franey, in his retirement, continued as the Chaplain for the Poor Clares in Rockford, an office he had held since 1957. Bishop O'Neill appointed Father Thomas C. Brady the Vicar General for the Diocese of Rockford on August 3, 1987.

The year of 1988 marked Bishop O'Neill's 45th anniversary of ordination to the priesthood in March, and his 20th anniversary as Bishop of Rockford in October. Bishop O'Neill also made his fourth *ad limina* visit to Rome that year

◆ **Hesed House.**

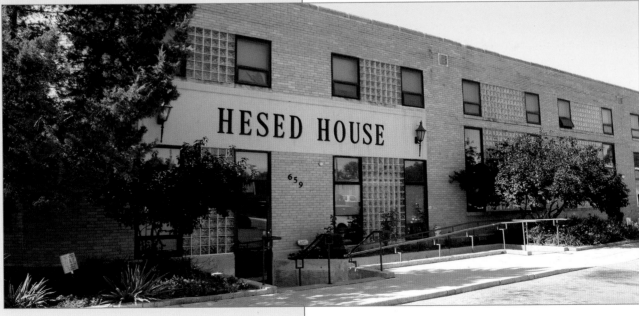

LOUIS JOSEPH FRANEY
1903 – 1989

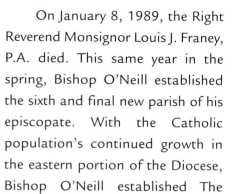

Louis J. Franey was ordained to the Sacred Priesthood on March 26, 1932, at Saint James Pro-Cathedral, Rockford, by The Most Reverend Edward F. Hoban. One week prior to the end of his second assignment on May 25, 1937, Father Franey was appointed the Vice-Chancellor of the Diocese of Rockford by Bishop Hoban. This year marked the beginning of a half-century of dedicated, capable and uninterrupted service to the Church by Father and then Monsignor Louis J. Franey, P.A.

Perhaps what Monsignor Franey loved most in all of his years of priestly life and service was his assignment as the Chaplain for the Poor Clares of Corpus Christi Monastery in Rockford. He served them as Chaplain from September 19, 1957 to October, 1988.

The Right Reverend Monsignor Louis J. Franey, P.A., died on January 8, 1989, in Rockford and his funeral Mass was offered by Father Thomas C. Brady, Vicar General in the Chapel of Corpus Christi Monastery on January 12, 1989. Monsignor Franey is buried in the Cloister Cemetery of the Poor Clares, the only non-Poor Clare to be so honored.

The Most Reverend Arthur J. O'Neill wrote to Monsignor Franey on July 2, 1987, accepting his request for retirement. Bishop O'Neill expressed very well the sentiments of all priests who, over so many years came to know and respect Monsignor Franey. Bishop O'Neill said, in part:

"Dear Monsignor Franey:

"It is with mixed feelings of regret and sincere appreciation that I write this letter to confirm our recent conversation that I am accepting the retirement which you submitted in writing several years ago. . . .

"You have a remarkable and unique record in your priestly service and dedication to the diocese. You came to the Chancery as Vice-Chancellor on June 1, 1937, and have ably served five of Rockford's Bishops as Chancellor and, later, Vicar General. In my own name and speaking for the priests of the diocese, there is a debt of gratitude that can never be repaid . . ."

On January 8, 1989, the Right Reverend Monsignor Louis J. Franey, P.A. died. This same year in the spring, Bishop O'Neill established the sixth and final new parish of his episcopate. With the Catholic population's continued growth in the eastern portion of the Diocese, Bishop O'Neill established The Church of Holy Apostles Parish in McHenry, and appointed Father Robert N. Sherry its first and founding Pastor. The McHenry County Deanery was now comprised of 17 parishes. On July 14, 1989, Bishop O'Neill appointed Father F. James Larson, the Pastor of St. Bernadette Parish, Rockford, and Dean of the Rockford Deanery, to be the Episcopal Vicar for Clergy and Religious. In November, Bishop O'Neill appointed Father Karl P. Ganss the Episcopal Vicar for Lay Spiritual Formation.

With the opening of St. Anne Center in Rockford and its growing popularity as a Catholic nursing facility, plans began to be formulated in 1990 for the construction of a Catholic independent living facility. It was to be constructed

◆ **ELCA Bishop Ronald Hasley and Bishop O'Neill sign a covenant between the Northern Illinois Synod and the Rockford Diocese, June 1992, at St. Peter Cathedral.**

on land adjacent to St. Anne Center and would bear the name St. Anne Place. Also, in 1990, Bishop O'Neill appointed Sister Joella Miller, O.P., to the position of Vicaress for Catholic Education, replacing the retired Father Robert J. Verstynen; Bishop O'Neill named Mr. Harry Koplin the head of the Office of Finance and Administration for the Diocese, replacing Father Beauvais who took a pastoral assignment.

1991 TO 1994

On July 1, 1991, Bishop O'Neill named Mr. John McGrath to head up the Diocese's Office of Ministry Formation and he has continued in this post to the present. Later in 1991 St. Catherine Parish in Freeport, established by Bishop Muldoon in 1921, closed due to a decline in numbers of Catholics in that area of the community. Father Charles K. McCarren was the Pastor of St. Catherine Parish at its close.

On September 29, 1991 Bishop O'Neill and Bishop Ronald Hasley, representing the Northern Illinois Synod of the Evangelical Lutheran Church in America, commissioned the creation of a covenant between the Rockford Diocese and the Synod. This historic covenant was the outgrowth of a dialogue between Catholic and Lutheran churches in the Rockford area. The completed covenant was signed by them at St. Peter Cathedral on Pentecost, June 6, 1992.

On March 30, 1992, Bishop O'Neill broke ground for St. Anne Place in Rockford. This marked the culmination of two years of extensive planning for the Diocese's independent living facility for senior citizens. The construction phase would last for about 18 months.

An extensive renovation of St. James Parish Church in Rockford (the Pro-Cathedral from 1908 to 1970) was completed in October 1992. Bishop O'Neill was the main celebrant of the Solemn Mass

◆ **Bishop O'Neill blesses the site of the future Aurora Central Catholic High School, May 1994.**

at which he consecrated the new, permanent marble altar. This celebration marked as well the 125th anniversary of this second church for St. James Parish, having been dedicated in October 1867, by the Right Reverend James Duggan, D.D., Bishop of Chicago.

December 14, 1992 was Bishop O'Neill's 75th birthday and, in keeping with Church law, he sent his letter of resignation to His Holiness, Pope John Paul II. Bishop O'Neill would continue in office as the Diocesan Bishop until such time as the Pope actually accepted his resignation.

March 27, 1993 marked the Golden Anniversary of ordination to the Sacred Priesthood for Bishop O'Neill and later this same year on October 11, 1993, Bishop O'Neill and the Diocese observed his 25th Anniversary as the seventh Bishop of the Diocese of Rockford.

September 30, 1993, was the official opening of St. Anne Place in Rockford. It opened with 103 of the 105 apartment units occupied and 12 duplex units and by early 1994, it was at full occupancy. ServantCor (Provena) was retained by the Diocese to administer the facility. In November 1993, Bishop O'Neill traveled to Rome to make his fifth and last *ad limina* visit to report to the Holy Father on the general status of the Diocese of Rockford.

Substantial change for the Diocese occurred the next year. It was Tuesday, April 19, 1994, that the announcement of the appointment of the eighth Bishop of the Diocese of Rockford was made both in Washington, D.C. by the Apostolic Nuncio, Archbishop Cacciavillan, and in Rockford by Bishop O'Neill.

His Holiness, Pope John Paul II had appointed Monsignor Thomas G. Doran, J.C.D., to be the eighth Bishop of the Diocese of Rockford and, at the same time, had accepted the resignation of The Most Reverend Arthur J. O'Neill from the See of Rockford. This was the first time in the Diocese's history that the See would be vacant for a reason other than the death or transfer of the Diocesan Bishop.

The episcopate of The Most Reverend Arthur J. O'Neill, D.D., spanned more than two and one-half decades in the life of the Diocese of Rockford and the Universal Church. The times proved to be much

◆ **The first diocesan class of permanent deacons, ordained in May 1975.**

◆ **Cardinal Joseph Bernardin listens at the Jubilee Mass for Bishop O'Neill, October 11, 1993, at the Metro Center, Rockford.**

different from those of any of his predecessors both for the Catholic Church and for the larger society and world. Throughout all the events both large and small in these times, Bishop O'Neill was that faithful and faith-filled point of reference for all of the Catholic faithful of the Diocese – the priests, the religious and the laity. From the earliest days of his tenure in 1968 through the last days of his time as Diocesan Bishop in 1994, Bishop O'Neill strove to fulfill the first role of every Bishop, to be a father to

all entrusted to his care. It is clear that Almighty God blessed his efforts and that they have borne good fruit.

THE VACANT SEE

In accord with the requirements of Church law that the Consultors of the Diocese meet within eight days of the See becoming vacant to choose an Administrator for the Diocese, they met on Friday, April 22, 1994 at the Chancery and Bishop O'Neill was elected the Diocesan Administrator. The members of the College of Consultors at that time were: Fathers Thomas C. Brady, William J. Clausen, Daniel J. Hermes, David D. Kagan, Gerald P. Kobbeman, F. James Larson, and Andrew J. Plesa.

In May 1994, with the plans having been completed in the latter half of 1993 and early 1994, Bishop O'Neill broke ground for a new Aurora Central Catholic High School on the far west side of the city of Aurora. In May 1994, St. James Parish, Rockford, received a prestigious civic award for the renovation of the parish church, called *The Heart of Rockford Award*. On May 21, 1994, Bishop O'Neill ordained his last class of men for the priesthood. Fathers Daniel J. Deutsch, John P. Earl, Martin G. Heinz and David A. Peck were ordained to the Sacred Priesthood at the Cathedral of St. Peter, Rockford.

As Diocesan Administrator, Bishop O'Neill oversaw the ordinary and daily business of the Diocese, and he named Father John J. Mitchell, Pastor of St. Bridget Parish, Loves Park, and Dean of the Rockford Deanery to assist him with all the plans for the ordination and installation of Bishop-elect, Thomas G. Doran, and Father Robert A. Balog to coordinate all of the liturgical ceremonies scheduled for Thursday, June 23, 1994, and Friday, June 24, 1994.

◆ **The staff of the Catholic Education Office and new principals, 1977.**

◆ **Bishop O'Neill with his parents, Lee and Clara O'Neill, on the occasion of his ordination as bishop of Rockford, October 1968.**

The Doran Years

Thomas George Doran was born on February 20, 1936 in Rockford, Illinois, the son of Robert J. and Gretchen Durst Doran. He attended St. James Pro-Cathedral grade school, graduating in 1950, and Campion Jesuit High School in Prairie du Chien, Wisconsin from 1950 to 1954. Thomas Doran then entered the college seminary and completed his classical and philosophical studies at St. Pius X Seminary at Loras College, Dubuque, Iowa from 1954 to 1958. Bishop Lane assigned him to pursue theological studies in Rome at the Pontifical Gregorian University and to receive his priestly formation at The Pontifical North American College, Vatican City. On December 20, 1961, Thomas George Doran was ordained to the Sacred Priesthood for the Diocese of Rockford in the Basilica of St. Peter in Vatican City by The Most Reverend Martin J. O'Connor, Rector of The Pontifical North American College. Father Doran completed his studies, receiving a License in Sacred Theology and returned to the United States in the summer of 1962.

Father Thomas Doran's first assignment was to be the Assistant Pastor at St. Joseph Parish, Elgin, and to teach Religion part-time at St. Edward Central Catholic High School from August 31, 1962 to August 18, 1963. His next assignment was to be the Assistant Pastor for St. Peter Parish, South Beloit, and to work part-time in the Chancery Office as a Notary for the Diocesan Tribunal from August 19, 1963 to September 1, 1965. Bishop Lane appointed Father Doran to be the Secretary to the Bishop on September 1, 1965 and take up residence at the Chancery on a full-time basis, and he served in this capacity, as well as being the Secretary of the Diocesan Tribunal and a Defender of the Bond, until Bishop O'Neill appointed him the Chancellor of the Diocese on January 1, 1969.

Father Doran served as Chancellor for the next 17 and one-half years. During these years he served also as the Secretary to the College of Consultors from 1969 to 1986, and pursued post-graduate studies in Canon Law in Rome from 1975 to 1978 obtaining a doctorate in 1978. Bishop O'Neill appointed him the Officialis of the Diocesan Tribunal and he served in this office from 1976 to 1984. He was appointed a member of the College of Consultors and served from 1981 to 1986, and he was appointed the first Episcopal Vicar for Catholic Education, serving from 1982 to 1984 in this office. On July 5, 1984, Bishop O'Neill

◆ **Bishop Thomas G. Doran, eighth bishop of the Rockford Diocese.
Motto: Hope is the anchor of life.**

SPES ANCHORA VITAE

◆ **Ordination of Bishop Doran as eighth bishop of Rockford, June 24, 1994.**

appointed Father Doran to be the Rector for the Cathedral of St. Peter where he served until July 18, 1986, continuing to serve also as the Chancellor of the Diocese.

When Father Doran's appointment to be a Prelate-Auditor of the Roman Rota was announced in the summer of 1986, he left his Cathedral assignment in July and then departed for Rome in the early autumn of 1986. The new Monsignor Doran served the Holy See and the Universal Church on the Roman Rota until Pope John Paul II appointed him to be the eighth Bishop of the Diocese of Rockford.

Thomas George Doran was ordained and installed as the eighth Bishop of the Diocese of Rockford on June 24, 1994, at the physical education center at Rock Valley College in Rockford. His Eminence, Joseph Cardinal Bernardin, Archbishop of Chicago, was the principal consecrator, with The Most Reverend Arthur J. O'Neill, Bishop Emeritus of Rockford, and The Most Reverend Joseph Galante, Bishop of Beaumont, Texas, being the co-consecrators. Father Robert A. Balog served as the Master of Ceremonies. Forty other archbishops, bishops, and abbots participated in the ceremonies, along with the priests of the Diocese, as well as its

permanent deacons. The total number of clergy, religious and laity who attended this Mass was estimated to be more than 4,000 people.

After his ordination and installation, on Monday, June 27, 1994, Bishop Doran confirmed in office Father Charles W. McNamee as the Chancellor and Father David D. Kagan as the Officialis, he reappointed Father Thomas C. Brady as Vicar General, the Episcopal Vicars as such for their Vicariates. Also on that day, Bishop Doran, in keeping with the revised Code of Canon Law (1983), created and filled a new diocesan administrative position. He appointed Father David D. Kagan to be the Moderator of the Curia.

Also according to Church law, when a see is vacant the various diocesan consultative bodies cease to function (except for the Consultors). Bishop Doran reconstituted the Presbyteral Council (Priests' Senate), and the Diocesan Finance Council by the end of the month of June 1994. During the months of August and September 1994, Bishop Doran met with the Presbyteral Council, the seven Deans, the Diocesan Consultors, the Diocesan Finance Council, and he attended all seven deanery meetings of the priests of the Diocese. His purpose was to hear from all concerned what they considered priorities of the Diocese for the next several years. Without exception, the promotion of vocations to the diocesan priesthood, planning for future parish development, and better youth and adult religious education were recommended as priorities.

◆ **Bishop Doran's first Chrism Mass on Holy Thursday, 1995.**

◆ Bishop Doran meets the press at St. Peter Cathedral's Fellowship Hall.

◆ Diocesan Pastoral Council members, John Krier, Sister Patricia Downey, OP, and Father Paul White, 2003.

August 18, 1994, marked the first of what has become an annual media luncheon hosted by Bishop Doran for members of the secular media. Its purpose is to provide a forum for the exchange of information and for the secular media to learn about the Catholic Church and its life and practices. This event is coordinated by the Office of Communications for the Diocese which also coordinates the Catholic Mass for Shut-in's. The media luncheon has given impetus to a weekly Monday morning radio program featuring Bishop Doran, as well as a daily 30-second morning reflection by Bishop Doran on a local Rockford television station.

On September 1, 1994, Bishop Doran made some further adjustments to the Diocesan Curia. He appointed Father F. James Larson, the Episcopal Vicar for Clergy and Religious since 1989, the Episcopal Vicar for Catholic Education. He then appointed Father Michael A. Binsfeld, Pastor of St. Mary Parish, Elgin, the new Episcopal Vicar for Clergy and Religious. On September 13, 1994, Bishop Doran gave formal permission for girls to serve at Mass in keeping with an earlier permission granted by the Holy See.

In November 1994, Bishop Doran attended his first general meeting as a member of the National Conference of Catholic Bishops in Washington, D.C. On November 17, 1994, Bishop Doran announced that three diocesan priests had been named monsignors by Pope John Paul II. Father Thomas C. Brady, Vicar General was named a Protonotary Apostolic Supernumerary of His Holiness, Father Charles W. McNamee, Chancellor, and Father David D. Kagan, Officialis and Moderator of the Curia, were named Prelates of Honor of His Holiness, all with the title of Reverend Monsignor.

On January 1, 1995, Bishop Doran appointed Monsignor David D. Kagan a Vicar General of the Diocese, and on January 25th he established as a formal diocesan position, the Parish Pastoral Associate. The Parish Pastoral Associate can be a religious sister or brother, a lay man or lay woman and, in certain cases, a permanent deacon. At present, there are six diocesan appointed Parish Pastoral Associates, three lay women, two lay men, and one permanent deacon.

During the season of Lent in 1995, Bishop Doran began a series of day-long seminars for teachers of religion in diocesan schools and parish religion programs on the Catechism of the Catholic Church. The approved English language translation of the Catechism had been published the prior year. These seminars were held at Marian Central Catholic High School, Woodstock, at St. Mary Parish, DeKalb, and at Aquin Central Catholic High School, Freeport. In the spring of 1995, the Diocesan Pastoral Council was established by

◆ **May crowning at St. Stanislaus Kostka Parish, Rockford, 1995.**

Bishop Doran in keeping with what Church law envisioned as a consultative group for the Diocesan Bishop in pastoral matters. Its first meeting was on June 3, 1995 at St. Rita of Cascia Parish, Rockford.

On June 1, 1995, Bishop Doran made the difficult decision to close St. Patrick Parish School in Rockford. A very low enrollment, rising costs and continuing deficits for the school and Parish were some of the reasons for this action. On June 11, 1995, Bishop Doran celebrated Mass at St. Patrick Parish, Rochelle, for a group of Young Adult Catholics and then held a town hall meeting with them to listen to their concerns and recommendations for parish and diocesan ministry in their regard.

Bishop Doran named Wayne M. Lenell, Ph.D., to succeed Harry Koplin as head of the Diocese's Office of Finance and Administration on July 1, 1995; he named Harry Koplin the Director of Catholic Cemeteries at the same time. Also, on July 1, 1995, Father Neal Kaminski, OFM Cap. was named the Diocesan Director of the Propagation of the Faith, succeeding Monsignor Raymond J. Wahl who had held this position since 1984. On August 1, 1995, Bishop Doran named Sister Patricia Downey, O.P. the new Superintendent of Schools for the Diocese of Rockford.

The autumn of this year was a time for dedications of major high school expansions for Bishop Doran. On September 24, 1995, he dedicated the new Aurora Central Catholic High School, located on North Edgelawn Drive in Aurora. On October 30, 1995, Bishop Doran dedicated a new classroom and auditorium addition at Boylan Central Catholic High School in Rockford.

A further sign of God's continued blessings on the Diocese of Rockford was manifested on October

◆ **Poor Clares Corpus Christi Monastery, Rockford.**

13, 1995. Given the growth in members of the Poor Clares of Corpus Christi Monastery in Rockford, eight nuns lead by Sister M. Dorothy, left Corpus Christi Monastery to establish a new community of Poor Clares in the Diocese of Joliet, in Minooka, Illinois. Thus, Annunciation Monastery came into existence there and was officially dedicated three years later in 1998.

The year of 1996 witnessed some institutional changes in the Diocese of Rockford, the creation by the Holy Father of more monsignors from among the diocesan clergy, and the introduction to the Diocese of a new group of priests, as well as Bishop Doran's first ordinations for the diocesan priesthood.

Fathers Michael A. Binsfeld, Thomas L. Dzielak, Alphonsus F. Harte, Daniel J. Hermes, John J. Mitchell, William H. Schwartz and Edward S. Wright were named Prelates of Honor to His Holiness, Pope John Paul II. Father Sylvester J. Eye, a priest of the diocese for 59 years, was named a Protonotary Apostolic Supernumerary to His Holiness and died shortly after receiving this high honor; Monsignor Raymond J. Wahl was elevated to the rank of Protonotary Apostolic Supernumerary to His Holiness at this time as well. These honors were conferred on our priests in January of 1996.

In February 1996, Bishop Doran began the Diocese's preparation for the Great Jubilee Holy Year of 2000 by appointing Father Eric R. Barr, Pastor of St. Joseph Parish, Aurora, and Chairman of the Presbyteral Council, to develop the liturgical, homiletic and devotional materials to be used by all the parishes for the next three years of immediate preparation for the Great Jubilee Holy Year.

In May, Bishop Doran ordained his first class of priests at the Cathedral of St. Peter. They were: Fathers Stanislaw Kos, Miroslaw A. Reikowski and Max J. Striedl. On June 2, 1996, Bishop Doran dedicated a new classroom addition for Marian Central Catholic High School in Woodstock. On June 18th Bishop Doran appointed Father Martin G. Heinz the full-time Diocesan Director of Vocations, an office he would hold and develop capably until May, 2002. June 30, 1996, marked the sale by the diocese, of St. Vincent-St. Joseph Home in Freeport to Provena Senior Services (formerly ServantCor). June 1996, was the month in which Bishop Doran introduced to the diocese, The Institute of Christ the King, Sovereign Priest. This group of priests has been approved by the Holy See to offer the Latin Mass according to the Roman Missal and rubrics of 1962. Father Brian A.T. Bovee was assigned to the diocese and began this apostolate in Rockford at Corpus Christi Monastery of the Poor Clares, and in Aurora at St. Joseph Parish.

July 1, 1996 marked a milestone in one of the longstanding diocesan ministries. Bishop Doran appointed Monsignor William H. Schwartz to be the Diocesan Scout Chaplain, replacing Monsignor Charles W. McNamee who had served in this post for forty-two years and was responsible for its development as a vital apostolate to the young boys and girls of the Diocese of Rockford.

◆ **Former residents and supporters gathered for a reunion in honor of the 100th anniversary of St. Vincent Orphanage in Freeport. Dave Thomas, an adoptee himself and founder of the Wendy's Hamburger Restaurant chain, was the guest speaker, July 21, 1996.**

◆ **Monsignor William Schwartz and Eagle Scout Michael Spencer pay tribute to Monsignor Charles McNamee.**

◆ **The Knights of Columbus throughout the diocese remember abortion victims through prayer, action and memorials like this one from Calvary Cemetery, Winnebago.**

In August 1996, Bishop Doran appointed a Steering Committee to develop a process to study the vitality of the parishes, agencies and the Diocese itself so that future planning for all would be more in keeping with what was truly effective and affordable. The process came to be known as With a Heart Renewed: Parish Consultations Process. The original members of the Steering Committee were: Monsignors David D. Kagan and Michael A. Binsfeld, Father F. James Larson, Mr. John J. McGrath, Mr. Thomas F. McKenna, and Dr. Michael J. Cieslak.

In the autumn of 1996, Bishop Doran authorized the review of the diocese's procedures and administration of St. Francis School for Exceptional Children in Freeport. Reductions of State funding and changing and increased State regulations made this review imperative.

The First Sunday of Advent, 1996, marked the beginning of the Diocese's immediate observance of the preparation for the solemn celebration of the Great Jubilee Holy Year of 2000. Throughout all of 1997 the Diocese celebrated the Year of the Son, the Lord Jesus. In December 1996, Bishop Doran celebrated his 35th anniversary of ordination to the priesthood.

With the work of the Parish Consultations Process Steering Committee making some significant progress, Bishop Doran appointed Father F. James Larson to be the Episcopal Vicar for the Parish Consultations Process on February 1, 1997. At the same time, the Bishop named Sister Patricia Downey, O.P., Superintendent of Schools, to be also the Secretary for Catholic Education for the Diocese of Rockford, to replace Father Larson. In February, Bishop Doran implemented the required parish visitation process as called for by Church law and he delegated the Deans to perform this task for the parishes of their respective deaneries every two years.

As he had done in 1995, Bishop Doran held four more study days on the Catechism in the months of February and March 1997 at St. Catherine of Siena Parish, Dundee, Boylan Central Catholic High School, Rockford, St. Mary Parish, DeKalb, and Marian Central Catholic High School, Woodstock. In May 1997, Bishop Doran ordained five men to the diocesan priesthood. It was in this same month that Bishop Doran authorized a comprehensive examination of all diocesan office buildings in order to determine their continued suitability and viability.

◆ **Every parish contributed to a diocesan quilt hanging at the Bishop Lane Retreat Center. The event pictured is the World Marriage Day dinner, 1994.**

On June 2, 1997, a major renovation of the Cathedral of St. Peter began and would take most of the rest of the year to complete. A most generous donation by Mrs. Frances Deming in memory of her late husband, made this renovation possible.

At the end of June Bishop Doran gave approval for the establishment of *Legatus* in the Diocese of Rockford. It is a group for Catholic business men and women that meets on a monthly basis for spiritual, educational and social renewal and exchange. Its first meeting was on June 24, 1997.

July 1, 1997 was the date of the appointment of Monsignor Thomas C. Brady, P.A., as the new Diocesan Director of Cemeteries. August 23, 1997, marked the formal beginning of the Parish Consultations Process. The work of the Steering Committee which had been meeting for a year was presented at a day-long meeting at Cliffbreaker's Restaurant in Rockford. Bishop Doran and Father F. James Larson, the Episcopal Vicar for the P.C.P., presented to all the priests, parish representatives and diocesan employees the purpose, scope and work of this process which was to be pursued over the next eighteen months throughout the Diocese. In sum, this was to be a direct consultation of as many Catholics as possible in the Diocese about the current vitality of their parishes, as well as seeking their advice about pastoral plans that could make their parishes more vital in the future. In the end, more than 55,000 Catholics participated in the P.C.P.

On November 30, 1997, after having consulted the necessary councils and others with a particular expertise, Bishop Doran canonically altered the status of St. Mary Parish in Rockford. Its status became that of a Shrine rather than a territorial parish. The dramatic demographic changes which had been occurring in this parish over many years made this difficult decision necessary. St. Mary's had few resident parishioners and it was no longer

◆ **Monsignor David Kagan was the keynote speaker for the newly formed Women for Faith and Family conference.**

◆ **John McGrath hands a lit candle to a parish representative at the opening ceremony to "With a Heart Renewed: Parish Consultations Process", August 1997.**

◆ **Sisters of the Immaculate Heart of Mary were among the women religious honored by the Knights of Columbus at their Annual Sisters' Night Out.**

able to meet the many responsibilities which every parish, large or small, must bear. Bishop Doran entrusted the care of the Shrine of St. Mary to the Institute of Christ the King, Sovereign Priest.

With the First Sunday of Advent, 1997, the second year of preparation for the Great Jubilee of 2000 began and would extend throughout 1998 as the year of God the Holy Spirit.

December 26, 1997, the feast of St. Stephen, Proto-Martyr, Bishop Doran issued his first pastoral letter to all of the Catholic faithful of the Diocese of Rockford. It was entitled: "On the Most Holy Eucharist."

◆ **Father David Beauvais visits with Father Clarence Thennes and Sister Dion Heine, principal at St. Francis School, at the 30th anniversary celebration for St. Francis Home for Exceptional Children, Freeport, 1998.**

In 1998, two more diocesan priests were honored with the title of Monsignor. Father Thomas E. Bales, Pastor of St. Mary Parish, Sterling, and Dean of the Sterling Deanery, and Father Robert B. Hoffman, Pastor of St. John Neumann Parish, St. Charles, and Dean of the Elgin Deanery were named Prelates of Honor to His Holiness, Pope John Paul II. The first five months of 1998 were devoted to the necessary preparations for Bishop Doran's first *ad limina* visit to the Holy See. That visit extended from May 21, 1998 to June 4, 1998. Just prior to leaving for Rome in May, Bishop Doran ordained six more men to the Sacred Priesthood for service to the Diocese.

Upon his return from Rome in June 1998, Bishop Doran formed a committee of priests, religious and laity from the Diocese to make the plans and preparations for the Diocese's celebration of the Great Jubilee Holy Year of 2000. This Jubilee 2000 Committee was chaired by Monsignor Schwartz, Rector of the Cathedral.

During the month of July 1998, Bishop Doran invited the head of the NCCB Committee for Hispanic Ministry to evaluate the Diocese's programs, progress and level of support for its

Hispanic Ministry apostolate. Mr. Ron Cruz spent part of the month of July and then returned the following September to complete his comprehensive review. He had much praise for all those dedicated to this ministry and its programs, as well as the level of diocesan support both in full and part-time personnel and the financial resources dedicated to this ministry.

In September 1998, Bishop Doran transferred ownership of the Knights Community Complex from the Diocese to Boylan Central Catholic High School for its use and program development.

The highlight of the year of 1998 occurred on Tuesday, September 29, 1998 with the dedication of the altar at the recently renovated Cathedral of St. Peter. Francis Cardinal George, OMI, was the principal celebrant of the Mass of Dedication, Bishop Doran, Bishop O'Neill and 10 other bishops from the region were joined by the priests, religious and laity of the Diocese at this concelebrated Mass. This Mass also commemorated the 90th anniversary of the diocese. The year of 1998 was also Bishop O'Neill's 55th anniversary of ordination to the Sacred Priesthood and his 30th anniversary as a bishop.

◆ **Martin House executive director Ron Thomas shows an award given to the agency for its service to people living in the inner city.**

In November 1998, Bishop Doran introduced to the diocese the Congregation of the Sisters of the Immaculate Heart of Mary of Nigeria. Their first mission was to staff St. Elizabeth Catholic Community Center in Rockford and they now serve in Catholic nursing homes in Rockford and in Freeport.

On December 1, 1998, tragedy struck Sacred Heart Parish in Aurora with the suspected arson fire and destruction of the Parish Church.

With the First Sunday of Advent in 1998, the third year of preparation for the Great Jubilee of 2000 began with the celebration of the year of God the Father throughout 1999 and up to Christmas Eve when the Great Jubilee Holy Year of 2000 would begin.

On December 26, 1998, again the feast of St. Stephen, Proto-Martyr, Bishop Doran issued his second pastoral letter to the Catholic faithful of the diocese and this was titled: "On the Sacrament of Penance or Reconciliation".

Adjustments in diocesan ministries continued in the first half of the year of 1999. On January 1, 1999, the Fourth Street Bridge project in Rockford was discontinued due to changes in State funding and State priorities. January also saw the formation of a committee to review all aspects of the status of St. Francis School for Exceptional Children in Freeport. The committee completed its work by March and recommended its closure since the new State regulations were found to be impossible for the facility or the Diocese to fully implement. Bishop Doran reluctantly accepted the recommendation and St. Francis closed at the end of the summer in 1999.

A first for the Diocese occurred in January 1999 and then again in May 1999. Two former Anglican clergymen had been received into full communion with the Roman Catholic Church and in January were ordained transitional deacons by Bishop Doran

◆ **Former Anglican clergymen, Addison Hart and Dean Smith, are ordained transitional deacons by Bishop Doran in January 1999. Both were ordained priests in May 1999.**

and then were ordained to the diocesan priesthood with three other men in May. While it may not seem unusual, both men came to the Church and the priesthood under the terms of what is called the *Pastoral Provision*. More precisely, this governs those Anglican clergy who are married and while Father Dean M. Smith is not, Father Addison H. Hart is married and, with the prior permission of the Holy See, Bishop Doran was able to ordain him a Roman Catholic priest.

June 24, 1999, marked Bishop Doran's Fifth Anniversary as the eighth Bishop of the Diocese of Rockford. July 31, 1999 marked the retirement of Monsignor Charles W. McNamee as Chancellor and the appointment of Monsignor David D. Kagan to be the Chancellor ad interim on August 1, 1999. Not long before Monsignor McNamee's retirement, he was elevated to the rank of Protonotary Apostolic Supernumerary by His Holiness, Pope John Paul II on May 11, 1999.

In September 1999, the Final Report and Recommendations of the Parish Consultations Process were completed and submitted to Bishop Doran which he accepted in May of the following year. The P.C.P. process was a distinct benefit to the parishes, diocesan agencies and the Diocese itself since it had achieved what it set out to accomplish – a study of the vitality of each parish and how each parish can be helped in achieving greater vitality through mutual cooperation and diocesan assistance. More and better ministry to our Catholic youth and young adults, more and better religious education for all Catholics and a more active involvement of the Catholic laity in Church life, both parish and diocesan, were among the most often-repeated recommendations.

◆ **Diane Kryzanski and Coni Schwandt prepare to process more than 55,000 parish surveys that were collected during the first phase of "With a Heart Renewed: Parish Consultations Process."**

A near tragedy was avoided in October 1999, when a fire broke out in the Youth Ministry Center at the Bishop Lane Retreat Center. The fire spread quickly rendering the building a total loss but, thanks be to God, no one was using the facility at that time. Plans were quickly formulated and approved by Bishop Doran to build another facility and construction began within a few months. On December 1, 1999, the Diocese purchased 19 acres of land in northern Boone County in the Village of Poplar Grove for future parish development.

With the approach of Christmas Eve, 1999 and the official beginning of the Great Jubilee Year 2000, the Jubilee 2000 Committee which Bishop Doran had appointed the prior year to prepare the diocese's celebration of the Holy Year completed its work

THE GREAT JUBILEE OF 2000

The first official celebration in observance of the Great Jubilee of 2000 came on Christmas Eve, 1999. Every parish and other institution with a chapel

◆ **Home visits were made across the diocese during the United in Faith campaign.**

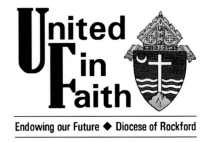

received a special Jubilee Cross to be hung near its main entrance. As the Holy Father opened the Holy Door of St. Peter Basilica in the Vatican, so Bishop Doran and all pastors and chaplains did the same on that Christmas Eve, inaugurating the Jubilee Holy Year of 2000. Special devotions and pilgrimages with indulgences attached were arranged for the Catholic faithful of the Diocese, and were observed in specially designated parish churches throughout the Diocese during the entire course of the Holy Year.

The Jubilee Year of 2000 witnessed a significant change in how Bishop Doran would govern the daily business of the Diocese. It was at the beginning of this year that Bishop Doran undertook the first diocesan capital campaign to insure financial support for the current and any future ministries serving a very rapidly growing Catholic population which was fast becoming far more diverse than ever before.

In March of 2000 the first diocesan capital campaign began. The theme of this campaign was: "United in Faith – Endowing Our Future", and for the remainder of the year 2000 and throughout 2001, the campaign would continue under the

◆ **Bishop Doran ceremoniously opens the door of St. Peter Cathedral on Christmas Eve, 1999, to begin the Holy Year.**

direction of Mr. David Hougan, Director of the Office of Stewardship Development, seeking to achieve a target of $35 million. This total would be permanently endowed through deposit in The Catholic Foundation for the People of the Diocese of Rockford. The earnings would be distributed to give financial support to the following diocesan priorities: Catholic schools, Religious Education and Youth programs, seminarian education and the continuing education of priests, needy parishes and schools, and priest retirement.

The spring and summer months of the Jubilee Year of 2000 were filled with significant moments for the Diocese. On May 2, 2000, Bishop Doran established the Diocesan Planning Commission and named Dr. Michael J. Cieslak, Director of the Office of Research and Planning the chairman, and the other six original members named by the Bishop were:

Monsignors Michael A. Binsfeld and David D. Kagan, Father Joseph B. Linster, Dr. Wayne Lenell and Mr. William Easton. This commission was formed as a result of recommendations from the Parish Consultations Process.

The date of May 17, 2000, marked the Silver Anniversary for the first class of men ordained as Permanent Deacons by Bishop O'Neill.

Bishop Doran ordained eight men to the Sacred Priesthood as part of the Holy Year class, on May 20, 2000. They were Fathers Carl E. Beekman, Michael G. Black, Stephen O. Folorunso, John C. Fritz, Brian D. Grady, Ricardo F. Hernandez, Uriel Lopez and Dean E. Russell.

◆ **Jubilee Confirmation at the Metro Center, Rockford, June 11, 2000.**

June 11, 2000, Pentecost Sunday, was a day of firsts for the Diocese of Rockford. Bishop Doran, assisted by ten other archbishops and bishops, three abbots, and five monsignors, administered the Sacrament of Confirmation in two afternoon ceremonies to more than three thousand young people from across the Diocese. The Metro Center in Rockford was reserved for this great occasion and it was filled to capacity twice. Confirmation 2000 was the high point of the Diocese's celebration of the Great Jubilee Year of 2000.

◆ **Rockford native and Augustinian priest, Father Richard Palmer preaches at a special Mass honoring Our Lady of Guadalupe in the Jubilee year. This celebration was part of the Hispanic Ministry Program.**

Michael A. Binsfeld who was appointed the Pastor of St. Elizabeth Ann Seton Parish in Crystal Lake, and who would die suddenly the very next year. Also on this date, Bishop Doran appointed Father Glenn L. Nelson to be the Chancellor of the Diocese.

On July 1, 2000, Bishop Doran announced a major realignment of the diocesan administrative structure. The Episcopal Vicar system was changed to a Diocesan Departmental system, with only the Episcopal Vicar for Clergy and Religious retained. There would be four main departments under which all diocesan apostolates and services would be supervised. The departments are: Educational Services, Financial and Administrative Services, Pastoral Services and Social Services; each would have a director and an assistant director. The directors and assistant directors for the four departments were respectively: Sister Patricia Downey, OP, and Mr. John McGrath; Dr. Wayne Lenell, CPA, and Mrs. Jodi Rippon, CPA; Father John A. Slampak, STL, and Mrs. Lorrie Gramer; Mr. Thomas McKenna and Mr. Jason Christiansen. All would work with the Moderator of the Curia to provide Bishop Doran with the best information and advice in order for him to administer the Diocese's growing and more complex array of ministries and services.

On July 1, 2000, Bishop Doran appointed Father Eric R. Barr, Pastor of St. Rita of Cascia Parish, Rockford, to be the new Episcopal Vicar for Clergy and Religious. He succeeded Monsignor

During this same Jubilee Year, four diocesan priests were honored with the promotion to the rank of monsignor and one other monsignor was elevated in rank. Fathers Eric R. Barr, Episcopal Vicar for Clergy and Religious, Joseph F. Jarmoluk, Pastor of St. Peter Parish, Geneva, P. William McDonnell, Pastor of St. Thomas Aquinas Parish, Freeport and Dean of the Freeport District, and William J. Clausen, Pastor of St. Mary Parish, Maple Park and Dean of the DeKalb District, were named Prelates of Honor to His Holiness, Pope John Paul II, with the title of Reverend Monsignor. Monsignor William H. Schwartz, Rector for the Cathedral of St. Peter was named a Protonotary Apostolic Supernumerary by Pope John Paul II.

◆ **Rock 2000 brought hundreds of teens together to celebrate faith and promote vocations.**

On September 2, 2000, the Apostolic Nuncio announced that Bishop Doran had been appointed by Pope John Paul II to be a member of the Supreme Tribunal of the Apostolic Signatura in Rome. Bishop Doran would fulfill the duties of this position for the next five years, in addition to his many responsibilities as the Bishop Rockford.

In the month of November, 2000, construction was completed on the new youth center which replaced the old center destroyed by fire. Bishop Doran approved the naming of the center The Holy Family of Nazareth Youth Center and dedicated it so that the first group was able to make use of it in December, 2000.

The year of 2001 was devoted to pursuing to a successful completion the Diocese's first capital campaign. From January to December, each parish conducted its part of the campaign. One of the features of this campaign was that each parish would share in the campaign's success by receiving a portion of the funds the parish raised to use for its own further development.

As a result of Bishop Doran's consultations with the Presbyteral Council, the College of Consultors and the Diocesan Pastoral Council during the years of 2000 and 2001, preparations were begun under the direction of Monsignor David D. Kagan for another Diocesan Synod. This preparatory stage occupied most of this year of 2001 and set in motion the immediate work of the Synod in the following year.

On March 2, 2001, Pope John Paul II, once again appointed Bishop Doran to another Roman Congregation. It was announced by the Apostolic Nuncio that Bishop Doran was to be a member of the Congregation for the Clergy, in addition to his other duties and responsibilities. Like his appointment the year before to the Church's highest court, this appointment was for five years.

In May, Bishop Doran ordained five more men to the Sacred Priesthood for service to the Diocese.

◆ **The diocese serves many ethnic populations. Catholics with a Philippine heritage celebrated Simbang Gabi in December 2002, at St. John Neumann Church, St. Charles.**

All paused in shock as the terrorist attacks of September 11, 2001, unfolded before the world. Bishop Doran called for and led the Catholic faithful in special prayers for the victims, their families, our nation and for peace at that time of national crisis and grief. Bishop Doran authorized a special collection to be taken up in all parishes of the Diocese the weekend of September 15-16, 2001, to assist with immediate relief in the aftermath of the attacks on New York and Washington, D.C. The Diocese forwarded to Catholic Charities, U.S.A. the donations of the Catholic faithful in the amount of $277,375.91.

Preparation work for the next Diocesan Synod had progressed to the point that on November 30, 2001, Bishop Doran appointed Monsignor David D. Kagan the Promoter of the Synod and charged him with implementing the Synod's process.

◆ **St. Elizabeth Catholic Community Center meets a variety of social and corporal needs including feeding the hungry. This photograph shows the Thanksgiving dinner in 2002.**

◆ **Bishop Doran speaks to First Communicants at St. Mary's Oratory, Rockford.**

In December, 2001, Bishop Doran celebrated his 40th anniversary of priestly ordination. December, 2001 brought the "United In Faith" capital campaign active phase to a close and a final report of the campaign's success was submitted to Bishop Doran. A brief summary of the results showed that the diocesan target had been surpassed by more than $7 million in pledges and that 94 of the 104 parishes exceeded their individual targets. The pledge redemption period would continue through December, 2006.

In the months of January and February, 2002, the Synod Preparatory Commission met on an almost daily basis to prepare the actual Synod Directory. This Commission, appointed by Bishop Doran, was composed of 21 persons chosen from among the clergy, religious and laity of the Diocese. At the Mass of Chrism on March 28, 2002, Bishop Doran formally announced his decision to convoke the Fourth Synod of the Diocese of Rockford on September 28, 2002.

In May, Bishop Doran ordained six men to the Sacred Priesthood for service to the Diocese. At mid-year, after making the required consultations, Bishop Doran altered again the status of St. Mary Shrine in Rockford to that of an Oratory. He confirmed the continued administration of the Oratory by the priests of the Institute of Christ the King, Sovereign Priest. May, 2002, was the month when Bishop Doran appointed Father Aaron R. Brodeski to be the Director of Vocations for the Diocese of Rockford, succeeding Father Martin G. Heinz who had also been Pastor of Holy Angels Parish in Aurora since June 30, 2000.

In July 2002, Bishop Doran announced his decision to reinstitute the Vicariate for Hispanic Ministry, given the continued growth and development of the Ministry and he appointed Father Arquimedes Vallejo the Episcopal Vicar for Hispanic Ministry on August 1, 2002.

On July 10, the Diocese purchased 36 acres of property in Lake in the Hills for future parish development. Also in July, 2002, as part of the acceptance of the final report of the "United In Faith" capital campaign, Bishop Doran appointed a Permanent Committee of clergy, religious and laity from the Diocese to oversee the investment and distribution of funds gathered from the campaign. The first meeting of this group took place on August 5, 2002.

On August 16, 2002, two more firsts were achieved in the diocese. Bishop Doran appointed the first Associate Publisher for *The Observer*, Dr. Owen Phelps who, until then, had been the Editor. Bishop Doran then appointed the first female Editor for *The Observer*, Mrs. Penny Wiegert.

On August 29, Bishop Doran issued the decree for the convocation of the Fourth Synod of the Diocese of Rockford.

In mid-September, 2002, after five years of careful study and examination, Bishop Doran purchased the property owned by the Dean's Foods Company at the tollway on the east side of Rockford. The property of ten acres and a 70,000 square foot office building would serve as the new central administration building for all diocesan offices which, until this time, had been located at eight different sites in Rockford. The purchase price for the land and buildings was $6,087,500. During the third week of October, 2002, all 26 diocesan offices closed and moved to the new location and by the following Monday, the Diocese was once again open for business.

On Saturday, September 28, 2002, the Fourth Synod of the Diocese of Rockford was convoked by Bishop Doran at the Cathedral of St. Peter in Rockford. The Synod Directory was approved by the participants and recommended to Bishop

Doran for his acceptance and promulgation which he did on October 18, 2002. So that copies of the new Synod Directory could be published in English and Spanish and distributed to the Catholic faithful of the Diocese, the Synod statutes became effective on the Solemnity of Mary, Mother of God, January 1, 2003.

◆ **Bishop Doran and Pope John Paul II.**

◆ **Diocesan Administration Center, Rockford.**

◆ **Bishop Doran dedicates the new mausoleum at St. Mary/St. James Cemetery, Rockford in 2003.**

The year of 2003 was the occasion for Bishop Doran to make his second ad limina visit to the Holy See to report to the Holy Father on the general status of Catholic life in the Diocese of Rockford. The Bishop made his *ad limina* visit in May of 2003, spending the preceding months in preparation for this visit.

One might say that the year of 2003 was the year of the priesthood in the Diocese of Rockford. In January, four more diocesan priests were honored by being promoted to the rank of monsignor. Father Joseph B. Linster, Pastor of St. Patrick Parish, St. Charles, Father James W. McLoughlin, Pastor of St. Mary Parish, Woodstock, and Dean of the McHenry County District, Father Glenn L. Nelson, Chancellor and a Vicar General of the Diocese, and Father Thomas J. Dempsey, Pastor of St. Elizabeth Ann Seton Parish, Crystal Lake were named Chaplains to His Holiness by Pope John Paul II. This year of 2003 was a significant year for Bishop O'Neill since he celebrated his 60th anniversary of ordination to the Sacred Priesthood and his 35th anniversary of ordination as a bishop.

In May, 2003, Bishop Doran ordained the single largest class of men to the Sacred Priesthood in the 95 year history of the Diocese. Those ordained priests of the Diocese in 2003 were: Fathers Godwin N. Asuquo, David M. Austin, David C. Finn, Lorenzo Gonzalez, Phillip A. Kaim, Joel Lopez, Cesar C. Pajarillo, James W. Parker, Steven M. Sabo, Ariel Valencia and Kenneth Wasilewski.

◆ **In 2003, Bishop Doran ordained the largest class of men to the priesthood in the history of the diocese.**

On July 31, 2003, the diocese sold the vacant Seton Center, its former main office building and the once St. Thomas High School on West State Street in Rockford.

In the month of October, 2003, Bishop Doran reconstituted and reorganized the Diocesan Ecumenical Commission. He appointed Father Addison H. Hart, Director of the Office of Ecumenism, to be the chairman of the Commission. Those appointed by Bishop Doran to be members of the Commission were: Monsignors Thomas L. Dzielak and David D. Kagan, Fathers Michael G. Black and Joel Rippinger, OSB, and Dr. Paresh Dixit.

In May, 2004, Bishop Doran ordained two men to the diocesan priesthood and on June 24, 2004, Bishop Doran observed his 10th Anniversary as the eighth Bishop of the Diocese of Rockford.

In October, 2004, three more priests of the diocese were elevated to the rank of monsignor. Father Robert J. Willhite, Pastor of St. Rita of Cascia Parish, Aurora, and Dean of the Aurora District was named a Prelate of Honor of His Holiness, Pope

John Paul II. Fathers Thomas J. Monahan, retired, and Arquimedes Vallejo, Episcopal Vicar for Hispanic Ministry, were named Chaplains to His Holiness by Pope John Paul II. On October 18, 2004, Bishop Doran appointed Monsignor David D. Kagan to be the Chaplain for the Poor Clares of Corpus Christi Monastery in Rockford.

On Christmas Eve of 2004, the world witnessed the massive destruction of life and property in the wake of a tsunami which struck Indonesia and the other countries of that area of Southeast Asia. Not only did Bishop Doran call all Catholics of the Diocese to prayers for all affected, he also authorized a special collection for immediate relief to be taken up in all the parishes of the Diocese on

◆ Helen Reier and Rheta Zellner received the blessing for consecrated virgins from Bishop Doran in 2003.

◆ Father Brian Grady is pictured in the October 2004 life chain in Rockford, one of many held each year in the diocese.

◆ St. James Parish, Rockford, was among the many diocesan parishes that responded to the needs of Hurricane Katrina victims in 2005.

◆ Bishop Doran attempts to quiet chancery personnel as they watch live coverage of the announcement of the new pope April 21, 2005.

the first weekend of the New Year. As a result of that collection and the generosity of the Catholic faithful, the Diocese was able to forward to Catholic Relief Services a donation in the amount of $425,429.81.

On April 1, 2005, another first in the Diocese's history occurred. Bishop Doran announced the hiring of Mrs. Ellen Lynch Harrison as the Diocese's first full time, in-house General Counsel. Her responsibilities would be to oversee all legal matters for the Diocese itself, and all of its parishes and other institutions and agencies, as well as to coordinate and supervise the Diocese's Office of Human Resources.

On April 2, 2005, the Diocese along with the rest of the world mourned the death of our beloved Pope John Paul II. Bishop Doran directed that all churches, chapels, oratories and diocesan buildings be draped in black during the nine days of official mourning. Seventeen days later, April 19th, God the Holy Spirit, graced the Universal Church with a new Vicar of Christ. Joseph Cardinal Ratzinger, who took for himself the name Benedict XVI, had been elected in one of the briefest conclaves in recent Church

history. Bishop Doran ordered the bells of all our churches to be rung in thanksgiving. This date was also the 11th Anniversary of Bishop Doran's appointment as the eighth Bishop of Rockford.

In May, 2005, Bishop Doran ordained four men to the Sacred Priesthood. On June 4, 2005, Bishop Doran broke ground for the new church building for The Church of Holy Apostles Parish in McHenry. On August 15, 2005, Bishop Doran appointed Father Michael A. Kurz to be the Judicial Vicar for the Diocese of Rockford. He succeeded Monsignor David D. Kagan who had held this office for the prior 20 years.

At the end of August, 2005, disaster struck again and this time it was Hurricanes Katrina and Rita which devastated the Gulf Coast region of the United States. The hardest hit areas were the States of Mississippi and Louisiana. Bishop Doran, again, called on the generosity of the Catholic faithful of the Diocese and a special collection was taken up in all parishes the weekend of September 3-4, 2005. The Diocese forwarded to Catholic Charities, U.S.A. a total amount of $840,319.54.

BISHOP MULDOON'S CHAPEL

In 1917 Bishop Muldoon moved from St. James Pro-Cathedral Rectory to a private residence at 1704 National Avenue, Rockford. Probably within a short period of time, Bishop Muldoon had renovated the unfinished attic on the third floor to become his private chapel. After Bishop Muldoon died in 1927, Bishop Hoban lived in this house until 1929, when the Chancery and Bishop's Residence were built.

It is assumed that much of the chapel was disassembled before the Diocese sold the house in 1931. Significant remnants of Bishop Muldoon's chapel, however, remain today, 78 years after Bishop Hoban moved out. This includes a hand-painted reproduction of Bishop Muldoon's crest on the landing of the staircase leading to the chapel, and a cross and two stars – representing Bishop Muldoon's motto "For God and for country" – carved into the wood of an archway at the chapel entrance.

In 2005 the owners of the house, Rick and Monica Wilfong, donated to the Rockford Diocese several items from Bishop Muldoon's chapel. These include an elaborate candle stand and a set of custom-designed electric light fixtures, with the glass globes in the shape of a bishop's miter.

◆ **Pluman Petrov and Mike Rigali discuss how to remove the painting from its frame.**

After the house was sold, the next owners, Michael and Nicole Ranz, told the Diocese that they were willing to donate from the chapel an oil painting of the Assumption of the Blessed Virgin Mary into heaven. The only problem was that the painting was four feet wide and seven feet high. Diocesan workers attempted to remove the painting from the chapel but found that it was too large to navigate through the rather narrow staircase leading to the chapel.

The Diocese enlisted the help of Michael Rigali, from Daprato Rigali Studios, Chicago, a firm specializing in church art restoration. In September 2006, an artist from Daprato Rigali Studios carefully removed the oil canvas from its frame, which enabled it to be carried down the stairs. As of March 2007, this firm is restoring the painting.

◆ **Diocesan workers Mark Parsek and Brian Heinkel look for a way to move the painting of Mary's Assumption down the staircase. Behind them is Bishop Muldoon's crest, painted on the wall.**

On December 23, 2005, Bishop Doran appointed the Diocesan Centennial Committee to which he gave the task of planning for the celebration of the 100th anniversary of the establishment of the Diocese. Monsignor David D. Kagan was named the chairman of the committee and the other eight members appointed by the Bishop at the time were: Monsignors Eric R. Barr, Glenn L. Nelson and Arquimedes Vallejo, Sister Patricia Downey, OP, Mrs. Barb Farrah, Mrs. Sally Mullen, Mrs. Penny Wiegert and Dr. Michael Cieslak. Consultants to the Committee were named as well and they were: Father Joseph P. Naill, Mrs. Anne Hayes and Mr. John Krier.

The month of January, 2006, marked a significant anniversary for one of the longest, continuous diocesan apostolates to the sick and infirm. January 23, 2006, was the 40th anniversary of the Diocese's Mass for Shut-in's on the Rockford television station WREX; this apostolate has been coordinated by the Diocesan Office of Communications since 1982.

With the beginning of the Lenten Season of 2006, and at the direction of Bishop Doran, the Diocese undertook a four-year, adult religious

◆ Bishop Doran blesses Catholic couples married 25 and 50 years at the annual Silver and Gold Mass. This photograph is from the 2004 event at St. Peter Cathedral.

education program entitled *Why Catholic?* Its purpose is to better inform the Catholic men and women of the Diocese in the basics of the Catholic faith, the practices and liturgical and devotional life of the Catholic Church and it is entirely based on the four pillars of the *Catechism of the Catholic Church.* Two six-week sessions are held in all the parishes of the Diocese each of the four years and it has had an enthusiastic reception by the laity and their pastors.

On May 20, 2006, Bishop Doran ordained nine more priests for service to the Diocese.

The Poor Clares of Corpus Christi Monastery in Rockford observed a milestone on the feast of St. Clare, August 11, 2006. Bishop Doran was the main celebrant of a Pontifical Mass of Thanksgiving on the occasion of the 90th Anniversary of the Poor Clares coming to the Diocese of Rockford in 1916.

◆ Bishop Doran celebrates Easter Mass for shut-ins on Rockford television station WREX. The TV Mass is in its 40th year.

At the end of this month of August, in keeping with the request of the United States Conference of Catholic Bishops, a special second collection was taken up in the parishes of the Diocese to provide direct financial aid to the Diocese of Biloxi, Mississippi, and the Archdiocese of New Orleans, Louisiana. Both had been devastated the year before by hurricanes. Another $176,977.26 was forwarded to the Conference of Bishops for a total, two-year diocesan contribution to this relief effort of $1,017,296.80.

In September, 2006, the Diocese was honored when Sister Patricia Downey, O.P., Director of the Department of Educational Services, received the *Spirit of Saints Francis and Clare Award* from the University of St. Francis in Joliet, for her many years of dedicated service to God's people in her religious life as a Catholic educator.

Bishop Doran reorganized and reconstituted the St. Elizabeth Catholic Community Center Advisory Committee on October 3, 2006. This Center was a project initiated by the Catholic Woman's League of Rockford, founded by Bishop Muldoon in 1909 and, with his support, the League started this Center in 1911.

The Diocese of Rockford and its official newspaper *The Observer*, hosted the Midwest Regional Meeting of the Catholic Press Association on October 19-20, 2006, at the Diocesan Central Administration offices.

The upcoming 45th anniversary of Bishop Doran's ordination to the Sacred Priesthood would be overshadowed by the news announced on December 13, 2006. Monsignor David D. Kagan and the Office of Communications and Publication had the somber task of announcing that Bishop Doran had been diagnosed with lung cancer and would require surgery. On December 14, 2006 doctors removed approximately one-fourth of Bishop Doran's left lung at the Mayo Clinic in Rochester Minnesota. Bishop Doran returned to the Diocese for a long recuperation process in December of 2006. In the meantime, special prayers and Masses were said in parishes and in schools for the bishop's quick return to good health.

At the Mass of Chrism at the Cathedral of St. Peter, concelebrated by Bishop Doran and the priests of the Diocese on April 5, 2007, Bishop Doran made the official announcement of the Diocese's Centennial Celebration. He announced that the year of observance and celebration would open on Sunday, September 23, 2007, with a diocesan-wide, Solemn Pontifical Mass at the Northern Illinois University Convocation Center in DeKalb. All the parishes and other diocesan institutions would receive a supply of the liturgical and devotional materials to be used during this year.

◆ **Bishop Doran awards diplomas in May 2005 to graduates of the Diocese's only Catholic School of Nursing. The OSF Saint Anthony College of Nursing is operated by the Sisters of the Third Order of St. Francis.**

◆ **Pope Benedict XVI and Bishop Doran.**

The materials were to be used for both private and communal prayer and devotion in celebration of 100 years of faith.

The year of observance and celebration was scheduled to close on Tuesday, September 23, 2008, the actual date of the Diocese's establishment, with a Solemn Pontifical Mass at the Cathedral of St. Peter in Rockford, with Francis Cardinal George, OMI, Archbishop of Chicago, scheduled to preside in the Sanctuary and preach.

Also scheduled in honor of the diocesan centennial would be seven deanery-wide confirmation ceremonies, one in each of the seven deaneries.

TO BE CONTINUED . . .

The history of the Diocese of Rockford, like that of the Universal Church, is not cyclical but linear. It is a history of the living faith of God's people on pilgrimage to eternity. While this written rendition of almost 100 years stops at this point in time, our faith, our hope, and our charity live on and continue to increase under the guidance of our Chief Shepherd, Thomas George Doran, eighth Bishop of the Diocese of Rockford.

PARISHES OF THE DIOCESE OF

Rockford

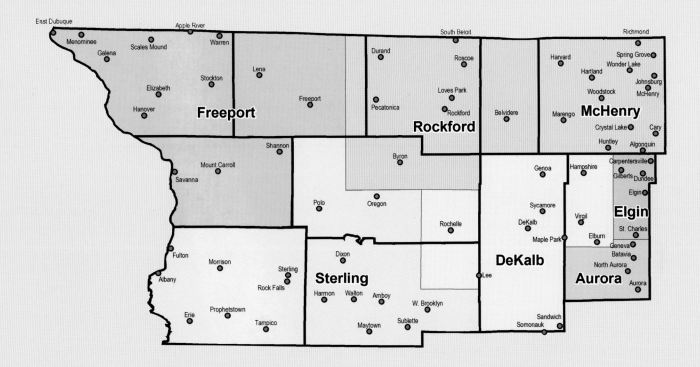

St. Patrick Parish

St. Patrick Parish had its origins in St. Patrick Church, Coffey's Corners, which was originally named St. Columbanus. St. Columbanus was an Irish saint from West Leinster, Ireland, who lived around the year 543.

Prior to 1877 Catholics living in the area attended Mass at Fulton or Mass was said in their homes, or the Dublin school. In 1877 Mr. Edward Coffey purchased land at the northeast corner of what is now Archer and Stern Roads, south of Albany. This land was called Coffey's Corners by the local people.

In 1877 Father John J. Kilkenney (1873-1884) built a church on the land donated by Mr. Coffey, the principal benefactor of the church until his death in 1916. Twenty-six families registered as parishioners of the newly renamed mission of St. Patrick of the Docia. The church was not dedicated until 1883. It could be seen for many miles distance by those on the west, south, and east. It was bounded on the north by timber and hills. A wing was added during the pastorate of Father James L. Moloney (1894-1908).

St. Patrick was popularly known as the Docia mission, since it was located near Meredosia Road. The earliest records from this mission are the baptism of Edward, son of John Kennedy and Anna Matthews, which took place on January 3, 1869. Sponsors: Patrick Kennedy and Bridget Lahey. The ceremony was performed by Father Francis X. Nighe. The first marriage license was granted to James Lyons and Margaret Shelly on November 27, 1869.

Until 1904 Mass was celebrated only once a month at St. Patrick, as priests had to travel on the tortuous roads from Fulton. From 1904 to 1929 parishioners were able to attend Mass at their parish

◆ **St. Patrick Church on Second Avenue and South Church Street.**

◆ **St. Patrick Church, formerly St. Columbanus, Coffey's Corners, circa 1896.**

twice a month. Beginning in 1929 Mass was offered every Sunday and holyday of obligation. The promise of a weekly local Mass was made much easier in 1930 with the arrival of a concrete highway (Route 84) between Fulton and Albany. The priests still had five miles of country dirt road to travel, however.

In 1948, Father John T. Egan (1929-1948) purchased the former Presbyterian church in Albany. After remodeling it was used by the people of St. Patrick Parish as their parish church: A small portion of the church at Coffey's Corners was placed alongside the new church, and the original church was razed. The first pastor of St. Patrick Parish in Albany was Father Myles F. Callahan (1948-1957). Father Callahan resided at Immaculate Conception Parish in Fulton

In 1967, while Father William F. McMahon (1965-1969) was pastor, a new church was built in Albany to replace the frame structure purchased in 1948. Bishop Loras T. Lane dedicated the new

◆ **St. Patrick Church interior.**

St. Patrick Church in Albany on October 20, 1967. Father Edward R. Hughes (1969-1975) was appointed pastor, September 2, 1969 and completed the renovation of the church in late 1973 and early 1974.

As of March 2007 the pastor is Father James R. Keenan. Approximately 50 families make up the parish in Albany.

◆ **St. Patrick Church.**

St. Margaret Mary Parish

◆ **St. Margaret Mary Church.**

St. Margaret Mary Parish in Algonquin comprises one of the oldest settlements along the Fox River in McHenry County. By 1844, a large Bohemian settlement had been founded and thus Catholic services first began in 1845. In 1911, Bishop Peter J. Muldoon appointed Father Peter J. Hogan (1911-1915) to serve Algonquin with twice-a-month services. Mass was celebrated in Gallahan's Hall, north of the Northwestern Railway tracks. St. Margaret Mary Parish, built on land bought along the banks of the Fox River, was organized in 1915 as St. Margaret Parish, a mission of SS. Peter and Paul in Cary. The total of 26 families that made up the parish in 1915 grew steadily over the years and was greatly increased by the building boom during and just after World War II. In June, 1954, Bishop Raymond P. Hillinger appointed Father Raymond N. Eipers (1954-1962) as first resident pastor in Algonquin. One of Father Eipers' first acts as pastor was the purchase of a building for use as a rectory. The small mission church built in 1915

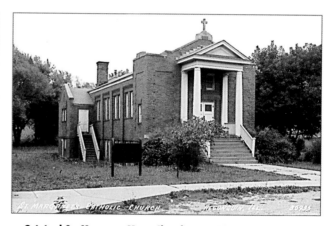

◆ **Original St. Margaret Mary Church, circa 1915.**

had long been inadequate, so in 1955 a ten acre plot was purchased for a future parish center. The land, located on Illinois 62, a block east of the Fox River, was to be the site of a combination school and church building, plus a house that was renovated for use as a convent. With the Dominican Sisters of Springfield in charge, the school opened in September, 1955, with 130 pupils in its first four grades.

◆ **St. Margaret Mary School 3rd and 4th grade class, 1956.**

◆ **Farm on Illinois 62, the site of the current church.**

The original mission church was converted into four additional classrooms, and was used by the parish during the 1960's. The old church was abandoned and the congregation moved into the new basement church, housed in the school building, on March 9, 1958. The construction of a new rectory was completed the same year. During the pastorate of Father P. William McDonnell (1979-1991), a new church was built. The new church, which seats 750 people was dedicated on Aug. 28, 1983 by Bishop Arthur J. O'Neill. At that time the parish served about 2400 families.

◆ **Baptismal Font**

An event that stands out in the parish's history happened on June 14, 1985 when TWA passengers were taken hostage by terrorists on Flight 847 from Athens to Rome. One of the passengers was the pastor of St. Margaret Mary Parish, Father P. William McDonnell, who was leading a Holy Land pilgrimage which included other parishioners. Father McDonnell was released on June 16 and returned to celebrate Mass on Sunday, June 23 for his grateful parishioners.

Under the pastorate of Father Michael J. Tierney, the current pastor, the parish expanded its ministries in 2000 to serve the large Polish population of the area when it began offering Mass in Polish each Sunday. In 2001 ten acres next door to the church, along with the former Eastview School at 451 E. Algonquin Road, were purchased from School District 300. A donor provided the funds to renovate and upgrade the school, which began housing St. Margaret Mary's K-8 students in the fall of 2004..

As of March 2007 the pastor is Father Michael J. Tierney. Approximately 3400 families are currently registered at St. Margaret Mary Parish.

◆ **Sister with "angels" at 1957 event.**

St. Patrick Parish

◆ **Choir in 1880.**

The history of the Amboy parish dates back to 1853, when it was a mission of St. Patrick Parish in LaSalle. Father Mark Anthony, C.M., offered the first Mass in 1853 in Michael Egan's home which was a log cabin on a farm at the east end of Amboy. Before that it was a common sight on Sunday morning to see Catholic families, some in buggies, some on foot, going to Maytown to the little log church at Sandy Hill. The little log church had been built in 1847 and dedicated to St. Michael.

In 1856, Father F. Bray (1856-1857) became the first resident pastor of Amboy. He purchased lots at the corner of South Mason Avenue and Center Street. It was on this site that the first Catholic Church was built, but unfortunately the nearly completed structure burned down before it was ever used. Until the church was rebuilt, Mass was offered in the Exchange Block building.

Under the direction of Father Joseph Vahey (1858-1859), plans were formulated for the rebuilding of St. Patrick Church. It was completed in the spring of 1859. The sacrament of confirmation was administered for the first time at St. Patrick in June of 1863 by Bishop John Duggan of Chicago.

Under the pastorate of Father M. J. Clarke (1859-1868), property was purchased for St. Patrick Cemetery. In 1869, Father Clarke

◆ **St. Patrick's parishioners, circa 1859.**

was succeeded by Father W. D. Murphy (1869-1873) who purchased the first rectory, which was on the site of the present one. In 1871, the church was enlarged to meet the needs of the growing congregation.

While Father Francis A. Keenan (1873-1885) was pastor, he began plans to build a new larger brick church. As was the first church, so this new building was threatened by disaster before its completion. On June 27, 1884, a violent wind storm caused the north wall to spread. The completion of the church went ahead under the direction of Father John A. Coughlin (1885-1890). Archbishop Patrick A. Feehan of Chicago dedicated the church on June 27, 1886. Father Joseph S. Gallagher (1895-1912) built the present parish hall in 1900. In 1910 Father Thomas J. Cullen (1910-1929) was appointed administrator of the parish and one of his first projects was the decoration of the church. In 1914, Father Cullen sold the old rectory at Amboy and had it moved and in its place erected the present brick rectory. In 1920 the parish bought two lots across the street from the church and on these lots built the first parochial school in Amboy.

◆ **Church dedication June 27, 1886.**

In July of 1929 Father Robert C. Troy was appointed pastor, a position he held until his death in February 1966. Under Father Troy's leadership during the depression years, a new pipe organ was installed, and the interior of the church was extensively remodeled, including the installation of a complete set of stained glass windows. Later, Father Troy had the church redecorated again, this time adding a new altar, in keeping with the decrees of the 2nd Vatican Council. In 1961, a new entrance was built on the front of the church.

While Father Joseph J. Reikas (1966-1967) was pastor in 1966 some remodeling was done on the parish rectory. Father Reikas was succeeded by Father John E. Reuland (1967-1970) in October of 1967. Father Reuland was instrumental in creatively restructuring the parochial school system in Amboy during his short time as its pastor. In 1968, grades 1 through 6 were accepted at St. Anne School, the parish school, while grades 7 and 8 attended the public school. Grades 5 and 6 also shared classes with the public school.

Father Robert P. Donavan (1970-1977) took up the duties of pastor in Amboy in February of 1970 and it was necessary for him to announce that the school would close at the end of that school term. In the summer the convent was torn down and the sisters who remained to continue teaching the religious education classes resided in a nearby apartment. In 1971 the sisters left and St. Anne School building was sold in February, 1973.

In 1986, during the pastorate of Father Anthony J. Becker (1984-1992), the school building was repurchased. After remodeling, eight religious education classrooms on the first two floors and apartments on the third floor were created.

Improvements, including a new lift for the church, were made in 2000. A 15-foot cross from the estate of the parents of Father Francis P. Daleiden (1993-2001), the pastor at the time, was erected at the parish cemetery the same year.

In preparation for the 150th anniversary of the parish founding, painting, restoration and structural repairs were begun in 2005 under the direction of the pastor, Father Aaron R. Brodeski (2003-2006). These repairs were completed in 2006.

As of March 2007 Father Carl E. Beekman is the parochial administrator. Approximately 370 families are currently registered at St. Patrick Church.

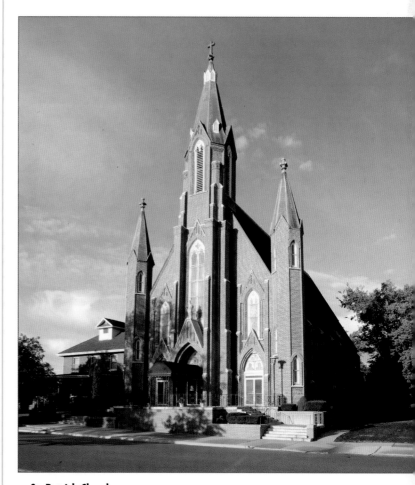

◆ **St. Patrick Church.**

◆ **St. Patrick Church interior.**

ST. JOSEPH PARISH

Located near the Wisconsin border in the center of Jo Daviess County is the parish of St. Joseph in Apple River. Early Catholics in the area were attended somewhat irregularly from the nearby town of Galena and by missionaries from Freeport. One of these missionaries, Father Peter Corcoran, supervised the completion of a church in Apple River in the year 1863. Regular services were held by missionaries at St. Joseph's until 1868, when the first resident pastor, Father C. Schilling, was appointed.

◆ **St. Joseph Church, circa 1863.**

Father Schilling's term of just over a year was followed in 1869 by that of Father Patrick McElhearne (1869-1870). In 1870, Father Joseph Kindekens (1870-1878) began an eight-year pastorate that was to see the establishment of a parish cemetery and the enlargement of the church for the growing congregation. The newly renovated church was blessed and placed under the protection of St. Joseph on November 21, 1871.

Father John E. Shannahan, appointed in 1885, was pastor at Apple River for sixteen years. Father Joseph S. Gallagher, pastor from 1901 to 1902, purchased a house next to the church and converted it into a permanent rectory.

The next pastor, Father Thomas F. Leydon (1902-1907), had a new foundation constructed next to the rectory and had the church building moved. The church was also remodeled as was the rectory. The original church remained in use until the early 1920's; the rectory until 1916. Father William M. McGuire (1914-1918) had begun his pastorate in 1914 and completed the rectory work two years later. He was absent for a time while he served as an Army Chaplain, 1918-1919, but the present church had been started before that military service. The new brick church was completed and dedicated by Bishop Peter J. Muldoon on July 1, 1923.

Father McGuire was succeeded in June, 1926 by Father John T. Egan (1926-1929) who made extensive improvements to the parish hall. During the pastorate of Father Russell J. Guccione (1932-1940) the church was repaired and redecorated. Father Edward J. Connolly, who had been pastor from 1929 to 1933, returned as pastor in 1950. This was due to the death of Father Flavian C. Voet, pastor from 1940 to 1950. During Father Connolly's second pastorate (1950-1952), the interior and exterior of the Church were decorated and the cemetery was improved. In the spring of 1953, while Father Norbert M. Richter (1952-1957) was pastor, a new organ was installed.

During the pastorate of Father Daniel D. Tranel (1973-1983) the men of the parish donated their

◆ **Laying the cornerstone of the current church, 1922.**

time to remove the old church roof and replace it with a new roof. While Father Everett J. Hiller was pastor (1985-2000) the church was made handicap accessible, was air-conditioned, and new lighting was installed. Also the rectory was sold since priests serving St. Joseph Parish generally reside in Warren. During the pastorate of Father Miroslaw A. Reikowski (2000-2002), the Vondra Family *Glory of God Memorial Garden* was established next to the church.

As of March 2007 Father Brian D. Grady is the parochial administrator. Approximately 75 families are currently registered at St. Joseph Parish.

◆ **St. Joseph Church interior.**

◆ **St. Joseph Church.**

◆ Church service, circa 1940.

◆ Father Albert J. Neidert with altar boys, circa 1920.

In the northeast section of Aurora known as the "Big Woods," over one hundred Catholic farming families, with the approval of Bishop Thomas Foley of Chicago, established a parish on March 25, 1875, the feast of the Annunciation of the Blessed Virgin Mary.

The material needed was, for the most part, furnished by the farmers, and with their own hands they erected a church, school, and pastor's residence. This original school was later replaced by a larger structure, enrolling 100-110 pupils until 1920. The first three teachers were laymen. In 1886, two Sisters from St. Francis Convent, Milwaukee, Wisconsin, were engaged to teach in the school. They were succeeded in 1906 by the Sisters of St. Francis of Assisi, also of Milwaukee and then, in 1908, the Sisters of St. Francis of Mary Immaculate, of Joliet.

Annunciation's first priests were Franciscan Fathers from St. Peter's Church in Chicago. Then, in 1876, Bishop Foley appointed Father William Schamoni as the parish's first resident pastor. Three months later, Father John B. Kanzleiter (1876-1883) became pastor. Father Kanzleiter supervised the moving of the school, originally built one mile from the church, to the property adjoining the church.

In July of 1883, replacing Father Kanzleiter, Father Henry Bangen (1883-1921) began his thirty-eight years as Annunciation's pastor. During those years, the church's property was tripled, and the two grottos, Lourdes (1910) and Calvary (1912) were constructed. In duplicating the design of the original grotto in Lourdes, France, the stone for the shrine was obtained from parish farmers clearing their land of "hardheads." The latter shrine was also formed by using natural materials native to the parish. Annual pilgrimages were made to the grottos shortly after World War I began. Chicagoans regularly made all-day spiritual outings to Annunciation on Sundays.

In marking the parish's fiftieth jubilee in 1925, major renovations were undertaken in the parish under Father Albert J. Neidert's (1921-1933) direction. Father Neidert's pastorship also saw the

◆ School children's choir.

original rectory destroyed by fire in 1926, shortly after the building of the new school. The present rectory rests on the original rectory foundation.

In 1933, the Benedictine Order took over Fox Valley High School, transforming it into Marmion Military Academy. At this time, the Benedictines were also given charge of Annunciation Parish. In July of that year, Father Lambert Enslinger, O.S.B. (1933-1934), became the parish's first Benedictine pastor.

Under the pastorate of Father Lawrence Riebenthaler, O.S.B. (1942-1963), the church was elaborately redecorated in 1948. Father Lawrence also saw the completion of the school in 1963. Also in 1963, Father Maurice Patrick, O.S.B. (1963-1972), became Annunciation's eighth pastor, under whom a large debt was liquidated ahead of schedule, once again affirming the parish's vow to financial stability.

In July of 1972, Father Sebastian Crow, O.S.B. (1972-1986), was appointed pastor. Under Father Sebastian, the church was completely renovated and air-conditioned in time for celebrating the parish's 100th anniversary in 1975.

As of March 2007 the pastor is Father Mario Pedi, O.S.B. Approximately 800 families are currently registered at Annunciation Parish.

♦ **Annunciation interior, before 1945.**

♦ **Annunciation of the Blessed Virgin Mary Church.**

HOLY ANGELS PARISH

Holy Angels Parish was formed May 1, 1892, from territory originally part of St. Mary's Parish. Father W. J. McNamee (1892-1898) of Chicago was appointed its first pastor. Aurora, at the time, was part of the Chicago Archdiocese.

The first Mass was celebrated by Father McNamee on May 2, 1892 in temporary quarters on the third floor of a theater, Sweet's Academy, on River Street. A few weeks later the Advent Church on Locust Street was purchased. The following year, a house was acquired to serve as the rectory. Also acquired was additional property for expansion. The church was solemnly blessed in October, 1892, by Archbishop Patrick A. Feehan of Chicago.

The Diocese of Rockford was established in 1908 and Aurora was included in its boundaries. During the pastorate of Father James A. Quinn (1909-1927), ground was broken for a combination church and school at Locust Street and Galena Boulevard in July of 1910. The structure, now gone, was dedicated by Bishop Peter J. Muldoon on January 26, 1911. The cost of this structure was a then awesome $40,000! A building on Galena Boulevard was purchased to function as a convent for the Dominican Sisters of Springfield, Illinois, who had come to the Rockford Diocese and to Holy Angels in 1911 to staff the parish school.

An indication of the vitality of the maturing parish was its offspring. Just as St. Mary's was the parent to Holy Angels, so too, Holy Angels was the mother-church to St. Peter's, which began life as a mission church in 1925, and became independent in 1929.

In the early 1950's, new needs confronted the Holy Angels Parish community which necessitated a bold move—a new parish plant in a new location within the existing parish boundaries. A tract of land in the geographical center of the parish and in the heart of the expanding residential district was available and was purchased for the site of the relocated Holy Angels parish plant. Under the pastorate of Monsignor Frederick F. Connor (1932-1966), construction was begun on the new eight hundred seat church.

The new church on Lancaster Avenue at Hardin Street was dedicated February 3, 1952, by Bishop John J. Boylan. The rectory was blessed at the same time. The new school was opened in 1960, and the convent was built the following year. The parish complex was completed in 1970 with the opening of the Religious Education Center. The creation of the Center reflected an important development in the total parish education program.

◆ **Father D. O'Brien standing outside the first Holy Angels Church, circa 1900.**

Monsignor Connor died in 1966 after a pastorate of thirty-four years. Father Edward J. McIsaac (1966-1968) was then appointed pastor. He died suddenly on July 19, 1968. While attending Father McIsaac's

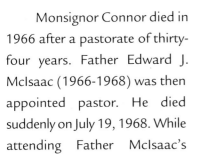

◆ **"Angel" window leading into the adoration chapel, designed by Lynn Simantz.**

funeral on Monday, July 22nd, the priests of the Diocese were shocked to learn of the death of Bishop Loras T. Lane earlier that morning.

Father Raymond N. Eipers (1969-1971) was appointed pastor in January of 1969. In 1970, he had the church renovated to conform to new liturgical directives for parish worship.

In celebration of the 100th anniversary of the parish, the church was again renovated during the pastorate of Father Gerald P. Kobbeman (1987-2000). The entire project grew out of a parish survey taken when it was time to do an extensive cleaning of the church. The old confessional became the new shrine to the holy family. A baptistry with flowing water was added to the interior of the church. Seating was rearranged to accommodate a redesigned altar space. New carpeting and tile, refinished pews, and new altar furniture completed the renovation project. Bishop Arthur J. O'Neill rededicated the church on May 2, 1992.

In 2003, while Father Martin G. Heinz was pastor, the church was redesigned to be more traditional in appearance. Along with repainting, the following new items were installed: altar, pews, carpeting, lighting, and sanctuary. The choir loft was extended and new stained glass windows were added. Bishop Thomas G. Doran rededicated the church on July 20, 2003.

For more than three decades, the Holy Angels Parish Food Pantry has extended a helping hand for needy families in the area. Seventy volunteers help provide food to about 2100 families twice a month. A truck purchased with donations is used three or four times a day, six days a week, to pick up food donated from various sources.

As of March 2007 the pastor is Father Martin G. Heinz. Approximately 2500 families are currently registered at Holy Angels Parish.

◆ **Holy Angels Church interior and exterior**

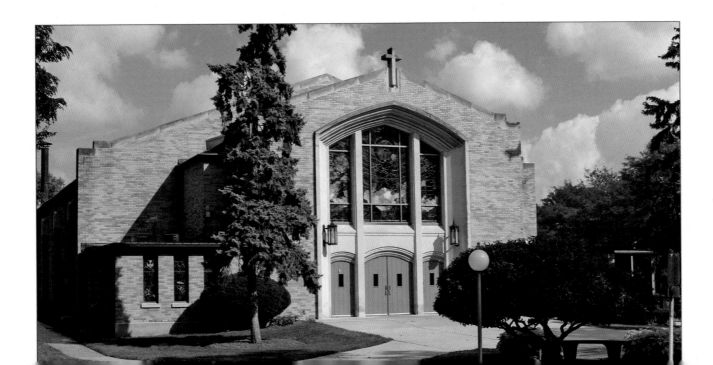

OUR LADY OF GOOD COUNSEL PARISH

In 1908, Peter Hilgen and Conrad Reuland, sought permission from Father Charles Schnueckel, pastor of St. Nicholas, to start a new parish in the southeastern section of Aurora. Before he could give permission, Father Schnueckel died suddenly on October 14, 1908, shortly after Aurora had become part of the newly created Diocese of Rockford, with Auxiliary Bishop Peter J. Muldoon of Chicago as its first bishop.

On the 8th of February, 1909, Peter Hilgen and Conrad Reuland then presented to Bishop Muldoon a petition with sixty-nine signatures, asking him to establish a parish in the southeast end of Aurora. Bishop Muldoon granted their request and on April 26, 1909, the feast of Our Lady of Good Counsel, he appointed Father Leon M. Linden (1909-1943) the first pastor.

Plans for a combination school, convent, hall and rectory, to be built on the corner of Talma Street and Seventh Avenue, were approved by Bishop Muldoon on the 4th of July, 1909. The Bishop laid the cornerstone on September 26, 1909 and dedicated the church on Sunday, May 1, 1910.

While the church was being built, services were held in the hall of St. Mary School.

The parish school, occupying rooms on the second floor of the combination structure, opened on September 10, 1910 with the Dominican Sisters from Adrian, Michigan staffing the school.

In 1911, a rectory was built north of the church. Father Linden lived there until July 19, 1924, when he moved into the new rectory at 620 South Fifth Street.

The school year of 1925-1926 brought with it a change in the teaching staff of Our Lady of Good Counsel School. The Dominican Sisters withdrew from the school and were replaced by the School Sisters of St. Francis from Milwaukee.

The silver jubilee of the parish was celebrated with a Solemn Mass offered by Bishop Edward F. Hoban on April 26, 1934.

The first parish credit union in Aurora was opened at Our Lady of Good Counsel on June 19, 1935, at the invitation of Father Linden. Father Linden died on July 1, 1943, and Bishop John J. Boylan appointed Father Herman A. Meilinger (1943-1960) to be Good Counsel's second pastor.

By the fall of 1951, additions to the school and convent were completed. On Sunday, May 11, 1952, Father Meilinger broke ground for the new church. On Sunday, September 7, 1952, Bishop Boylan laid the cornerstone. The new church was dedicated on Tuesday, October 12, 1954.

The parish celebrated its Golden Jubilee on April 26, 1959 with Bishop Loras T. Lane celebrating

◆ **Father Leon Linden, circa 1909, with his first automobile.**

◆ **The church and rectory on Talma Street, circa 1917.**

◆ **Father Leon Linden, OLGC's first Pastor, June 23, 1918.**

◆ **The parish Sodality, circa 1909, meeting in the church hall.**

the Jubilee Mass. By this time the parish had grown to 998 families and the school enrollment was 727 pupils.

In 1961, Father Sylvester J. Eye (1960-1973) proposed an addition of twelve classrooms, gymnasium, cafeteria, and other facilities to the parish school. Father Eye blessed the cornerstone of the new addition on Sunday, October 7, 1962. Bishop Lane blessed the new school on Sunday, June 9, 1963.

In an effort to preserve parish history the old church bell, which was solemnly blessed on January 11, 1910, was moved in September 1980 from the old church to the bell tower of the new church.

The parish celebrated its diamond jubilee on April 26, 1984, with Bishop Arthur J. O'Neill as principle celebrant. Concelebrating with Bishop O'Neill were former pastors and priests ordained from the parish. Another special parish event took place on October 17, 2004, when former pastors, religious sisters and parishioners gathered for a special Mass marking the 50th anniversary of the church's dedication.

As of March 2007 Father David R. Engbarth is the parochial administrator. Approximately 800 families are currently registered at Our Lady of Good Counsel Parish.

◆ **Our Lady of Good Counsel Church.**

Sacred Heart Parish

The first Catholic church in the city of Aurora was dedicated to the Sacred Heart of Jesus. In the winter of 1848, Mr. I. E. Labrie, a very popular and influential citizen, went to the parish priest of Bourbonnais to explain the necessity of a Catholic mission in Aurora. The following February Father Louis A. Courjeault came to Aurora where he celebrated Mass in an old school house and led a three-day mission. This convinced Father Courjeault that Aurora was in great need of a Catholic place of worship and such reports were sent to Bishop James O. Van de Velde, the second bishop of Chicago.

In February 1851, Bishop Van de Velde bought a tract of land, for church purposes, and soon a chapel was constructed on Broadway, north of Claim Street.

◆ **Father G. Kerston.**

In the meantime Father Courjeault was succeeded in Bourbonnais by Father F. Lebel, who for one year administered Aurora as a mission, once every month, and later became the first resident pastor.

After one year of existence the congregation was found to have steadily increased by the arrival of a large number of Irish and German immigrants. In December 1852, the church was greatly damaged by a windstorm. The building was sold and divided into two private residences.

A second Sacred Heart Church was built on the West side, at the corner of Pine and Spruce streets. It burned down on November 8, 1869.

Meanwhile the French members of the first Sacred Heart Church had separated from their mother church and were building a new church at the corner of Columbia and Union streets. The first Mass was celebrated by Father Clark on December 8, 1869, just a month after fire destroyed the original Sacred Heart Church. Since there was now no church of that name, the French chose it for their newly constructed church.

Services were not held regularly until February 17, 1871, when Father G. Kertson was placed in charge. A public school located nearby made any future expansion impractical, so a new location was sought. A site at the corner of State and Fulton Streets was purchased, and a rectory built there in 1871.

In 1875, under the direction of Father A. Martel (1874-1879), who had become the first resident pastor, the church was moved to the corner of State and Fulton streets. Father Martel opened the first parish school in the basement of the church.

◆ **Sacred Heart Church, circa 1900.**

◆ **Former Sacred Heart School.**

He was succeeded in 1879 by Father P. F. X. Chouinard, C.S.V. (1879-1884) who obtained a bell for the church tower. He also began construction on a parish school before he was succeeded in 1884, by Father Jacques Cote (1884-1896). Father Cote completed the school and built galleries in the church. He secured services of the Sisters of the Congregation of Notre Dame to teach in the school.

Father E. J. P. Therien (1896-1900) built the original brick church and made many necessary improvements in the rectory. The altars and stained glass windows were added by Father J. C. LeSage (1900-1905). He bought the school property from the Sisters of Notre Dame and built a parish hall there. In 1904, the Sisters of St. Joseph took charge of the school. Failing health forced Father LeSage to resign in 1905.

In 1913, while he was the pastor, Father J. C. Simard (1905-1947) expanded the school and made repairs to the rectory. The cemetery was improved, and in 1917, a heating plant was installed for the church, school and hall.

The congregation of Sacred Heart Parish was severely affected by the depression of 1929. Many parishioners remember Father Simard sharing his own inadequate sustenance with them.

Father J. Urban Halbmaier (1948-1959) was given the rather touchy assignment, in April, 1946, of going to Aurora ostensibly as Father Simard's assistant, but with the understanding from Bishop John J. Boylan that he was to strengthen the floundering parish, since Father Simard had been incapacitated for nearly ten years.

A quonset hut was erected for use as a hall where the parishioners could hold functions and regain some measure of financial stability. Father Simard was to have dedicated the hall but before the dedication he died on August 11, 1947.

Father Halbmaier administered the affairs of the parish and was appointed pastor on October 28, 1948. In January, 1948, the rectory was turned over as a convent to the sisters, who previously had lived in the rear of the school. The church was repaired and the electrical fixtures rewired. The convent was renovated and in 1950, a new rectory was built. Early in 1950, the school was begun; it was completed in October of 1950 and dedicated that same month by Bishop Boylan.

In the late 1970's, the parish experienced a change in population as the neighborhood began to change. At that time about one third of the new parishioners were Hispanic. The demographic change accelerated during the next twenty years and by the late 1990's the parish was about 95% Hispanic.

On December 1, 1998, 130 years after the original Sacred Heart Church burned to the ground, Sacred Heart Parish once again lost its church to a fire. Thankfully, there was no loss of human life and no one was hurt or seriously injured. The burned-out shell of the church building could not be saved for reconstruction. In 2005, Sacred Heart Parish began a campaign to rebuild from the 1998 fire. The mostly Hispanic parish has called the rebuilding committee esperanza- the Spanish word for "hope."

As of March 2007 Father J. Robert Camacho is the pastor. Approximately 500 families are currently registered at Sacred Heart Parish.

◆ **Sacred Heart after December 1, 1998 fire.**

◆ **Sacred Heart Church.**

St. George Byzantine Catholic Parish

On Sunday, April 17, 1955, Monsignor Louis J. Franey, Chancellor of the Rockford Diocese, represented Bishop Hillinger at the reconciliation of the Romanian parish of St. George with the Holy See. The parish, an off-shoot of the parish of St. Michael, had its beginning in the disagreements of 1932. It was incorporated in 1934, with Father John Vuc as its pastor, but had not previously been recognized by Rome.

On November 10, 1935, the cornerstone for a new church was laid. Only the basement was built at that time and services were held there until enough funds were gathered to enable the building of a superstructure and thus complete the plans for a new church. This dream was not realized until July 1967.

Reconciliation had been initiated some years previously and was finally made possible by the 1955 decisions of the Supreme Sacred Congregation of the Holy Office, and of the Sacred Oriental Congregation.

The sadness of the past was transmuted into joy on this Feast of the Resurrection according to the Eastern Rite, when Father Vuc and Augustine Ratz, representing the people of the parish, repeated the Profession of Faith in the presence of Monsignor Franey and Monsignor John Kruk, representing the Sacred Oriental Congregation for the Romanian Faithful. A Mass of Thanksgiving followed, with Father Vuc as celebrant.

Father Vuc remained as pastor until October 21, 1964 when he resigned due to his ill health. Negotiations for a Romanian Catholic priest of the Byzantine Rite began immediately and Father Louis Puscas was appointed pastor of St. George, effective February 1, 1965 by Bishop Loras T. Lane, Bishop of Rockford.

In the spring of 1966, Bishop Lane approved architectural plans for a superstructure to be built over the existing basement structure. Construction began in the fall of 1966. The first Divine Liturgy to be celebrated in the new church was on July 27,

◆ **St. George Byzantine Catholic Church, Aurora**

1967. Bishop Lane dedicated the new church of St. George on Sunday, May 26, 1968.

On December 4, 1982 Pope John Paul II established the Apostolic Exarchate for the Romanian Byzantine Rite, and Father Puscas was appointed Exarch. On June 26, 1983 Father Puscas was ordained as Bishop. On March 26, 1987 the Apostolic Exarchate for the Romanian Byzantine Rite was elevated to the Rank of an Eparchy (Diocese) and Bishop Puscas was promoted as its first Eparch. The Jurisdiction of the Romanian Catholic Diocese of Canton extends territorially to all of the United States.

St. Joseph Parish

Some German families living in northeast Aurora did not benefit much from the construction of the new church of the Annunciation at Big Woods in the 1870s. They still had to walk a considerable distance to St. Nicholas Church and had to cross a number of railroad tracks. A committee approached Father Charles Schnueckel, Pastor of St. Nicholas, to talk the matter over and as a result, a meeting was held on the evening of July 17, 1898. Father Schnueckel, his assistant Father John Schmitt, and two hundred men were present for this meeting. Father Schnueckel discussed the advantages and disadvantages of establishing a new parish, and then put the question to those assembled, asking whether or not they were ready to assume such obligations. It was decided unanimously to separate from the mother parish of St. Nicholas.

Father Schnueckel put Father John F. Schmitt in charge of the preliminary work. During the next month Father Schmitt and his committee secured the permission of Archbishop Patrick A. Feehan and purchased property north of Mountain Street between High and Root Streets. On September 28, 1898, ground was broken for a combination church and school. Archbishop Feehan formally appointed Father Schmitt (1899-1940) pastor of St. Joseph

◆ **Monsignor John F. Schmitt.**

Parish on February 1, 1899. The cornerstone was laid by the Chancellor of the Chicago Archdiocese, Father F. J. Barry, on August 30, and on October 1, 1899, Father Schnueckel offered the first Mass in the new church. The following November the school opened, staffed by the School Sisters of St. Francis. Bishop Peter J. Muldoon, then Auxiliary Bishop of Chicago, dedicated the church and school on September 28, 1902.

A convent was built in 1902; in 1903, land was purchased for a cemetery. A rectory was built in 1908. A $45,000 addition was built on to the church and school in 1925; it contained four classrooms, a kitchen and dining room. Three years later the sisters' convent was enlarged. On July 9, 1930, Father Schmitt was raised to the rank of domestic prelate with the title of Right Reverend Monsignor. Ten years later, on April 17, 1940, Monsignor Schmitt died, after forty years of service to the people of St. Joseph Parish.

Father Joseph J. Weitekamp (1940-1963) was appointed to succeed Monsignor Schmitt on May 22, 1940. The entire parish plant was renovated and redecorated. A Crucifixion group was erected in the cemetery in 1941; an additional four and one-half acres were procured there in 1947. On Sunday, November 6, 1949, the parish, now grown to more than five-hundred families, celebrated its first fifty years. Bishop John J. Boylan presided at the Mass.

In 1954, plans for a contemporary-style new church were drawn up. On the feast of the Assumption ground was broken; Bishop Raymond P. Hillinger preached on the occasion and turned the first shovel of earth. Father Weitekamp laid the cornerstone on October 21, 1955, and the first Mass in the new church was celebrated by the pastor, with his two brothers as deacon and subdeacon on the Feast of St. Joseph, March 19, 1956. Bishop Lane

◆ **St. Joseph Church, circa 1909.**

◆ **Father William P. Staff.**

consecrated the main altar on April 11, 1957 and returned to dedicate the church on May 1, 1957, the Feast of St. Joseph the Worker.

On October 17, 1961, plans were drawn up for building a new school. Due to a fire on January 18, 1962, the rectory was destroyed and Father William P. Staff, the young assistant, died in the fire. It was then necessary to consider building a new rectory in addition to the building of a new school. Work was begun on both buildings on June 8, 1962 and the work was half completed on both buildings when Father Weitekamp died on May 19, 1963. Father Paul A. Tuchlinsky (1963-1976) was appointed pastor on June 5, 1963 and by August 15, 1963 both the rectory and school were completed and ready for occupancy.

In 1974, St. Joseph Parish celebrated its Diamond Jubilee with Bishop Arthur J. O'Neill concelebrating the Jubilee Mass on April 7, 1974.

Groundbreaking ceremonies for a new activity center were held in 1994. In 1995, the original church built in 1899 was razed to make room for the new center. On December 1, 1995, the pastor, Father Eric R. Barr (1991-1997), welcomed Bishop Thomas G. Doran and Bishop Arthur J. O'Neill for the dedication of the new St. Joseph Activity Center.

An original artifact from St. Joseph's 1899 church was rededicated on October 12, 2003. The bell that once hung in the old church's bell tower was placed outside the existing church. An inscription on the bell reads, "St. Joseph Parish – a credit to the poor."

As of March 2007 Father Jerome L. Leake is the pastor. Approximately 800 families are currently registered at St. Joseph Parish.

◆ **Cornerstone and bell from original church built in 1899.**

◆ **St. Joseph Church.**

St. Mary Parish

In the winter of 1848, Mr. I. E. Labrie, an influential citizen, went to Bourbonnais to explain to the parish priest there the needs of the 700 Aurora Catholics. After occasional visits by Father Louis A. Courjeault, Bishop James O. Van de Velde, the second bishop of Chicago, was persuaded, in September 1850, to come to Aurora to administer Confirmation.

Returning in February 1851, Bishop Van de Velde bought nineteen and a half acres for a church which was soon built and dedicated to the Sacred Heart. Father Courjeault was succeeded in Bourbonnais by Father F. Lebel, who said Mass in Aurora once a month. In a short time, he became the first resident pastor at Aurora.

The arrival of many Irish and German immigrants increased the size of the congregation, which had been predominately French Canadian. A severe windstorm,

◆ **Father Thomas F. Leydon at pulpit, 1894.**

on December 24, 1852, did considerable damage to the church. The property was sold to the railroad and a new site was secured at the corner of Pine and Spruce Streets. Here the second Sacred Heart Church, was built by the pastor, Father Zuker.

During the pastorate of Father Walter Powers, the Germans decided to provide themselves with a church at which they could hear their own language; the French shortly after followed suit.

On the morning of November 8, 1869, a fire completely destroyed the second Sacred Heart Church. Father T. B. Murphy (1869-1877) and his congregation set about building a new church, this time in East Aurora, where most of the English-speaking Catholics lived. By now, the Germans already had their own parish (St. Nicholas) and the French Canadian church was only a month away from completion. The new church was dedicated July 7, 1872, having been paid for, in large part, by the insurance money from the fire. With the change in location came a change in name; the church in East Aurora was named St. Mary.

Father P. A. McLaughlin (1894-1907) built the first parochial school in 1902, and obtained services of the Sisters of Providence from St.-Mary-of-the-Woods, Indiana.

◆ **St. Mary Church.**

During Father John P. McGuire's years as pastor (1913-1929), many improvements were made in the parish buildings, without placing a high indebtedness upon the parishioners. During Father Daniel A. Feeley's tenure (1929-1933), plans were drawn up for extensive repairs to the church.

Father Feeley retired in 1933, and was succeeded by Father Charles R. Kelly (1933-1965). Father Kelly began carrying out the plans made by his predecessors by repairing the towers on the church. In 1937 work was begun on renovating the church and rectory. This work was completed in 1938 at a cost of $140,000. Bishop Hoban consecrated the new altars on October 1, 1938 and dedicated the church the following day, October 2, 1938. A Wick pipe organ was installed on November 29, 1953.

In the summer of 1957, another remodeling project was begun under the pastorate of Father Kelly, and the heating plants were changed to allow for air conditioning in the church.

On October 8, 1972, St. Mary Parish celebrated its 100th anniversary and at the same time Father Edward J. Connolly (1964-1971), who retired as pastor of St. Mary Parish in September, 1971, celebrated his 50th anniversary in the priesthood.

The church was repainted and redecorated in 1972, in keeping with the last renovation done in 1938 under the pastorate of Father Kelly. The sanctuary was carpeted throughout and matching carpet covered the aisles. Appropriate new furniture was placed in the sanctuary as was the Baptismal font. The pulpit was moved to the side of the main altar with the center gates from the altar rail being incorporated into its base. The original altar, installed in 1938, was moved forward to comply with the new liturgy initiated by the Second Vatican Council, and the sanctuary floor was raised two steps. The tabernacle, which rested on the main altar, was placed on a new marble repository.

In 1975, under the pastorate of Father Richard W. Paddock (1971-1987), St. Mary School was renovated as a Parish Center and Area Center for Religious Education. In October of 1988, under the

◆ **School students outside the parish school, 1902.**

pastorate of Father Albert F. Rennell (1987-1994), the statue of Mary was moved in front of the parish center as a new shrine to the Blessed Mother.

As of March 2007 Father Timothy R. Piasecki is pastor. Approximately 400 families are currently registered at St. Mary Parish.

◆ **Ambo.**

St. Michael Byzantine Catholic Parish

The Romanian people in Aurora originally came to the "New World" seeking better living conditions and opportunity. Their first thought was the building of a church where they could gather to ask the grace and blessing of God upon their endeavors. For this purpose a missionary priest, Father Epaminonda Lucaciu called them together on July 21, 1907 in the auditorium of St. Nicholas School. After the celebration of the first Mass in the Romanian language, the Romanians of Aurora, determined to establish the parish of St. Michael. Immediately a public collection was begun and through many sacrifices, in a short time, they arranged a chapel where they might offer Mass.

The number of faithful increased rapidly with groups arriving from the mother country. The construction of the first Romanian church began in 1908. On July 4, 1909, the church was dedicated by Bishop Peter J. Muldoon. Seeing his work practically completed, Father Lucaciu left for Trenton, New Jersey after having introduced Father John Pop as the new pastor. During his pastorate the "Romanian Home" was erected in 1916, and on July 18, 1917, the dedication of the new church took place by Bishop Muldoon. The old church was transformed into a school. Only three years after having been appointed pastor, Father Pop died on October 23, 1919.

After a brief interval, Father Aurel Hategan arrived to serve as pastor until September 12, 1920 when Father Leon Manu was appointed. Father Manu built a new garage and purchased a home for the sisters. The rectory was renovated, the entire church redecorated and additional school space was provided under Father Manu's administration.

Father Manu was succeeded by Father John Vuc who administered the parish from May 30, 1930 to November 12, 1932. This was the time of a lamentable split in the parish, with Father Vuc starting St. George Parish. This parish was not recognized by the Holy See until 1955, when there was a reconciliation.

Lacking a Romanian priest to send to St. Michael, Bishop Hoban sent Father Joseph A. Rzeszotko to administer the parish until 1935. On June 18, 1935, Father Basil Marchis assumed administration of the parish. During Father Marchis' 41 year pastorate, St. Michael Parish, after the initial difficulties through which it passed, progressed both spiritually and materially.

Beginning with the choir balcony, steeple and eaves of the church, everything was repaired or replaced from beginning in 1936. That year a new roof was put on the school and the exterior and interior painted by the parishioners. The parishioners repaired the sisters' home and made needed repairs to the parish home. In addition the cemetery grounds were enlarged and a bridge was built over a low area.

In 1941, Father Marchis was named honorary dean by Bishop Alexander Rusu of Aaia Mare, Romania. In 1946, Father Marchis was made a Papal Chamberlain with the title of Very Reverend Monsignor by Pope Pius XII. On November 10, 1955, the Holy Father conferred upon Monsignor Marchis the honor of a domestic prelate, together with the title of Right Reverend Monsignor.

Payment of the last dollar on the old debt of $72,000 was made in 1952. As a token of gratitude and a sign of devotion in that Marian Year, a Fatima Shrine was erected in the parish garden. In 1956 the parking area was enlarged; the heating plant was modernized; the church basement and kitchen were completely remodeled; and the auditorium was refurnished.

For the celebration of the 50th Jubilee of the parish in 1957, the church was extensively remodeled. Improvements continued in 1962 when a new rectory was built on the location of the original parish house.

St. Michael School was closed in 1966 due to the lack of teaching sisters and the increased cost of operating the school.

St. Michael Parish continued under the authority of the Bishop of Rockford until December 4, 1982 when Pope John Paul II established the Apostolic Exarchate for the Romanian Byzantine Rite. On March 26, 1987 the Apostolic Exarchate for the Romanian Byzantine Rite was elevated to the Rank of an Eparchy (Diocese). The jurisdiction of the Romanian Catholic Diocese of Canton extends territorially to all of the United States.

◆ **St. Michael Byzantine Catholic Church, Aurora.**

ST. NICHOLAS PARISH

◆ **St. Nicholas Church.**

◆ **Corpus Christi Altar.**

The number of German Catholics attending the original Sacred Heart Church on the west side of Aurora in its early years grew with the flow of immigrants into the city. Many did not speak English and the leaders in this group believed that its spiritual growth would be facilitated by the establishment of another church, in which the customs, hymns and language of the fatherland would be retained. St. Nicholas Parish was founded February 16, 1861, with a list of contributors to the building fund representing 205 German families. A frame church was built at the corner of Liberty and High Streets and was dedicated to St. Nicholas on April 27, 1862. Father Joseph Mueller, C.Ss.R.

(1862-1863), a Redemptorist priest and Pastor of St. Michael Parish, Chicago was appointed to be the first pastor and the Redemptorist Fathers continued to be in charge of the parish until June, 1863.

In 1864, Father Joseph Westkamp (1863-1865), the first resident pastor, built a parochial school, a small house with two classrooms. In the same year he also built a modest rectory for himself.

During Father H. Lierman's pastorate (1865-1880), the parish expanded due to an influx of immigrants from Luxembourg, Westphalia and the Rhenish province. It was necessary for Father Lierman to enlarge the church and also the school.

The years of Father Charles Schnueckel's pastorate (1880-1908) were, for St. Nicholas Parish, the golden age of uninterrupted progress. As soon as Father Schnueckel arrived in 1880, he immediately added four classrooms to the school. He also engaged the School Sisters of St. Francis to teach in the school. In 1882 he began the erection of a new parish church, a beautiful structure of Gothic architecture. When the church was completed in

◆ **Graduating class from 1913.**

1887, he at once started building another addition of four more classrooms to the school. A rectory was built in 1889; a convent was purchased for the sisters and in 1900 a parish hall was built to complete the parish buildings. Father Schnueckel died suddenly, October 14, 1908.

Father Peter J. Weber (1908-1923) was appointed the next pastor. The recent building program had understandably left a large indebtedness on the parish and Father Weber's main task at first was the reduction of the debt, which he did in a very short time with the supported effort of the parishioners..

Father Magnus A. Schumacher (1923-1966) came to St. Nicholas on August 20, 1923 and remained as pastor for 43 years. During his long pastorate he engaged in an extensive renovation of the entire parish plant. In 1941, the whole church interior was remodeled; in 1944 the parish hall was renovated and a bowling alley constructed; the cemetery was beautified in 1946; a new convent was built in 1954 and a new school was built in 1955. Also under Father Schumacher's pastorate, the church was again renovated in 1965, bringing it up

◆ **St. Nicholas interior, circa 1890.**

◆ **St. Nicholas interior.**

to the liturgical standards of the Second Vatican Council.

In 1973, shortly after Father Sylvester J. Eye (1973-1979) arrived, the St. Nicholas convent was leased to the Diocese to be the center of the apostolate to the Spanish speaking Catholics of the area. It is now known as Centro Cristo Rey. (Christ the King Center).

In 1974, an agreement was made between St. Therese Parish and St. Nicholas Parish to combine the 7th and 8th grades of the schools.

St. Nicholas Church became the first officially designated historical landmark in Aurora. In 1988, the then 95-year-old structure was granted the designation by unanimous vote of the Aurora Preservation Commission.

Since both St. Nicholas and Sacred Heart Parishes closed their old schools in the spring of 1990, the children from both parishes attend a new school housed in the former St. Nicholas school building. Because both parishes have many Hispanic families, it was decided to name the new school in honor of the late Archbishop Oscar Romero of San Salvador who was assassinated at Mass in 1980 for speaking out on behalf of the poor.

As of March 2007, Father Oscar Cortes is the parochial administrator. There are approximately 2000 families currently registered at St. Nicholas Parish.

St. Peter Parish

◆ **Former St. Peter Church.**

◆ **Construction of current church in 1963.**

What is now St. Peter Parish originally was within the territory of Holy Angels Parish. Tradition has it that Bishop Peter J. Muldoon felt there were some fallen away Catholics in this area. He prevailed upon Father James A. Quinn, Pastor of Holy Angels, to put up a mission church. Father Quinn did so rather reluctantly for he felt that it could not support itself and would not last. A temporary chapel was built, named after St. Peter in honor of Bishop Muldoon, and put into service on Easter Sunday, April 12, 1925.

Father Joseph W. Rojemann was assigned as assistant to Holy Angels, and was appointed to develop the new area. He went to work with great zeal and a parish hall was soon built. Bishop Edward F. Hoban granted Father Rojemann's request of making the mission a parish in the spring of 1929. Father Rojemann (1928-1936) was appointed the first pastor, and immediately secured a rectory and a convent for the sisters who would eventually staff St. Peter School.

In March, 1936, Father Rojemann was transferred and Father Joseph A. Rzeszotko (1936-1984) was appointed to take his place. In spite of serious

financial problems, the first of the new pastor's undertakings was the decoration of the church. As times grew brighter, so did the financial condition at St. Peter.

By the late 1940s the area was being hemmed in by industrial development. In October 1948 a tract of slightly more than five acres across the street from the church was purchased, along with other vacant lots adjacent to the buildings.

The parish celebrated its Silver Jubilee on May 7, 1950, and the Silver Jubilee of its pastor, Father Rzeszotko, in April, 1953.

In 1955, a drive was conducted to secure funds for a building program. A new school was built on the property across the street from the church and the new school opened its doors in 1959 staffed by the Springfield Dominican Sisters. Five years later plans were begun for a new church and rectory. On May 31, 1964, ground was broken and on Easter Sunday of the following year, 1965, the first Mass was offered in the new church.

Father Rzeszotko was named a monsignor in 1965. He was pastor at St. Peter for 48 years, from 1936 to 1984.

◆ **St. Peter Church.**

◆ **Exterior mosaic.**

◆ **St. Peter Church interior.**

In 1968 a new convent was built, thus completing the building program. The new buildings were directly across the street from the original parish facilities. Each building was paid for as it was completed.

In the mid-1960s the old church was transformed to the Saint Vincent DePaul Center, operated by Marie Wilkinson. From this center food, clothing and furniture were distributed to the poor of Aurora.

After the arrival of Father Ronald A. Jones (1998-2002), the rectory was remodeled and religious education was expanded.

The "little mission" has grown and flourished since its inception in 1925. St. Peter Parish celebrated its 75th anniversary in May of 2000.

As of March 2007 the pastor is Father George Glover, O.S.B. There are approximately 400 families currently registered at St. Peter Parish.

St. Rita of Cascia Parish

St. Rita of Cascia Parish was established in 1927. The Augustinian Fathers were in charge of the parish, with Father Cornelius Ford, O.S.A. (1927-1933) serving as the first pastor. During the early years of the parish, all services were conducted in the chapel of the Fox Valley High School, which was also operated by the Augustinians. In the summer of 1933, a transfer was arranged and the Augustinians moved to Rockford, taking charge of St. Thomas High School and St. Mary Parish. At the same time, the Benedictine Fathers assumed responsibility for Fox Valley High School on North Lake Street, which then became Marmion Military Academy and included boarding facilities. Father Michael A. Kissane (1933-1954), a diocesan priest, became the Pastor of St. Rita of Cascia.

In 1935, the church of St. Rita, a portable building, was dedicated. In August of 1949, six acres of property were purchased on the northern limits of the city of Aurora on North Lake Street. Two adjoining acres were purchased in June, 1955, which included a residence.

Because of the rapid growth of this section of Aurora in those years, plans had to be made

◆ **The church on Lake Street.**

immediately for expansion. In June, 1954, the Sisters of Mary Immaculate of Joliet, Illinois agreed to teach in the proposed school after its construction.

When the Indian Creek Public School was vacated, the parish rented it for the school year, beginning, in 1956.

At this time the property purchased by the parish on North Lake Street began to be encircled by commercial establishments. Many were of the opinion that this was not the proper area to build a

◆ **St. Rita of Cascia Church.**

◆ **May Crowning, 1957**

◆ **Indian Creek School, 1959.**

parish complex. A determination was made that the location of the parish should be further to the west, more to the center of the area covered by St. Rita. As a result, property was purchased on Indian Trail, the location of the present parish. Two residential homes were part of the property purchased. One home was to serve as a rectory and the other home for the parish custodian.

Ground was broken in the fall of 1959 for a twelve room school, a gym-church, and a convent. St. Rita School officially opened to students in September, 1960. Dedication of all buildings took place in the spring of 1961. Later it was determined that the school needs would be better met with additional classrooms, and the school was enlarged to sixteen rooms. All of the building and accomplishments of St. Rita Parish during these years was under the leadership and inspiration of Father Thomas P. Bermingham (1954-1969). For his dedication to his parish, he was elevated to the title of Right Reverend Monsignor in January, 1964.

It was during the pastorate of Monsignor Raymond J. Wahl (1969-1973) that the Diocese decided that the North Aurora area was increasing in population so fast that a Catholic parish should be established in that area. When this was done in 1970, approximately three hundred families were transferred from St. Rita to the new Blessed Sacrament Parish of North Aurora.

In 1972, the residence used as a rectory for St. Rita's priests was disposed of and a new rectory to serve the needs of the pastor and his associates was constructed adjacent to the church. At this time it was determined that a gymnasium should be built to help serve the needs of all segments of the parish. The decision was also made to remodel the gym-church as the permanent space for worship.

After five years of study and planning together, St. Rita of Cascia parishioners settled into their newly renovated worship space and newly added gathering space. The culmination of the project took place when Father Robert J. Willhite welcomed Bishop Thomas G. Doran for the official blessing during a Mass of Dedication on July 28, 1996.

As of March 2007 Monsignor Robert J. Willhite is the pastor. There are approximately 1600 families currently registered at St. Rita of Cascia Parish.

◆ **St. Rita School first grade class, 1961.**

St. Therese of Jesus Parish

◆ **Original church interior.**

It is quite probable that this parish is the first one anywhere to be dedicated to the Little Flower (St. Therese of Lisieux), for Bishop Peter J. Muldoon selected the patron on May 25, 1925, the very day of her canonization. Monsignor Magnus A. Schumacher, Pastor of St. Nicholas, had taken a census of the extreme eastern part of the city of Aurora to determine exactly how many Catholics lived there. Property had been bought with the idea of erecting a mission there. Monsignor Schumacher recommended, rather, that the area be constituted an independent parish.

On receiving the report that about one-hundred and fifty Catholic families were in the area, Bishop Muldoon abandoned the thought of simply establishing a mission and decided to erect a parish at once with a resident pastor.

Father Charles A. Henkel (1925-1965) was appointed the first pastor of St. Therese Parish in July, 1925. In the letter of appointment, Bishop Muldoon promised Father Henkel "hard and strenuous work" and stated that "the Little Flower will guide and direct you." The first Mass for the new parishioners was offered in St. Nicholas Hall on Sunday, August 9, and a few weeks later, arrangements were made for the pastor to celebrate Sunday Masses in the auditorium of the Oak Park School, situated within the boundaries of the parish.

That August, plans were drawn up for a one-story flat-roofed building, to be used temporarily as a church, and to be finished later with the addition of one or two stories as a combination church and school. Ground was broken in September. Enthusiasm to have a parish school right away was such that Bishop Muldoon was persuaded to consent to the addition of the second story, as a school and convent.

The building was completed by the end of July, 1926. A bungalow had also been built to serve temporarily as a rectory. Mass was celebrated for the first time on August 1, 1926. Bishop Edward F. Hoban presided at the dedication of St. Therese Church shortly after his appointment to the Diocese. That fall, the school was opened with an opening enrollment of 130 students under the charge of the School Sisters of St. Francis, of Milwaukee.

◆ **Convent groundbreaking, 1948.**

◆ **Dedication of current church, 1966.**

◆ **Baptismal Font.**

◆ **St. Therese of Jesus Church.**

During the depression the parishioners were severely challenged in supporting their parish; most were either on relief or working short hours. Father Henkel counted himself lucky to be able to pay his operating expenses and meet the interest on the debt. It was not until 1947 that the debt was finally liquidated.

In 1948, a new convent was started. It was completed the following year, releasing the former living quarters for conversion into classrooms. A rectory was built in 1952 and completed in 1953.

In October of 1964, Father Henkel began the construction of a new church but before his work could be completed he passed away on June 22, 1965 and Father Clement P. Petit (1965-1970) assumed the pastoral duties of St. Therese. Father Petit completed the building of the church. Bishop Loras T. Lane dedicated the new church on October 2, 1966.

Father Herman A. Porter (1970-1979) assumed the pastoral duties at St. Therese in February of 1970. At his request, a Resale Shop was opened in a five room house that once served as the parish rectory. The shop raised more than $143,000 for the parish over the 28 years it was open. During Father Porter's pastorate many Hispanic families began moving into the parish area.

In 1982, to meet the demands of the growing Hispanic population, Bishop Arthur J. O'Neill asked the Missionaries of the Sacred Heart for assistance. The order provided Father James Campbell, MSC (1982-1991) as pastor; he had served several years in Colombia where he had opportunity to practice Spanish. During his pastorate, Father Campbell put the parish on a solid financial basis and oversaw important repairs to parish facilities.

Father Gerald Paul, MSC, was parish administrator from May 1994 to January 1995. During this time the convent, which became vacant when the sisters left the parish several months earlier, was leased. Under the pastorate of Father Joseph T. Muller, MSC (1995-2005), the Resale Shop was transformed into parish offices, and an outdoor shrine to St. Therese was erected with the last funds from the shop.

As of March 2007 the pastor is Father Michael Miller, MSC. There are approximately 600 families currently registered at St. Therese of Jesus Parish.

HOLY CROSS PARISH

Some time in the year 1854 a Father Sullivan came from Aurora to offer Mass in the farm home of John Lonergan, east of the village of Batavia. A scant dozen Catholics assembled in the Lonergan home for this first Mass. Undaunted by the small congregation, Father Sullivan persevered in his missionary effort. Within a few months, he had rented a single room in a block on Batavia Avenue immediately north of Wilson Street, and so slight was the increase of Catholics that this small chapel was adequate for six years

The care of the small mission was assumed by Father Patrick O'Dwyer of St. Charles. In 1860, Father O'Dwyer had inspired his small flock with courage to purchase the former Congregational Church which adjoined the chapel then being used.

Whether Father O'Dwyer had overestimated the resources of his Batavia congregation or whether their own desire for a church had carried them

◆ **Former Holy Cross Church, circa 1897.**

beyond their financial depth, is a matter of conjecture, but it is a matter of record that the people were threatened with the loss of their church because of their failure to meet the payments. In this crisis, Owen Kavanaugh and John Findley rose as leaders in a determined effort to save the church. They went from home to home receiving the pitifully small donations which the impoverished Catholics were able to give. Kavanaugh himself gave up a sorely needed overcoat to help supply the need. Despite their sacrifices, the Catholics were unable to raise the sum required, and the church was saved only through additional help given by generous non-Catholics.

Marriages, from 1857, were recorded in a special register for Batavia. Baptisms, however, were recorded in the parish register of St. Patrick Church, St. Charles, until February of 1866.

It is with the arrival of Father Michael Prendergast, O.P. (1870-1875) as the first resident pastor of St. Charles that the history of Holy Cross Parish properly begins.

Father Prendergast must have been hopeful of the growth of the Batavia mission for he purchased

◆ **Holy Cross School Dedication, May 7, 1961.**

◆ **Holy Cross School Dedication Mass, May 7, 1961.**

◆ **Adoration Chapel.**

the Kemp property on the east side at the corner of Wilson and Van Buren, a commanding site in that day, and soon left St. Charles to take up residence in Batavia. St. Charles now became the mission from Batavia and not long after Turner Junction, now West Chicago, was placed in the care of the pastor of Batavia. The territory served by the pastor of Holy Cross then embraced the present areas of the parishes in Batavia, St. Charles, Geneva and West Chicago. St. Patrick Parish in St. Charles soon regained independent status but West Chicago remained a mission of Batavia for many years, in fact, it wasn't until the coming of Father George Ratz (1893-1907) that West Chicago was severed and Elburn became the mission of Batavia.

Father Dominic Spelman (1876-1893) arrived in Batavia to continue as pastor for seventeen years until the coming of Father George Ratz in 1893. Father Ratz was a native of Freeport. In all probability, he was the first American born pastor of Holy Cross, and was born within the limits of what is now the Diocese of Rockford. He was also a former Lutheran who had been converted in his early adult life. The zeal of the convert and the desire of a native son were combined in Father Ratz.

The year 1896 was a year of financial panic and frightening to people who depended upon steady employment for the necessities of life. The lack of money, however, did not deter Father Ratz from building a church, nor did it discourage his people. In place of money, they gave materials and long devoted hours of grueling labor. A parishioner, William Shannon, was the owner of a quarry and many of the men of the parish were stone masons, jobless because of the depression. These men quarried the Shannon stone, cut, dressed and set it.

The cornerstone of Holy Cross Church was laid in the spring of 1896 and the church was completed early in the summer of 1897. Father T. Mooney, Chancellor of the Archdiocese of Chicago, dedicated the new church on June 15, 1897.

Acknowledgement must be made of the generosity of non-Catholics while the Catholics were striving to build their church; the large tower bell was donated by a non-Catholic.

In 1909, Father John P. McGuire (1909-1913) devoted himself to building the rectory which adjoined the church. In 1911, Elburn was constituted an independent parish and Father Daniel P. Drennan was appointed the first pastor. The boundaries of Holy Cross had been gradually reduced, first by the withdrawal of St. Charles, then by the severance of West Chicago, and later by the new status granted to Elburn.

It was early in the pastorate of Father Daniel Lehane (1913-1929) that the so-called Batavia plan of released time religious instruction was inaugurated. An agreement was reached between the School Board of Batavia and the churches of the city whereby every elementary school pupil in Batavia would be released on Thursdays for two consecutive periods of religious instruction in the church designated by parents. The Sisters of Mercy conducted the religious instruction classes until 1953, when Bishop John J. Boylan persuaded the Daughters of the Holy Heart of Mary to come to Holy Cross to teach religion to the children.

Father William J. Donovan (1929-1967) succeeded Father Lehane as pastor and served as pastor of Holy Cross for the next 38 years. In November of 1945, Pope Pius XII named Father Donovan a domestic prelate with the title of Right Reverend Monsignor.

In 1959 work was begun on a one-story building which would consist of four classrooms and a multi-purpose hall, serving as a gymnasium and assembly room for the school.

The Missionaries of the Sacred Heart assumed the pastoral responsibility of the parish in 1969 with Father Raymond J. Costello, MSC, (1969-1982) being appointed the first MSC pastor. In 1988, the MSC's decided to no longer staff Holy Cross due to a shortage of priests within their order. Bishop Arthur J. O'Neill assigned Father Stephen J. St. Jules (1988-2001), a diocesan priest, as the new pastor.

A new church was built during the pastorate of Father St. Jules. A Mass of Dedication was celebrated by Bishop O'Neill on April 8, 1994. The new church has seating for 1200 people, compared to the old church, which seated 300 people. This increase in seating reflects the growth in Batavia's population, from about 3,800 in 1897, when the first church was built, to about 20,000 when the new church was completed in 1994. Just as the parishioners of 1896 built their church with their own hands, the parishioners of 1994 built the parish's new rectory with all volunteers.

As of this writing, the parish is constructing an Education-Community Center under the pastorate of Father Daniel J. Deutsch. Construction is expected to be completed in fall 2008.

As of March 2007 Father Daniel J. Deutsch is the pastor. There are approximately 3,000 families currently registered at Holy Cross Parish.

◆ **Holy Cross Church**

St. James Parish

In the early days, Belvidere was one of a number of settlements in the area which were attended by missionary priests of the Chicago Diocese. When Father Patrick McMahon became the first pastor of Donnelley's Settlement (which later became Hartland) in 1844, he used to travel on horseback over the trails which served as roads, offering Mass in pioneer homes. Belvidere was on his route and he said Mass here regularly up to 1850, usually in the home of Cornelius Connelly.

Father Hugh Brady succeeded Father McMahon and kept up the practice of visiting the Catholics of Belvidere. Since the town was on the route from Chicago to Galena, Bishop James O. Van de Velde passed through it with some frequency; he noted in his diary that on September 18th, 1851, "a lot has been purchased for the erection of a church."

Father John A. Hampston (1851-1854), newly ordained, was appointed in the autumn of 1851 as pastor of Belvidere, with the neighboring towns in his charge. Father Hampston built the first St. James Rectory at the corner of Lincoln Avenue and Burgess Street, but he lived in it a very short time as it soon

◆ **Graduating class from 1935.**

became evident that Rockford was growing faster than the neighboring communities. By 1853, Father Hampston had moved to Rockford where he established St. James Parish. Belvidere was to continue as a mission church of Rockford until 1864.

William Gilman donated to the Belvidere parish a site at the corner of Church and Caswell Streets and work began on construction of a church. Bishop Anthony O'Regan came from Chicago to lay the cornerstone.

Father John P. Donelan (1860-1864) was appointed pastor and made his first visit to Belvidere on Saturday, June 19, 1860. It was he who provided the impetus for the erection of the first small stone church which was used until 1866; he also purchased land for a cemetery with his own money.

In July 1864, the Rockford and Belvidere parishes were separated and Father Patrick McGuire (1864-1893) was named the first resident pastor in Belvidere. Here he labored for almost twenty-nine years. In 1886, he built the present church which was dedicated by Archbishop Patrick A. Feehan, of Chicago, on March 28, 1889. Two years later, Father McGuire enlarged the cemetery by several acres.

In the short time Father J. C. Murphy (1907-1909) was pastor, he remodeled the rectory, put a new roof on the church, redecorated the church and

◆ **St. James Church and rectory, 1893.**

◆ **St James interior.**

◆ **St. James School students in 1950, grades 5-6.**

installed a steam heating plant. Cement walks were laid and, in addition, the parish debt was greatly reduced.

On September 10, 1909, Father Joseph P. Joyce (1909-1929) was appointed pastor of St. James. In the first year of his pastorate, he built a four-room parochial school at a cost of $25,000 and purchased a convent for the School Sisters of Notre Dame of Milwaukee, who were engaged to teach. On the occasion of the celebration of the fiftieth anniversary of the establishment of the parish, an effort was made to retire the school debt. A former parishioner, Roger Sullivan of Chicago, promised a gift of one-third of all that the parish would raise. A fund drive raised $21,000 and Mr. Sullivan made good his promise with a donation of $7,000.

In July of 1933, Father Leo W. Binz (1933-1936) was named pastor. He became a Monsignor in January of 1934, a Bishop in 1942 and, in 1949, he went to Dubuque as Coadjutor. In 1954, he became Archbishop of Dubuque and in 1961 became Archbishop of St. Paul.

Father John T. Egan (1948-1954) became pastor in 1948. He renovated the church and the rectory. Father Edward J. Connolly (1954-1960) took up his work in April of 1954 and continued the improvements begun by his predecessor, completing many of them.

The basement of the church was renovated and remodeled into a parish hall with kitchen, rest rooms, and stage facilities. The parish hall seats approximately 300. The old parish hall was razed to

◆ **Religious vocations were promoted by having students wear the garb of priests and sisters.**

provide room for a new convent, completed in 1956. A four room addition to the school, including a large cafeteria, was completed in 1958. The cemetery was enlarged to six acres.

Father Charles K. McCarren (1965-1979) was appointed pastor in 1965 and during his term the church was renovated.

The interior of St. James Church underwent an extensive renovation project in 1982 during the pastorate of Father Robert R. Miller (1979-1991). Bishop Arthur J. O'Neill celebrated Mass and blessed the new altar during a rededication in July of 1982. The church celebrated its centennial in 1986.

In October of 1990, the Bracken family, whose membership in the parish goes back more than 75 years, donated 22 acres of land, northwest of the city, to St. James Parish for future parish expansion.

A new parish center attached to the school was completed in 1993 while Father Richard M. Russo (1991-1995) was pastor. The building houses parish offices, meeting rooms, two classrooms and a multi-purpose room.

While he was administrator in May of 2001, Monsignor David D. Kagan (2001-2002), dedicated a shrine to Our Lady of Guadalupe. The painting had been blessed on her feast day, December 12, 2000, by Bishop Emeritus Arthur J. O'Neill. Jose Aguado and Antonio Delgadillo built the shrine which is in the interior of the church.

As of March 2007 Father Thomas E. Brantman is pastor. There are approximately 2200 families currently registered at St .James Parish.

◆ **St. James Church.**

st.James catholic church

ST. MARY PARISH

The first Catholic settlers in the Byron area traveled to Oregon, Seward, Rockford and other towns to attend Mass and receive the other sacraments.

In 1894, Mr. W. I. Caldwell, a Catholic gentleman of the Byron area, consulted with Father John J. McCann of St. Mary Parish in Oregon about the possibility of building a church in Byron. Father McCann offered the first Mass in Byron's G.A.R. Hall on April 20, 1895. Attendance grew until it became necessary to rent the opera house, where Mass was offered

◆ **Le Fleur family shrine located on what was once their homestead, on the corner of Kishwaukee and Crestview Roads.**

every other Sunday beginning August 25, 1895.

A fund drive was held to raise funds for a church building. Ground was broken September 20, 1895 and on June 3, 1896, Archbishop Patrick A. Feehan came from Chicago to dedicate St. Mary Church.

The Catholic people purchased six city lots for use as a cemetery, but later established the present cemetery of four acres at the west end of Byron.

The parish was served by the pastors of St. Mary in Oregon until Father Paul E. Kunkel

◆ **St. Mary Church.**

(1954-1967) was appointed on March 7, 1954 as the first resident pastor of St. Mary by Bishop Raymond P. Hillinger. At this time St. Peter Parish in Davis Junction became a mission of the Byron parish.

In December of 1966, Bishop Loras T. Lane assigned Father Edward S. Wright (1967-1970) to be pastor of St. Mary in Byron and its mission, St. Peter in Davis Junction. During Father Wright's pastorate, the rectory was purchased and furnished, additional property was acquired and the mission at Davis Junction was closed in September, 1969.

Father Thomas J. Monahan (1970-1977) was appointed by Bishop Arthur J. O'Neill in October of 1970. The first action taken under Father Monahan was the planning for a new church. A pledge campaign began on March 17, 1974 and Mass was offered for the last time in the original church on July 22, 1974. Demolition of the building and preparation of the site began the following day.

Nine months later, in April of 1975, the new building was completed. Bishop O'Neill dedicated the new St. Mary Church on April 20, 1975.

On Memorial Day in 1994, a monument to the unborn children of abortion was dedicated by the Pastor of St. Mary Parish, Father John W. Cahill (1989-1995). The stone monument in St. Mary Cemetery was donated anonymously by a monument company.

◆ **St. Mary Church interior.**

A new parish center was dedicated by Bishop Thomas G. Doran on August 28, 1994. The new 13,000 square foot center has four offices, along with thirteen classrooms for religious education, and is accessible to the handicapped.

Bishop Doran joined Father John A. Slampak (1995-1999), pastor, and the faith community of St. Mary Church in celebrating the parish's 100th anniversary on August 20, 1995.

As of March 2007 Father Timothy L. Doherty is the pastor. There are approximately 600 families currently registered at St. Mary Parish.

◆ **St. Mary Church, circa 1900.**

ST. MONICA PARISH

St. Monica Parish in Carpentersville, formerly known as Meadowdale, had its beginnings in 1954 as a mission church of St. Catherine of Siena Parish in Dundee.

Father John F. Regan, Pastor of St. Catherine's in Dundee (1950-1957), acquired the Curtis Candy Company experimental farm on Route 25 through the generosity of Leonard W. Besinger.

With the help of many of the parishioners, Father Regan converted one of the barns on the property into a chapel, named Siena Chapel and in the fall of 1954, Father Regan officially opened the mission in Meadowdale. In three short years, the mission had grown to such an extent that Bishop Loras T. Lane officially established it as an independent parish in honor of St. Monica on October 1, 1957.

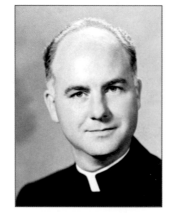

◆ **Father Edmund Petit.**

Father Edmund P. Petit (1957-1964), formerly associate at St. Mary's in Woodstock, was named the first resident pastor and Father Thomas W. Neville, the associate at St. Catherine in Dundee, was appointed the associate pastor. Another one of the buildings on the premises was furnished as a rectory for Father Petit and Father Neville.

In 1962, the original church building was renovated for use as a catechetical center, and on September 16, 1962 the building was dedicated by Bishop Lane.

Father Petit was transferred in August of 1964 and Father Neville (1964-1970), who had left as an associate in 1959 returned as the parish's second pastor on August 17, 1964. It was under Father Neville's leadership that plans were made to build a new church.

Groundbreaking ceremonies for the new church were held on March 24, 1968. The new church, which seats a thousand people, faces Route 25 and was completed in August of 1969. It was formally dedicated by Bishop Arthur J. O'Neill on November 2, 1969.

◆ **Father Thomas Neville, left, and parishioners at the future site of St. Monica Church in 1968.**

◆ **Father Adolph Weideman relaxes at St. Monica's Fest in the early 1970s.**

◆ **St. Monica Church interior.**

On September 12, 1982 Bishop O'Neill joined with the Pastor, Father Bernard J. Mullane (1974-1986), and former pastors, Father Petit and Father Neville, in concelebrating Mass on the 25th anniversary of the parish.

As of March 2007 the pastor is Father Moises Apostol. There are approximately 2200 families currently registered at St Monica Parish.

◆ **St. Monica Church.**

SS. Peter and Paul Parish

Catholics moved into the Cary area from Barrington and Woodstock, probably in the 1850's or 1860's. Cary was first attended from Woodstock. Mass was first celebrated in the home of James Neeley, an early trustee. Later, Mass was celebrated in the ice house. Along with Crystal Lake, Algonquin, and Dundee, Cary was one of the churches to grow out of Hartland-Woodstock-Gilberts sources. In 1872, about thirteen Catholics from Bohemia built the church of St. John Nepomucene near Fox River Grove. St. John's never did become a parish, however, because it did not have the population growth of nearby Cary.

Father Joseph M. Lonergan organized the Cary congregation in the year 1911. He resided in Barrington at the time, but saw to it that Mass was said every Sunday in Cary, and once a month at St. John Nepomucene. The cornerstone for the Cary church was laid in 1912 and the church construction was completed in 1913 when it was dedicated to Saints Peter and Paul.

The first resident pastor at Cary was Father Joseph L. Gies (1913-1914), who had served as Father Lonergan's assistant at Barrington. While Father Gies was an assistant to Father Lonergan, the construction of the church took place. Father Gies was appointed pastor at Cary when Father Lonergan left to be a chaplain in WWI. Father Gies served only

◆ **Drawing of the original church with inset photographs of Fathers Joseph Gies and Joseph Lonergan.**

a year before he died, and he was succeeded by Father Edwin A. McCormick (1914-1915). Father Lonergan returned briefly to the parish after Father McCormick was transferred to Crystal Lake in 1915 and Father Theodore B. McCormick (1917-1918) took Father Lonergan's place as administrator in 1917.

Father Francis A. Kilderry (1918-1958) began a 40 year term as pastor in July, 1918. During Father Kilderry's time as pastor, groundbreaking ceremonies were held for the parish school and convent on July 2, 1929. The new building was dedicated later during

◆ **SS. Peter & Paul Church.**

◆ School orchestra, probably from the 1940s.

◆ SS. Peter & Paul School students, 1938.

that same year by Bishop Edward F. Hoban. The school was staffed then, and is still staffed, by the Dominican Sisters of Springfield, Illinois. Father Kilderry served as pastor until his death in 1958.

Father C. Alfred Dietsch (1958-1975) was appointed pastor of SS. Peter and Paul Parish in December of 1958. During Father Dietsch's 17 years as pastor, he completely rebuilt the parish plant. At the time Father Dietsch was appointed pastor, the plans for the relocation of the parish complex, from the old site on Route 14 and First Street to the present location, were being formulated. The Holy Name Society had already purchased fifteen acres. Six and one half more acres were purchased to complete the parish property.

Through the untiring efforts of the parishioners and with the guidance of Father Dietsch, the school, and temporary church building, was built. The dedication ceremonies were held in October of 1960, with Bishop Loras T. Lane officiating.

Bishop Lane urged Father Dietsch to begin immediately the construction of the rectory so that the priests would be close to the church. The rectory was ready for occupancy in December 1962. Next, plans were formulated for the construction of the new convent. The convent was completed in 1967.

The year 1969 seemed the opportune time to lay plans for the new church, the focal point of a parish. The church was constructed during 1970 and dedicated in the summer of 1971. On November 21, 1972, the entire parish plant was dedicated. Father Dietsch served the parish until he retired on November 1, 1975, when Father Andrew J. Plesa (1975-1987) was appointed the pastor of SS. Peter and Paul in Cary.

The church was rededicated in September of 1990 due to the remodeled sanctuary which was raised and recarpeted. An immersion pool for baptisms was also completed at this time during the pastorate of Father Donald M. Ahles (1988-2003)

Bishop Thomas G. Doran, joined by Father Ahles, dedicated a new church addition on September 16, 1995. At the same time, SS. Peter & Paul Parish celebrated the 25th anniversary of their church.

In 2002, a 33,000 square foot addition to the school was completed. Thanks to two anonymous donations totaling nearly $5 million, work on the project began in June of 2001. On August 25, 2002, Father Ahles welcomed Bishop Thomas G. Doran who blessed the new addition.

As of March 2007 the pastor is Father Stephen J. St. Jules. There are approximately 3200 families currently registered at SS. Peter and Paul Parish.

St. Elizabeth Ann Seton Parish

◆ **Site of the future St. Elizabeth Ann Seton Church, 1981.**

◆ **Father Joseph Kulak at the groundbreaking of the parish, 1981.**

On December 13, 1978, Bishop Arthur J. O'Neill announced the appointment of Father Joseph F. Kulak (1978-1995) as the founding pastor of St. Elizabeth Ann Seton Parish. The parish was named in honor of the first native-born U.S. citizen to be canonized a saint. On December 31, 1978, the first Mass for the parish was celebrated in the auditorium of Crystal Lake South High School. Mass was celebrated in this auditorium until a new church was built for the parish.

Groundbreaking ceremonies were held for the construction of a new church on February 1, 1981. The rectory and land were donated by St. Thomas the Apostle Parish in Crystal Lake, where many St. Elizabeth parishioners belonged before their parish was formed.

The church was dedicated on April 24, 1982 by Bishop O'Neill. The Mass was concelebrated with Father Kulak, Pastor. A Eucharistic Chapel that seats 50 is included in the church building and a stained glass window that depicts the life of St. Elizabeth Ann Seton occupies one side of the narthex, directly behind the baptismal font.

A bronze crucifix in the sanctuary of the church was dedicated on June 3, 2001. The corpus of Christ is six feet tall and weighs over 450 pounds and is mounted on teak wood. The crucifix was donated

by Marian Stello in honor of her parents, Cal and the late Jennie Basile.

On September 9, 2001, under the pastorate of Father (now Monsignor) Thomas J. Dempsey, a

◆ **Bronze crucifix donated by Marian Stello.**

◆ The stained glass window depicting the life of St. Elizabeth Ann Seton.

The new parish center was dedicated and blessed by Bishop Emeritus O'Neill, assisted by Monsignor Dempsey, on March 16, 2003. The new 34,000 square-foot building is attached to the church and has a large reception hall with seating for 500, a kitchen, meeting rooms whose walls can be extended or contracted to form larger and smaller rooms, a bride's room and toddler room, parish offices and a large, still-unfinished area upstairs.

As of March 2007 Father Phillip A. Kaim is the parochial administrator. There are approximately 2900 families currently registered at St. Elizabeth Ann Seton Parish.

◆ Statue of the parish's patroness.

groundbreaking ceremony was held for the construction of a new two story parish center. Bishop Thomas G. Doran officiated at the ceremonies.

◆ St. Elizabeth Ann Seton Church.

St. Thomas the Apostle Parish

◆ **St. Thomas the Apostle Church on Pierson Street, 1925-1968.**

In May 1922, St. Thomas the Apostle Parish in Crystal Lake received its first official resident pastor. Some seventy-five years before, the parish had its beginning.

The beginning was in the year 1846 in a place known as North Barrens, about four miles west of Crystal Lake along Illinois 176. The actual site of that first church (a log structure) was on the grounds of Mt. Thabor cemetery. The structure was called the Little Church in the Bush by the Algonquin Township residents around Crystal Lake, and the Little Church in the Woods by the Grafton Township residents of Huntley. Both areas attached themselves to the church.

A large influx of Catholics into the Crystal Lake area came in 1846. The congregation grew rapidly, and it became a mission church of St. Mary Parish, Woodstock, when that church received its first resident pastor, Father Bernard O'Hara in 1855. By 1877, when Father Thomas F. Leydon was Woodstock's pastor, weekly Mass had to be said in the larger quarters of Fitch's Hall in Crystal Lake.

Under the supervision of Father Leydon, property was purchased (from Thomas Leonard, Sr.) on Pierson Avenue and a frame church was constructed, with the first Mass being said in 1881.

In 1905, Barrington and Crystal Lake were separated from Woodstock and each was made a separate parish. Each town had its own church; both communities financed the rectory which was built in Barrington.

In 1908, the Diocese of Rockford was formed from the Chicago Archdiocese. Barrington, where the jointly-financed rectory was located, was in the Chicago Archdiocese, with Crystal Lake, of course, part of the Rockford Diocese. An arrangement was made whereby the Diocese of Rockford was allowed jurisdiction in the Barrington section of the parish. This arrangement lasted into the pastorate of Father Edwin A. McCormick (1915-1955).

Crystal Lake returned to a mission status in 1911 when Father Lonergan was appointed pastor of Barrington. In 1913, Crystal Lake became an independent parish, and Father Lonergan was its pastor; he continued, however, to reside in Barrington.

On May 2, 1922, Father Edwin A. McCormick was appointed the first permanent pastor of Crystal Lake. Following a donation of four city lots in 1922 by Mrs. Libby Duffy Reynolds, Father McCormick began construction of a parish plant. Excavation for the rectory began on June 1, 1922, with its completion coming in March, 1923. An item in Father McCormick's notebook states: "March 3, 1923: I burned my electric lights for the first time."

Ground was broken for the church June 27, 1924. It was dedicated July 12, 1925, by Bishop Peter J. Muldoon.

Attention was turned next to a school, with work beginning on that in June, 1927. It opened in September of that year with 60 pupils under the supervision of the Springfield Dominican Sisters. Also acquired that year was a house to be used as a convent. An addition to the convent was completed in 1952.

◆ **St. Thomas the Apostle Church.**

◆ **The interior of the church on Pierson Street, shown at the Duffy wedding, 1957.**

◆ **The graduating class of 1946.**

The parish acquired a Catholic cemetery—the Catholic section of Crystal Lake Memorial Park Cemetery—in 1953. Father McCormick's 40 years of pastoral leadership ended with his death on December 13, 1955.

Following the appointment of Father Burwell E. Beddoes (1957-1962), plans for a massive building project took form. The parish had grown to 850 permanent families, with an additional number of summer residents. Plans were formed in December for a new school building, a new rectory and a remodeling program to convert the old rectory into a larger convent. The new school building was dedicated by Bishop Loras T. Lane on May 10, 1959.

In August, 1964, Father Leo H. Ambre (1964-1979), arrived to begin his care of the Crystal Lake area Catholics. The parish had grown to over 2,000 households, and another parish was being considered for the city. After meetings between Bishop Loras T. Lane and Father Ambre, it was decided to retain the one parish situation, at least for a time, but there would be an additional church built.

The site chosen for the new structure was on the north side of the city, on Illinois Route 176 and Oak Street. Ground was broken March 20, 1967. Hexagonal in shape, the church seated over 800 persons around its contemporary altar. Rather than calling the new building a mission church, parishioners referred to it as St. Thomas on Oak Street while the original church was referred to as St. Thomas on Pierson Street. The parish celebrated the completion of the new structure on Easter Sunday, April 14, 1968.

A new rectory was purchased at 445 Dartmoor Drive in June of 1975 during the pastorate of Father William M. McKinstra (1975-1978).

Due to the growth of the community, a new parish was established in Crystal Lake in 1979 and named St. Elizabeth Ann Seton Parish. St. Thomas the Apostle Parish gave the new parish the rectory on Dartmoor Drive, the land for the new church and $500,000 to be paid over a ten-year period.

Father Geoffrey D. Wirth (1987-2001) was appointed pastor in 1987 and immediately made plans for renovation and expansion. Extensive renovations were made to the twenty-year-old physical plant in the spring of 1988. A renovated parish center at 272 King Street was blessed on September 17, 1989. Ground was broken in October of 1994 for a new addition to the parish school on King Street and a new community center at the main church on Oak Street. The new buildings were dedicated on December 17, 1995 by Bishop Thomas G. Doran.

As of March 2007 the pastor is Monsignor Daniel J. Hermes. There are approximately 3400 families currently registered at St. Thomas the Apostle Parish.

◆ **St. Thomas the Apostle Church interior.**

CHRIST THE TEACHER PARISH

Christ the Teacher University Parish, frequently referred to as the Newman Center, is the worshipping community of Catholic students from Northern Illinois University, as well as permanent parishioners, most of whom are faculty and administrative members of the university.

The Newman Club at Northern Illinois State College began in the school year 1941-1942, under the leadership of Dr. Marguerite O'Connor. During the 1940's the spiritual needs of the students were served by priests of St. Mary Parish in DeKalb.

In September of 1950, a frame building at 618 College Avenue was obtained by Father Charles K. McCarren for the first Newman Student Center on the campus. Fr. McCarren borrowed $2,200 from his mother and $3,500 from the DeKalb Trust and Savings Bank to buy the house. This building was later torn down by the university to make way for a new university library. September, 1951, marked the beginning of Father Hubert V. McGinn's twenty year career in the city of DeKalb as chaplain to the students of Northern Illinois University.

It soon became apparent, because of the ever increasing enrollment at NIU, that a new facility would be needed for serving the Catholic student population. In August of 1957, two and one-half acres of farmland at 512 Normal Road was purchased as a site for the permanent chapel and center. This property came complete with farmhouse, sheep shed, and a crop of soybeans. Father McGinn was appointed the first full-time chaplain by Bishop Loras T. Lane in September of 1957.

In June of 1960, Bishop Lane blessed the cornerstone of the new Newman Chapel, and the following September, regular Sunday services began. The Knights of Columbus played a very important role in the building of the Newman Center. Councils from around the Rockford Diocese contributed generously so that the Center could be built to serve the spiritual needs of Catholic students at NIU. By this time, the enrollment at Northern Illinois University had substantially increased and there were overflow crowds of students at all the Sunday Masses.

At the formal dedication of the new Newman Center, the Newman Club at NIU was recognized in September of 1964 as the most outstanding Newman Club in the nation, with a registered membership of over 1000 students.

October of 1964 marked the beginning of a unique program which continues to this present day. It is a cooperative arrangement between the Newman Foundation and Loyola University of Chicago to offer credit courses in theology to students at NIU. The first courses began in the fall of 1964 and were taught by Dominicans from River Forest, Illinois.

◆ **Bishop Lane at the dedication of the Newman Center Chapel.**

◆ **The Newman Center had its origins in the Newman Club.**

◆ **Newman Catholic Student Center / Christ the Teacher Church.**

The education programs and the Newman Center expanded to such a degree that a new educational wing was constructed and later dedicated in August of 1965.

December 11, 1966 marked another major turning point for Christ the Teacher, Newman Center. It was the establishment of Christ the Teacher as a university parish—a unique status among Newman Centers throughout the country.

Membership of Christ the Teacher University Parish was to be primarily composed of the academic community of Northern Illinois University. This included Catholic students and Catholic members of the administrative and teaching faculty. Father Hubert V. McGinn was installed as pastor in December of 1966 by Monsignor Magnus A. Schumacher, Dean of the Aurora Deanery.

In the fall of 1970, Sister Evelyn Derezinski, a member of the Sisters of Mercy, became a member of the Newman staff. The following summer Father Daniel J. Hermes and Father P. William McDonnell also joined the staff. This increase in staff marked the beginning of the gradual expansion of programs that were designed to reach out to students. Along with the expansion of the Newman staff came a gradual renovation of the Newman Center in order to make it a more comfortable and attractive place for students to congregate. The highlight of this renovation was the addition of a meditation chapel in back of the large chapel, in the area which used to be for the choir.

The summer of 1970 marked the beginning of Father Robert B. Hoffman's ministry as the second pastor of Christ the Teacher University Parish. Fr. Hoffman established the Newman Center's endowment fund

(initiated by a generous bequest from a diocesan priest, Fr. John Vaughn) to maintain and develop Newman's ministries. At graduation in the spring of 1982, NIU recognized Fr. Hoffman's contributions to the entire university community by presenting him with the F.R. Geigle Outstanding Service Award.

On December 2, 1995, the library at the Newman Center was dedicated to Father Stephen K. Potter, former pastor and director of the Newman Center for 11 years, from 1984-1995. Father Potter helped develop the library into one of the largest collections of Catholic theological texts in northern Illinois.

A dedication ceremony and Mass celebrated by Bishop Thomas G. Doran on February 13, 2000, marked the culmination of a large renovation project. Under the leadership of Father Stephen J. Knox, the 40-year-old chapel was completely remodeled.

As of March 2007 Monsignor Glenn L. Nelson is the pastor. About 9,000 members of the NIU Catholic community (students, faculty, and staff) are part of the Newman Catholic Student Center / Christ the Teacher Parish, as are about 550 registered families.

◆ **Christ the Teacher Church interior.**

St. Mary Parish

From 1850, the parish of St. Mary in DeKalb was attended from the cathedral in Chicago. At that time Mass was said in the homes of Catholic pioneers and in the town hall. When the weather was pleasant, outdoor Mass was celebrated in a nearby grove of trees..

In December, 1861, DeKalb received its first resident pastor, Father John B. Murray (1861-1865). It was during his stay that the first church was built.

Bishop Thomas Foley of Chicago purchased land in 1874 for the use of St. Mary Church. The land became St. Mary Cemetery.

Father P. James O'Connor (1894-1895) saw the start of the present blue Bedford stone church. He moved the old church and rectory farther back on the property and the foundation was begun at the corner of Fourth and Pine Streets.

In December, 1899, Father James A. Solon (1899-1940), the next pastor, completed the church which was dedicated by Bishop Peter J. Muldoon, Auxiliary Bishop of the Chicago Archdiocese, on October 9, 1901. Father Solon also built a rectory west of the church in 1904. It was built of the same blue Bedford stone, matching the church.

The parish school, started in 1911, was completed in 1913. Ninety pupils enrolled that year; there were thirteen in the graduating class. In 1922, St. Mary Hospital was erected and dedicated on October 19th of that year. A large portion of the school, as well as one-third of the cost of the hospital's construction, was the personal contribution of Father Solon.

After forty years of service to the parish, Monsignor Solon died September 25, 1940. He was succeeded by Father Charles H. Quinn (1940-1955). Father Quinn purchased land in 1944 that almost doubled the size of the cemetery. In 1949, he purchased a new house for use as a convent across the street from the church.

Father Quinn added a new wing to the school with eight classrooms and more modern facilities in 1953-1954. The school has been staffed by the School Sisters of Notre Dame as well as by dedicated lay faculty members.

During the pastorate of Father Clement W. Caine (1962-1967), a new convent and rectory were constructed. The old convent and temporary rectory were demolished. The south parking lot opened in 1968.

◆ St. Mary Church and rectory, circa 1890.

◆ Laying the cornerstone of the current church.

◆ **St. Mary rectory, circa 1920.**

◆ **From the early years of the Twentieth Century.**

The older wing of the parish school was completely remodeled in 1971 and adapted to serve as a parish center. Father Harold L. Nilges (1970-1983) also had offices constructed for parish and area religious education directors and secretaries.

A tragic fire, set by an arsonist on the night of November 23, 1973, severely damaged the church. The entire sanctuary area of the church was destroyed and the beautiful new pipe organ was almost totally ruined by the extreme heat. The school gymnasium was converted into a temporary church.

A Liturgy of Thanksgiving in the restored church was celebrated on July 6, 1974. On May 16, 1976, St. Mary Parish celebrated the 75th anniversary of the construction of the present church with a special Mass offered by Bishop Arthur J. O'Neill. He also dedicated and blessed the newly restored church.

During the pastorate of Father William H. Schwartz (1983-1995), a seven-year renovation project was completed. The parish celebrated this event with a rededication in the summer of 1989. The school continued to grow and in order to make more classroom space, the parish offices moved from the convent to the rectory. A private home was purchased on Fisk Avenue to serve as the rectory. To accommodate the growing number of students, the parish purchased the former Notre Dame High School on Gurler Road in 1994. This facility is still being used as the parish school.

Father Karl P. Ganss (1995-2003) welcomed Bishop Thomas G. Doran on September 8, 1996 for the dedication Mass of the newly renovated St. Mary School. The house on Fisk Avenue was sold. The parish offices returned to the former convent and Father Ganss moved back to the rectory.

In October of 2001, the parish celebrated the 100th anniversary of the dedication of the new church.

As of March 2007 Father Kenneth J. Anderson is the pastor. There are approximately 1400 families currently registered at St. Mary Parish.

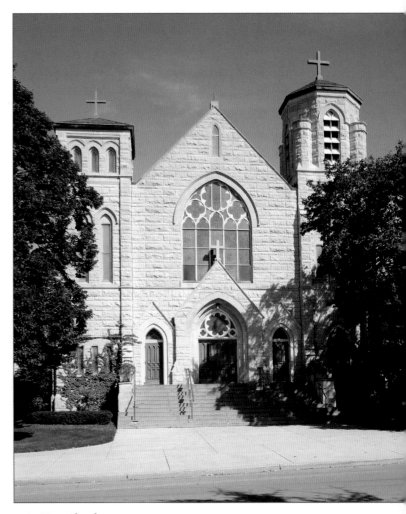

◆ **St. Mary Church.**

ST. ANNE PARISH

◆ **St. Anne Church**

The beginning of St. Anne's dates to 1928 when Rockford's first Bishop, Peter J. Muldoon, appointed Father Thomas G. Flynn (1928-1933) to organize a parish on the north side of Dixon. Property was purchased at East Morgan Street and North Dement Avenue for the erection of a new church, and ground was broken in the summer of 1928.

Mass was celebrated in the Knights of Columbus Hall for a time until the completion of the church section of what was to have been a combination building. A house, historically interesting as one of the oldest in the area, was purchased to be used as a rectory. On July 28, 1929, the church was dedicated by Bishop Edward F. Hoban.

During the depression years, Father Clement W. Caine (1933-1940) dedicated himself to the task of guiding the expanding parish and meeting the many problems of the time. Father Caine, in spite of the depression, managed to reduce the parish debt.

On May 22, 1940, Father Ronald L. French (1940-1957) was appointed pastor and remained for 17 years. During this period, the parish continued to grow with new demands being made on the parochial facilities. Father French completely resolved the parish debt as he saw the parish double in size. Wishing to open a parochial school, Father French purchased the old North Central School. He also extensively remodeled the

◆ **Father Thomas G. Flynn.**

rectory. By 1957, the parish had grown from the original 55 families to 265 families.

Father Myles F. Callahan (1957-1974) began his 17 years as pastor on March 4, 1957. Realizing the present and anticipating the future needs, Father Callahan, in December of 1957, obtained an option on 10 acres of land about one-half mile north of the old church with the intention of erecting a new parish plant. In July of 1958, the optioned property was purchased. In May 1959, plans were initiated for the new building. Ground was broken on October 18, 1959, and after a year of construction, the new St. Anne's, including a combination church and school and a separate parish administration building, was completed.

The first Mass was celebrated in the new church on December 23, 1960 for the many parishioners whose prayers, help and generosity really built the church. Father Callahan welcomed Bishop Loras T. Lane to St. Anne's on June 11, 1961 to formally dedicate the new parish buildings. St. Anne School opened for the first time on August 31, 1964. Three School Sisters of Notre Dame and one lay teacher were on the faculty.

St. Anne Parish celebrated its 50th anniversary on September 10, 1978 with Bishop Arthur J. O'Neill concelebrating the Jubilee Mass with the pastor, Father William M. McKinstra (1978-1987).

◆ **Knights of Columbus shrine.**

Under Father McKinstra's leadership, the church was remodeled and redecorated. On July 26, 1981, Bishop O'Neill celebrated the Mass of Rededication.

As of March 2007 Father Michael E. Morrissey is the parochial administrator. There are approximately 600 families currently registered at St. Anne Parish.

◆ **Church on E. Morgan Street and N. Dement Avenue.**

◆ **St. Anne Church interior.**

St. Patrick Parish

The rapid early growth of the Dixon Catholic community made it the mother church of many parishes in the southwest portion of the Rockford Diocese. The first resident pastor, Father James Fitzgerald (1854-1856), was sent to Dixon in 1854 by Bishop Anthony O'Regan of Chicago, when the parish had about twenty-five families. Previous to that time, Mass had been celebrated in private homes, both in the town of Dixon and in the surrounding countryside, by traveling missionaries.

Father Fitzgerald began the work of organizing the Catholics of the vicinity into a congregation. The first Mass was said in the Old Court House.

Father Fitzgerald was succeeded in July 1856, by Father Thomas Kennedy (1856-1859) who built the old frame church on Highland Avenue, between Fifth and Sixth Streets. Father John Tierney came immediately on the departure of Father Kennedy, probably as assistant, because Father Michael Ford (1859-1862) came as pastor the same month and the same year, April 1859. Father Tierney died in 1860 and Father Ford died in 1862 and was buried in Dixon, but the people of Sterling, who were attended by Father Ford and very fond of him, stole his body in the middle of the night and re-buried it in Sterling.

Father Louis F. Lightner (1863-1869) was a Polish nobleman and a doctoral graduate of a Roman university. During his pastorate he made plans for a new church and saw to the laying of the foundation before he was transferred.

During Father Michael McDermott's pastorate (1870-1874), the church was completed and a house was bought for a rectory. The old church was then used as a school building and the former rectory became a convent for the Sinsinawa Dominican Sisters who taught in the school.

The cornerstone of the church was laid by Bishop Thomas Foley, of the Diocese of Chicago, on June 23, 1872, and on November 2, 1873, he dedicated the completed church.

It was during Father Eugene Gray's pastorate (1882-1885) that the school was discontinued. Father James Treacy (1885-1892) succeeded him in February of 1885. On May 7, 1887, a tragic fire gutted the church, but it was not long until it was rebuilt. Although in ill health most of the time, Father Treacy was an energetic and accomplished man; illness forced his retirement from the active priesthood in June of 1892.

Father Michael J. Foley (1892-1929) came to Dixon in June, 1892, and remained as pastor until his death in 1929. The parish school was reopened in 1897, again with the Dominican sisters from Sinsinawa in charge. During his pastorate, Father

◆ **St. Patrick Church interior, 1911.**

◆ **School fundraising campaign, circa 1960.**

Foley built the present rectory, but died on September 16, 1929, before it was ready for use.

Father James J. Clancy (1929-1930) was the first pastor to occupy the new parish rectory. Father Thomas L. Walsh (1930-1950) became pastor in 1930. He paid off the parish debt incurred with the building of the rectory. In 1935, a house was acquired as a convent, and the sisters moved from the school building in which they had been living. The following January this new convent was partially destroyed by fire, but was rebuilt in the spring. Additional classrooms were provided in the school building and the interior of the church was renovated.

Father Thomas S. Green (1950-1957) was assigned to Dixon as pastor in May 1950. He constructed an addition to the convent, and provided additional classrooms for the school. The residence north of the church was purchased for future use.

Father Sylvester J. Eye (1957-1960) came to St. Patrick's on August 6, 1957. During his pastorate a new grade school was constructed on the site of the old St. Mary School.

In March of 1960, Father William Boland (1960-1972) succeeded Father Eye. During Father Boland's pastorate an extensive church renovation program was completed, including the installation of a new altar, sanctuary fixtures, interior painting and tuckpointing of the building and re-leading of the beautiful stained glass windows.

On October 28, 1973, Father James A. Molloy (1972-1977), pastor, and the people of St. Patrick Parish celebrated the Centennial of their church. Bishop Arthur J. O'Neill celebrated the Mass.

St. Patrick's Day, 1985 brought Bishop O'Neill to St. Patrick Parish for the dedication of the Holloway Catholic Community Center. During the pastorate of Father Gerald P. Kobbeman (1977-1987), Mary Holloway donated $1 million in securities and land in memory of her husband. Mrs. Holloway's parents were married at St. Patrick Church in 1893.

Extensive renovations to the church were completed while Father John L. Stringini was pastor (1987-1999). While parishioners were aware of the need for renovations, the issue was strikingly made public when Bishop Thomas G. Doran was celebrating

◆ **St. Patrick Church.**

Confirmation. A huge paint flake came fluttering down from the ceiling and the bishop, unaware that his microphone was on, said to the pastor, "My lord, John, when are you going to do something about this church?" Plans for renovation began immediately. The rededication took place on September 20, 1998 with Bishop Doran celebrating the Mass.

Father Robert W. Jones oversaw the completion of the renovation of the rectory in 2003. On July 11, 2004, Bishop Thomas G. Doran celebrated Mass in honor of the parish's 150th anniversary.

As of March 2007 Father Robert W. Jones is the pastor. There are approximately 900 families currently registered at St. Patrick Parish.

◆ **St. Patrick Church altar.**

St. Catherine of Siena Parish

◆ **Statue of St. Catherine of Siena in the narthex of the church.**

St. Catherine was organized in 1912 by Father Joseph M. Lonergan, while he was pastor of parishes at Barrington and Crystal Lake. In the early days, Catholics in the area of what was to become Dundee were served by the priest who lived in Elgin, but who was actually the pastor of the "Barrens" parish. The "Barrens" church was located about one mile east of Gilberts and about one mile north of Elgin; it was the only church in northern Kane County until 1851, when St. Mary was constructed in Elgin.

After St. Mary's was built, Dundee was part of the Elgin parish, and the few Catholics living in Dundee at the time used to hire a "bus" to take them to Mass in Elgin. It is said that winter's cold as well as summer's heat saw capacity loads cheerfully braving the ten-mile ride.

The first Mass at Dundee was offered July 8, 1912, with thirty-five Catholics present. A table with cigar boxes, covered with linen handkerchiefs, served as the altar. Over the next two years, Mass was regularly offered in a variety of private homes.

Bishop Peter J. Muldoon dedicated the first church of St. Catherine in May 1914. Two principal donors to that church were Mrs. Catherine Morrison, who provided funds for a fifth of the entire debt, and Mrs. Charles Becker, who donated the altar furnishings and clerical vestments.

The pastor at Barrington and Crystal Lake took care of Dundee area Catholics until 1917. At that time Father Leo M. Keenan (1917-1929) was appointed pastor of the Dundee and Gilberts parishes. Father Keenan resided at the St. Joseph Hospital in Elgin until 1920, when a rectory was purchased.

During Father Keenan's stay at Dundee, the church was fully decorated, the sanctuary carpeted and work in the rectory completed. In 1927, the school was built under Father Keenan's direction and was staffed by the Sisters of Mercy.

The population expansion in the Dundee area between 1940 and 1950 brought additional students to the school. Eventually, a new convent was purchased to accommodate the additional Sisters of Mercy who had come to staff the expanding school.

◆ **Original St. Catherine of Siena Church, 1914-1983.**

◆ **Stained glass window of the Last Supper.**

During the term of the Dundee parish's fifth pastor, Father John F. Regan (1950-1957), a mission church was established at Meadowdale (later called Carpentersville) and by 1957 it was large enough to acquire its own resident pastor.

When the new school at St. Catherine, begun in 1963, was completed in 1967, the old church and school buildings were abandoned. They remained abandoned and unused until 1972 when, during the pastorate of Father Bruno E. Daukas (1972-1987), they were sold, along with the convent and rectory buildings.

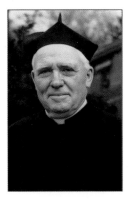

◆ **Father Joseph M. Lonergan.**

◆ **St. Catherine of Siena Church.**

On May 8, 1983, ground was broken for a new 700-seat church located at the intersection of Routes 72 and 31. It was the culmination of a 20-year building program, started in the 1960's with the school and gym. The gym, which was used as the sanctuary, was returned to a multi-purpose gymnasium after the new church was finished.

Father Daukas, Pastor, welcomed Bishop Arthur J. O'Neill on September 9, 1984 for the dedication of the new church.

As of March 2007 Father Richard A. Rosinski is the pastor. There are approximately 2100 families currently registered at St. Catherine of Siena Parish.

ST. MARY PARISH

The first Mass was celebrated in what is now the Durand parish in 1836 in the Patrick Fenlon home at Fenlon Settlement, about three and one-half miles north of Durand. In all probability, Father Samuel C. Mazzuchelli, O.P. of Galena offered this first Mass. For the next several years Mass was offered once a year in private homes by priests from either Galena or Chicago. It is known that Father John Guiguen, who resided near what is now Lake Forest, used to travel out this way, even as far as Galena.

Until 1862, Mass was said at irregular intervals not only in homes at Fenlon Settlement, but also in the home of Matthew Doyle and also the Lennon, Fox and Ryan homes.

The cornerstone of St. Mary Church was laid in 1862 at Durand by Father Michael J. Hanley of Freeport. The church was opened for services sometime in 1863, although the deed was not transferred until 1867 to the Archdiocese of Chicago.

In 1872, Durand was attached as a mission to the parish at Pecatonica. This situation prevailed with the exception of four years, from 1885 to 1889, when Father Eugene Gray (1885-1889), was appointed pastor. He took up residence in Davis in order not to show preference for either parish.

Father Daniel A. Feeley (1909-1913) was appointed by Bishop Peter J. Muldoon as the first resident pastor on July 1, 1909 and was given St. Patrick, Irish Grove as a mission. He immediately set about building a rectory on a lot adjoining the church property. The rectory was completed in 1910 and reliable sources say it was dedicated by Bishop Muldoon in 1911. Father Daniel J. Considine (1913-1920) succeeded Father Feeley in November of 1912. He purchased the land for the present cemetery in 1917.

Father Edward A. Cerny (1925-1930) was appointed pastor in 1925. In May of 1926, the first shovel of dirt was turned to begin construction on a new church and the first Mass celebrated in the new church was Midnight Mass, December 25, 1926.

◆ **St. Mary Church.**

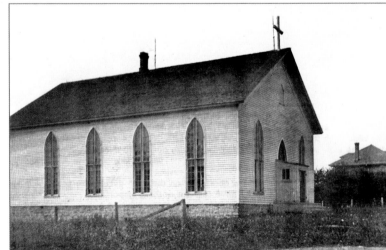

◆ **Original St. Mary Church, 1862-1926.**

Due to the illness of Bishop Muldoon, the solemn dedication of the new church was postponed until October 28, 1928, when Bishop Edward F. Hoban, second Bishop of Rockford, came to St. Mary's for the dedication.

Father Joseph A. Driscoll (1933-1960) was appointed pastor on December 8, 1933 and served for twenty-seven years.

During Father John J. Kilduff's pastorate (1960-1965), the church was renovated in keeping with the liturgical changes of the Second Vatican Council.

Father Paul E. Fry (1965-1966) came in 1965 and began a program of remodeling the rectory and church that would continue for several years.

Father Alphonsus F. Harte was the administrator of the parish for one month until

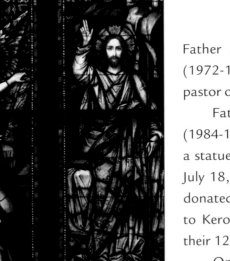

Father Aloysius J. Neumann (1972-1984) was appointed pastor on September 20, 1972.

Father Karl P. Ganss (1984-1995), Pastor, dedicated a statue of the Holy Family on July 18, 1993. The statue was donated as a special memorial to Keron and Anne Walsh by their 12 surviving children.

On August 29, 2004, during the pastorate of Monsignor Eric R. Barr, Bishop Thomas G. Doran rededicated St. Mary Church and consecrated its new altar. The parish had spent several years renovating the 80-year-old church. Parishioners volunteered many hours helping with the renovations.

As of March 2007 Monsignor Eric R. Barr is pastor. There are approximately 500 families currently registered at St. Mary Parish.

◆ **St. Mary Church interior, showing the new altar.**

◆ **New mural of the Annunciation.**

ST. MARY PARISH

Of the earliest days of this parish very little is known. Dubois, a French fur trader, arrived in this vicinity in company with Julien Dubuque in 1788 and they were the first white settlers. Apparently they only remained a few years and nothing is known of any settlers between that time and 1832 when the town was platted out and named "Dunleith," which was later changed to East Dubuque. It was too close to Dubuque, Galena, and Sinsinawa to have much independence in the days of extreme scarcity of priests.

In the 1830's and 1840's, Catholics were not numerous, but we know that Father Samuel C. Mazzuchelli visited the settlement every six weeks. There are records to show that as early as 1833 services were held in Dubuque, and from the time Dubuque had resident priests, the people on the Illinois side of the Mississippi were also attended quite regularly. Sometimes the priest from Sinsinawa Mound, Wisconsin, would come, and so it is not odd that the early records of St. Mary, East Dubuque, are found in Dubuque, Sinsinawa Mound, and Galena.

A company was formed at Dunleith by Gregoires Freres and a site donated for a Catholic church. This church was named St. Thomas and was built by 1857. It is not clear how long the church bore this name but it is likely it endured until 1882, when the second church was built.

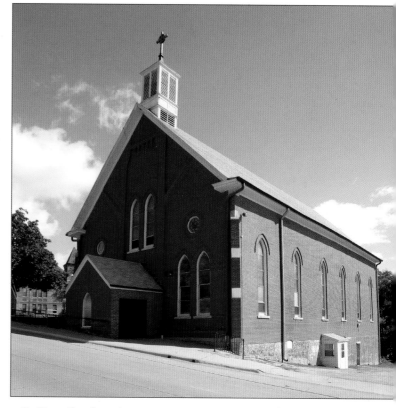

◆ **St. Mary Church.**

Tradition has it that on March 17, 1866, about one hundred Catholics from East Dubuque attended Mass at Dubuque, crossing the Mississippi River on the ice. On returning, the ice broke away and floated down the river with the East Dubuque Catholics aboard. A bone chilling wind had arisen and these people endured a panic-filled nightmare, expecting imminent death, when about four hours later, the ice floe crashed into a sand bar. All were saved.

A school of sorts was conducted during Father O'Reilly's day. Classes were held in the church; after Mass the Blessed Sacrament was removed and a partition placed lengthwise through the church so that the upper and lower grades were divided.

When the parish of St. Mary was established in 1868 with Father J. C. Murphy (1868-1870) as pastor, it was deemed wise to discontinue the school.

Father John McMahon was in charge from 1877 to 1880 and he also took charge of the mission at Vinegar Hill where he offered Mass every

◆ **Bishop Loras T. Lane at St. Mary, circa 1960.**

◆ **St. Mary interior prior to Vatican II.**

◆ **St. Mary Church interior.**

Sunday. Father Peter J. Gormley (1880-1882) was the next pastor and he also attended Vinegar Hill.

In 1882, Father Jean F. Berube (1882-1898) came to replace Father Gormley. He purchased property for a convent and a school; he built a church and rectory.

Father James A. Solon (1898-1899) had the church plastered, improved the rectory and reduced the debt. Father Solon was succeeded by Father P. James O'Connor (1900) and Father Thomas A. Burke (1900-1903), who built a chapel and had a hall made under the church.

Father Peter J. Gallagher remained as pastor of St. Mary for 33 years, from 1903 until he died there in 1936. In addition to liquidating the parish debt, he modernized the entire parish plant. He built a parish school in 1924. In 1935 and 1936, a renovation program was completed in the school.

A church hall was built and a new foundation provided during the pastorate of Father John J. Hackett. In 1952, property for a school addition was purchased and, in 1955, two rooms were added to the school. Father Hackett had completed 24 years of pastoral service when he died in November 1960.

It was during the time that Father John F. Tuchlinsky (1960-1970) was pastor, that the parish built its new school on Illinois 35, on the north edge of the city. The property at that site was also sufficient for future construction of a church, rectory and convent.

While Father Raymond O. Holmgren (1970-2001) was pastor, the interior of the church was renovated in November of 1973. In the fall of 1987, a new roof was put on the rectory and in 1988, additional remodeling was done to the rectory. Father Holmgren served as pastor for 32 years until his retirement in 2001.

The church was renovated and redecorated in 1993 in time to celebrate the 125th anniversary of the founding of the parish. Since St. Mary is the home parish of Bishop Arthur J. O'Neill, his 25th anniversary as a Bishop and 50th anniversary of his ordination to the priesthood were also celebrated the same year. In his honor, the church hall was named the Bishop O'Neill Hall.

As of March 2007 Father James W. Parker is the parochial administrator. There are approximately 650 families currently registered at St. Mary Parish.

◆ **St. Mary Church, circa 1900.**

ST. GALL PARISH

Elburn area Catholics were dependent on missionaries or lengthy travel to attend Mass until the early 1850's. In 1851, Father William Feely, Pastor of "The Barrens" Church near Gilberts, began the construction of a church at Barney's Hill, midway between Elburn (then called Blackberry) and Maple Park (then known as Lodi). It was the Milnamow family who donated the site for that first area church in 1851. This church was named St. Mary Church.

Only the exterior of St. Mary Church, better known as "Hill Church," had been completed when the territory was divided and Elburn was placed in the care of pastors in St. Charles. The first pastor in that city, Father Patrick O'Dwyer, then finished the frame church near Elburn. This church building was moved afterwards to DeKalb and only the cemetery remains.

◆ **Father Daniel Drennan.**

Prior to the building of St. Gall's, Masses were celebrated in several Elburn homes, as well as in Reed's Hall. In 1869, Michael Tierney, John McMahon and William O'Donovan secured title to property on the southeast side of Elburn and obtained permission to begin planning the stone church that was to be completed the following year.

The first St. Gall Church in Elburn was built in 1870, while the parish was a mission of St. Patrick Parish, St. Charles. The first Mass in the building was celebrated New Year's Day, 1871, by Father Patrick O'Dwyer, who had been pastor in St. Charles from 1853 to 1860. It was Father O'Dwyer who had completed the first Elburn area church, St. Mary Church, in 1853.

In 1872, the year after the first St. Gall church was finished, Elburn became a mission of Maple Park's pastor, Father Richard H. McGuire. In later years, St. Gall's was transferred back to St. Charles and later to Holy Cross Parish, Batavia.

In 1911, three years after the creation of the Rockford Diocese, Elburn became independent and received its first resident pastor, Father Daniel P. Drennan (1911-1921).

The first St. Gall church served Elburn Catholics for about 55 years or until the arrival of Father Robert C. Troy (1924-1929), the parish's third pastor. Like the original Hill Church, the first St. Gall building also went on to other use. Its lumber and other materials were used in the construction of shelter houses at Elburn Forest Preserve and Lions Park.

In 1924, Father Troy purchased property on Shannon Street (Illinois 47) and supervised the construction of the present church. The first Mass there was celebrated on Christmas Eve, 1925.

Father Edward A. O'Brien (1929-1930) was appointed Elburn's fourth pastor. The depression caused too much of a financial drain on the congregation, so Elburn again reverted to mission status. It was attended by Father James W. Friedrich

◆ **St. Gall Church, 1870-1925.**

◆ St. Gall Church.

(1930-1940), chaplain at the Illinois Training School for Boys in St. Charles.

The parish had been growing during the late 1930's, and it continued with more vigor after the appointment of Father Leonard J. Guzzardo (1940-1959) as resident pastor in 1940.

The Sisters of St. Francis, stationed at Virgil, began conducting religious instruction classes in

◆ Father Edward C. Fanning celebrating Mass, circa 1959.

Elburn. In 1952, a new rectory was built adjoining the church. In 1956, a new baptistry and cry room were constructed and new tile floors laid in the church. Two years later, in 1958, the church was completely redecorated during Father Guzzardo's pastorate.

From the depths of the depression days which saw the parish relegated back to mission status, St. Gall grew to a thriving parish of 110 families by 1958.

In July of 1970, a new parish hall, which had been begun by Father Harold L. Nilges (1967-1970), was completed under the pastorate of Father Robert F. Devine (1970-1974).

Father Thomas J. Dempsey (1974-1978) was appointed pastor of St. Gall's on July 3, 1974. Under his direction, the church was renovated and

◆ St. Gall Church interior.

redecorated during the winter of 1974 and spring of 1975. Bishop Arthur J. O'Neill rededicated the church on Sunday, October 19, 1975.

The church was once again renovated and redecorated in 1989 during the pastorate of Father Richard W. Paddock (1987-2003).

In February of 2003, after two years of planning, St. Gall Parish purchased and installed a new organ in the choir loft. Keeping focused on the future, the church decided to buy the new organ for use in their present church as well as at their future location on the corner of Route 47 and Hughes Road.

As of March 2007 the pastor is Father Karl P. Ganss. There are approximately 800 families currently registered at St. Gall Parish.

St. Joseph Parish

Like many other national groups, German Catholics in Elgin wanted to be instructed in the truths of their religion in their native tongue. They wanted to sing the hymns with which they were familiar and it seemed only proper that they be instructed in a language they could understand without difficulty. In the summer of 1887, a group of Germans obtained an option on the Presbyterian Church on Villa Street. Later Archbishop Feehan, Archdiocese of Chicago, authorized its purchase for $4,000.

♦ **Father Bernard Westarp.**

Father Bernard Westarp (1887-1895) was appointed first pastor over a congregation of about seventy families. After he was at St. Joseph a few months, Father Westarp opened a parochial school in the church basement; Mr. H. F. Anthe was the teacher during these first years.

Father Arthur Riss (1895-1901) succeeded Father Westarp in 1895. He was able to secure the services of the Sisters of the Third Order of St. Francis of Mary Immaculate, from Joliet, Illinois, as teachers in the parish school.

Since the parish had grown to over a hundred families and had outgrown its facilities, Father Joseph Rohde (1901-1914), the third pastor of St. Joseph, purchased property in 1902, and work was begun on the church and school, both of which are still in parish service. Structures then standing on the new property were used for a rectory and convent. Ground was broken in May, 1902. Bishop Peter J. Muldoon, then Auxiliary Bishop of Chicago, laid the cornerstone on June 21, and the congregation celebrated the first Mass in the new church on August 15, of the same year.

Father Henry J. Hauser's pastorate (1914-1926) was a period of great expansion for the parish. Additional land was purchased, and there was a large increase in the congregation. Some of the growth

♦ **St. Joseph Church.**

♦ **Father Arthur Riss with school division 1, circa 1895.**

◆ **Father Frederick J. Brummel on the 25th anniversary of his ordination to the priesthood, June 10, 1935.**

◆ **St. Joseph Church interior.**

was due to the first Elgin Hispanics, who worked in the foundries and settled in the Dexter-Douglas area, in the shadow of St. Joseph. This Hispanic growth would continue in subsequent decades.

Monsignor Alfred A. Heinzler (1939-1945) became pastor in 1939. Plagued by poor health, Monsignor Heinzler nevertheless was able to keep the parish in excellent physical repair, and, financially repaired many of the ravages of the depression. He died August 9, 1945.

Another period of expansion for the parish took place during the pastorate of Father Joseph W. Rojemann (1945-1955). The membership increased, and the era of prosperity following World War II enabled Father Rojemann to make many improvements. A large gymnasium and three classrooms were added to the school. The interior of the church was completely renovated. The convent was enlarged and a residence adjacent to the parish property was purchased for the caretaker. Additional property was secured for playground facilities and parking space.

During the pastorate of Father Henry M. Schryer (1957-1983), work on a new school was begun in 1962. It was dedicated on Sunday, April 21, 1963, by Bishop Loras T. Lane when the parish celebrated its 75th Anniversary. Father Schryer was charged with the task of ministering to three distinct parish populations. He heard confessions in English and German,

and helped with the growing Spanish-speaking population. Beginning at this time the Diocese of Rockford has tried to provide pastors for St. Joseph who are fluent in Spanish.

On August 20, 1989, during the pastorate of Father David R. Engbarth (1986-1992), Bishop Arthur J. O'Neill blessed the newly remodeled St. Joseph Church. Two major features of the renovations were making the 86-year-old building handicap accessible and putting in a central air-conditioning system.

Due to the large increase in parishioners, beginning in October 1996, the parish rented the lodge-like building called Wonderland Ballroom located about one block south of the church. The parish used this facility for two additional Masses until June of 2002 when these Masses began being held in the school gym. These two Masses were in addition to the nine held in the church.

For over twenty-two years, St. Joseph Parish, with the help of more than 80 volunteers, has held an annual Thanksgiving Day dinner for the needy of the Elgin community. The grateful recipients total around 1000 each year.

As of March 2007 Father John P. Earl is the parochial administrator. There are approximately 2500 families currently registered at St. Joseph Parish.

St. Laurence Parish

Elgin's third parish was established by Bishop Edward F. Hoban on September 28, 1928. Prior to the establishment of St. Laurence Parish, all Catholics in the community had attended either St. Mary or St. Joseph Churches. Father Laurence C. Prendergast (1928-1944) was appointed by Bishop Hoban as the founding pastor of St. Laurence Parish.

On coming to Elgin, Father Prendergast lived at St. Joseph Hospital and began to offer Mass for Catholic residents on the west side of the Fox River in the building owned by the Knights of Columbus at 10 Villa Street. Parishioners in the new parish attended Mass in these temporary quarters until September 8, 1929, when they built a Tudor Gothic structure housing a church with capacity for 450 people and a school giving accommodations to 240 pupils. This structure was built on the northwest corner of Jewett and Standish Street.

Father Prendergast took up residence in February 1929 in a house at 573 Standish Street. While the church building was being completed he offered daily Mass in the rectory.

Monsignor John P. McGuire laid the cornerstone for the new St. Laurence Church on March 4, 1929. The sacrifice of the Mass was offered for the first time in the new St. Laurence Parish Church on September 15, 1929. Three days later the parish school opened with an enrollment of 140 students. The Sisters of Mercy, whose motherhouse was then at Aurora, had accepted responsibility for instruction of the children. Bishop Hoban formally dedicated the new parish building on Sunday, November 24, 1929.

During Father Prendergast's administration of St. Laurence, money was borrowed for the purchase of property and construction of parish buildings. In December 1933, the parish debt was $131,440. During the years of the depression it had been necessary to borrow money to pay interest on the debt.

Mt. Hope Cemetery, established in 1910, was administered by the pastor of St. Mary Parish, Elgin. In April, 1929, Father Prendergast was named superintendent of the cemetery and made responsible for its maintenance and administration. This cemetery is located within the territory of the Archdiocese of Chicago and Rockford Diocese continues to be responsible for its care.

On April 4, 1954 Father Philip L. Kennedy (1954-1963) was appointed pastor of St. Laurence. In 1954, the Silver Jubilee of the parish was celebrated with a Mass offered by Bishop Raymond P. Hillinger. Stained glass windows had been installed and the church completely redecorated and refurnished for the occasion. Additional work was done in the convent and the school.

◆ **The first wedding at St. Laurence was November 28, 1929, when William Weber married Marie Hebeisen.**

◆ **Knights of Columbus building used for the first Mass, 1928.**

◆ **St. Laurence Church**

◆ **Monsignor Philip Kennedy with St. Laurence school children, circa 1960.**

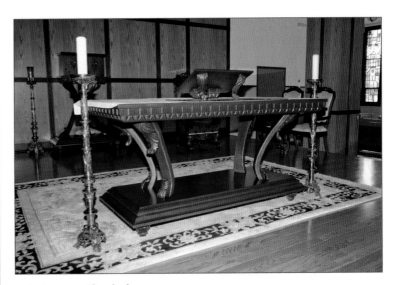

◆ **St. Laurence Church altar.**

In 1956, two temporary classrooms were added at St. Laurence School to provide for an enrollment of 375 students and in 1957 another temporary classroom was added.

Father Philip E. O'Neil (1969-1983) was appointed to the pastorate of St. Laurence on June 6, 1969. The church was completely renovated and remodeled in the summer of 1971 and the church was formally rededicated on November 28, 1971 by Bishop Arthur J. O'Neill.

A new parish center and library-learning center was blessed by Father O'Neil on August 22, 1982.

Father Joseph F. Kulak, pastor, and the parishioners of St. Laurence Church celebrated the completion of a major renovation project with a Mass by Bishop Thomas G. Doran on June 1, 2003.

As of March 2007 Father Joseph F. Kulak is the pastor. There are approximately 1200 families currently registered at St. Laurence Parish.

◆ **St. Mary Academy at 112 Villa Street, 1886.**

◆ **Laying the cornerstone of the current church, July 31, 1898.**

The first record of Mass being celebrated in Elgin dates back to 1840. The celebrant was Father Maurice de St. Palais, a pioneer priest who came from Vincennes, Indiana.

In 1842, the Reverend John Guiguen, also of Vincennes, occupied a log cabin near the present town of Lake Forest, Illinois. From there he made trips on horseback visiting Catholic settlers wherever he could find them, "baptizing the children, saying Mass and speaking words of encouragement to the people of the wilderness." In 1843, under the guidance of Father Guiguen, the Catholic people west of the Fox River began building the first church, known as the "Barrens" church. Its location was near the present village of Gilberts. The following year, 1844, Father Guiguen was recalled to Vincennes and the church was never fully completed.

In January 1845 Father John Faughnan (1845) was appointed the first pastor of Elgin. In 1848, the fourth pastor was named. He was Father William Feely (1848-1853). The parish which Father Feely served included Elgin, Dundee, Huntley, St. Charles, Geneva, Sycamore and the "Barrens", near Gilberts, plus other communities no longer existing.

Father Feely built a cobblestone church at the corner of Gifford and Fulton Streets in 1851. He was succeeded in 1853 by Father James Gallagher (1853-1858), who completed the church; it was dedicated August 26, 1855.

His successor was Father Terrence Fitzsimmons (1868-1877) who came from Hartland, March 8, 1868. An apostle of temperance, Father Fitzsimmons founded, in 1872, an organization known as the Young Men's Catholic Temperence and Benevolent Association. In 1874, ground was broken for what

◆ **St. Mary Church.**

◆ **First Communicants, 1900.**

became known as St. Mary Academy. Before the building was completed, a depression passed over the country.

Father Fitzsimmons' successor was Father John Mackin (1877-1899) who remodeled and enlarged the old church. Then he persuaded the Sisters of Charity of the Blessed Virgin Mary to take over the unfinished school and assume its obligations. A few years later he built a rectory on Gifford Street, on a lot adjoining the church property. Late in the fall of 1896, Father Mackin began the erection of the present church, but he did not live to say Mass in it. The cornerstone was laid July 31, 1898; he died August 24, 1899, and the first services held in it were those of Father Mackin's funeral.

Father F. A. Lynde, who had been an assistant under Father Mackin, was appointed administrator until the arrival of the next pastor, Father John J. McCann (1899-1918), on December 29, 1899. Father McCann obtained land for use as a parish cemetery.

In 1912, the Sisters of Charity of the Blessed Virgin Mary, who had opened the Academy in 1880, left Elgin, and the Dominican Sisters of Adrian, Michigan took over.

Father Hercules E. Ouimet (1918-1949) became pastor at St. Mary on July 7, 1918. He installed new windows in the church and had it redecorated. A new home for the sisters was purchased. He also built a new grade school and had the rectory moved to its present location.

Father John T. Smith (1949-1952), who came to St. Mary in 1949, immediately began an extensive program of redecorating and refurbishing the church, school, rectory and convent.

Father Walter J. Ryan (1952-1957) succeeded Father Smith on September 4, 1952. He continued the program of renovation and brought it to a conclusion, as well as substantially reducing the debt.

Father Anthony J. Becker (1967-1973) was named the pastor on May 22, 1967. Father Becker remained until July 17, 1973, when the Society of the Missionaries of the Sacred Heart from Aurora assumed the parish and appointed Father Robert Cell, M.S.C. (1973-1983), as the parish's first and only M.S.C pastor. In 1976, the church was renovated, redesigning the altar space to incorporate liturgical changes brought forth by Vatican II.

St. Mary Parish celebrated the dedication of a new hospitality center on October 15, 1989 with Bishop Arthur J. O'Neill and Father Michael A. Binsfeld (1983-1994), Pastor. The new facility is connected to the historic 1898 church structure and the rectory. It features a large 2000 square foot hospitality room on the upper level. The lower level consists of a multi-purpose room and other facilities, including an archive room to house all parish records dating back to the founding of St. Mary Parish under the name Immaculate Conception in 1851.

To help celebrate the church building's 100th birthday, Father Thomas J. Dempsey (1994-2001), Pastor, and his parishioners completed a nine-month refurbishing project. Bishop Thomas G. Doran celebrated a centennial Mass on July 26, 1998.

St. Mary is the oldest parish in Elgin. It is located in the heart of the Elgin historic district, on the east side of town.

As of March 2007 Father Edward J. Seisser is the pastor. There are approximately 1300 families currently registered at St. Mary Parish.

◆ **St. Mary Church interior.**

St. Thomas More Parish

◆ Construction of the original church, 1960.

◆ Laying the cornerstone of the original church, June 5, 1960.

On March 23, 1959, Bishop Loras T. Lane created the new parish of St. Thomas More by dividing St. Laurence Parish and giving the new parish 15 acres to build a church. The founding pastor, Father Walter C. Roberts (1959-1970) arrived at St. Thomas More on Friday, April 10, 1959, and celebrated the first Sunday Masses two days later at the Highland Avenue School Gym. Weekday Masses were offered at St. Laurence Church until a temporary church could be constructed.

Father Roberts resided at the Chateau Louise in Dundee from April 11, 1959 until May 11, 1959 when he moved into the first rectory on Commonwealth Avenue.

In September of 1959, the groundbreaking ceremonies for the new church and school were held and Father Roberts celebrated the first Mass in the temporary church on September 4, 1960.

The school officially opened in September of 1960 for grades 1 through 5 with Sister Helena, O.P., serving as the first principal. One grade was added thereafter each year until the school reached the capacity of eight grades.

Bishop Lane solemnly blessed the church and school on April 22, 1961.

In August of 1964, Father Roberts put the sisters "on Easy Street" by purchasing a private home to be used as a convent which just happened to be located at 1431 Easy Street. Before this, the sisters lived in a rented house on Jewett Street across from St. Laurence School.

In July of 1966, construction on a new rectory was begun and on October 22, 1966 Father Roberts moved into his new residence.

On January 6, 1970, Father Willis L. Bradley (1970-1975) was named the second pastor of St. Thomas More Parish. During his five and one half years as pastor, Father Bradley continued the work of retiring the parish debt.

During the pastorate of Father James V. McKitrick (1975-1979), a new St. Thomas More Church was built. The new church was dedicated on February 4, 1979 by Bishop Arthur J. O'Neill who

◆ The groundbreaking for the current church, June 22, 1977.

was the principal celebrant of the Mass. The new church seats 700 people. The Community Activity Center was added to the former church and school building and serves as a multi-purpose area for parish activities

On June 1, 1979 Father Joseph B. Linster (1979-1991) was appointed the fourth pastor of St. Thomas More. The new pastor had his work cut out for him. Not only was there an existing parish debt of $959,000, for the new buildings, but many crucial decisions had to be made about organizing the new facilities. Under Father Linster's pastorate, not only was the debt retired but a new fund drive was begun to build a parish center and to add a kindergarten and pre-school.

Bishop O'Neill celebrated Mass and dedicated the new parish center on September 13, 1992. Father Robert R. Miller (1991-1995), Pastor, concelebrated with Bishop O'Neill. The new parish center consists of a 7,000 square foot wing built onto the existing school. In addition to the new wing, the original church was remodeled and dedicated as

◆ **St. Thomas More Church interior.**

Roberts Hall in honor of Father Walter C. Roberts, the founding pastor of St. Thomas More.

On June 25, 2006, during the pastorate of Father Geoffrey D. Wirth, Bishop Thomas G. Doran celebrated the Mass of Dedication for the renovated and expanded church building. A gathering space, five meeting rooms, storage space, and new offices for parish staff were all added.

As of March 2007 Father Geoffrey D. Wirth is pastor. There are approximately 2500 families currently registered at St. Thomas More Parish.

◆ **St. Thomas More Church.**

St. Mary Parish

◆ **Our Lady of Sorrows Church was the fourth church for Elizabeth, 1882.**

It seems that the church of Elizabeth began as early as 1843, attended by priests from St. Michael Church, Galena.

By 1846, the care of Elizabeth was given to the first pastor of New Dublin. In 1848, it was given to St. Mary Church, Galena and continued to be attended from Galena until 1866.

In 1849, Elizabeth had a log church on the south side of town called St. Elizabeth. In 1853, land was acquired for a larger church and a year or two later, a second log church was built at what is now 209 Madison Street. By 1864, there was need for yet a larger church and, in 1865, using the combined resources of the Germans and the Irish, a brick building was bought on the site where the present church stands, on the northwest corner of the intersection of Catlin and Washington Streets. It was remodeled and called St. Thomas Church.

Elizabeth was attended briefly, in 1866-1867, from St. Joseph Church, Apple River. In 1867, Elizabeth was again given into the care of St. Mary Church, New Dublin and was attended from there one Sunday a month. In 1880, it was given to the care of Father George Ratz (1880-1884), the first resident pastor of St. John the Baptist Church, Savanna.

On December 19, 1880 the land for St. Mary Cemetery was acquired.

By 1881, the brick church building, somewhat dilapidated when it was purchased, so continued to decay that it was replaced by a frame structure which seated one hundred people. This church was

◆ **Laying the cornerstone of the current church, October 15, 1913.**

◆ **Father John K. Nilles on the steps of the rectory, circa 1913.**

◆ **St. Mary Church interior.**

dedicated to Our Lady of Sorrows. By 1908 the parish became popularly known as St. Mary, though diocesan records officially called it Our Lady of Sorrows until about 1928.

In 1884, Father Francis J. Antl (1884-1887) became the pastor of Savanna and continued to care for Elizabeth. He built a school and convent just north of the church. The school was at first conducted by a lay teacher, then by the Sisters of St. Francis.

Father Joseph Ruetershoff (1887-1891) became the first resident pastor of St. Mary, Elizabeth in August, 1887. He built the rectory.

As class sizes diminished, the school/convent was no longer necessary. The 1910-1911 term was the final one for St. Mary School.

On the 16th of February, 1913, at a parish meeting, the decision was made to build a new church on the site of the old church. The cornerstone for the new and present church was laid by Bishop Peter J. Muldoon on October 15, 1913. Bishop Muldoon dedicated the new church on May 14, 1914. This brick church, massive in appearance, seats 260 people. Father John K. Nilles (1912-1914) was pastor during the building of the new church.

In 1930, about a year after Father John L. Daleiden (1929-1933) came to St. Mary, the school building was torn down.

Father Paul A. Tuchlinsky (1944-1950) was made pastor in March of 1944. During Father Tuchlinsky's time, St. Mary's acquired its pipe organ. Father Tuchlinsky remained until April 20, 1950 when he was succeeded by his brother, Father John F. Tuchlinsky (1950-1960).

The nine stained glass windows in the church were refurbished and cleaned in 1982 while Father Raymond M. Hettermann (1974-1988) was pastor. He also had a new statue of the Blessed Mother hand-carved from white stone. It is a life-size image and replaces the smaller 30-year-old cement statue that was damaged by the elements over the years. The statue was blessed at a May crowning on May 17, 1986.

In 1991, during the pastorate of Father Ronald J. Conro (1988-1999), a handicapped accessible entrance was constructed. Central air conditioning was installed in 1992.

As of March 2007 Father Christopher J. Kuhn is pastor. There are approximately 200 families currently registered at St. Mary Parish.

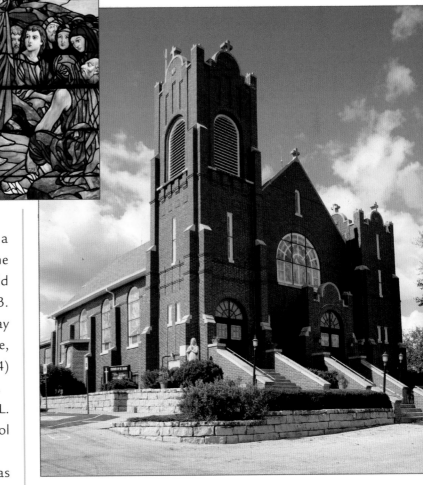

◆ **St. Mary Church.**

St. Ambrose Parish

On December 8, 1917 Mass was offered for the first time in Erie by Father John V. Walsh (1917-1920). Father Walsh had been appointed pastor of St. Catherine Parish, Prophetstown, and its Erie mission two months earlier. From December 1917, until October 1919, Mass was said in a hall of the Shellhammer Building in Erie.

In 1919, Father Walsh purchased a house in Erie at the corner of Main and Water (now 5th) Streets. Renovations on the house were begun by Father Walsh and completed later by Father John T. Egan (1920-1921). While various improvements were made to the former residence, so that it resembled a neat chapel, it became apparent by 1933 that its size was inadequate for the growing Catholic population.

During the pastorate of Father Ambrose M. Weitekamp (1933-1946), a new church was built in Erie, named by Bishop Edward F. Hoban as St. Ambrose, in the pastor's honor. Until then the mission parish had no name and was known simply as "the mission of St. Catherine." On November 29, 1936, Bishop Hoban dedicated the little brick church and administered Confirmation to 50 people. A local newspaper article provided a preview of the dedication: "An event not likely to occur again in the next century will take place in Erie Sunday,

◆ **Father Ambrose Weitekamp.**

◆ **St. Ambrose Church.**

◆ **Parishioners gather in 1924 in front of the house that had been renovated to serve as their chapel.**

◆ **St. Ambrose Church interior.**

when members of St. Catherine's Catholic congregation hold dedicatory services in their beautiful new Roman design brick church." This church is still in use.

Between 1946 and 1961, many changes were made to the interior of the church. Special services were held on December 10, 1961 to celebrate the Silver Anniversary of the church building. This occurred while Father Thomas W. Neville (1960-1964) was pastor.

In 1981, during the pastorate of Father Vincent J. Shindelar (1980-1986) a church hall was built behind the church. This building serves as the location for all parish social and fund-raising events. In 1986 the church basement was totally remodeled to make classrooms available for the parish youth program.

A 50th anniversary was celebrated to mark the church building date in 1986 while Father William

F. Morrissey (1986-1994) was pastor. On July 10, 1988, Father Morrissey dedicated a newly erected Pieta Monument in the St. Ambrose section of the Erie Cemetery.

In 1993, major renovation and redecorating was done to the church during the pastorate of Father Morrissey. The altar area was redone, and all of the church's statues, stations of the cross and baptismal font were repainted and new carpeting was added. By the fall of 1994, stained-glass windows were installed. Also in 1993, a parish library with hundreds of videos, books and magazines was established.

St. Ambrose Parish continues to be attended from Prophetstown.

As of March 2007 Father Francis Wawryszuk is the pastor. There are approximately 100 families currently registered at St. Ambrose Parish.

St. Joseph Parish

St. Joseph had its beginning in 1862, when the German population separated from St. Mary Parish in Freeport and built its own church.

The Bishop of Chicago, James Duggan, agreed to the split and appointed Father John Westkamp (1862-1863) as the first pastor. St. Mary Parish kept the church and gave the new parish $500 plus the school building and the organ.

The German Catholics now had a priest without a pulpit and an organ without a church. On June 4, 1862, the old Baptist church was purchased. By August 3, they were ready to celebrate the first Mass in their new parish. The old school was moved next to the church and an additional lot bought. Father Westkamp left Freeport in May 1863, and was succeeded by Father Ignatius Baluff (1863-1874) in June of the same year.

A rectory was not provided until March 1865. To provide more much needed space, two galleries were built on either side of the church in 1868 and new benches were bought. In 1870, four acres of land were purchased for a cemetery. The present stone church was begun in the fall of 1871. Bishop Thomas Foley laid the cornerstone in June 1872, and he dedicated the church on the Fourth Sunday in Advent, 1872. The church cost $25,000. In the following year, repair work was done on the rectory.

◆ **Father Nicholas Berg at groundbreaking for the school, 1954.**

Then, in February 1874, Father Baluff left Freeport.

On March 11, 1874, Father Clemens Kalvelage (1874-1929) became the next pastor of St. Joseph Parish. The most immediate problem at the time was debt reduction. It was nearly all-absorbing, as there was a great gap between the expenses incurred by the building program and the wealth of the parishioners. But hard work and generosity brought the sum down to $2,200 by 1880, and new additions and repairs could be thought of: a pulpit, stations, and other improvements.

In January 1881, a steeple was begun, and on August 7, an eight-foot cross was put in place to become the highest point in Freeport. Bells were provided and were blessed December 4, 1881.

In January 1883, pledges were begun for a new school. On September 30, it was dedicated and classes opened on October 2. In 1885, new pews were purchased; in 1886, a high altar. Later that year more suitable side altars were donated.

Monsignor Kalvelage served the parish of St. Joseph for over fifty-six years. He retired June 30, 1929.

When Father Nicholas J. Berg (1929-1959) became pastor in July 1929, the entire school was redecorated and new benches installed in the upper grades in time for the September opening. The following year, the sacristies, which were still equipped with gas lights, were modernized. Considerable modernization was undertaken in the rectory that same year.

For the diamond jubilee in 1937, the church was redecorated. The convent was remodeled to provide private rooms and a chapel.

◆ **Monsignor Kalvelage with school class, circa 1893.**

In 1950, a new roof was put on the church. A new floor, pews, heating plant, and electric clock and Angelus chimes were provided.

While Father Berg was pastor, a school was built on property which became available in 1952. It was adjacent to the church. The Sisters of the Immaculate Heart of Mary served St. Joseph School for 104 years, having left in June of 1972. A year later the convent was razed.

Father John L. Daleiden (1960-1972) was installed as pastor on January 17, 1960, and the Centennial Year of St. Joseph's was celebrated in 1962. That year the church was renovated and decorated. St. Joseph's was not only the first church in the Rockford Diocese, but also possibly the first in the Midwest, to be renovated for the new liturgy in accordance with Vatican II.

In 1967, a new rectory was built and the old rectory was demolished. It was also during Father Daleiden's administration that ten acres of land were acquired in Chapel Hill Cemetery. Father Daleiden later erected a shrine in St. Joseph's Garden of Chapel Hill Cemetery.

Renovation plans, including making the church handicapped accessible, began in the fall of 1999. Parishioners and Father John W. Cahill (1995-2006), Pastor, joined in a Mass of rededication celebrated by Bishop Thomas G. Doran on April 2, 2000. A crucifix, formerly hung in the church and dating back to 1872, was found, cleaned and is now the centerpiece of the sanctuary.

A special Mass on September 15, 2002 celebrated the parish's completion of three years of renovations. A new statue of St. Joseph was erected in front of the church in the spring of 2003. Below the statue is a marble sign, made from the old marble side altars in church, which identifies the statue.

In the spring of 2005, Father Cahill had a new roof put on the school and had extensive renovations and remodeling done to Berg Hall.

As of March 2007 Father Burt H. Absalon is pastor. There are approximately 400 families currently registered at St. Joseph Parish.

◆ **First Communion, 1962.**

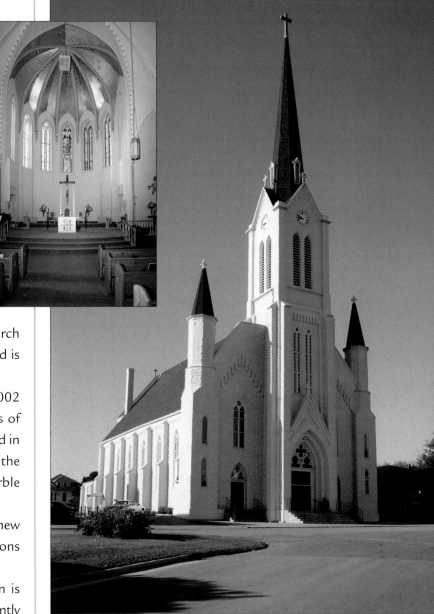

◆ **St. Joseph Church interior and exterior.**

ST. MARY PARISH

One of the first Masses offered in what was to become the Rockford Diocese took place early in the fall of 1827 when Father Francis Vincent Badin celebrated Mass in the cabin of Simon Brady, near Kellogg's Grove in Stephenson County.

The year of that first Mass was well before white settlers had arrived in Freeport and before the Blackhawk War.

The mother parish of St. Mary was St. Mary of the Mound at New Dublin, which had a small log church as early as 1836. Missionaries and priests from Galena paid irregular visits to that church.

In 1846, Father John Cavanaugh (1846-1854) was assigned to the New Dublin area. He resided at New Dublin for a time, offering Mass at the home of his sister, Mrs. Thomas Egan, when he visited Freeport. In 1851, the first St. Mary Church was built on the present site in Freeport.

Father Cavanaugh also had charge of the growing parishes in Elizabeth, Rockford, Mount Carroll, Plum River, Savanna and Warren. It was Father Cavanaugh who moved the parish center to Freeport.

Father Ferdinand Kalvelage (1854-1859) built the second St. Mary Church, laying the cornerstone for the brick structure in July 1855. Lumber for that building was hauled by oxen from Savanna. Father Ferdinand Kalvelage was the uncle of Monsignor Clemens Kalvelage of St. Joseph Parish, Freeport.

During the term of Father Thomas O'Gara (1859-1866), the German population of Freeport was given permission to build a national church, St. Joseph. Father John Westkamp organized that parish. St. Mary's kept the existing church, but gave $500, the school building and the church organ to the new parish.

It was Father O'Gara who purchased the first section of land for Calvary Cemetery in 1859.

During the next 24 years a number of priests served as pastor, including Father Michael J. Hanley (1867-1869), who built a two-story brick rectory in 1867 and began to organize the parish school; Father F. J. Murtaugh (1870-1871), who bought a building for conversion into the school in 1869; Father Thomas F. Mangan (1877-1887), who supervised extensive remodeling on the church, and Father Michael Welby (1887-1890), who began plans for a new church before he died in 1890.

The cornerstone of the present church was laid in August 1890, during the pastorate of Father William A. Horan (1890-1899). The structure cost $40,000 and was consecrated by Archbishop Patrick A. Feehan of Chicago on September 13, 1896. At that time, it was one of only two consecrated churches in Illinois. St. James in Chicago was the first. On the day of consecration, multiple Low Masses were offered between 5 A.M and 7 A.M. in the

◆ **St. Mary School fire, December 1956.**

convent chapel and the basement chapel, followed by the formal consecration at 7 A.M. by Archbishop Feehan. Immediately after the consecration, Archbishop Feehan offered a Low Mass at one of the newly consecrated altars. About 10:00 A.M a Pontifical High Mass was celebrated by Bishop Maurice F. Burke, of the Diocese of St. Joseph, Missouri; this Mass did not end until 1 P.M. Finally at 7:30 P.M. Bishop John Janssen, of the Diocese of Belleville, presided at a "most impressive vespers service."

◆ **St. Mary's second church with the original church on the far left, circa 1855.**

◆ **May Crowning, May 3, 1896.**

During Father Charles F. Conley's term (1924-1964), 12 acres were added to the cemetery, a new organ was installed and the church was renovated. He became a Domestic Prelate, with the title of Rt. Rev. Monsignor in 1932. Monsignor Conley was the first priest ordained for the Rockford Diocese on April 10, 1909.

Tragedy struck St. Mary Parish in December 1956, when fire destroyed the school. With the slogan "A rosary a day, and a monthly day's pay," the parish launched a fundraising campaign for a new school. It was rebuilt in two years during the pastorate of Monsignor Conley. In September 1963, St. Vincent Orphanage discontinued their campus school and all children were sent to the three Freeport parish schools; twenty children from the orphanage were enrolled at St. Mary's.

In May 1965, under the pastorate of Father John F. Regan (1964-1969), the church was redecorated to comply with the liturgical directives of the Second Vatican Council. Father Regan was elevated to the status of Monsignor by Bishop Loras T. Lane in May 1966.

In December 1966, the Dominican sisters moved into a new convent. In June 1975, however, the sisters had to withdraw their service to St. Mary Parish. The parish grade school was closed in spring 1976 due to continuing financial problems and dropping enrollment.

In spring 1987 a major redecorating project began, in preparation for the parish's 100th anniversary of the building of St. Mary Church. The large round window of the Assumption of Mary behind the altar, which had been plastered over in the 1965 redecorating, was uncovered.

On September 16, 1990, while Father Donald D. DeSalvo (1988-1992) was pastor, Bishop Arthur J. O'Neill led the parish in celebration of the 100th anniversary.

On January 11, 1992 Father DeSalvo announced that St. Mary would close on June 30, 1992 due to financial debt, a shortage of priests, a changing neighborhood, the physical condition of parish property and the geographical proximity of St. Mary to St. Joseph Parish. A series of intense meetings and consultations with the Diocese were held over the next several months. During this time, in April 1992, the body of Father Horan was exhumed from the winter chapel and buried in Calvary Cemetery. On June 14, 1992 Bishop O'Neill announced that St. Mary would remain open "while more extensive consultation takes place" about the challenging issues facing the parish.

September 13, 2006 marked the 110th anniversary since St. Mary Church was consecrated. Father Burt H. Absalon welcomed Monsignor David D. Kagan, Vicar General, representing Bishop Thomas G. Doran and Bishop Emeritus Arthur J. O'Neill for a special anniversary Mass on September 17, 2006 to celebrate the occasion. Also, the renovated parish center was dedicated.

As of March 2007 Father Burt H. Absalon is parochial administrator. There are approximately 300 families currently registered at St. Mary Parish.

◆ **St. Mary Church.**

St. Thomas Aquinas Parish

◆ **St. Thomas Aquinas Church.**

◆ **St. Thomas Church on Harlem Avenue, 1922-1974.**

◆ **Interior of the Harlem Avenue church.**

St. Thomas Aquinas Parish was established on December 4, 1921, by Bishop Peter J. Muldoon. Father William G. McMillan (1921-1929) was the first pastor.

The cornerstone of the one-story church building had already been laid in May, 1921. The building was completed in the following year and was dedicated May 28, 1922. Father McMillan continued to live at the St. Joseph Rectory until a residence was purchased in March 1923, at the corner of Harlem Avenue and West Stephenson Street.

In September 1929, Father Daniel O'Connell (1929-1936) was appointed to succeed Father McMillan. During his pastorate, a second floor was added to the building, providing four classrooms, two rooms of which were opened in September 1931, by the Dominican Sisters of Sinsinawa. For almost twenty years, the sisters teaching at St. Thomas lived in the convent at Aquin High School. In 1932, Father O'Connell sold the rectory and moved into a rectory at 11 North Harlem, immediately adjacent to the parish property.

Father Alexander S. McIsaac (1936-1954) became the next pastor in August 1936, during a period of expansion for the church. Unfortunately, ill health began to affect Father McIsaac and Father Arthur J. O'Neill (later Bishop of Rockford) was appointed administrator on October 4, 1954. Later,

St. Thomas Aquinas Church interior.

May Crowning, May 31, 1964.

upon the resignation of Father McIsaac, Father O'Neill (1957-1967) was appointed pastor on June 9, 1957.

By the 1956-1957 school year, the enrollment had grown to 225 students and it became necessary to erect temporary classrooms in the parish hall. Enrollment continued to increase so four classrooms and a gymnasium were constructed in 1963.

In January of 1967, Father James J. Murphy (1967-1971) became pastor and worked with the parishioners in paying off the parish debt. Serious thought was given to the possibility of constructing a new church and parish center on a site west of the city.

In 1970, the three parishes in Freeport consolidated their educational programs, with St. Mary School and St. Thomas School retaining grades 1 through 5 and St. Joseph School taking over grades 6 through 8.

Father Louis J. Pesut (1971-1973) became the pastor on June 15, 1971. At that time, lay committees were established, an architect was contracted, the new church was designed and plans were put out for bids.

On October 2, 1973, Monsignor Raymond J. Wahl (1973-1978) became pastor of the parish. Because of the preliminary work that had been done under Father Pesut, it was possible to have ground breaking ceremonies for the new church on October 21, 1973. The laying of the cornerstone took place on June 30, 1974. On December 15, 1974, Bishop Arthur J. O'Neill, the former Pastor of St. Thomas

Parish, came back to dedicate the church and the new adjoining parish center which also contains the rectory. The new church site is adjacent to Highland Community College.

During the pastorate of Father Thomas L. Dzielak (1978-1990), a new rectory was built in 1988. Father David E. Beauvais was pastor from July 1990 until 1992.

Father P. William McDonnell was appointed as pastor on July 15, 1992. Shortly thereafter he oversaw a large building project including the expansion and remodelling of the church, completed in 1995. Bishop Thomas G. Doran dedicated the new addition on December 6, 1995. Among many other improvements, the 11,332 square foot addition includes an education wing and a fellowship hall named the O'Neill Center in honor of Bishop O'Neill. The entire facility is handicapped accessible. In November 2000 Pope John Paul II elevated Father McDonnell to the rank of monsignor.

On November 26, 2000 a new Our Lady of the Blessed Sacrament Chapel was dedicated by Bishop Doran. Mr. Dick Edler and his family donated the building in memory of his late wife, Jeanne. Other parishioners provided funds in memory of their loved ones for furnishing the 95-seat chapel and for the stained glass windows.

As of March 2007 Monsignor P. William McDonnell is pastor. There are approximately 1000 families currently registered at St. Thomas Aquinas Parish.

Immaculate Conception Parish

◆ **Rectory and church, circa 1901.**

The geographical location made Fulton one of the earliest settlements in the territory that comprises the Rockford Diocese. Situated in Whiteside County, on the Mississippi River, the area attracted a number of traders in the early 1830's. At that time, it was known as the "Narrows of the Mississippi".

Other name changes came before it was decided to name the town after the inventor, Robert Fulton. It also had been known as Mississippi and Baker's Ferry (John Baker of Maryland was the town's founder). Fulton's official founding came in 1835, with survey work starting in 1836.

Early Catholics were attended by priests from the Dixon and Sterling area, with Mass being said in private homes. Their numbers swelled after the railroad arrived in 1851 and a sawmill was erected in 1853. The need and desire for a permanent church grew throughout the 1850's.

In 1861, a committee formed by Father William Herbert of Sterling sought the permission of Bishop James Duggan of Chicago to build a church in Fulton. It was granted, and land was bought at the corner of 16th Avenue and 8th Street. The first Mass was said in the new church on Christmas Day 1863.

Father John Daly was appointed the first pastor at Sterling in June 1863; he also attended the Catholics in Fulton. Father Francis X. Nighe began attending

Fulton in 1867, coming at regular intervals. In 1868, he arranged to stay in town from Saturday to Monday when he made his visit. He furnished the sacristy with a bed and stove, sometimes cooking his own meals, other times eating with Thomas Martin and his family. It was at this time that he began keeping records at Fulton.

Father James J. McGovern (1869-1870) became the first resident pastor at Fulton in August 1869. He purchased the property at the site of the present parish buildings, bought a house and had it moved to the new site. He asked for donations to pay for these expenses.

The second pastor of Immaculate Conception Parish, Father Peter J. Gormley (1870-1873), arrived in September 1870. Early in 1871, he had the old church moved to the new property and placed on the lot next to the rectory.

The next pastor at Fulton was Father John J. Kilkenney (1873-1884), who arrived in October 1873. He built churches at Morrison and Coffey's Corners, and also attended Savanna.

Father Maurice Stack (1884-1893) was appointed pastor in May of 1884. He built a new rectory in 1890, which was in service until the late 1940's.

Father James L. Moloney (1894-1908) was Fulton's next pastor, coming in July of 1894. In 1905, plans were begun for a new church and a collection was taken up. Father Moloney donated $1,175 himself. The new Church of the Immaculate Conception was dedicated by Bishop Peter J. Muldoon, then Auxiliary Bishop of Chicago, on February 17, 1907.

Father James J. Clancy (1909-1929) became the first pastor appointed to Fulton by the first Bishop of the Rockford Diocese, Bishop Peter J. Muldoon, in February of 1909. In 1925, the church

◆ **Father James Clancy.**

◆ **Confirmation, March 23, 1952.**

was completely redecorated, and an organ was purchased the following year. In 1927, a new heating plant was installed.

Father John T. Egan (1929-1948) came in 1929 and began to plan for a parish school. Property was purchased, but the depression set in, necessitating postponement of the school.

Father Myles F. Callahan (1948-1957) built the present rectory on the site of the old one in 1950. It was during Father Callahan's pastorate that the mission church of St. Peter's in Thomson (built in 1914) was closed. In 1949, it was decided to close the church and sell the building. Father Callahan had just completed large-scale renovations and redecorations in the Fulton church when Father Walter C. Roberts (1957-1959) was appointed pastor on March 4, 1957.

Father Edward R. Hughes (1969-1975) was appointed pastor September 2, 1969 and renovated the church in late 1973 and early 1974.

During the pastorate of Father Frank C. Draude (1975-1983), many improvements were also made to the church. The pipe organ was completely rebuilt, the church was redecorated and carpeting and new pews

were installed. While Father Kenneth J. Anderson was pastor (1994-2000), more than a dozen stained glass windows, originally installed in 1906, were restored.

In 2002 Father James R. Keenan became pastor and soon began a program of repair and restoration of the church in advance of its 100th anniversary. The bell tower was completely rebuilt and the original bells were removed so that a new Carillon electronic bell system could be installed. Restoration of the amber windows under the bell tower was also completed. On September 23, 2006 Bishop Thomas G. Doran celebrated the 100th anniversary Mass for Immaculate Conception Church.

As a matter of historical interest, President Ronald Reagan's parents were married at Immaculate Conception Parish in 1904.

As of March 2007 Father James R. Keenan is pastor. There are approximately 150 families currently registered at Immaculate Conception Parish.

◆ **Immaculate Conception Church.**

◆ **Immaculate Conception Church interior.**

St. Mary Parish

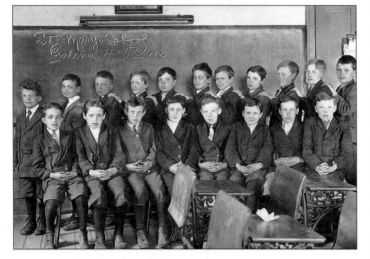

◆ **Fifth and sixth grade classes at St. Mary School, circa 1925.**

◆ **St. Mary Church interior, circa 1939.**

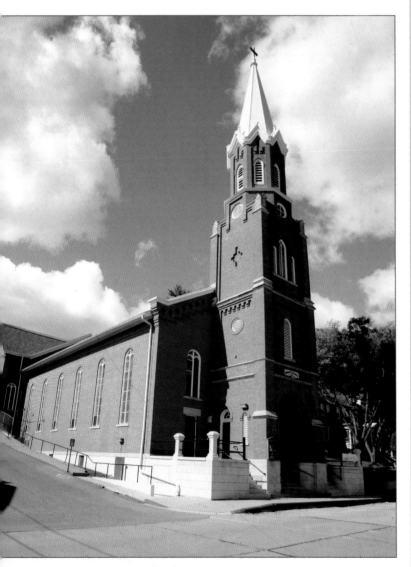

◆ **St. Mary Church.**

St. Mary Parish was organized in October 1850, for the specific purpose of caring for German Catholics in Galena and the lead miners around that city.

In that month and year, Bishop James O. Van deVelde, second Bishop of the Chicago Diocese, left Chicago with Father Rodericus Heimerling and headed toward Galena. Among purposes of the trip, according to the Bishop's diary, was a plan to visit the faithful along the way and conduct a meeting of German Catholics in the historic lead mining city.

Committees were formed for the construction of a church, and Father Heimerling (1850-1856) was appointed St. Mary's first pastor.

The first church of the parish was purchased from St. Michael Parish in Galena shortly after St. Mary's was organized. The building had originally been a Baptist church, but it had been converted into a school by St. Michael's. The frame building was moved to the present site of St. Mary Church on Franklin Street, just a few blocks from St. Michael's.

The parish's second pastor, Father Bernard Herderer (1856-1861), began his appointment in 1856. During his five-year term, missionary work was of major concern. His records show that services were conducted in the Irish settlement of Vinegar Hill, Elizabeth, Pilot Knob, Rush, Hanover, Spruce

Father William Bally and First Communicants, circa 1880.

Creek, Guilford and Plum River. Services were also held at Hazel Green, Wisconsin.

The basic part of the present parish church was constructed during the pastorate of Father Peter Fischer (1861-1862). It was built through the use of architectural plans by Father Samuel C. Mazzuchelli, the revered Dominican missionary who had been St. Michael's pastor from 1835 to 1843.

By the time St. Mary's was constructed, Father Mazzuchelli was working in the Benton, Wisconsin, area, but he nevertheless took an active interest in the Galena work. When the church was finished, Father Mazzuchelli donated a marble altar which later served as a side altar.

The frame building that had served as a church for the first 11 years of St. Mary's history was sold and moved across the street from the parish buildings. That first building was to see many more uses made of it, including time as a barber shop, saloon, blacksmith shop, paint store and wagon shop.

In 1862, Father William Bally (1862-1914) began a pastorate that was to span over 50 years. One of his first projects was the purchase of eight acres of land on the south side of the city for a cemetery. The first parish school was finished in 1864, and the sanctuary was constructed as an addition to the church in 1867. The 1870's marked other building projects by Father Bally. He supervised the construction of the huge steeple in 1875, and the rectory was built the following year. Stained glass was also installed in the church in 1867, with the high altar that was in use until 1928, being completed in 1878. The painting of the Assumption was

St. Mary's first church building, purchased from St. Michael Parish, circa 1850.

installed over the main altar in 1878, and it has been there since that year, for over 129 years.

Another term of unusual length was started in 1914 when Father John K. Nilles (1914-1940) was appointed the fifth pastor of St. Mary's. He served until his retirement in January 1940. Among the physical contributions he made to the parish was a new gallery for the children, the raising of the church floor, the enlargement of the cemetery, the renovation of both the church and rectory, and an addition to the school.

Father Paul A. Tuchlinsky (1950-1963) was appointed in April 1950, and began a massive renovation program. The work had been started in preparation for the parish's centennial which was delayed until June 1951.

In January 1967, Father William F. Morrissey (1967-1975) was appointed pastor and the church was totally redone during his pastorate. The work retained the historical associations of the building and, at the same time, provided for a renewed liturgy.

The school closed in 1974 and was sold.

Upon arriving in November of 1975, Father Patrick D. Corbally (1975-1983) found the rectory and parish hall in need of attention. A program of renovation was immediately begun. It was completed in March of 1976.

In the late 1980's and early 1990's, under the pastorate of Father Daniel D. Tranel, the interior of the church was renovated. A ramp for the handicapped was also installed, along with an electronic bell system and a new public address system.

As of March 2007 Father Daniel D. Tranel is pastor. There are approximately 400 families currently registered at St Mary Parish.

ST. MICHAEL PARISH

Galena is not only the locale of one of the oldest white settlements in Illinois, but also the home of St. Michael Parish, the oldest parish in the Diocese of Rockford. Bishop Joseph Rosati of St. Louis appointed a pastor here in 1832, five years before the first parish was established in Chicago.

The community began as a fur-trading post, probably in 1810, and in 1821 a permanent settlement was established. The missionaries who visited in the early years called it Fever River, not because of any noxious atmosphere, but after a French trader named LaFevre. The name of Father Stephen T. Badin is frequently listed among the early missionaries who visited Galena as well as the nearby Irish mining settlement of Vinegar Hill as early as 1825. A year after Father Badin's first appearance, the settlement was platted and in 1827 it was officially named after the ore that brought prosperity to the town: Galena.

In 1827 Bishop Rosati came to St. Louis, which had been made a diocese in July of the previous year, as its first bishop. One of the first problems confronting him on his arrival was a petition from a committee of Irish workers in the lead mines that a priest be sent to live among them and minister to the needs of Catholics in the district. Stern necessity dictated the Bishop's answer: a shortage of priests made compliance impossible.

Father Francis V. Badin, brother of Father Stephen Badin, the first priest ordained within the original Thirteen Colonies, spent several weeks in Galena in the fall of 1827 and again in the summer of 1829. His records show that outside of Prairie du Chien, his parish, Galena was the center of his

missionary activity.

Bishop Rosati made several attempts to secure a priest for the Galena territory, and finally in 1830 was able to send Father Joseph Lutz as a missionary priest with faculties extending over a territory which included Prairie du Chien, Galena and Sangamon City.

Finally, on August 22, 1832, Father John McMahon (1832-1833) was appointed as the first resident pastor in what is now the Diocese of Rockford. The first Masses were celebrated in a rented house in Galena. According to the author of the first diocesan history, Father Cornelius Kirkfleet, O. Praem., "The history of the proto-pastor of the Rockford Diocese is strange, indeed."

John McMahon left Dublin, Ireland, for the United States in 1825 with his wife Judith. Pious by nature and childless, they agreed to separate in order to devote their lives to religious matters. Judith returned to Dublin where she intended to become a Dominican sister, but because neither she nor her husband was able to provide a dowry, no convent would accept her. Instead, she took a perpetual vow of chastity and was appointed by the Archbishop of Dublin as Superioress of the Penitents' Asylum, Dublin. Bishop Rosati entered John McMahon in St. Mary Seminary at the Barrens. After dispensation from the marriage vows was granted by Pope Pius VIII, John McMahon was ordained on November 20, 1830.

In the 1924 diocesan history, Father Kirkfleet wrote, "Though not a great theologian, as appears from his letters to the Bishop, the good Rev. McMahon was a zealous

◆ **Father John McMahon**

pastor." The strenuous life occasioned by this zeal made one frontier winter all his strength could sustain. He fell victim to the cholera, raging at that time in epidemic proportions, and died June 19, 1833. This man who had given his life so that others could enjoy the consolation of religion, died without the comforting presence of a fellow priest or the Eucharist.

Bishop Rosati was unable to send another pastor to Galena until 1834. In the year intervening, a Jesuit, Father C. F. VanQuickenborne (1833-1834), was sent to investigate religious conditions at Dubuque and Galena. In addition to giving Catholics the opportunity to receive the sacraments while he was among them, Father VanQuickenborne settled the financial questions left after the death of Father McMahon, and made definite recommendations concerning the building of the first church.

Father Charles J. Fitzmaurice (1834), an Irish priest educated in France, was accepted into the Diocese by Bishop Rosati and was sent immediately to Galena. Father Fitzmaurice solicited funds for building churches in Dubuque and Galena. He labored night and day visiting his cholera-stricken parishioners until on December 21 of that first year of his pastorate, he too was felled by the disease and the Catholics of Galena were again without a priest.

In a sense, the sacrifices of Father McMahon and Father Fitzmaurice were a prologue to the history of the church in Galena and in the Rockford Diocese. For an entirely new era began with the appointment in 1835 of the saintly, dynamic Dominican, Father Samuel C. Mazzuchelli (1835-1843) as pastor in Galena.

Father Mazzuchelli is one of the giants in the history of American Catholicism. He was a man of immense energy, imagination and great personal magnetism.

In July 1835, Father Mazzuchelli arrived in Galena. Here he ministered to the needs of the two hundred Catholics and began collecting funds for a church, having found, he wrote, "not a vestige of the sacred things necessary for the celebration of the Holy Sacrifice." Father Mazzuchelli bought a site on Bench Street and made plans for a church.

◆ **St. Michael Church interior, circa 1932.**

Father Mazzuchelli was named the parish's third pastor in the summer of 1835. The cornerstone for the first church was laid that September. At that time St. Michael Parish included all of Jo Daviess County and parts of Stephenson County.

In April of 1838, Bishop Loras visited Galena: the first time a bishop officiated within the territory of what is now the Diocese of Rockford.

The construction of the first church received not only the pastoral supervision of Father Mazzuchelli, but also his physical labor and talents as general contractor and architect. While it was being built, a frame building was constructed on the lot and used as a combination church and dwelling.

The main church was first used in 1839, but the building wasn't completed until 1842. It was blessed by Bishop Peter R. Kenrick of St. Louis in July 1842. St. Michael Church cost $14,000, a fantastic sum in those days. But as Father Mazzuchelli was quick to point out, it was not wealth that erected St. Michael's, but "the expenditure of time, joined to economy, to tireless perseverance, to disinterestedness, and, above all, to good will."

In 1843, Father Mazzuchelli accompanied Bishop Loras to the Provincial Council of Baltimore as theologian. At the close of the sessions he sailed for his native Milan to collect his inheritance and to solicit funds from the Society for the Propagation of

◆ **Father James T. Donohue with the school band, circa 1940.**

the Faith for his missions in the United States. Using these funds he purchased many locations, the most noteworthy being an eight-hundred acre tract for Sinsinawa College.

When he left for Europe in 1843 Father Mazzuchelli turned St. Michael Parish over to his assistant, Father Remigius Petiot (1843-1848), who then became its fourth pastor in 1843.

On November 28, 1843, the new Diocese of Chicago was established with Bishop William J. Quarter as its first Ordinary, separating Galena from the territory of St. Louis and from the administration of Dubuque. Bishop Quarter made his first visit to Galena to administer the sacrament of Confirmation in August of the following year.

On his second visit to Galena Bishop Quarter brought with him his brother, Father Walter Quarter, and two Sisters of Mercy, who established a house here, eventually building a convent at Main and Broad Streets. The convent flourished for almost ten years when the rapid development of the area around Chicago made it necessary to recall the sisters to the Motherhouse.

Evidently Father Petiot felt himself unsuited for the life of a missionary, for in 1848 he resigned his pastorate and entered the Capuchins. Father Bernard McGorisk (1848-1854) succeeded him on May 28, 1848. Father McGorisk was the first priest ordained in the Diocese of Chicago.

Unsuited or not, Father Petiot must have been an able administrator, for Father McGorisk found his parish in excellent health, both spiritually and temporally. The first church was barely six years old and the parish almost out of debt. Galena was at its height of population and prosperity. The congregation was sufficiently large to warrant the building of a new church on the east side of town, which was

given into the charge of Father Dennis Dunn, then assistant to Father McGorisk. In the early months of his pastorate the first Catholic school in the territory was opened by the Sisters of Mercy and it lasted 10 years. It was also at this time that the scene of mining changed from Galena to California. The gold rush to California took many miners from Galena.

Father Patrick McElhearne became the sixth pastor of St. Michael Parish in 1854. On April 1, 1856, a fire broke out which destroyed a large section of Galena, including St. Michael Church. Undaunted, Father McElhearne began immediately to plan for reconstruction, and in less than a week ten thousand dollars had been collected for a new church which was also designed by Father Mazzuchelli.

In 1857, Father McElhearne was transferred to Springfield and was succeeded at St. Michael by Father John Larkin (1857-1862). At this time Mass was celebrated in the Sisters of Mercy convent. Later the basement of the present church was used until the church itself was sufficiently enclosed to permit its use. Evidently hard times had fallen on Galena for Father Larkin was obliged to stop construction temporarily because of lack of funds.

In 1862, Father Walter Powers (1862-1869) became the eighth pastor. In spite of the fact that this was the period of Civil War, which took a heavy toll in Galena, Father Powers managed to complete the building of the church by the end of 1863, and also to direct the construction of a sacristy at the Vinegar Hill mission. The new St. Michael's opened in December of 1863.

In 1869, Father Powers exchanged parishes with Father Patrick Farrelly of Joliet. In the twenty years of his pastorate at St. Michael Father Farrelly (1869-1889) made many improvements. He brought with him an organ which he later placed in the church; at the time of his death it was learned that he had willed it to the parish. In 1870, Bishop Thomas Foley came to Galena to bless the church.

In 1871 new altars were installed and special paintings for the Stations of the Cross were hung. The cathedral glass windows were put in under Father Farrelly's direction. An imposing flight of

Father Charles O'Callaghan

stone steps was built at the entrance to the church. In 1884, the square church towers were finished.

Father Farrelly opened the first Catholic parochial school, Annunciation School, and built the school and parish hall. Annunciation School ended up serving the Catholics of St. Michael Parish for many decades, before closing in 1969.

At the death of Father Farrelly in 1889, Father Charles J. O'Callaghan (1889-1893) was appointed to take his place. Shortly after he arrived Father O'Callaghan purchased a new rectory, but he was the only pastor of St. Michael Parish to live in it.

In 1893, Father O'Callaghan was transferred and succeeded by Father John E. Shannahan (1893-1928). One of Father Shannahan's first official acts was to sell the new rectory in order to reduce the parish debt. He rented rooms until a new rectory was completed in 1897; this is the rectory in use today.

In a few years Father Shannahan had paid off the entire debt. Within a year of the establishment of the Diocese of Rockford in 1908, he had the church redecorated. In 1921 he purchased for the parish the convent which had previously belonged to the Dominican Sisters.

Father James T. Donohue (1928-1943) became the twelfth pastor of St. Michael in November, 1928.

◆ **St. Michael Church.**

During his pastorate extensive renovation took place in the school, church and cemetery. These years will be remembered as the time of a great nationwide depression. Also they were years of great hardship in Galena, for the time of lead-mine prosperity had long since passed. Father Donohue and his successors, Father Joseph A. Driscoll (1943) and Father Joseph T. Healey (1943-1946), were hard pressed to maintain such a large physical plant through such difficult years.

◆ **St. Therese Shrine**

Father Russell J. Guccione (1946-1952) was appointed to St. Michael when Father Healey was sent to St. James Pro-Cathedral in Rockford as Administrator in 1946. He completely redecorated the rectory and began an extensive program of renovation in the church: work on the foundation of the Sanctuary, remodeling the Sanctuary and new pews.

When Father Edward J. Connolly (1952-1954) was transferred to Belvidere in 1954, Father Vincent L. Cottam (1954-1957) came to Galena. On May 30, 1955, a fire broke out at the main altar destroying the Sanctuary and causing great damage to the entire church. Father Cottam saw to the rebuilding of damaged portions and the complete redecoration of the interior of the church.

Father John P. Dolan (1957-1968) assumed the pastoral responsibilities of St. Michael Parish from July 1, 1957 until June 28, 1968 when Father Robert F. Devine (1968-1970) was appointed the pastor. During Father Devine's pastorate the main body of the church was carpeted, new heating systems were installed in the church, rectory and convent, and the basement of the present church was renovated and converted into a parish hall. Father Devine began the renovation of the rectory before he was transferred and this renovation was later completed during Father Weideman's pastorate.

To replace Father Devine, Father Alfred P. Kruk (1970-1974) was appointed pastor on July 10, 1970. During Father Kruk's time he enlarged the floor area of the sanctuary of the church, put a new roof on the church and rectory and continued the renovation of the rectory.

Father Kruk served as pastor for three and a half years until July 3, 1974, when Father Adolph H. Weideman (1974-1976) was appointed pastor.

◆ **Grades 1-6 from Annunciation School, circa 1921.**

◆ **Annunciation School.**

◆ **St. Michael Church interior.**

Under Father Weideman's direction, the interior of the church was completely renovated, including installing the most modern sound system available and rewiring the church. A new roof has been put on the convent and it was remodeled to provide a home suitable for family living. Under Father Weideman's leadership and direction, the rectory renovation which had been begun during Father Devine's pastorate, was completed. Father Weideman continued to administer the parish until his untimely death on May 9, 1976.

In June, 1976, Father James W. McLoughlin (1976-1983) was appointed to succeed Father Weideman as pastor of St. Michael Parish. Father McLoughlin had served as the diocesan Director of Religious Education for seven years before being assigned to Galena.

During the pastorate of Monsignor Raymond J. Wahl (1983-1996), a Mass of Thanksgiving was celebrated by Bishop Arthur J. O'Neill on August 25, 1991. St. Michael Church had been undergoing renovations since 1985, the year that air conditioning was added to the 134-year-old building. Over the last six years, the pews were stained to resemble the original pews, the interior of the church was painted and carpeted, the light fixtures were replaced and the kneelers were recovered.

No history of St. Michael Parish would be complete without a mention of St. Mary Parish, Vinegar Hill. This was a distinctly Irish community a few miles north of Galena. At one time it was a parish of over a hundred families; but it was abandoned around 1900 as its families were absorbed by surrounding parishes. Almost always it was supplied with priests out of Galena. Previous to the establishment of St. Michael Parish, visiting missionaries made Vinegar Hill one of their regular stops and Mass was celebrated at the home of John Furlong, as early as 1824. A church was built in 1843. More information can be found in this history book, in the section on closed parishes.

As of March 2007 Father Daniel D. Tranel is pastor. There are approximately 400 families currently registered at St. Michael Parish.

St. Peter Parish

◆ **St. Peter Church.**

It appears from the Diary of Bishop James Van de Velde, Bishop of Chicago, that he visited Geneva in 1852 with a view of locating a parish there. However, a mission church had been built in St. Charles the year before, and the plan was not carried out. In 1860, the Catholics in Batavia built a church, and for the next fifty years Geneva Catholics attended one of these two neighboring missions. It was not until the coming of Bishop Peter J. Muldoon and the establishment of the Rockford Diocese that Geneva obtained a church..

On July 5, 1911, Bishop Muldoon appointed Father Theodore B. McCormick (1911-1914) the first pastor of Geneva. On July 23, the first Mass was offered in what had been the Unitarian Church with 132 people present. Shortly afterwards, an unused Swedish Methodist Church was procured and leased for one year. By April, 1912, property at the corner of James and Fifth Streets was purchased and plans for a church and rectory were drawn up. Bishop Muldoon laid the cornerstone on Labor Day,

◆ **St. Peter Church on James and Fifth Streets, 1913-1958.**

September 2, 1912, and celebrated the dedication Mass the following Memorial Day, May 30, 1913.

In April of 1952, Father Walter C. Roberts went to St. Peter as an assistant pastor. After the death of Father Francis S. Porcella (1939-1956) in 1956, Father Roberts was made administrator. He continued to administer the parish for the next seven months. A complete program of remodeling was initiated in 1955.

◆ **Groundbreaking for the Kaneville Road church, 1958.**

◆ **St. Peter Church interior.**

During Father Ronald L. French's pastorate (1957-1966), the school and temporary church were built in 1958 on Kaneville Road. Later, a new rectory and convent were constructed.

One event that stands out in the history of the parish occurred on June 14, 1985. Father James W. McLoughlin (1983-1997), Pastor of St. Peter's, was one of the passengers taken hostage by terrorists while on TWA Flight 847 from Athens to Rome. Father McLoughlin was leading a Holy Land pilgrimage which included other parishioners. While other passengers, including Father McLoughlin's mother, were shortly released after the hijacking, Father McLoughlin was held in captivity in Beirut, Lebanon until his release on June 30, 1985. Father McLoughlin's homecoming was joyously celebrated by the parish and the Geneva community. A shrine to the Blessed Virgin Mary was erected in front of the Parish Center in thanksgiving for the safe return of all the hostages.

◆ **Bishop O'Neill accompanies President Ronald Regan on his 1982 visit to St. Peter School.**

Over the years, St. Peter Parish has been the recipient of visits from several famous people. Joe Wise, well-known folk singer and liturgist, presented two concerts, one in 1981 and again in 1982. Chicago Bears kicker Bob Thomas has also been a

◆ **One of St. Peter Parish's Barn Sales.**

guest speaker. The most famous, however, was President Ronald Reagan who came to teach a lesson in civics to the eighth graders at St. Peter School in April of 1982.

September of 1987 saw the parish's first Barn Sale being held. This Barn Sale continued annually through 1996. Over $1 Million was contributed to the Building Fund through these sales.

On October 17, 1993, Bishop Arthur J. O'Neill presided at the dedication Mass of the new St. Peter Church on Kaneville Road. The new church seats up to 1200 people. Father McLoughlin, Pastor of St. Peter, stated that it was the fulfillment of a dream people had in 1911 when they built the first church on James Street. That church seated 100 people.

During Monsignor Joseph F. Jarmoluk's pastorate, a newly renovated and expanded St. Peter School was dedicated on September 13, 2003 by Bishop Thomas G. Doran. The remodeled Parish center and the newly constructed Adoration Chapel were also both blessed that day by Bishop Doran before the Mass.

As of March 2007 Monsignor Joseph F. Jarmoluk is pastor. There are approximately 3000 families currently registered at St. Peter Parish.

St. Catherine of Genoa Parish

◆ **Original St. Catherine of Genoa Church, 1924.**

It was on September 1, 1912 that the first Catholic church in Genoa was dedicated by Bishop Peter J. Muldoon. The dedication came just three months before the death of Father Casper J. Huth, the pastor of St. Charles Borromeo Parish in Hampshire and the priest who first provided Genoa Catholics with regular services.

Father Huth served in Hampshire from 1885 until his death January 9, 1913. On the first Sunday of each month he would travel the short distance west into DeKalb County and celebrate Mass on the second floor of the old James Kiernan building in downtown Genoa.

After a series of meetings in 1911 with Genoa Catholics, Bishop Muldoon bought several lots on Emmett Street for the possible construction of a church. In February, 1912, the Bishop sent Father Thomas J. O'Brien to Genoa for purposes of a census and fund drive. Father O'Brien soon had an ample amount of subscriptions and work began on a church.

Among other large donations was $1,000 from Miss Elizabeth Finkler of Chicago in memory of her mother, Catherine. The gift was one-fifth the total cost of the new church, so the church was named St. Catherine.

One of the altar boys for the Bishop's dedication on September 1, 1912, was William R. Warner, who returned 25 years later to serve as the parish's pastor.

Father O'Brien (1912-1926) was appointed as the first pastor. In 1913, he supervised the construction of a rectory next to the church, and in 1916, he provided St. Peter Mission Church for Catholics living in Kirkland. The mission church was used for only about a decade, however, since many of the Catholic families moved away.

The movement of families also hit the Genoa parish during the Depression years in the 1930's. Father William M. McGuire (1930-1936), who in 1930 became pastor of St. Catherine, saw the parish membership drop to about the level of 52 families, the number which made up the parish when it was organized 20 years earlier.

During Father William R. Warner's pastorate (1937-1960), the parish grew in 20 years to about 125 families, numbering about 325 Catholics.

Father James A. Molloy (1963-1972) was named St. Catherine's ninth pastor in May, 1963. A 25-acre section of land in the southeast part of Genoa was bought in 1965. Two years later, in September, 1967, ground was broken and work began on the very modern structure on Stott Street which now houses the church, rectory, meeting rooms, eight classrooms, and offices. The first Mass in the new church was celebrated by Bishop Arthur J. O'Neill on December 8, 1968. Bishop O'Neill also dedicated the new church on October 12, 1969.

◆ **In 1988 Sister Marianne Nilges and Kathleen Coffey stand in front of the monument donated to the parish cemetery by Kathleen and Jane Coffey.**

◆ **St. Catherine of Genoa Church interior.**

Built not long after Vatican II, St. Catherine Church was designed in the round to incorporate sweeping changes in the liturgy. A central altar is the focal point of the structure. The building won an award as an outstanding religious edifice in 1968.

The parish's old church on Emmett Street was sold and converted into an apartment house.

St. Catherine of Genoa Parish observed its 75th anniversary with a Mass of Thanksgiving celebrated by Bishop O'Neill on October 17, 1987. Father Harold L. Nilges (1983-1999), Pastor, was one of the concelebrants.

A new 12-foot granite shrine in St. Catherine of Genoa Cemetery was dedicated by Father Thomas C. Brady in a special ceremony on September 18, 1988. The shrine was donated by Kathleen Coffey.

October 10, 1993 brought several celebrations to the parish. Father Nilges, Pastor, and his sister, Sister Marianne Nilges, pastoral minister, celebrated 10 years at St. Catherine Parish. At one time, they were the only brother and sister pastoral team in the U.S. Father Nilges celebrated his 40th anniversary of ordination while Sister Marianne celebrated her 45th anniversary of profession of vows. The parish also celebrated the 25th anniversary of the building of the new church complex on Stott Street.

◆ **Father William Warner.**

A bequest of $273,000 from Jane and Kathleen Coffey in 1997 was used to retire the debt of the complex built in 1967.

As of March 2007 the pastor is Father Timothy J. Seigel. There are approximately 550 families currently registered at St. Catherine of Genoa Parish.

◆ **St. Catherine of Genoa Church.**

St. Mary Mission

In 1835 George Tyler, a recent convert to Catholicism, rode on horseback west from Cincinnati to the Elgin area. He came to a spot a few miles north of Elgin, camped under a thorn-apple tree beside the creek which now bears his name, and in that neighborhood marked his claim and built a house. A number of Irish families began to move into the neighborhood and the place became known as the "Barrens" or the "Irish Settlement." In 1837, the first Mass was celebrated in Tyler's cabin by Father Maurice de St. Palais, later Bishop of Vincennes, Indiana.

The first missionary to minister to the Catholic people of this area was the first pastor of Chicago, Father St. Cyr. Around 1841 Father John Guiguen moved to Lake County, near what is now Lake Forest. He had pastoral responsibility for serving all Catholics within Kane, McHenry and DeKalb counties. Under his direction construction began in 1841 or 1842 on the "Barrens" church, which was located where the Gilberts cemetery now stands. This building was never fully completed and in 1855 Father Gallagher built a large frame church in Gilberts because of the railroad station there. This church was about a mile west of the first church.

In 1863 Fathers Giesen and Bradley, Redemptorist missionary priests, came to Gilberts and after preaching a mission erected the Redemptorist cross still honored in the present church.

In 1872 Gilberts was attached to the newly-formed parish at Huntley. In 1915 Bishop Peter J. Muldoon gave responsibility for Gilberts to the pastor of Cary. This arrangement lasted until 1917, when Bishop Muldoon separated Gilberts and Dundee from Cary and appointed Father Leo M. Keenan (1917-1929) pastor of both. Since that time St. Mary, Gilberts has been attached to St. Catherine Parish, Dundee.

During the pastorate of Father William M. McKinstra (1987-2000), the entire church was renovated to prepare for the parish's 150th anniversary, celebrated in 1991. In 1992 the church was placed on the National Register of Historic Places by the United States Department of the Interior.

As of March 2007 Father Richard A. Rosinski is pastor. There are approximately 90 families currently registered at St. Mary Parish.

◆ **Historical recognition of St. Mary Church came in 1992.**

◆ **St. Mary's centennial celebration, 1941.**

◆ **St. Mary Church interior and exterior.**

St. Charles Borromeo Parish

Scattered throughout Hampshire, Burlington and Rutland townships in the early 1870's were less than two dozen Catholic families, who attended Mass in the towns nearest their respective farms, Huntley, Gilberts or Sycamore. The long distance as well as the bad condition of the roads made these trips real hardships and naturally often caused long lapses between trips to church, especially in the winter and spring.

Still, those of Irish descent were fairly well cared for, as priests of that nationality were stationed at the above named towns. The German speaking faction, however, was seriously handicapped because many of them could not speak English. The Vicar General of the Diocese of Chicago became informed of this condition and occasionally sent Father William Delaporte from Naperville to Sycamore to give the German speaking Catholics an opportunity to go to the Sacraments. To still further accommodate these old parishioners

Father Delaporte would come to Burlington at times and hear confessions, say Mass and give Holy Communion in several homes. This duty was later transferred to Father Clement Duerr, a German speaking priest, who had come to take charge of the Huntley parish.

Although the number of Catholics was small, both nationalities felt the need of a church within easy access. They obtained permission from the Administrator of the Chicago Diocese to canvass the families for funds for the erection of a church.

In 1875, Hampshire was chosen for a site, located almost equal distance between the two churches the Catholic families had been attending in Huntley and Gilberts, and the station in Burlington. The site at Hampshire had been surveyed and the town had every indication that it was growing. Mr. William Shatters, in 1875, bought and paid for the lots now occupied by the parochial school and church.

A frame church was built in 1878 at a cost of $1,525. Father Peter J. Gormley (1875-1878), who was pastor of Huntley at the time, took charge of it. He was followed by Father Charles Rosenbauer, C.Ss.R. (1878-1881) in 1878. The church was named after his patron saint, St. Charles Borromeo. His first Mass was offered in the church where there were no pews and a store box was used for an altar. In 1879 the rectory was built.

In 1880, Hampshire, which had grown to a population of 600, had improved transportation facilities and families from Genoa, Kingston and Kirkland were brought to Mass on a milk train. At this time the parish numbered 60 families.

Father Casper J. Huth (1885-1913) arrived in 1885; he guided Catholic activities for 28 years. It was at this point that it became necessary to enlarge

◆ **The first St. Charles Borromeo Church, 1887.**

◆ **Father Clement Petit at the groundbreaking for a school addition, April 2, 1962.**

◆ **First Communicants with Father Casper J. Huth, July 20, 1901.**

the church facilities. A 26-foot addition was added in 1886 at a cost of $770.

As the parish continued to grow, both Father Huth and his parishioners foresaw the necessity of a much larger church. Accordingly, lots west of the church were purchased for the sum of $800. In the spring of 1908, the new church was begun. The new church was built in Gothic style and constructed of red pressed brick with cut stone trim, a slate roof and a steeple 120 feet high. It has a seating capacity of 500. The cost of construction was $25,000. The old church was remodeled into a parish hall.

In anticipation of church expansion, Father Frederick J. Brummel (1921-1927) purchased property in 1923 which would later provide a site for a convent.

Father Francis P. Heckinger (1927-1933) came to assume the responsibilities at Hampshire in 1927. During his pastorate, a parochial school was constructed. The old wooden building, which had been the first church, then a hall, was torn down and in 1928 the construction of the school began.

Father Herman A. Meilinger (1933-1943) came to the parish in 1933 from Harmon. During this period, financial difficulties were great, but a parishioner, Conrad Reh, deeded to the parish his farm valued at $17,000 as well as two houses and lots to ease the situation.

◆ **Construction of the current church, summer 1908.**

◆ **St. Charles Borromeo Church interior.**

During Father Nicholas J. Thiry's pastorate (1943-1951), a Kilgen pipe organ was installed in the church, playground equipment was purchased, the interior of the rectory was decorated, and the parish debt completely paid off. In 1951, Father Thiry resigned from the pastorate due to ill health.

Father Sylvester J. Eye (1951-1957) became the pastor in 1951 and during his pastorate the church was redecorated, with a new heating plant and floor covering among the many improvements made in the church.

Father Clement P. Petit (1957-1965) came to Hampshire as pastor and during his pastorate a new convent was purchased and a major addition to the school was built and dedicated in May, 1963.

In 1975, a new rectory was built on the same site to replace the 100-year-old structure. The generous bequest of parishioner William Joseph McAuliff made this possible.

After major remodeling and renovation under the supervision of Father William J. Clausen (1979-1986), the church was rededicated by Bishop Arthur J. O'Neill on December 9, 1984.

In 2001, St. Charles Borromeo Parish celebrated its 125th anniversary and in November of 2004, a statue of the parish's patron saint was dedicated. The six-foot tall bronze statue of St. Charles Borromeo was donated by the family of Alfred and Milly Reiser in their memory.

A 25-acre parcel of land was purchased in 2004 for future use. Located on Getzelman Road, the property is adjacent to the parish's 120-year-old cemetery.

As of March 2007 the pastor is Father Joseph P. Nicolosi. There are approximately 850 families currently registered at St. Charles Borromeo Parish.

◆ **St. Charles Borromeo Church.**

St. John the Evangelist Parish

St. John the Evangelist Parish has a mixed history of independence, and the southern Jo Daviess County congregation has a very long history.

The first recorded Mass was celebrated in the open air along the banks of the Apple River, at the site of the long-departed Craig's Mill. Celebrant of the Mass was the famed Dominican missionary, Father Samuel C. Mazzuchelli. Since the previous fall, Father Mazzuchelli, working out of Galena and Dubuque, had been traveling both south as far as Burlington, Iowa, and north to Prairie du Chien, Wisconsin. On August 16, 1840, he stopped to care for Catholics in the Hanover area.

The small settlement near Apple River became a station for irregular visits by Galena pastors. Such visits, however, were rare because of the limited number of settlers in the mid-1880's. Usually, attendance at religious services required traveling north to the town of Galena.

◆ **Father Thomas Walsh.**

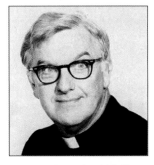

◆ **Father John Kilduff**

In 1887, Hanover Catholics built a church and received a pastor. The congregation was placed on a mission status under St. Mary Parish, Elizabeth. The latter parish, located just north of Hanover, had received its first resident pastor, Father Joseph Ruetershoff, in August 1887.

Acquiring Hanover as a mission, Father Ruetershoff moved immediately to have a church constructed in the town. The new church was named the Church of the Holy Face and services were conducted on the second and fourth Sunday of the month.

Hanover remained a mission until October 1925, when Bishop Peter J. Muldoon came to administer Confirmation and approved a committee petition for independent status of the parish.

The town had grown through the booming business of the Hanover Woolen Mill, and Catholics were now numerous enough to warrant the change. Father Thomas L. Walsh (1926-1928) was appointed the following spring as the first resident pastor at Hanover.

During Father Walsh's two-year stay, the frame church was enlarged through the addition of a sacristy and a basement. A new bell was installed, the interior was renovated and the entire building veneered.

In the one-year term of the second pastor, Father Edward J. Connolly (1928-1929), the new church was dedicated by Bishop Edward F. Hoban and renamed St. John the Evangelist.

When Father Joseph T. Healey (1939-1943) assumed the pastoral duties, he supervised major repairs to the church and was instrumental in the planning and building of the massive Craig Manor, a government housing project.

◆ **Mass of Thanksgiving after the ordination of Father Stephen Wilbricht, CSC, April 13, 1997.**

◆ **St. John the Evangelist Church interior.**

◆ **St. John the Evangelist Church.**

With the advent of World War II, the Hanover parish was swelled by Catholics from the Savanna Ordnance Depot.

A year after Father James F. Mulcaire (1948-1952) became pastor, the woolen mill closed, bringing both economic hardship to the community and a migration of families. That situation changed shortly with the start of the Korean conflict and the resulting increased activity at the nearby ordnance plant. There were some 150 families in the Hanover congregation in 1952. Major repairs were made to the heating system and land was purchased for a rectory garage.

In 1954, the new pastor, Father John J. Kilduff (1954-1960), instituted such major projects as new sidewalks and church woodwork, as well as repairing the church's foundation, but the town's economic health was once more getting strained. By 1960, the parish was down to about 80 families.

In 1960, Father Kilduff was transferred and the Hanover parish reverted to mission status under the pastor of St. Mary Parish, Elizabeth. That status changed again late in 1960 when Father William F. Morrissey became pastor in Elizabeth. Hanover and Elizabeth were now operated under a dual-parish system, with the pastor of St. Mary Parish being made the administrator of St. John Parish. The dual arrangement continued for 10 years.

Under Bishop Arthur J. O'Neill, Hanover once more acquired independent status. In September 1970, Father Robert C. Williams (1970-1973), was appointed resident pastor of St. John the Evangelist Parish, Hanover.

In the early 1970's, during the pastorate of Father Williams, the church interior was renovated and the present-day stone entrance was constructed.

During the pastorate of Father Michael A. Librandi (1992-1999), all the parish buildings were renovated and redecorated in 1992.

In cooperation with other churches in town, the St. Anne Society of St. John's has coordinated a Christmas bazaar for more than 42 years, since 1964.

As of March 2007 Father Christopher J. Kuhn is pastor. There are approximately 125 families currently registered at St. John the Evangelist Parish.

St. Flannen Parish

The Catholics in Harmon were ministered to by the priests of St. Patrick Parish, Dixon, as far back as 1870. Previous to that time, there were the usual infrequent visits of traveling missionaries when Mass was celebrated in pioneer homes. Most frequently, Masses and baptisms were held in the home of Owen Burns, which was next door to the present rectory.

In May 1870, Father Michael McDermott (1870-1874) came as pastor to Dixon, and assumed duty also at Harmon, which was a mission. On his visits, he offered Mass in the school house and initiated the building of a frame church. Father Cornelius J. Kirkfleet, O. Praem., the first historian of the Diocese, dates the

◆ **Original church fire, December 25, 1911. Note the figure at the lower right peering at the fire from behind the tree.**

erection of the church to sometime during 1873, since convention attributes its construction to Father McDermott who was transferred to Bloomington in 1874. This belief has been challenged, however, since the Baptismal Registry reports baptisms were still performed in the house of Owen Burns as late as the early 1890's. Father David A. Murphy (1933-1964), stated that this was not necessarily a contradiction, as it is quite possible that adults could safely attend Mass in a poorly heated, or even unheated, church while baptisms might more conveniently have taken place in a private home, particularly one that had been used for the celebration of Mass so many times previous to this.

It is certain that St. Flannen was established as an independent parish on October 5, 1898, when Father D. E. McGrath (1898-1902) was appointed its pastor. He built the first rectory, a frame building, just east of the church. He also secured five acres of land for a parish cemetery.

Disaster struck the parish during the pastorate of Father Thomas Smith (1905-1912). Fire destroyed the church and rectory on Christmas Day 1911. In the summer of 1912, the present church and rectory were begun and the cornerstone of the present church was laid by Bishop Peter J. Muldoon in September 1912.

The new church and rectory were completed by Father Patrick H. McKeown (1912-1917). On May 26, 1914, Bishop Muldoon returned to dedicate the new church.

During Father Thomas M. Moore's years as pastor (1917-1928), the entire remaining parish debt was removed and a fund of over $6,000 was left, presumably for the building of a parish school.

A fire in the sacristy shortly after Father Thomas Walsh's (1928-1930) arrival in 1928 necessitated the redecoration of the church. A school

◆ **St. Flannen Church interior, 1917.**

◆ **St. Flannen Church.**

bus was acquired in 1929 at the request of Bishop Edward F. Hoban, so both high school and grade school children could benefit by attending Catholic schools in Sterling.

In May of 1933, Father David A. Murphy (1933-1964) came to begin a pastorate that was to last over 30 years. In addition to installing new heating plants in the parish buildings, Father Murphy also supervised another redecoration project for the church in 1947.

Father James F. Lafferty (1964-1978) was appointed pastor of St. Flannen on May 26, 1964. It was during Father Lafferty's pastorate in July of 1967 that St. Mary Parish in Walton was made a mission parish of St. Flannen. Also during his pastorate, in November 1973, Father Lafferty extensively renovated the church in Harmon.

◆ **Father David Murphy.**

On September 26, 1987, during the pastorate of Father Richard R. Kramer (1979-1992), Bishop Arthur J. O'Neill celebrated a Mass of Rededication in observance of the church building's 75th anniversary.

Minor improvements to parish facilities were made during the pastorate of Father Thomas P. Dolan (1993-2003). Improvements and repairs included a new roof for the rectory garage, in 1993, and a new roof for the church and rectory, in 1994. A new sidewalk to the front and back of the rectory was also put in during Father Dolan's pastorate.

As of March 2007 Father Carl E. Beekman is parochial administrator. There are approximately 35 families currently registered at St. Flannen Parish.

ST. PATRICK PARISH

◆ **The first St. Patrick Church, built in 1856, is here shown in 1911.**

◆ **St. Patrick Church interior, June 1932.**

On December 6, 1836, Andrew Donnelley with his sister and brother-in-law, Katherine and Francis Short, and a few others, arrived in Hartland by horse and wagon from Lowell, Massachusetts. They camped in what is now the southwest corner of Greenwood Township, the Shorts staking their claim there. After spending the winter in Chicago, the party returned in the spring of 1837, and Mr. Donnelley took up his claim in what is now the southeast corner of Hartland Township. He later built an inn, and the place became known as Donnelley's Settlement. While in Chicago, they met Father John St. Cyr who promised to visit them in their new home. Father St. Cyr was the first pastor in Chicago, having been sent there in 1837 by Bishop Rosati of St. Louis.

◆ **Aftermath of the fire that destroyed the original church in 1913.**

In the summer of 1837, Francis Short traveled by horseback into Chicago and guided Father St. Cyr and an Indian out to Donnelley's Settlement where Mass was said for the first time in McHenry County. The Indian came along to guide the priest back, for there were no roads, and they had to follow trails. From that time on, Mass was said at intervals at the various homes of the early settlers. Until there was a resident pastor, and later in the 1870's when for some years the parish was administered from Harvard by Father Dominic F. Egan, the priest would stay with various families so that all their neighbors might have a chance to attend Mass and receive the sacraments.

A variety of priests came out for Mass to the little settlement from time to time. According to the diary of Bishop William Quarter, Donnelley's Settlement was one of the most important missions of the Diocese.

In 1844, Bishop Quarter ordained Father Patrick A. McMahon (1844-1850) and appointed him that summer as pastor at Donnelley's Settlement or Hartland as it is now known. Unfortunately, his health was poor and Bishop Quarter soon was forced to send Father John Faughnan, also newly ordained, to assist him.

During the pastorate of Father Patrick Hampston (1853-1856), a new church was built in 1856. It served the growing congregation for over half a century until it burned to the ground in 1913. It was during the pastorate of Father Thomas Kearney (1909-1929) that this historic church burned. The location selected for the new church was across the road, on high ground so that it might be seen from a long distance. It was solemnly dedicated by Bishop Peter J. Muldoon on August 15, 1914.

◆ **Aftermath of 1941 church fire.**

Much needed improvements to the church and rectory were made during the pastorate of Father Edward A. O'Brien (1930-1933).

In 1941, the church was once again completely destroyed by fire. Despite the fact that the parish had decreased to a mere 15 families (many had lost their farms in the great depression and moved to the city), they all rallied and came forth with generous donations even with the very poor economic conditions for the typical farmer. A new church was built on the original foundation at a cost of over $35,000. Leaving only a small debt of $8,000 which was soon paid off, the new church was blessed by Bishop Edward F. Hoban in July of 1942, shortly after the appointment of Father John M. Dording (1942-1960) as pastor. In 1953, Father Dording had the church completely redecorated.

During Father F. James Larson's administration of the parish (1972-1973), the interior of the church was remodeled. During the administration of Father Michael J. Tierney (1975-1978), both the interior and exterior of the rectory were renovated and the church tuck-pointed.

In order to celebrate the parish's Sesquicentennial,

the church was redecorated and recarpeted in 1986, during the pastorate of Father Lawrence M. Urbaniak (1984-1999)

On December 22, 2002, St. Patrick Parish celebrated four years of renovations to the parish church. Father Joseph P. Naill, assisting at St. Patrick 2001-2004, concelebrated Mass with Bishop Thomas G. Doran who dedicated the church's new altar.

As of March 2007 Monsignor James W. McLoughlin is pastor. There are approximately 200 families currently registered at St. Patrick Parish.

◆ **St. Patrick Church.**

St. Joseph Parish

The early Catholic settlers of the Harvard area depended upon the parish in Hartland for their religious needs. The first Mass to be said in McHenry County was in what was then known as Donnelley's Settlement. The first Mass was said sometime in the summer of 1837 by Father John St. Cyr who traveled to Donnelley's Settlement on horseback from Chicago. In 1844, Father Patrick A. McMahon was appointed by Bishop Quarter of Chicago as the first pastor at Donnelley's Settlement. Father McMahon served not only Donnelley's Settlement but also all the Catholics in the McHenry area, including those who lived in the area now known as Harvard.

Since 1850, Catholics in this area were attended somewhat irregularly by priests out of Holy Name Cathedral in Chicago. Between visits, Harvard Catholics attended Mass at St. Patrick Parish, Hartland, when they were able.

The first Mass celebrated in Harvard was on Christmas day in 1859 by Father Terrence Fitzsimmons, Pastor at Hartland. The Mass was celebrated in a grocery store which was owned by Michael O'Neil, a great uncle of Monsignor Philip E. O'Neil, who was ordained for the Rockford Diocese in Harvard on May 27, 1954.

In 1866, property was bought on Front Street and the Catholics in the area began to build what was known as "The Log Cabin Church" since the foundation and the supports were trees that the farmers felled on their ground. This frame building was completed sometime in 1866, and the first Mass was said there in that same year.

◆ **Stained glass window depicting the ordination of Fathers Thomas Brady and Philip O'Neil, 1954.**

In 1869, Father Dominic F. Egan (1869-1890) took up residence at Harvard, thus becoming Harvard's first resident pastor. He purchased the property directly behind the present St. Joseph Church and built a small rectory there. He also purchased land for a cemetery and Hartland continued to be served from St. Joseph Parish in Harvard. This continued until 1883 when the two parishes were separated.

Father James E. Hogan (1890-1894) succeeded Father Egan of St. Joseph Parish in 1890. He saw the immediate need for a new and larger church, for the membership of the parish had grown to eleven hundred parishioners. Although the times were hard and money was scarce, work began on the plans for a new church. The cornerstone for the present church was laid on July 4, 1891. Father Hogan himself labored on the building, working with the bricklayers in his spare time.

In 1915 Father Daniel A. Feeley (1912-1929) bought the "Cottage Hospital" and converted it into a temporary rectory. At this time he also bought property for a school which opened in September of 1916. The school was staffed by the Sisters of the Holy Cross.

Father Leo M. Keenan (1929-1950) was pastor during the rough years of the Depression. In spite of the tight money, Father Keenan did as much repair work to the church, convent and rectory as was possible.

When Father Joseph T. Healey (1950-1983) came in July of 1950, his first task was to renovate the school. The old convent was torn down and ground was added to the school playground which was completely blacktopped. The sisters then moved into the house across the street from the school.

When the school and convent were renovated, Father Healey decorated the church. The high altar

◆ **The first St. Joseph Church, built in 1866.**

◆ Monsignor Meilinger, Archbishop Binz, Bishop O'Neill, Cardinal Cody, Bishop Grady, Bishop Grutka, and Monsigner Healey at St. Joseph's centennial Mass, 1969.

◆ St. Joseph Church interior.

was refurbished, new stained glass windows were ordered and the church was air-conditioned.

The decorating of the church was completed in the early spring of 1954. Later, when the stained glass windows were installed, one of them was to depict the ordination of former parishioners Father Thomas C. Brady and Father Philip E. O'Neil by Bishop Raymond P. Hillinger. The other windows depict most of the former Bishops of Rockford officiating at some function at St. Joseph Parish.

In 1963, Monsignor Healey, who was elevated to Monsignor that year, broke ground for a new rectory. A new convent was built in 1965. The convent, however, was not to be a permanent need for the Sisters of the Holy Cross. Due to the small numbers of religious vocations to their community, the sisters, were forced to withdraw from St. Joseph Parish School in June 1971.

In 1966, the parish in Harvard was one hundred years old. The celebration of the centennial was put off until the church could be renovated, meeting with the changes brought about by the Second Vatican Council. The church was repainted and an entirely new sanctuary was designed.

The renovation of the church was completed by 1969 and on October 19, 1969, the centennial of the parish was officially observed with a Mass concelebrated by Bishop Arthur J. O'Neill, Archbishop Leo Binz (Archdiocese of St. Paul and Minneapolis), Bishop Thomas Grady, (Archdiocese of Chicago), Bishop Andrew Grutka (Diocese of Gary) and priests who had been ordained from the parish, along with priests who had served the parish as associate pastors. The homily was delivered by His Eminence, John Cardinal Cody of

Chicago. In August of 1981, Monsignor Healey welcomed Bishop Arthur J. O'Neill as the main celebrant of a Mass marking the rededication of the 90-year-old church and the consecration of its new altar.

Numerous renovations to the church were completed during the pastorate of Father Richard R. Kramer (1994-2003). Bishop Thomas G. Doran blessed the remodeled altar on August 10, 1997.

Father Kramer dedicated a Memorial of Life on October 17, 1999. The memorial is engraved with the words "I call you by name, remember the unborn."

As of March 2007 Father Daniel E. Peters is pastor. There are approximately 600 families currently registered at St. Joseph Parish.

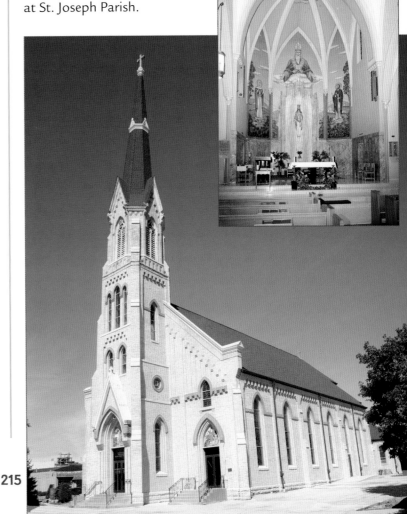

◆ St. Joseph Church interior and exterior.

St. Mary Parish

◆ **St. Mary Church.**

Previous to the year 1870, the Catholic people of Huntley and the immediate vicinity attended either the "Little Church in the Woods," known as the North Barrens, located about four and a half miles northeast of Huntley, or the church near Gilberts, known as the South Barrens.

It was in 1851 that Thomas S. Huntley platted land in what was known as Huntley Grove and donated sites for a village and three churches, Catholic, Congregational, and Lutheran.

By the time of his action, the Chicago and Northwestern Railroad had reached the Huntley area. The land set aside for Catholic use was located on the south end of town.

Meetings of a building committee had been held in 1870 and 1871 at John Kelley's blacksmith shop. Funds were collected in the summer of 1871 and work began on the church at the site which had been donated by Mr. Huntley.

◆ **The first St. Mary Church, 1924.**

Catholics in the Huntley area finished building their first church shortly after the first resident pastor, Father Clement Duerr (1873-1877), arrived in the McHenry County parish in July 1873. Father Duerr also served Gilberts as a mission.

◆ **Interior of the first St. Mary Church, which was built in 1873.**

Soon after Father Duerr began his four-year pastorate, he supervised the construction of a rectory across the road from the church. Father Desire D. Miller (1909-1917) built the second rectory.

As the 1930's began, so too did plans for new church buildings. A more centrally located site was chosen on North Woodstock Street and the church and adjoining rectory were completed in 1931 at a cost of $75,000. Father Ivon A. Esser (1930-1934) had been named pastor in June 1930.

Huntley remained predominately an Irish and German farming community until 1938, when several industrial firms finally opened plants. The two biggest firms were the Dean Foods Milk Plant and the Union Special Sewing Machine Company.

Father L. Dudley Day (1938-1980) arrived on July 22, 1938. Among other accomplishments early in the service of Father Day was the liquidation of a $70,000 depression-era debt within seven years.

A dance and an auction were held in 1997 to celebrate the 125th anniversary of St. Mary Parish and on December 5, 1999 groundbreaking for a new church took place.

The first Mass in the new church took place on November 10, 2001 during the pastorate of Father Robert M. Garrity (1995-2004). The dedication was on November 18, 2001 with Bishop Thomas G. Doran officiating as celebrant.

The new church combined elements of the former church on North Woodstock Street with modern amenities. A new, imported crucifix from Europe hangs above the altar, while restored, 100-year-old hand carved walnut-framed Stations of the Cross from Germany line the walls. Most of the church's windows were removed from a Franciscan girls' school in New Jersey and stored in Ohio for more than half a century. The 26 stained-glass windows were purchased through donations from parishioners.

The new church fronting Kreutzer Road accommodates 1200 people with room for expansion. Besides the large worship area, the building has nine classrooms, a bride's room, office space and meeting rooms.

As of March of 2007 Father Stephen J. Knox is pastor. There are approximately 4000 families currently registered at St. Mary Parish.

◆ **Laying the cornerstone for the second church, November 30, 1930.**

◆ **St. Mary Church interior.**

St. Patrick Mission

A mission of the Durand parish since 1909, Irish Grove is one of the oldest Catholic settlements in northern Illinois, and home to one of its oldest Catholic churches, St. Patrick. Father Remigius Petiot, then Father Samuel C. Mazzuchelli's assistant at Galena, and later pastor there, offered the first Mass at Irish Grove in 1841. Later, under the direction of Father Petiot, a log cabin church was built at Irish Grove. Both Father Petiot and Father Mazzuchelli, O.P., attended the Irish Grove church.

There are conflicting reports about the early history of the Irish Grove parish. It was attended by priests out of New Dublin and Freeport for several years. Father John Cavanaugh, later pastor in Freeport, came to Irish Grove twice a year, at least as early as 1847.

◆ **Replica of the original log cabin church, circa 1842.**

Later, a Father James Fitzgerald visited Irish Grove and liked it so well he decided to make it the center of his priestly work. He built a house in the church yard, but died on one of his missionary journeys and it was never used as a rectory. Later it was removed from the church property.

A Father P. McLaughlin attended the parish from 1855 to 1859 when Father Thomas O'Gara came to Freeport and had charge of the surrounding

◆ **St. Patrick Church.**

◆ **The current St. Patrick Church, in an earlier time.**

◆ **St. Patrick Church interior.**

missions. Father O'Gara built a second church at Irish Grove in 1862. It was in that year that Father Michael J. Hanley took charge, and Irish Grove, in the same way as Durand, was attended from Freeport until 1872, when it too, was transferred to Pecatonica.

Father Eugene Gray lived in Davis and served as pastor from 1885 to 1889. Perhaps he comes as near as being a resident of Irish Grove as any priest before or since his time. Until then, all the priests had come from other places to attend the spiritual needs of St. Patrick, Irish Grove.

The third church at Irish Grove was built by Father Michael J. Sullivan who was pastor at Pecatonica from 1894 to 1899. In 1909, Father Daniel A. Feeley (1909-1913) was appointed the first resident pastor at Durand with Irish Grove as a mission. Since that time, the history of the parish corresponds very closely with the mother parish.

On September 28, 1942, the centennial of the parish of Irish Grove was celebrated with a Mass offered by Bishop Edward F. Hoban.

In 1973, during the pastorate of Father Aloysius J. Neumann (1972-1984), a lot across from the church was purchased to be used as a parking lot. This was a much needed improvement in the church property. Father Neumann also directed a remodeling of the church's interior.

Father Karl P. Ganss (1984-1995), Pastor, and the people of St. Patrick Parish welcomed Bishop Arthur J. O'Neill who celebrated a 150th anniversary Mass on September 20, 1992.

As of March 2007 Monsignor Eric R. Barr is pastor. Families currently registered at St. Patrick Parish are included in those registered at St. Mary in Durand.

◆ **The second church, built in 1862.**

St. John the Baptist Parish

The first Germans arrived in Johnsburg on August 2, 1841, making this an exclusively German Catholic center, one of the oldest in the state. There is a tradition that Bishop Brute, of the Diocese of Vincennes, was in this territory in 1838, and baptized four children here.

◆ **St. John the Baptist Church.**

The first settlers were Nikolaus Frett (from whose headstone the exact date of arrival is known), Jacob Schmitt, Nicolaus Adams and John Baptist Mueller. They were joined the following year by others who emigrated from the same section of the old country—Coblenz, Eiffel and vicinity.

The first chapel was built here in 1843 by Fred Schmitt, in fulfillment of a vow made while threatened by an ocean storm experienced while crossing.

This chapel was built of logs on the Schmitt farm and was used by the settlement for almost 10 years, mainly for private devotions. In 1853, it was

◆ **Father Hubert Fegers standing in front of the third St. John church, 1880.**

replaced by a brick chapel. This is still standing at Chapel Hill Golf Club but is not in use as a chapel.

In 1878, the Miller chapel was built on the Miller farm. It is still standing on the corner of Wilmot and Ringwood Roads. The Miller family has Mass once a year in the chapel.

These chapels are not to be confused with St. John the Baptist Parish Church. However, the Johnsburg settlers and their descendants had many processions to both of these chapels, where they would go in groups to pray for good crops, favorable weather conditions, and for the sick and needy. Mass was celebrated at these chapels on occasion.

The second parish church in Johnsburg was being built in May 1850, when the Most Rev. James O. Van deVelde, Bishop of Chicago, visited the region. The frame building was used by missionaries until 1852, when the first resident pastor, Father John Jaconnett (1852-1853), was appointed.

Father Clement Venn (1866-1868) began building the third parish church in 1868. Father Henry Mehring (1884-1908), eventually completed the third church, which was destroyed by fire in 1900. Father Mehring then built the present St. John Church. He served 24 years as pastor.

It was during Father William Weber's pastorate (1914-1930) that the church was redecorated in 1927,

◆ **A fire destroyed the third St. John church, 1900.**

in time for the 25th anniversary celebration. Father Weber also had the Lourdes Grotto constructed, which was dedicated by Bishop Peter J. Muldoon on May 24, 1921.

Father Anthony J. Vollman (1930-1938) succeeded Father Weber in 1930. He erected the Via Dolorosa and the Shrine to Our Lady of Perpetual Help on the church grounds.

The present parish school was constructed in 1953, during the pastorate of Father Joseph M. Blitsch (1949-1963). The education of parish children has been carried on since 1850, despite losing the first large-scale building to fire in 1945. The school still has one member of the School Sisters of St. Francis on staff.

On May 24, 1975, the parish celebrated the 75th anniversary of its present church.

While Father Leo J. Bartel (1970-1983) was pastor, a rededication weekend was held on November 17 and 18, 1979, to celebrate the restoration of the church. The extensive repairing and remodeling project took over two years to complete.

St. John the Baptist Church was designated as a historical site by the McHenry County Historical Society in November of 1983. The landmark status was the first awarded to a church in the area.

◆ **Father Stephen Wolfgarten, pastor 1908-1912.**

In 1988, Father John C. Holdren (1983-1994), Pastor, held a rededication of the parish's newly restored cemetery chapel.

In November 1992, under the pastorate of Father Holdren, a building project began for a parish hall, offices, classrooms and conversion of the former convent into classrooms and meeting rooms.

In November 1993, Bishop Arthur J. O'Neill blessed the new facility.

During July 2006, the parish came under the direction of the Congregation of the Resurrection religious order with Father Gerald Watt, C.R., as pastor.

A project to restore the stained glass windows in the church will begin in the fall of 2006.

As of March 2007, Father Gerald Watt, C.R. is pastor. There are approximately 1,300 families currently registered at St. John the Baptist Parish.

◆ **St. John the Baptist Church interior.**

St. James Parish

St. James Parish, located in the east section of Lee County, can trace its beginnings to the mid-1860's in Twin Grove, an unincorporated area about two miles west of the town of Lee.

Twin Grove had first been settled by a William Moore in about the year 1840, but a Catholic group did not settle there until 25 years later. As the Civil War drew to a close, about a dozen immigrant families settled the region and immediately began planning for a church. A stone building was completed in 1867 on land donated by John Herrmann in Willow Creek Township.

In Lee itself, St. James Church was built in 1878 and dedicated on June 17, 1878. The church had been constructed under the supervision of Father Edward Froelich, Pastor of St. Patrick Parish in Rochelle from 1876 to 1879. It was therefore attached to Rochelle as a mission, which it remained for almost 30 years.

In 1906 Father Michael J. Hanley (1906-1908) was appointed as St. James' first resident pastor, with the Twin Grove church becoming a mission of the Lee parish. In 1893, when Father Thomas Finn became pastor of the Rochelle church, he was assigned the Twin Grove Mission. He arranged to have a German speaking priest of Aurora, Father John F. Schmitt, look after their needs until Twin Grove was attached to Lee in 1907.

St. James Church had been built just four years after the village of Lee was incorporated in 1874. Plans for the church had been started three years before the completion time by pioneer settlers John Kennedy, James Kirby, M. P. Harris, and Bernard Malloy. On October 13, 1875, Kennedy donated an acre of his farm for the church site, and the quartet took just three days to raise $3,000 from area Catholics.

The church underwent its first renovation program while Father Finn was in charge. He renovated the church building, installed a heating plant, had shelter sheds (for horses) built, and purchased land for a rectory. The rectory was built next to the church after Father Hanley was appointed Lee's first pastor in 1906.

Shortly after Father William P. Quinlisk (1912-1924) became pastor at Lee in 1912, the church at Twin Grove was labeled "unsafe for occupancy" by a state inspection department. It was decided at this time to abandon the church, and Twin Grove area Catholics became a part of the Lee congregation.

It was in 1949 during the pastorate of Father James W. Curran (1933-1960) that the fifty-year-old shelter sheds were destroyed by a fire which itself threatened the church. In 1952, two lots east of the rectory were purchased.

◆ **St. James Church.**

◆ **Foresters Court 817, in 1915.**

◆ **Father James Curran in the living room of the rectory.**

During Father Edward J. Connolly's pastorate (1960-1964), vast improvements were made on the church and rectory.

Between 1964 and 1970 Father Raymond O. Holmgren authorized some major repairs on the church. Meanwhile funds were being set up for the new building program in the parish. This program was not initiated until Father Clement P. Petit succeeded Father Holmgren as pastor on January 8, 1970.

A Social and Educational Center was constructed at the cost of $75,000 and the center was blessed by Bishop Arthur J. O'Neill on September 16, 1973.

During Father Petit's pastorate (1970-1986) the church was completely remodeled and redecorated. St. James Parish marked its 100th anniversary with a jubilee Mass celebrated by Bishop Arthur J. O'Neill on June 18, 1978.

As of March 2007, Father Perfecto Vasquez is the parochial administrator. There are approximately 200 families currently registered at St. James Parish.

◆ **St. James Church interior, circa 1950.**

◆ **St. James Church interior.**

St. Joseph Parish

The first Mass in the Lena area was celebrated by Father Ignatius Baluff in 1860 at the farmhouse of Anthony Doll, located just over a mile west of the village. Father Baluff was a missionary priest who worked extensively in the Sublette and Shannon regions, as well as Lena. In 1863, Father Baluff began an eleven year pastorate at St. Joseph Parish, Freeport.

Prior to the arrival of Father Baluff, Catholics in the Lena area were attended by priests from Galena, starting in the late 1830's, and from New Dublin, after 1844.

Lena itself was laid out in 1854 by Samuel F. Dodds, in conjunction with the Illinois Central Railroad. It became an important shipping point for grain and stock, serving as the center of trade for Stephenson County farmers. It was incorporated as a town in 1866, just four years before Catholics erected their first church. Earlier services had been held in an old schoolhouse, and later in a stone building that had been a high school.

Another noted missionary of the period, Father Edward Froelich, supervised the construction of the first St. Joseph Church in 1870.

◆ **St. Joseph Church.**

◆ **The first St. Joseph Church, right, next to the current church before its remodeling.**

The rectory at St. Joseph is made up of two houses. The front part of the house was built on St. Joseph's property in 1886. The back part of the house was the original rectory at New Dublin. The New Dublin Parish was administered by St. Joseph's beginning in 1890. When New Dublin was closed, the house was moved to St. Joseph and attached to the rectory there, in order to double the size of the house. The first resident pastor at St. Joseph Parish, Father M. Orth, arrived in Lena in 1888, twenty-eight years after the date of the first Mass and 18 years after the first St. Joseph Church was constructed.

The frame building that was the original church is still used by the parish. It forms the base of the present parish hall, a functional and well-cared for building just west of the present church.

◆ **The second St. Joseph Church, built in 1895.**

The second St. Joseph Church was erected in 1895, under the third pastor, Father John Rempe (1892-1896). That building served the parish until it was destroyed by fire in May 1937. A modern fireproof church was constructed by Father Arthur M. Kreckel (1929-1939) and dedicated by Bishop Edward F. Hoban on June 26, 1938.

In November 1954, a Marian Year Grotto was built between the rectory and the church and was dedicated by Bishop Raymond P. Hillinger.

Renovations and improvements have continued through the years at Lena, including an extensive remodeling project in both the church and parish hall by Father John W. Ryan (1960-1965), during the first three years of his pastorate at Lena.

In 1978, the addition of a narthex to the 40-year-old church provided a space for entry, a cry room, confessional, inside stairs and rest rooms. The remodeling project was completed under the leadership of Father Michael J. Shanahan (1974-1980).

A lot directly across the street from the church property on which there was an old house and a new two-car garage was purchased in 1978. The house was razed and the garage moved to the rear of the rectory.

In 1991, during the pastorate of Father Salvatore J. Guagliardo (1988-1999), a new entrance for the handicapped was added to the church.

During Father Michael A. Librandi's pastorate (1999-2003), Neil Petsche cleaned up the Marian Grotto for his Boy Scout Eagle Project when he was a senior in high school. Neil was killed while serving in the military. His father, Dave Petsche, as a tribute to Neil, improved the grotto in October 2005.

An annual Strawberry Festival continues to be held in June, as it has been for over 25 years.

As of March 2007, Father Brian D. Grady is parochial administrator. There are approximately 200 families currently registered at St. Joseph Parish.

◆ **St. Joseph Church interior.**

St. Bridget of Erin Parish

◆ **The circus tent used for the first parish Masses in 1946.**

The parish of St. Bridget of Erin was founded in 1946. Previous to this time St. James Pro-Cathedral had maintained a mission interest in Loves Park, which later developed to the point that an autonomous parish could be set up. That portion of St. James Parish, north of Spring Creek Road was separated by Bishop John J. Boylan and established as an independent parish, under the pastorate of Father Raymond P. Gordon (1946-1983), who had been an associate for thirteen years at the pro-cathedral.

When Father Gordon went to Loves Park, he had five empty lots at his disposal, but no building, nor was any building made available to him for saying Mass.

Refusing to give up when the public school refused to rent him a building, Father Gordon ordered a large circus tent and on the Feast of the Assumption in 1946, the first Mass was said on parish grounds for the 67 families listed as members of the new parish.

A few weeks later, a house next to the church property was purchased and Mass was said each Sunday in this residence. On December 8, 1946, Bishop Boylan presided at the groundbreaking ceremonies for the new church. At that time, ground was broken for a foundation on which the Catholic chapel from Camp Grant would be reassembled. The parish had purchased the chapel, had it dismantled and later, after the foundation was prepared, brought the disassembled chapel out in sections to the St. Bridget property and reassembled it on the newly built foundation. The first Masses were said in it on Mother's Day, 1947. On June 29, Bishop Boylan

◆ **Father Raymond Gordon.**

blessed and dedicated the chapel to St. Bridget. This was the first new parish established by Bishop Boylan.

The parish continued to grow rapidly and soon the chapel was inadequate. New property was sought, but many property owners were reluctant to sell when they discovered the Catholic Church was the purchaser. Through a series of anonymous purchases, several neighboring lots to the north, and

◆ **St. Bridget of Erin Church.**

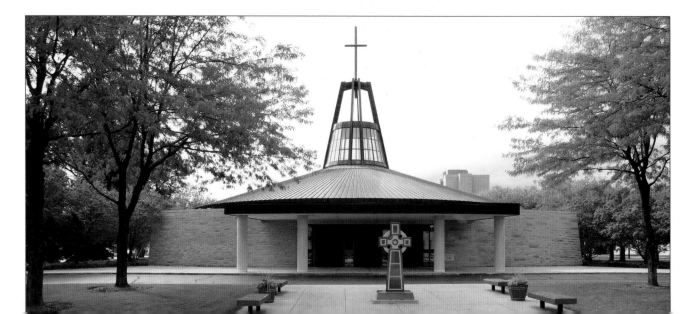

◆ **The first permanent church, a chapel from Camp Grant.**

◆ **Parish center.**

the areas connecting them, were acquired until finally a solid tract of some twenty-four acres was owned by the parish.

At the direction of Bishop Raymond P. Hillinger, on November 21, 1954, work was begun on a school and gym at the new site.

On Pentecost Sunday, May 20, 1956, the building was blessed and the first Mass was celebrated in the gymnasium, which served as the church.

St. Bridget School officially opened in October 1953 when the first kindergarten class was welcomed. In August of 1955, Mother Mary Gerald, O.P., sent five Dominican sisters from Adrian, Michigan, to teach in the school.

In September 1957, enrollment had increased to 580. Soon afterward the new wing was completed providing five new classrooms, a church hall and kitchen facilities.

A new convent was built in 1961.

A new church was built during the pastorate of Father (later Monsignor) John Mitchell. The blessing and Mass of Dedication was celebrated by Bishop Arthur J. O'Neill on October 30, 1988. The 25,000-square-foot church seats 1,000 people. There are a series of stained glass windows in the adjoining Blessed Sacrament chapel. The windows were designed by Virginia Broderick, internationally renowned liturgical artist. Outdoors, there is a new meditation garden with the Stations of the Cross.

An addition to St. Bridget School was dedicated and blessed on September 26, 1995, during the pastorate of Father Mitchell. The addition included two classrooms and an adult education center.

St. Bridget Church marked its 50th anniversary at a special Mass celebrated by Bishop Thomas G. Doran on August 18, 1996.

In the fall of 2004, a new 13,500-square-foot parish center was built. It houses a 4,200-square-foot social hall, a large gathering space, kitchen and three meeting rooms. Bishop Doran blessed the building in November 2004.

For 61 years, since 1946, the parish has celebrated its "birthday" with an ice cream social held every year on the Sunday closest to the Feast of the Assumption, August 15.

As of March 2007, Monsignor John J. Mitchell is pastor. There are approximately 2,100 families currently registered at St. Bridget of Erin Parish.

◆ **Parish center interior.**

CHURCH OF HOLY APOSTLES PARISH

Bishop Arthur J. O'Neill established the Church of Holy Apostles in July 1989. This was the first new parish in McHenry in 95 years. Father Robert N. Sherry was appointed the parish's first pastor. On September 23, 1989, the first Mass for the parish was celebrated at the Tamara Royale Inn with 400 persons in attendance. On Thanksgiving Day, 1989, the parish moved to occupy a 6,000-square-foot building in the Tonyan Industrial Park.

On September 20, 1992, a dozen people representing all Holy Apostles broke ground at the present site. The church was dedicated by Bishop O'Neill on November 28, 1993.

In September 1994, Holy Apostles dedicated its new freestanding, fish-shaped bell tower. The bell was commissioned in France by one of Napoleon's bodyguards, Bartholomaeus Theiss. The Theiss family immigrated to the United States in 1846 and the bell was placed at a church, one of the oldest in the Diocese, in Lee County. The church was known first as Theiss Church and then the Perkin's Grove Catholic Church. When the church was vandalized, Richard

◆ **Baptismal font.**

Theiss removed the bell for safekeeping. His daughter, Marge McCarthy, and the McCarthy family, donated the bell to the Church of Holy Apostles.

◆ **Holy Apostles Church.**

◆ **Bishop O'Neill at the adoration chapel groundbreaking, 1998.**

Parishioner Jason Glaw, 16, completed the construction of a gazebo on the parish's property in 1998. This was done as Jason's Eagle Scout project. Parishioners donated money for the materials and Jason's dad and friends helped with the project. The gazebo is used for wedding pictures and a nativity scene at Christmas, as well as at other times.

On Father's Day in 1998, ground was broken for a 6,000-square-foot addition, which included eight classrooms, meeting room, office, storage space and restrooms. A connecting corridor to the original parish building has a foyer and three offices.

On November 1, 1998, the Feast of All Saints, ground was broken for the All Saints Perpetual Eucharistic Adoration Chapel, which was dedicated on the Feast of the Assumption, August 15, 1999, by Bishop Thomas G. Doran and Bishop Emeritus O'Neill. The chapel gives everyone a place to pray 24 hours a day, seven days a week.

Angels Wing, housing classrooms and offices, opened in February 1999. Noah's Ark Preschool opened in September 1999.

On Good Friday, April 13, 2001, the new Holy Apostles Cemetery and columbarium were blessed. Additional land was dedicated for cemetery use, allowing space for another 1,800 burials or inurnments.

Construction on a new rectory, begun in early 2002, was ready for occupancy in July.

Father Sherry remained as pastor when, on June 5, 2005, a groundbreaking ceremony for a new church was held and, after several delays, construction began on October 24, 2005.

The Church of Holy Apostles produces its own one-hour television program, along with its weekly "Mass with Father Sherry." The parish is affiliated with CTNA and has access to all EWTN and F&V programming. The television ministry began in February of 1992.

As of March 2007, Father Robert N. Sherry is pastor. There are approximately 2,400 families currently registered at Church of Holy Apostles Parish.

◆ **Adoration chapel interior.**

◆ **Adoration chapel.**

St. Mary Parish

Until 1894, the German Catholics in McHenry were dependent upon the parish at Johnsburg for services in their own language. German missionaries on their way to the church of St. John the Baptist in Johnsburg would stop in McHenry to care for the Germans there. During the time of Father Hubert M. Fegers, who came to Johnsburg in 1868, the German community here was considered a mission of that parish.

In 1894, Father Frederick J. Kirsch (1894-1901), a German speaking priest, was appointed the first resident pastor of St. Mary Parish, McHenry. He offered the first Mass at St. Mary's on August

◆ **Father Mathias Barth with First Communicants, circa 1901.**

15, 1894, in a building which had been used as a public school. Soon after Father Kirsch's arrival he made plans to build the present St. Mary Church. Dedication of the church took place on the Feast of the Assumption, August 15, 1898, just four years from the date of the first Mass celebrated by Father Kirsch.

After a suitable place of worship was built, priority was placed on a parish school. Classes could be conducted in the old school building. Atmosphere was not essential, learning was.

The School Sisters of St. Francis operated the district school in Johnsburg and their services were requested for McHenry. They continued to administer the educational program through the years, but left the parish in the early 2000's.

During the pastorate of Father Edward Berthold (1915-1921), tragedy struck the parish in 1917 when fire heavily damaged the church and destroyed the rectory. The church was repaired, but the parish got

◆ **St. Mary Church.**

◆ **Father Mathias Barth, pastor 1901-1907.**

◆ **St. Mary Church fire, 1917.**

◆ **Father Charles Nix with the graduating class of 1923.**

along without a rectory until Father Charles S. Nix (1921-1960) became pastor on August 10, 1921, the first day of what was to become 39 years of service to the parish.

Father Nix, who was named a Monsignor in 1935, supervised the immediate construction of a new rectory. In 1937, Monsignor Nix built a new school building, which was to serve as a community school for the children of St. Mary and St. Patrick parishes until 1951 when the people of St. Patrick's built their own school. Bishop Edward F. Hoban dedicated the new school on November 7, 1937. In 1956, Monsignor Nix added four classrooms and a gymnasium to the growing parish school.

Father Eugene C. Baumhofer (1960-1979) was named the pastor of St. Mary's on November 22, 1960, the beginning of his 19 years as pastor.

For at least 30 years, the parish enjoyed the services of Benedictines from Marmion Abbey for much needed assistance on weekends, holy days and at the holiday seasons.

St. Mary Parish celebrated its diamond jubilee of the founding of the parish during Masses of Thanksgiving on Sunday, September 21, 1969. The pastor, Father Baumhofer, also celebrated 25 years in the priesthood on that day. To mark the jubilee, extensive renovation of the church and the Mary Chapel (the church basement) was carried out.

In 1970, St. Mary and St. Patrick consolidated their parish schools to form Montini Primary Center and Montini Middle School. In 1989, the Church of Holy Apostles School consolidated with St. Mary and St. Patrick.

The rectory was refurbished and plans were made for the conversion of St. Mary Chapel to St. Mary Family Hall in 1993 during the pastorate of Father Thomas E. Burr (1991-2006).

The parish's 100th anniversary was celebrated in 1994 and Montini Catholic School celebrated its 25th anniversary in 1995.

For over 25 years, the parish has held an annual rummage sale in June. The proceeds go to the Montini Catholic School.

As of March 2007, Father Robert A. Balog is pastor. There are approximately 800 families currently registered at St. Mary Parish.

St. Patrick Parish

St. Patrick Parish, McHenry, was founded in 1840 by Father Maurice de St. Palais. Father de St. Palais had been sent to Chicago by Bishop Simon Brute, of Vincennes, whose jurisdiction extended to the northeastern portion of Illinois.

The McHenry parish, one of the pioneer parishes in the Rockford Diocese, was only one of Father de St. Palais' missionary activities, but the French priest only remained a short time in Illinois. He returned to Vincennes after the Chicago Diocese was created and he later became Bishop of Vincennes.

Despite St. Patrick's early formation, nearby Hartland had established a church four years earlier. It was to this church that McHenry area residents went for major church functions.

The Masses offered before St. Patrick Church was built were said in homes, primarily those of James Wall, John and Michael Sutton, George Frisby and Mrs. Mary Behan.

The first St. Patrick Church was built in 1853 on land donated by James Gibbs. The building cost $700 and was to serve the parish for almost 20 years. Mr. Gibbs also had donated land for a cemetery.

The second parish church was built by Father Peter Birch in 1872, which also was the year that McHenry was incorporated— in spite of the fact that the first settler had arrived some 36 years earlier.

Father P. M. O'Neill (1876-1906) was the first long-term pastor of St. Patrick. He built an addition to the church in 1883. Father O'Neill also replaced the rectory and had charge of the missions of Richmond, Wauconda and Fox Lake.

◆ **Father Maurice de St. Palais.**

◆ **St. Patrick Church.**

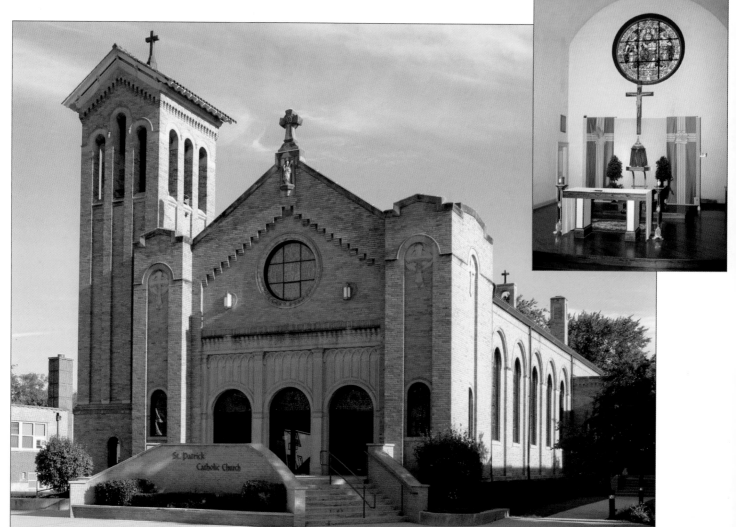

◆ First St. Patrick Church, 1853.

◆ First St. Patrick Church interior.

Father Martin J. McEvoy (1915-1926) began planning a new church in 1921. The cornerstone was laid in August 1922, with Bishop Peter J. Muldoon officiating. The new church was dedicated on St. Patrick's Day, March 17, 1923.

Father William A. O'Rourke (1926-1950) became pastor in February of 1926 and was to remain until his death in 1950. Among his many achievements was a substantial reduction of the parish debt and redecoration of the church. Father O'Rourke joined with Monsignor Charles S. Nix in building the St. Patrick-St. Mary School in 1937. This school served the children of both parishes until St. Patrick Parish built its own school in 1951.

◆ Father William O'Rourke.

It was in 1951, under Father Edward C. Coakley (1948-1965), that the parish school was built, making possible a separation from the school that served both parishes in McHenry since 1937. During that year a convent was also secured. Four new classrooms were added to the school, and the convent was doubled in capacity. The school was staffed by the Sisters of Mercy.

Under the pastorate of Father Leonard J. Guzzardo (1965-1969), the church was enlarged in 1965 by opening the wall separating the winter chapel from the main church. The church hall and rectory were remodeled, a new garage was added and the parking area was resurfaced.

In 1966, land was purchased for a new cemetery south of McHenry on Barreville road. A new central heating system for the church, school and rectory was installed in 1967.

During the pastorate of Father Edmund P. Petit (1969-1986) a committee composed of pastors and members of both St. Patrick and St. Mary Parishes began studying the feasibility of combining the parish schools once again. The schools were consolidated for the school year 1970-1971 under the new name of Montini Catholic School in honor of Pope Paul VI. With the consolidation, the St. Patrick's building became the Montini Primary Center, serving grades one through four, and the St. Mary's building became the Montini Middle School, for grades five through eight.

In 1970, Father Petit redecorated the interior of the church to conform to the norms of Vatican Council II.

Bishop Arthur J. O'Neill was welcomed by Father Petit for a rededication ceremony on July 22, 1984. The new rectory was dedicated, along with the church's new parish center. The two-story Parish Center and Administrative Building contains 7,800 square feet, 3,900 on each level.

Under the pastorate of Father James V. McKitrick (1986-2000), an extensive remodeling project was undertaken in 1988 in anticipation of the 150th jubilee year in 1990.

In 1989, a pipe organ was donated by Howard V. Phalin in memory of his wife, Evangeline. The same year, a shrine to the Holy Family in the church and a memorial statue in the Angel Section of St. Patrick Countryside Cemetery were also donated.

As of March 2007, Father Joseph P. Naill is pastor. There are approximately 1,200 families currently registered at St. Patrick Parish.

St. Mary of the Assumption Parish

About 1853, Father Patrick O'Dwyer became the first resident pastor of St. Patrick Parish, St. Charles. Shortly after this he built the first church in what is now known as Maple Park. This wooden structure was built on the northeast corner of the current Watson and Keslinger Roads, and was then known as "Barney's Hill". This site is about four miles east and south of Maple Park. In these days Maple Park was officially known as Lodi.

Father O'Dwyer said Mass here occasionally for Catholics, many of whom left Ireland in the 1840's during the potato famine. Sometimes priests came from DeKalb—Father John McMullen, later the first Bishop of Davenport, Iowa, and Father John B. Murray, who was pastor at DeKalb in 1861.

This early church was eventually moved to DeKalb. In 1861, Lodi was attached to DeKalb as a

◆ **First St. Mary Church.**

mission. The Reverend John McMullen erected a new and larger church in Lodi. Lodi became known as Maple Park in 1863.

◆ **St. Mary Church.**

◆ **Bishop Muldoon and clergy of the Diocese at the dedication of the current church, May 25, 1914.**

◆ **St. Mary Church interior.**

Father Richard H. McGuire came to Maple Park as the first resident pastor in 1871. In 1899 a pipe organ was built in Boston by the Hook and Hastings Organ company for a church in Joliet.

◆ **Dedication of current church, May 25, 1914.**

When the Joliet parish constructed a new church in 1923 the organ was purchased by St. Mary Parish and moved to the Maple Park church.

Father John H. Whelan (1913-1918) became pastor in 1913. On September 1, 1913, construction was begun on the present church and rectory. Mass was celebrated in the chapel attached to the church on February 15, 1914, and in the church itself the following Sunday. Bishop Peter J. Muldoon dedicated the church on June 25, 1914, under the title of St. Mary of the Assumption.

When war was declared, Father Whelan enlisted in the army as a chaplain and left the parish in June, 1918. The following July, Father Francis S. Porcella (1918-1939) came to Maple Park as its pastor. He remained twenty years.

In 1967, under the pastorate of Father James C. Novak, OSB (1961-1969), an Education Center was built. This center, now known as the Novak Center in honor of Father Novak, is still used for CCD classes, as well as many parish activities..

In 1994, under the pastorate of Father Patrick D. Corbally (1985-1994), the old St. Mary Cemetery south of town was rededicated. Also that year, the Madonna della Strada Shrine was erected in front of the church.

As of March 2007 the parochial administrator is Father Joachim Tyrtania. There are approximately 250 families currently registered at St. Mary of the Assumption Parish.

SACRED HEART PARISH

The start of organized Catholic activity in Marengo coincides with activity in both Rockford and Belvidere, but its growth was not as rapid as in those cities.

In 1851, the newly ordained Father John A. Hampston (1851-1854) was sent to take charge of the stations of Rockford, Belvidere, and Marengo. Father Hampston soon settled in the most convenient location, Belvidere. A year later, he moved again, to the faster-growing town of Rockford and began the first Catholic church in Rockford. This became St. James Pro-Cathedral.

In the fall of 1854, Father George Hamilton (1854-1855) was appointed to take Father Hampston's place. He continued to care for Belvidere and Marengo, as did subsequent pastors, until 1864 when Belvidere became an independent

◆ **Laying the cornerstone of the church, July 19, 1908.**

parish. In July 1864, Father Patrick McGuire (1864-1893) was appointed as pastor of Belvidere, with Marengo being a mission.

Prior to the arrival of Father Hampston, Catholics in the Marengo area either went to the historic St. Patrick Church in Hartland or were provided with services by the missionary activity of that northern McHenry County parish. A pastor had been in residence at Hartland since 1844.

When Father Hampston began his mission work, Marengo had not even been incorporated as a village. The town, named after a village in northern Italy, was incorporated in 1857.

Two years later, members of an Episcopal congregation built a church in the downtown area. That church would later serve Catholics for over 40 years.

Mass in the early Marengo years was celebrated in Lansing Hall, also downtown. When Father McGuire became pastor in Belvidere, he negotiated the purchase of the

◆ **Sacred Heart Church.**

Episcopal church and dedicated it to St. Patrick. Another purchase of Father McGuire in 1874 was land north of the city for use as a cemetery.

Marengo became an independent parish in 1902, when Father Francis B. Swanson (1902-1907) was appointed first resident pastor. He purchased a building on North Taylor Street for use as a rectory. The present church was constructed next to the rectory during the service of the second resident pastor, Father Daniel J. McCaffrey (1907-1921). A church built in 1907 at a cost of $30,000 was named (and the parish renamed) in honor of the Sacred Heart.

◆ **Father Daniel McCaffrey.**

The former church building was sold to the Republican News and the newspaper firm moved it to face on Prairie Street.

During Father Daniel P. Drennan's term (1921-1936), the church was redecorated (1924), the cemetery improved (1927) and property for a school was purchased (1929) but, because of the depression and the lack of growth of the parish, the school was never built.

In 1936, Father Daniel O'Connell (1936-1963) began a Marengo pastorate that was to last for 27 years, until his death on August 17, 1963.

During his pastorate, Father John W. Ryan (1965-1975) completely remodeled the church, bringing it up to the standards of the Second Vatican Council. He also updated the rectory and parish hall.

Many improvements, including central air conditioning for the church and construction of the parish office building, were completed while Father John W. Cahill (1975-1983) was pastor. Sacred Heart Church celebrated its 75th anniversary on June 12, 1983, with a Mass offered by Bishop Arthur J. O'Neill.

In July 1983, Father Philip E. O'Neil (1983-2003) became pastor. In 1988, construction began on a major addition to the church facility, including a two-car garage, classrooms and meetings rooms, a chapel, a modern kitchen, four new restrooms, a community area and a chair lift accessible to any floor. Upon completion, Bishop Arthur J. O'Neill attended the dedication ceremony on September 11, 1988.

An extensive renovation of the church's interior took place in 1992. The new altar was blessed and the church was rededicated by Bishop Arthur J. O'Neill on October 4, 1992.

Sacred Heart Church honored its patron with the construction of a shrine located between the church and rectory. A gift from Ralph and Lorraine Deneen covered a major portion of the cost. The six-sided gazebo houses a hand-carved marble statue of the Sacred Heart of Jesus. Bishop Thomas G. Doran blessed and dedicated the shrine on October 31, 1999.

Father O'Neil, who was invested as a Monsignor in 1996, retired in 2003 after 20 years of service to the parish.

As of March 2007, Father Richard M. Russo is pastor. There are approximately 800 families currently registered at Sacred Heart Parish.

◆ **Sacred Heart Church interior.**

ST. PATRICK PARISH

In 1840, the William Dolan family came to settle in May Township and, on April 28, 1840, Father Parody, a Vincentian, said the first Mass in the Dolan family home. After this, Mass was said by Father Thomas O'Donnell, who came from Ottawa four times a year on horseback.

In 1847, a small log church dedicated to St. Michael was erected at Sandy Hill, three miles east of Maytown and about half a mile from the Dolan home. Local lore says William Dolan walked to Dixon carrying a pail of butter to exchange for the nails used to build the church.

In 1855, the brick church at Sandy Hill was built. For many years it was attended irregularly by priests from Ottawa and LaSalle. In 1859, Father M. J. Clarke came to Amboy and he attended the Maytown church, as well as the church at Perkin's Grove, as missions. Perkin's Grove later had a resident pastor but St. Michael's remained in the care of the Amboy pastors until 1880.

The area continued to grow with the influx of Irish settlers and, by 1870, its 60 families proved too large a congregation for the tiny St. Michael mission. Since most of the new families were moving west of

◆ **Father Francis Porcella with his horses Fanny and Flora, circa 1910.**

◆ **Father Francis A. Keenan.**

the church, Father Francis A. Keenan (1873-1880), Pastor at Amboy, purchased six acres of land west of Sandy Hill in 1875, and in 1876, a frame church was built and put under the patronage of St. Patrick.

The old church of St. Michael was not abandoned. In fact, in 1883, an addition was built. But 10 years later, in 1893, it ceased to serve as a parish church. In 1923, the walls were torn down, and a new front was added to the old sacristy, making a cemetery chapel as a memorial to the pioneer Catholics of St. Michael Parish.

Patrick Reiley's house served as a rectory for the priest serving Maytown and Sandy Hill. Bishop

◆ **St. Patrick Church.**

Thomas P.R. Foley of Chicago assigned Father George T. Ratz (1880-1881) as the first resident pastor of Maytown in 1880. Father Ratz lived in the former Reiley home. In the meantime, German Catholics had built St. Mary Church in 1875, as an offshoot of an earlier church in Perkin's Grove. Father Ratz was also put in charge of that church. His first work upon becoming pastor was to build a rectory near where the academy was to be built, and then to build the school itself. Mr. Reiley's estate had provided for the construction of an academy in 1879.

◆ **The first St. Patrick Church**

Six Benedictine sisters opened the academy in 1880, boarding girls and taking boys as day students. After approximately 10 years of successful operation, attendance fell and it was thought prudent to close it.

In 1906, Father William P. Quinlisk (1905-1909) served the three missions of St. Patrick, St. Michael, and St. Mary from Maytown.

Father Francis S. Porcella (1909-1918) was appointed pastor of the Maytown parish in 1909. The old academy, which had served as parish hall, was in need of extensive repair. Since it was located four miles from the church, Father sold the old building, and erected a new parish hall.

Father Cornelius J. Kirkfleet, O.Praem. (1918-1928), became pastor in 1918 and built the present brick church in 1919. During his tenure at Maytown, Father Kirkfleet wrote a biography of Archbishop Patrick A. Feehan and compiled the first History of the Rockford Diocese, published in 1924.

Father Ivon A. Esser (1928-1930) was appointed pastor of St. Patrick Parish and St. Mary's mission in August of 1928. He decorated the church and built a garage near the rectory.

Father J. Urban Halbmaier (1931-1943) became pastor in 1931 and was there for the 100th anniversary of the first Mass at Maytown, which was marked in 1940 with Bishop Edward F. Hoban in attendance.

Father John T. Smith (1943-1949) installed new heating plants in the church and hall, and had the church redecorated and tuck-pointed.

Father Sylvester J. Eye (1949-1951) was appointed pastor in 1949. He remodeled the rectory and enlarged the sanctuary. Changes were made in the hall in order that it could temporarily be rented to the public school system, which needed classroom space.

During the pastorate of Father Clement P. Petit (1951-1958) plans were made for modernizing and redecorating St. Patrick's, although the actual work was not done for several years.

During Father Bertram C. Jaeger's term (1958-1960), a shrine of St. Isidore was placed on the front lawn of the rectory.

It was during Father Charles E. Sherman's pastorate (1960-1964) that St. Mary Church was closed and combined with St. Patrick Parish.

In 1965, during Father Eugene D. Parker's pastorate (1965-1967), the church was redecorated and the old altars were removed. When Father Parker left in 1967, St. Patrick was placed in the care of Father Phillip Bajo (1967-1972), pastor of Sublette, until February of 1972 when Father William F. Boland (1972-1974) was made pastor of St. Patrick. Following his death, St. Patrick was once again placed under the care of the pastor of Sublette.

The church and parish hall were renovated by parishioners in the early 1990's while Father Thomas P. Dolan (1993-2003) was pastor. The old rectory was demolished and replaced with a parking lot for the elderly and disabled.

As of March 2007, Father Carl E. Beekman is parochial administrator. There are approximately 50 families currently registered at St. Patrick Parish.

Nativity of the Blessed Virgin Mary Parish

As early as 1838, Father Samuel C. Mazzuchelli, O.P., attended the spiritual needs of Catholic settlers and native Indians in what is now Menominee Township.

Mass was offered in the home of Joachim Lang until a frame church was built on the site of the present church. This frame church was probably erected in 1850.

The first pastor of Nativity B.V.M. Parish was Father Francis H. Kendeler who was appointed on February 14, 1864. The joy of the people of Menominee having a resident pastor was to be short-lived, his ministry terminating in premature death after just one short month.

◆ **Father William Verhoef.**

After an interval of two years, during which time the parishioners were served by priests from Galena, Father William Verhoef (1866-1877), a Crosier priest, was appointed to the parish in April, 1866. He erected the present brick church which stands as a lasting memorial to the zeal and energetic spirit of Father Verhoef and his parishioners. A year after its completion in 1877, Father Verhoef died at the age of 49. All the labor on the church was done manually by the parishioners and includes a 136–foot steeple.

Father Joseph Beinecke (1881-1887), came to the debt-free parish in 1881 and was able to take over the construction of a frame school almost immediately. A parishioner with a degree from the University of Osnabruch in Prussia, Mr. Herman Rojemann, was the first teacher, also serving as organist, sacristan and caretaker.

Father Paul Halbmeier (1887-1904) succeeded Father Beinecke in November, 1887. His pastorate, which lasted until 1904, has been the longest in the annals of the parish history. The rectory was built during these years and many notable improvements in the church were made, including the installation of a pipe organ and bells in the steeple.

Father Henry J. Hauser (1905-1914) came in 1905. He brought in the Franciscan Sisters of Milwaukee to teach in the school. By 1923, the old parish school had become a district public school, leased to the school district by the parish. Since all the pupils attending the school were Catholic, Catholic teachers were provided by the school district. When the Depression struck, the Menominee parish, almost entirely agricultural, was hard hit. To add to the hard times and sorrow of the parish at this time, Father Henry A. Hagen (1923-1933) became ill in 1930 and died in 1933.

◆ **Nativity of the Blessed Virgin Mary Church.**

◆ **Parishioners gather in the late 1800s.**

Bishop Edward F. Hoban appointed Father Joseph M. Lonergan (1934-1952) as the eleventh pastor at Menominee in 1934. Father Lonergan was the first pastor at Menominee who was not of German descent. During his pastorate of almost 20 years, the parish observed its centennial in 1938.

In the early part of 1952, with a new generation to be educated in their faith, everyone agreed a new school was necessary. Father Lonergan, foreseeing the difficulties of raising funds and securing teachers, realized the need of a younger priest than he to carry out the project. Father Henry M. Schryer (1952-1957) was appointed pastor, arriving at Menominee in September 1952. The new school was opened two years later, staffed by Dominican Sisters from Sinsinawa, Wisconsin.

Father Raymond M. Hettermann (1959-1963) arrived in June 1959, and during his pastorate the church was redecorated and, with his influence, land was purchased by the Holy Name Society for use as a playground and ball diamond, as were four and one half acres for additional cemetery ground.

In 1963, Father William H. Regnier (1963-1965) became pastor. He initiated liturgical changes in the church as a result of Vatican II. The communion rail was removed, and two communion stands and a portable altar facing the congregation were installed.

Further post-Vatican II changes were made under the leadership of Father Alphonsus L. Fitzgibbons (1966-1979), who was appointed pastor in September 1966. Under Father Fitzgibbons' direction and guidance, renovations took place, including refurbishing the historic church steeple, installing new heating equipment and a new roof on the school. Also at this time, the rectory was extensively remodeled.

During the administration of Father Bernard F. Dittman (1989-1999), the church was refurbished and made accessible to the handicapped.

Father Theodore V. Lewandowski (1999-2004) had the entire church steeple and the Crucifixion Scene in the cemetery redone.

For over 25 years, parishioners of Nativity of the BVM have joined with parishioners of St. Mary Parish in East Dubuque to ship donations by the semi-truck load, four to five times a year, to the Rosebud Indian Reservation in South Dakota. Later they added residents of Marks, Mississippi, to the list.

As of March 2007, Father Howard C. Barch is parochial administrator. There are approximately 200 families currently registered at Nativity of the Blessed Virgin Mary Parish.

◆ **Nativity of the Blessed Virgin Mary Church interior, 1914.**

St. Mary Parish

◆ **The first St. Mary Church, 1908.**

issionary priests from Dixon and Sterling said Mass in pioneer homes in Morrison until 1864, when Father John Daly, pastor at Sterling, supervised the construction of the first Catholic church in Morrison. Probably due to both the high number of early Irish parishioners in Morrison and the fact that the priests from St. Patrick in Dixon and St. Patrick in Sterling took care of the Morrison Catholics, the original church was dedicated as St. Patrick Church and remained St. Patrick until the turn of the 19th century, when it was rededicated as St. Mary Church.

Father John J. Kilkenney (1873-1884) began keeping records at Morrison and referred to it merely as "the Catholic Church at Morrison." It was during his pastorate that the church, built in 1864, was given its final construction touches.

In 1904, Father F. F. Hill, a Jesuit, urged the congregation to send a delegation to Chicago to plead for a resident pastor. The committee met with Bishop Peter J. Muldoon, then Auxiliary Bishop of Chicago, and Father Michael A. Bruton (1904-1905) was appointed as Morrison's first resident pastor.

Father Peter Gildea (1905-1906) became pastor in 1905. His pastorate is chiefly remembered because he built a rectory on Base Street, next to what Catholics thought was going to remain the church site.

During the pastorate of Father John R. Quigley (1917-1928), plans for a new church were made and much of the building material already taken to the Base Street site when it was learned that the Universalist church was for sale. Since the location was good and the price was tempting, plans for the new church were scrapped and the Universalist church was purchased. After remodeling, Mass was said in the new church for the first time on December 17, 1919.

◆ **Father Leo Bartel.**

In 1928, Father Alexander S. McIsaac (1928-1936) was named pastor. The parish records of the years of Father McIsaac's pastorate give evidence of extreme hardships caused by the Depression. Father McIsaac was succeeded by Father L. Dudley Day (1936-1938), who was able, in better economic times, to re-roof the church and the rectory.

During the term of Father Edward J. Connolly (1942-1949), the church and hall were extensively redecorated.

In the 1960s and early 1970s, the church was extensively remodeled during the pastorates of Father Charles W. McNamee (1963-1966), Father James F. McGuire (1966-1969), Father William I. Joffe (1969-1973) and Father Philip Kennedy (1973-1983).

In December 2003, during the pastorate of Father Leo J. Bartel (1983-2005), St. Mary Parish moved to a new location. The former church building, which was 130 years old, was not accessible to the handicapped and was developing potential safety problems. The need for more space and better accessibility became a top priority.

The former Unionville Auction Center at 13320 Garden Plain Road was acquired through the generosity of a parishioner. Through the kindness of the parishioner, St. Mary Parish was able

◆ **Stained glass windows from the old church.**

◆ **The second St. Mary Church**

to acquire five acres of land and the three-year-old building, as well as complete the extensive renovation, all without incurring debt. The parishioners transformed what was built as a large banquet hall into a worship space, parish hall and gathering space. Most all of the work was done by non-paid parishioners and friends. Many of the furnishings, including stained-glass windows, were moved from the old church building and reinstalled in the new space.

The conversion of the former auction center into a church was the first phase of the St. Mary project. The second phase will include the acquisition of an additional three to five acres of land, at no cost to the parish, for the construction of a larger church. The present church will then be converted into a full parish hall.

The 100th anniversary of St. Mary as a parish with a resident pastor was celebrated in 2004.

As of March 2007, Father William R. Antillon is parochial administrator. There are approximately 175 families currently registered at St. Mary Parish.

◆ **St. Mary Church interior and exterior.**

SS. John and Catherine Parish

Mass was first offered in Mount Carroll in 1881, when Father Anthony B. Buetter, who was pastor at St. Wendelin's in Shannon, came to Mount Carroll four times a year on the fifth Sunday of the month to say Mass in the Leo Phillips' home.

Irregular services continued until 1917 when Father John M. Clifford of Shannon was directed by Bishop Peter J. Muldoon to provide regular services (weekly, on a weekday). Again, there was no place for worship, so for some years Father Clifford offered Mass in private homes.

In 1924, Father Clifford supervised the construction of the Mount Carroll church on Jackson Street, across from the Shimer College campus, and attended the parish until his retirement in 1929. The church then became a mission of St. John the Baptist Parish, Savanna.

The practice of regular Sunday Mass in Mount Carroll began under the Savanna pastorate of Father Walter J. Ryan (1945-1952). The next pastor at St. John the Baptist, Father Edward J. McIsaac

◆ **Father Anthony Buetter.**

◆ **Father John Clifford.**

(1952-1963), redecorated SS. John and Catherine Church, adding a basement hall to the small white frame building.

Until the appointment of Father Matthew T. Rudden (1972), and the joining of Mount Carroll and Shannon parishes, the care of SS. John and Catherine was the responsibility of the pastor at Savanna.

Father James M. Weber (1972-1975) succeeded Father Rudden and, with his appointment, SS. John and Catherine Parish was no longer a mission church. The church was elevated to a parish by Bishop Arthur J. O'Neill in 1972.

In 1982, Father Charles K. McCarren (1982-1986), who was already serving as pastor of St. Catherine Parish in Freeport, was appointed pastor of SS. John and Catherine. The church was not affiliated with the Shannon parish during this time. For most of this time, catechism

◆ **The first SS. John & Catherine Church.**

◆ **SS. John & Catherine Church interior.**

◆ **SS. John & Catherine Church.**

classes were held at Shimer College, Mount Carroll Grade School, and in private homes.

Father McCarren purchased the present church on South Main Street in early 1983. The building was the former Mount Carroll Church of God. The new building offered two to three times as much seating in the church, plus six classrooms, an office, kitchen and roomy parish hall. Kneelers and Stations of the Cross installed in the new church were salvaged from the old St. Thomas High School in Rockford. Also installed was a marble baptismal font in which Father McCarren had been baptized. The statues, crucifix and altar were moved from the old church and placed in the new church.

A lot north of the church was purchased and is used for a parking lot. The old SS. John and Catherine church building was rented to the Church of Christ for a time and then sold at auction to a private individual in late 1986. It is now a private home.

In November of 1992, Father Joseph F. Jarmoluk (1992-1997) became pastor. He led the parish in major interior church remodeling in 1995. On July 13, 1997, Bishop Thomas G. Doran celebrated a rededication Mass.

In 2005, the kitchen was remodeled and chair lifts were installed during the pastorate of Father Moises A. Apostol (2002-2006).

As of March 2007, Father Dennis D. Atto is parochial administrator. There are approximately 125 families currently registered at SS. John and Catherine Parish.

BLESSED SACRAMENT PARISH

On Saturday evening, October 18, 1975, Bishop Arthur J. O'Neill dedicated Blessed Sacrament Parish in North Aurora, the only parish in the Rockford Diocese dedicated under the title of Blessed Sacrament.

The new parish began on October 4, 1970, with Father Edward S. Wright (1970-2004) as its first pastor. The parish began without any facilities at all for public worship and the congregation of the Blessed Sacrament Parish met in the Mercyville Auditorium for Sunday liturgies and religious education classes. Daily liturgies and meetings were held in the rectory on Chantilly Lane.

In 1972, the parish purchased eight acres of land and on June 1, 1975 the multipurpose building was completed and suitable for use. The multipurpose building served as the church, auditorium and religious education classrooms.

In 1981, a new rectory and parish center at 801 Oak Street was finished. It included living quarters and counseling and meeting rooms. With the completion of a 15-month "House-Give-Away" program, the parish was debt-free. The house being given away was the house at 15 N. Chantilly Lane

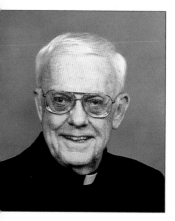

◆ **Monsignor Edward Wright.**

◆ **Tabernacle in the Blessed Sacrament chapel.**

◆ **Bishop O'Neill and Father Edward Wright at the groundbreaking of Blessed Sacrament.**

that the newly formed congregation bought in 1972. It was used as a temporary chapel, meeting room, and rectory.

During the pastorate of Father Wright, Bishop O'Neill dedicated the new Blessed Sacrament Church on September 16, 1984, the first parish he established as Bishop of the Rockford Diocese.

On April 21, 1996, founding pastor Father Wright was made a Monsignor. On July 4, 1999 Monsignor Wright blessed and broke ground for a new religious education center.

The Jubilee Year 2000 was a special one for Blessed Sacrament Church. Not only was the parish one of three pilgrimage churches in the Aurora Deanery, it also celebrated the 30th anniversary of its dedication.

On January 31, 2001, during the pastorate of Monsignor Wright, Bishop Thomas G. Doran dedicated the Blessed Sacrament Religious Education Center, a two-story, 16-room structure, which is connected to the rectory and parish hall.

As of March 2007 Father John A. Slampak is the pastor. There are approximately 600 families currently registered at Blessed Sacrament Parish.

◆ **Blessed Sacrament Church interior.**

◆ **Blessed Sacrament Church.**

St. Mary Parish

◆ **The first St. Mary Church.**

The recorded history of the Oregon parish may be said to begin in 1862 with the construction of a stone church at the cost of $1,600. There is an oral tradition, however, which goes back much further .

In 1838, a priest, whose name has been forgotten, left Chicago for Galena on horseback. Stopping in Elgin, he inquired of the hotel owner if there were any Catholics living between Elgin and Galena. He was told of a Francis Ryan whose home was between Grand Detour and Oregon. Two days later, after having crossed the Rock River, covered with mud and exhausted, he arrived at the Ryan homestead. Here he stayed four days, celebrating Mass each morning and baptizing the 1-year-old daughter of Michael Fenlon.

On his return from Galena, he stopped again at the Ryan homestead for three days before returning to Chicago. The magnitude of this event in the lives of those six Catholics visited can be truly appreciated from the fact that the Ryans had not seen a priest for four years previous to this time, and that in 1842, they moved to the Fenlon Settlement

◆ **The construction of St. Mary Church, 1889.**

◆ **St. Mary Church.**

Father Joseph Beinecke, pastor 1876-1881.

north of Durand, because Catholics there had the advantage of a priest's yearly visit.

Between 1842 and 1859 there is no available record of a visit of any priest in this neighborhood. However, during the years of 1859 and 1860, priests came from LaSalle and celebrated Mass in private homes. In 1861, Father Michael Ford came over from Dixon and offered Mass in an old country house, long since destroyed. Also, Father John Westkamp from Freeport attended the Catholics in Oregon.

In 1862, the Catholics of Oregon built their first church and from then on Father Louis F. Lightner came regularly from Dixon to celebrate Mass and administer the sacraments once a month.

In 1862, Oregon was made a mission of Sterling and the Sterling priests attended the parish.

In 1885, Father William Grunebaum was appointed the first resident pastor of St. Mary's.

Father Daniel Toomey built the present church and laid the cornerstone in 1891.

Father William P. Quinlisk (1905-1912) built the present rectory.

Father Arthur Kreckel, pastor 1939-1958.

During Father Norbert M. Richter's pastorate (1958-1964), land for a new school was purchased. Located west of Oregon on Illinois Route 64, at the top of Liberty Hill, the 21 acre site was well situated to serve both Oregon and Mount Morris. On September 25, 1959, Bishop Loras T. Lane of Rockford dedicated the new building.

The entire church building was renovated during Father Francis J. Bonnike's pastorate (1964-1967). An unusual mural was painted on the front wall of the interior of the church. A gift of the Bonnike family, it is entitled "The Manifold Presence of Christ in the Eucharist."

In 1967, major changes were made in the school program. The decision was made to concentrate on the first six grades, restoring the first grade that had been eliminated the year before, but eliminating the seventh and eighth grades.

Father Everett J. Hiller came on December 28, 1967. During his one year stay in Oregon, the rectory was remodeled.

It was during Father Charles E. Sherman's pastorate (1969-1972), in 1971, that St. Mary School closed. Shortly after the school closed, the convent was sold. On August 30, 1972, Father Salvatore J. Guagliardo (1972-1976) was appointed pastor of the Oregon parish. While he was pastor, he made some improvements to the rectory.

Father Anthony J. Becker (1976-1984) was named pastor in 1976, and in 1977, a project to put a basement in the church was begun. The hall has 3,600 square feet of space which includes a large open area, kitchen and restrooms. It is also handicapped accessible. Two stained glass windows from the earlier days of the church adorn the hall. Also, hanging in the hall is the cross from the top of the steeple that was hit by lightning in the mid-1900s.

A major renovation and redecoration of the church was finished in time to celebrate the church's centennial year. A new statue of the Holy Family, a gift from an anonymous donor, was installed in front of the church in March of 1991. Bishop Arthur J. O'Neill blessed the new statue, consecrated the new altar and rededicated the church on June 29, 1991, during the pastorate of Father William A. Budden (1984-2003).

The parish has had a Christmas Bazaar in December for many years. During Lent, the parish fish fry serves 800-900 meals each Friday.

As of March 2007, Father Richard R. Kramer is pastor. There are approximately 400 families currently registered at St. Mary Parish.

St. Mary Parish

In 1872, a parish was established comprising four missions: Pecatonica, Seward, Irish Grove and Durand. Father Peter Birch (1872-1874) was the first pastor. Previously, the area belonged to St. James Parish, Rockford. Occasionally priests from Rockford made the journey out to these missions, saying Mass in private homes. Father Birch said Mass in Seward at the church built on land donated by Lawrence McDonald with funds he collected.

The church of St. Thomas of Canterbury, Seward, was built in 1870-1871, but there was no church in Pecatonica when Father Birch arrived in 1872. Mass was celebrated in private homes and Father Birch lived in two rooms in the home of Thomas McDowell.

The present site of St. Mary Church was purchased in 1874 from Irvin French, and the small house on the property served as church and rectory. At that time there were about 12 families making up the parish.

◆ **Father Peter Birch.**

◆ **Father William Reedy.**

Father John E. Shannahan (1879-1883) became pastor in 1879 and built the first frame church. He was succeeded by Father John H. Ryan (1883-1885), who died of pneumonia in 1885.

Father Michael Sullivan (1894-1899) built a rectory in 1894 to replace the small building used earlier as church and rectory. He also built the church at Irish Grove.

When Bishop Peter J. Muldoon came to the new Diocese of Rockford, he separated the missions again. Father Daniel A. Feeley was named pastor of Durand and its mission, Irish Grove, and Father Hercules E. Ouimet (1909-1918) was assigned to Pecatonica and the mission at Seward in 1909. During Father Ouimet's tenure, four acres of ground were purchased for a cemetery in Pecatonica and in 1910 the Seward Church was remodeled.

The next pastor was Father William V. Reedy (1918-1954) who began his 36 years of service with his appointment in 1918. In the fall of 1919, pledges of $22,000 were received to replace the old frame church, which was inadequate for the growing congregation.

◆ **St. Mary Church and rectory, 1921.**

◆ **Laying the cornerstone of the current church, May 7, 1922.**

In January 1922, the rectory was destroyed by fire and rebuilding was started immediately. The cornerstone for the new church was laid by Bishop Muldoon on May 7, 1922, and the church was dedicated in December of the same year.

When Father Eugene C. Baumhofer (1954-1958) came in 1954, a broad program of renovation of the church, rectory and cemetery was initiated. The Seward church, St. Thomas of Canterbury, closed and its members joined the St. Mary congregation in Pecatonica.

In 2007, during the pastorate of Father Robert J. Sweeney, an addition, including rest rooms and an elevator large enough for a casket, were built.

For over 50 years, the parish has held a fall turkey or ham dinner on the third Sunday of October.

As of March 2007, Father Robert J. Sweeney is pastor. There are approximately 200 families currently registered at St. Mary Parish.

◆ **St. Mary Church.**

St. Mary Parish

St. Mary Parish was established in Polo in 1854; just a year after the town was laid out and named in honor of Venetian traveler Marco Polo. Two years after the establishment of the town, parishioners built the first church.

Catholic farmers living in the vicinity of what was to become Polo were cared for by missionaries in the late 1840s and 1850s. When the population began to expand in a central location, priests from Dixon made regular visits to the area, saying Mass in the homes of Catholic families.

In the early 1850s, there were many men from Ireland who came to this area to build the railroad. On Sundays, these men would take a handcar and go to Dixon, bringing back a priest to say Mass.

The town itself resulted from Illinois Central Railroad plans. The rail company intended to run through another Ogle County settlement, Buffalo Grove, but when residents there objected to right-of-way plans, the rail line was laid out to the northeast, through the farm of Mr. Zenas Aplington, the founder of Polo.

By 1856, a number of Irish railroad workers had settled in Polo and were living on the north edge of the town, at the end of Franklin Avenue, at a site known variously as Irish Polo and Irish Hollow. Zenas Aplington, a Baptist, donated a plot of land to St. Mary Parish, with the understanding that a church be built there within a year. By the winter of 1856, a small, white frame building was completed and occupied. This was the first church built in Polo.

There were about 40 families attending St. Mary Church at this time and services were held regularly by priests from Dixon. Father Thomas Kennedy (1855-1859) of Dixon was the first pastor. Polo remained a mission of Dixon until 1875, when it was attached as a mission to Freeport. In 1878, it had a membership 65 families.

During the Freeport pastorate of Father Thomas F. Mangan from 1878 to 1887, the little church was enlarged to about double its original

◆ **St. Mary Church.**

St. Mary Church with the steeple that was later removed.

St. Mary Church interior.

size. Twenty years later a lot was purchased at the corner of Dixon and Franklin Streets for a new church.

The present brick church was built in 1899, at a cost of about $12,000. The first services were conducted in the new church by Father John J. McCann on December 21, 1899. The church was dedicated, free of debt, on January 7, 1900. The original church was sold and moved to the 100 block of East Mason Street.

In 1906, St. Mary became an independent parish and received its first resident pastor, Father Sylvester J. O'Hara (1906-1909). Before he left, Father O'Hara bought a lot next to the church and work was begun on a rectory.

During the 20 years that Father James D. Burke was pastor (1945-1965), the church was redecorated and, in 1953, a basement hall with a modern kitchen and dining room was added to the church.

Father Leon DuFour, pastor in the 1890s.

Father James Burke.

Father Philip E. O'Neil (1966-1969) was appointed pastor on January 21, 1966. He renovated the church to be in line with the new liturgical norms of the Second Vatican Council.

Since Father Matthew T. Rudden's appointment (1972-1986), there have been improvements made to the church and church hall.

On November 24, 1974, St. Mary Parish celebrated the 75th anniversary of its present church.

Father Donald F. Smithes (1986-2000) was assigned as pastor on July 18, 1986. He organized a centennial celebration of the construction of the church building. That took place on January 16, 2000, and commemorated the dedication ceremony held on January 7, 1900.

On December 10, 2000, during the pastorate of Father John A. Hanrahan, a new statue of the Blessed Mother in front of the church was dedicated to the memory of Father Smithes as a memorial. Major renovation work on the church building also took place at that time.

As of March 2007, Father John A. Hanrahan is pastor. There are approximately 200 families currently registered at St. Mary Parish.

St. Catherine Parish

Originally, St. Catherine Parish was a part of St. Mary Parish in Tampico, and Catholics here attended Mass, when they could, at Tampico. John Murphy and his wife Rose moved to Prophetstown about 1875. He would engage the railroad handcar on Saturdays and take a group to Tampico to attend Mass on Sunday mornings.

Shortly after this time, Father Richard H. McGuire (1879-1885) from Tampico began to offer Mass in the home of John Murphy on the first Sunday of each month; he came by train on Saturday evening and returned the following Monday.

Prophetstown continued to be one of Father McGuire's commitments, even after the Murphy family moved to a nearby farm. Mass was regularly offered in a hall or in the home of another settler until Father J. A. Fanning (1885-1886) became pastor in Tampico. Mass wasn't regularly offered again in Prophetstown for about 30 years, until

March 23, 1916 when, Tampico pastor Father Leon X. DuFour came to say Mass at the home of Mrs. Elizabeth Leahy. Until November of that year, either Father DuFour or his assistant came to Prophetstown to celebrate Mass during the week rather than on Sunday.

In November 1916, Sunday Mass was started again by Father Theodore B. McCormick, who served as pastor of Tampico (1916-1917). He also supervised the construction of Prophetstown's church, which was dedicated by Bishop Peter J. Muldoon in May 1917, to St. Catherine. It appears that some pastors called the parish St. Catherine of Siena until about 1923.

◆ **Father Theodore McCormick.**

On October 1, 1917, Father John V. Walsh was appointed Administrator of the Prophetstown parish. In 1919, Father Walsh purchased a house in Erie at the corner of Main and Water (now Fifth) Streets. Renovations on the house were begun by Father Walsh and completed later by Father John T. Egan (1920-1921). The building was used as a church until Father Ambrose M. Weitekamp became pastor at Prophetstown in 1933.

Father David A. Murphy (1927-1933), the son of John and Rose Murphy at whose home the first Masses were celebrated in Prophetstown, served the parish. In 1928, Father Murphy built a rectory.

◆ **St. Catherine Church, circa 1920.**

◆ **St. Catherine Church.**

During the pastorate of Father Ambrose Weitekamp (1933-1946) a new church was built in Erie, named St. Ambrose, in his honor.

Between 1958 and 1960, during the pastorate of Father Robert P. Donavan (1957-1960), renovations were made to the church. The large stained-glass window was removed and replaced with double doors. The parking lot was added at this time.

In 1971, the stained-glass windows were installed and a new altar was added during the pastorate of Father Cletus A. Anger (1964-1980).

The old bell tower and bell were removed from the church in 1980 while Father Vincent J. Shindelar (1980-1986) was pastor. The cross that stood atop the bell tower was retained.

As of March 2007, Father Francis Wawryszuk is pastor. There are approximately 100 families currently registered at St. Catherine Parish.

◆ **St. Catherine Church interior.**

St. Joseph Parish

For approximately 75 years, St. Joseph in Richmond existed as a mission parish of St. Patrick's in McHenry—in spite of the fact that near its beginning the small congregation in the northeast corner of McHenry County actually had a pastor in residence.

The "resident pastor" circumstance came about in 1858 when Father Andrew Eustace (1857-1859), Pastor of St. Patrick in McHenry, moved his residence from McHenry to Richmond after he built a small log church in Richmond. Richmond was still in its mission status, but he chose to live there. He was the only pastor to do so until the Richmond congregation became a parish and received its first official resident pastor in 1925.

The church that Father Eustace had constructed served Richmond area Catholics for just over 40 years. A donation left to the parish by the Walsh family enabled its members to construct a new church in 1899. The frame building, located north of town across Twin Lakes Road and a bit north of the present parish cemetery, was dedicated on November 26, 1899, and renamed in honor of St. Joseph.

◆ **Father Karl Ostenkoetter.**

The second church was abandoned shortly after the parish acquired its independence. The parish attained independent status when Father Karl Ostenkoetter (1925-1930) became St. Joseph's first resident pastor. During his pastorate, the church built in 1899 was sold and Father Ostenkoetter arranged for the purchase of an unused Protestant church, which was renovated for use as St. Joseph's third church. The building was located a half block west of U.S. Highway 12 and a block south of Illinois 173, which later became the site of the parish school.

At the time Father John F. Blake (1934-1948) became pastor, Bishop Edward F. Hoban attached Hebron Township, formerly part of Hartland, to the Richmond parish. With this growth of the parish, it became necessary to build a new church.

Father Blake supervised the construction of the present rectory and helped draw plans for a new church. The rectory was moved to its present site, just north of the new church on U. S. 12, and the church's construction began in 1948.

Father Francis J. Miller (1948-1965) completed the building of the church. A new parish hall was available for Midnight Mass by Christmas of 1948, and the solemn dedication of the new church building took place on May 30, 1949, with Bishop John J. Boylan.

St. Joseph Parish celebrated its 50th anniversary as a parish on August 15, 1975, with a Mass concelebrated by Bishop Arthur J. O'Neill and Father Thomas W. Neville (1970-1989), pastor.

◆ **Father Thomas Neville.**

◆ **Building the religious education office, 1985.**

In 1995, during the pastorate of Father Joseph W. Kaiser (1991-2004), a new parish office and religious education office were built.

On March 19, 1999, the feast of St. Joseph, Bishop Thomas G. Doran celebrated a Mass of Thanksgiving to celebrate the parish's 100 years of patronage under St. Joseph.

The parish has held a St. Joseph's Day potluck for over 20 years.

As of March 2007, Father Stephen O. Folorunso is parochial administrator. There are approximately 400 families currently registered at St. Joseph Parish.

◆ **St. Joseph Church interior and exterior.**

ST. PATRICK PARISH

Previous to 1853 there is no record to indicate that any Catholic services were held in Rochelle for the early settlers. The railroad was built through this area in 1853 and 1854, and tradition has it that a priest, possibly from the LaSalle area, passing through once offered Mass here, probably in a home. In 1856, Father Thomas Kennedy, of St. Patrick Parish, Dixon, paid a visit to Rochelle and arrangements were made for Mass to be said on a regular basis. Rochelle was then made a mission from Dixon.

In 1857, construction of a church was started on the corner of North Eighth Street and Lincoln Avenue. Legend has it that the framework of the first church was destroyed by a windstorm, but the church was soon finished, and each month a priest from Dixon came to celebrate Mass.

Although the Rochelle Catholic community continued as a mission from Dixon, land for the current cemetery was purchased in 1867, and in 1868 Father Patrick Duhig (1868-1869) was appointed the first resident pastor. Shortly thereafter, he purchased a residence on North Seventh Street for a rectory.

During the pastorate of Father Edward Froelich (1876-1879), a new church bell, weighing 2250 pounds, was dedicated, and improvements were begun on the church. Completion of church improvements occurred during the pastorate of Father James Treacy (1879-1885).

The arrival of Father John J. Greene (1889-1890) spurred action to construct a new church. The existing church, later converted to a residence, was moved to South Sixth Street in early 1890, and construction of the new church was begun on the old church site in May 1890. Father Greene's sudden illness resulted in his

◆ **Aftermath of church fire, 1918.**

replacement by Father Anthony I. Carr (1890-1893) in July 1890. Construction proceeded swiftly to completion, and Archbishop Patrick A. Feehan dedicated the new church in December 1890.

The arrival of Father Thomas Finn (1893-1907) led to construction of a new rectory adjacent to the church in 1896. Before he concluded his Rochelle pastorate, Father Finn purchased a residence on Seventh Street to be used for a school. Father David J. Conway (1907-1909) opened the parish school in September 1908, with the Sisters of St. Francis of the Immaculate Conception, from Clinton, Iowa, as teachers.

Father Paul Bourke (1909-1926) finished paying the church debt, but later was faced with financial problems when, in June 1918, the church was destroyed by fire, during which the giant bell fell through the first floor and rested in the basement. The church was soon rebuilt at a cost of $35,000. Father Bourke liquidated this debt in a short time and in 1921 purchased additional property for a new school. He died suddenly at Rochelle in 1926.

Under Father Thomas J. O'Brien (1926-1950) a new school building was built in 1929 and the debt of $50,000 was liquidated during his pastorate. In July 1929, a convent was purchased. According

◆ **First Communicant, Helen Spath, 1913.**

to Father O'Brien, the parish did not suffer from the depression as severely as others in the diocese. In 1937, a new organ was installed in the Church, and in 1944 additional property for the cemetery was acquired.

◆ **St. Patrick Church.**

On November 3, 1948, Bishop John J. Boylan sent Father Thomas P. Lynam (1948-1954, administrator; 1954-1960, pastor) to administer the affairs of the parish at Rochelle. In April, 1951, four new bells, which had been cast, in part, from the previous giant bell, were blessed and installed in the bell tower. The parish newsletter reported in 1977 that, "On the feast of Corpus Christi, in 1952, the young seminarian Jim Larson could be seen on scaffolding ringing the bells by hand, much like Quasimodo did in The Hunchback of Notre Dame." This seminarian was ordained a priest and had a distinguished career in the Rockford Diocese, including several diocesan leadership positions.

With the passage of time, the need for larger facilities to accommodate parish growth became apparent. Following the arrival of Father Edward J. McIsaac (1963-1966) as pastor in June 1963, he purchased land on the east side of Rochelle for a new church.

In September of 1966, Father Francis P. Kennedy (1966-1999) assumed the pastoral duties at St. Patrick, a position that he would hold for almost 33 years. Under his direction, a new church was constructed in 1972 to replace the church building originally built in 1890. A new rectory was also constructed on the premises.

By 1972, the Sisters of the Immaculate Conception were unable to continue staffing St. Patrick Grade School. The lack of Sisters, rising costs of education, and small enrollment, resulted in closing St. Patrick Grade School in June 1972, and the building was subsequently sold. The convent was used for parish offices until it was sold in 1974.

To provide space for religious education classes and parish social events, Father Kennedy constructed a parish center in 1975, adjacent to the church. Bishop O'Neill dedicated the entire church complex on October 19, 1975. To meet continuing needs of the parish, Father Kennedy purchased a 12,000 sq. ft. building which was remodeled to serve as a learning center, and Bishop Arthur J. O'Neill dedicated it on December 15, 1990.

In October 2000, Father David A. Peck became pastor. He initiated several actions to revitalize the existing facilities and purchased a large parcel of land, near the new high school, for future growth and expansion of the parish.

As of March 2007, Father David A. Peck is the pastor. There are approximately 1200 families currently registered at St. Patrick Parish.

◆ **Father Thomas O'Brien with St. Patrick altar boys, circa 1940. The future Father F. James Larson is holding the banner.**

St. Andrew Parish

◆ **St. Andrew Church.**

In years before the establishment of the parish in 1950, Catholics from the Rock Falls area attended St. Mary and Sacred Heart Parishes in Sterling. The increasing industrialization of neighboring cities, already crowded, led to the rapid growth of the community of Rock Falls. Monsignor Andrew J. Burns, Pastor of St. Mary Parish, Sterling was alert to the needs of Catholics here, and largely through his efforts, Bishop John J. Boylan was prevailed upon to establish a parish in Rock Falls. Father Joseph J. Tully (1950) was appointed the first resident pastor in June 1950. The parish was named after St. Andrew the Apostle in honor of Monsignor Burns.

Father Tully, in the few months of his pastorate, very thoroughly laid the foundation for the new parish. A piece of property on the corner of First Avenue and East Tenth Street was given to the new parish by Leo Wahl of Sterling. Since it would have taken several months to obtain a suitable place for worship, Father Tully persuaded Mr. Wahl to switch the gift of this lot for an already constructed building at 800 Fourth Avenue, to be used as a temporary church while a new parish plant was being built. Mr. Wahl graciously consented to this arrangement, and the first Mass was said in that building on October 7, 1950.

◆ **Monsignor Michael Krug and Father Burwell Beddoes.**

After studying the trends in city development and population shifts, Father Tully purchased property at Eleventh Avenue and West Tenth Street. Preliminary plans were drawn up for a school building, but ill health necessitated Father Tully's resignation as pastor before he saw any of his plans materialize.

◆ **Father Burwell Beddoes with the First Communicants, May 18, 1952.**

◆ **St. Andrew, parish patron.**

On January 3, 1951, Father Burwell E. Beddoes (1951-1957) was appointed by Bishop John J. Boylan to continue Father Tully's well-begun work. Father Beddoes added to the Eleventh Avenue property and went ahead with the construction of the school. Ground was broken on November 21, 1951, and steady progress was made. On September 3, 1952, St. Andrew Grade School opened its doors to 202 pupils in the eight elementary grades. The Sisters of Loretto of Loretto, Kentucky, were contracted to staff the school and for this purpose four sisters came to Rock Falls in August of 1952.

On the Feast of Christ the King, October 26, 1952, the auditorium wing of the building was completed and the first Mass was celebrated in the new church. Bishop John J. Boylan blessed the new wing on the feast of St. Andrew, November 30, 1952.

During the three years he was pastor, Father William Boland (1957-1960) established the rectory at 700 Tenth Avenue, adjacent to the school.

Construction of the first parish church was begun in June of 1974. The school gym had served as the parish church for 23 years. The first Mass was offered in the new church on June 29, 1975, on

◆ **Father Joseph Tully.**

the Feast of SS. Peter and Paul. The new church, which seats 800, was dedicated on December 7, 1975, by Bishop Arthur J. O'Neill.

On October 8, 2000, Monsignor Thomas L. Dzielak, Pastor, joined Bishop Emeritus Arthur J. O'Neill in celebrating the 50th anniversary of St. Andrew Parish in Rock Falls. Following the Mass, Bishop O'Neill dedicated a statue of St. Andrew the Apostle, Fisher of Men, at the entrance of the church.

Monsignor Dzielak blessed and dedicated the new Divine Mercy Chapel at St. Andrew Church on Divine Mercy Sunday, April 3, 2005. The willingness of parishioners to do 90 percent of the construction, along with a generous monetary donation, made the chapel possible. It seats 36 and is connected to the church.

As of March 2007, Monsignor Thomas L. Dzielak is pastor. There are approximately 600 families currently registered at St. Andrew Parish.

HOLY FAMILY PARISH

In April 1962, Bishop Loras T. Lane established a new parish in Rockford. The property designated for the new parish was on a 23 acre tract of land in the northeast portion of the city. The property was designated to be not just a new parish, but also the new cathedral for the Rockford Diocese. Until a permanent name was chosen, the new community was to be called the "Cathedral Parish."

Bishop Lane appointed Monsignor Herman A. Meilinger (1964-1977) to be the parish's first pastor.

When the boundaries for the newly established parish were drawn, they included parts of St. James Pro-Cathedral Parish and St. Bridget Parish in Loves Park.

A vigorous building program was begun and in the fall of 1963, the eight-grade "Cathedral School" opened its doors for the first time. A convent to house the School Sisters of St. Francis, who staffed the school, was completed in October 1963, and the gymnasium, which was to serve as a temporary church, was ready for use the following spring. Two small, private homes at the far end of the property served as rectories for the priests assigned to the new parish.

During the same month, an architectural study of the new cathedral was under way in New York City under the direction of Brother Cajetan Baumann, O.F.M., a nationally renowned architect.

◆ **Construction site of Holy Family.**

The proposed drawing of the parish plant was to have a pyramid-like structure for the church, which was to have been 14 stories high with skylight lighting, circular driveway, meditation garden, and a separate chapel for the Blessed Sacrament. Because of the estimated high cost and Bishop Lane's untimely death in 1968, the plans never progressed beyond the drawing boards.

Following his ordination and installation as Bishop of Rockford in October 1968, Bishop Arthur J. O'Neill consulted with the priests of the Diocese regarding the feasibility of proceeding with the plans for the new cathedral. After much consultation and deliberation, it was decided not to proceed with the new cathedral. On October 11, 1970, St. Peter Church in Rockford was designated as the cathedral for the Rockford Diocese and what was to have been the "Cathedral Parish" was named in honor of the Holy Family.

This set before the more than 1,000 families of the still fledgling Holy Family Parish a new challenge: the building of a parish church, not a cathedral!

Shortly after this, Holy Family's boundaries were redrawn and 120 families were reassigned to St. James Parish. By then the Holy Family population had grown to 1,200 families, with the gymnasium still serving as the church. Both the choir loft and foyer were full at the five weekend Masses, despite the transfer of the families to St. James Parish.

◆ **Bishop Lane pointing out the property of the future Holy Family Parish.**

In August 1973, (11 years after the first groundbreaking), Bishop O'Neill and Monsignor Meilinger led groundbreaking ceremonies for Holy Family Church. Just two years later, in August 1975, Mass was celebrated for the first time in the new parish church. The solemn dedication of the church by Bishop O'Neill was held on June 13, 1976.

In September 1979, the new parish center was dedicated by Father Alphonsus F. Harte (1977-1989), Pastor. The center provided meeting rooms, counseling areas, a chapel and living quarters for the parish priests.

During the pastorate of Monsignor Daniel J. Hermes (1989-2001), a major addition was added to the school, a new pipe organ was installed in the church and a new Nazareth Adoration Chapel was constructed.

The school addition, dedicated by Bishop Thomas G. Doran in the fall of 1996, included a basement, a first floor with classrooms, and a second floor with computer lab, library and resource room.

The new pipe organ was dedicated on September 30, 2001, by Bishop Doran. The new organ has 3,199 pipes ranging in size from 2 inches to 32 feet. The pipe work was all made by hand in England, Germany, Holland and the United States.

As of March 2007, Monsignor Thomas E. Bales is pastor. There are approximately 3,000 families currently registered at Holy Family Parish.

◆ **Adoration chapel.**

◆ **Mass in the old school church.**

◆ **Holy Family Church.**

St. Anthony of Padua Parish

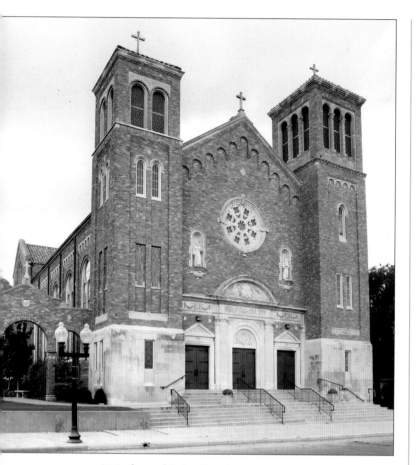

◆ **St. Anthony of Padua Church.**

In October 1906, the Reverend Anthony V. Marchesano (1909-1929) came from the Diocese of Cefalu, Italy, to America to visit his parents who were living in Chicago. Realizing the need for Italian-speaking priests in the Midwest, he was easily persuaded to obtain an extended leave of absence from his diocese in Italy, and for two years was stationed in Chicago.

Bishop Peter J. Muldoon, in view of the growing Italian community in Rockford, conferred with Father Marchesano, who agreed to come to Rockford to help establish the Parish of St. Anthony of Padua.

The first meeting of the newly-formed congregation was held at St. James Pro-Cathedral on Palm Sunday, April 12, 1909. After the Bishop's address, Father Marchesano explained the purpose of the meeting and more than 250 Italian families joined the new parish.

Masses were first said in the basement of St. Mary Church on Winnebago Street until St. Anthony Church and rectory were built in 1910. The one-story structure was dedicated by Bishop Muldoon on January 23, 1910, in colorful ceremonies attended by Italian dignitaries from all parts of the country.

In 1915, construction was begun on the second story, which was to be used as a school, and on September 7, 250 children registered. The Missionary Franciscan Sisters of the Immaculate Conception from Boston staffed the school.

◆ **The wedding of Thomas and Antonia Crapisi was the first wedding at St. Anthony Church, June 27, 1909.**

In 1919, the National Catholic War Council, at a cost of $13,000, erected a hall adjoining the church to be used for an Americanization school.

In the spring of 1929, Father Marchesano envisioned plans for a whole new parish, more adequate to care for the 1,200 souls in his charge. A gymnasium was completed and work on the church went forward, but Father Marchesano's health began to fail and he would not live to see his dream come to reality. In the summer of 1929, he left Rockford for Rochester, Minnesota, where he died on August 26, 1929.

Father John J. Flanagan (1929-1930), a long-time friend of Father Marchesano, volunteered to complete his work, since he was fluent in the Italian language. On August 18, 1930, Bishop Edward F. Hoban dedicated the new church.

◆ **The Columbian band, 1920.**

At the request of Bishop Hoban, the Franciscan Order of Friars Minor Conventuals took over the care of St. Anthony parish. Father Dominic Szymanski, O.F.M. Conv. (1933-1945), was appointed pastor on January 1, 1933. He bought property on Kent and Corbin Streets and converted it into a garden with a shrine to the Blessed Mother and St. Anthony. The old convent was sold and another larger home bought for the sisters in September 1942. In the 12 years of his pastorate, Father Dominic reduced the parish debt more than a third. He was transferred on August 29, 1945, and was succeeded by Father Maurice Bora, O.F.M. Conv. (1945-1957).

The church was redecorated in 1953. Chimes replaced the tower bell. A hall was built under the school building in 1956. Father Maurice further reduced the parish debt by nearly $150,000. On June 1, 1958, work was started on four modern classrooms and on August 24, 1958, the new school addition was blessed and dedicated to Father Marchesano and was known as "Marchesano School Annex."

In 1969, the new sisters' convent was completed and it was dedicated in 1971. The Missionary Franciscan Sisters of the Immaculate Conception lived in the convent and staffed the newly created St. Francis Consolidated School, which combined the three parish schools of SS. Peter and

◆ **Father John Daleiden at Father Marchesano's funeral, 1929.**

Paul, St. Anthony of Padua, and St. Stanislaus Kostka. Students in kindergarten through grade four attended classes at St. Anthony; those in grades five and six attended classes at SS. Peter and Paul, and grades seven and eight, St. Stanislaus.

Due to declining enrollment, St. Francis School closed at the end of the school year in 1985.

Construction on a memory garden began in August 2001 with a groundbreaking ceremony. The project was dedicated on October 7, 2001, with Father Anthony Labedis, OFM Conv., presiding. The garden honors the historic Italian-American community on Rockford's south side. Among other statues in the garden is a new statue of St. Anthony of Padua which is surrounded by a brick walkway. A 90-year-old fountain, which was formerly in service between the church and the school, was also placed in the garden, as was a large Celtic cross honoring the services of the Franciscan Irish Sisters early in the parish's history. Father Luke Poczworowski, OFM Conv. (1994-2005), was pastor during the construction.

St. Anthony Parish has held an annual St. Joseph's Altar since the early 1970s, continuing a tradition established in the 1920s by parishioners who would have the altars in their own homes. Sometimes three or more houses on one block would have St. Joseph altars.

As of March 2007, Father Anthony Labedis, OFM Conv., is pastor. There are approximately 1,100 families currently registered at St. Anthony of Padua Parish.

◆ **St. Anthony Church interior after the renovation, 1953.**

ST. BERNADETTE PARISH

◆ **Groundbreaking for St. Bernadette Church.**

◆ **Installation of Father Daniel Geoghegan as pastor, November 1957.**

On Sunday, October 20, 1957, Monsignor William G. McMillan announced to St. Peter Parish that its northwest section had been separated and that a new parish was being established there. A new parochial school had recently been completed at Rockton and Bell Avenues, and this school was to be the headquarters of the newly established St. Bernadette Parish.

On November 17, 1957, Bishop Loras T. Lane appointed Father Daniel B. Geoghegan (1957-1983) as pastor of the newly formed parish. Father Geoghegan found himself leader of a fully grown parish, with an estimated 800 families.

In the first year of existence, St. Bernadette School included first- to sixth-grade classes, with an enrollment of 449 children; in the second year, the school operated with all eight grades. The Sisters of Notre Dame taught in the school with the help of lay teachers.

Father Geoghegan built a rectory and convent in 1958 and, in 1961, the parish took another step in its overall building program. Between March and July 1961, the church, located in the 2300 block of Bell Avenue, was built at a cost of $100,000. A contemporary brick structure capable of seating 900, it features a cathedral glass entrance and windows, asphalt tile floors and a crying room.

On July 16, 1961, Bishop Loras T. Lane officially dedicated the church building.

Bishop Arthur J. O'Neill broke ground for a parish center on November 14, 1992. The 14,000 square foot structure includes a main room that seats 350 people and rest rooms which serve both the church and center. A kitchen, meeting rooms and storage space are also a part of the center. The parishioners and Father Matthew T. Rudden (1989-1999), Pastor, saw the completion of the center in October of 1993.

Rededication of the church took place on May 25, 1997, with Bishop Thomas G. Doran officiating at the Mass. Celebrating with the bishop was Father Rudden. The renovation included making a sanctuary into a side chapel and shifting the

◆ **St. Bernadette graduating class of 1959.**

direction of seating for the congregation, to face west rather than south.

Parishioners marked the completion of the renovation of their parish chapel with a Mass and dedication ceremony celebrated by Bishop Thomas G. Doran on February 11, 2002. The Our Lady of Lourdes Chapel, which seats between 30 and 40 people, was renovated during the pastorate of Father John L. Stringini (1999-2005).

As of March 2007, Father Kenneth J. Stachyra is parochial administrator. There are approximately 900 families currently registered at St. Bernadette Parish.

◆ **St. Bernadette Church interior and exterior.**

St. Edward Parish

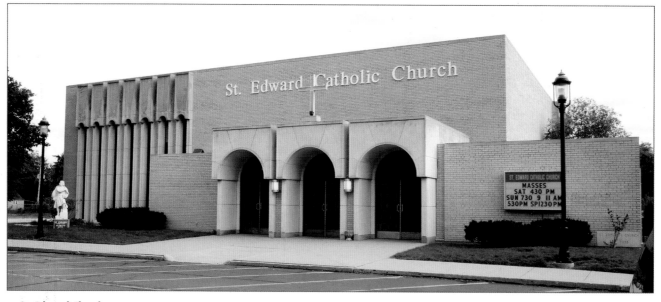

◆ **St. Edward Church.**

Shortly after his coming to Rockford in February 1928, Bishop Edward F. Hoban recognized the need to provide for the Catholics in the Grant Park district in southeast Rockford. The nearest church for these people was three miles away.

Fifteen acres of land were purchased in the 3000 block of Eleventh Street, and Father Thomas P. Bermingham (1929-1933) was appointed the first pastor. In the fall of 1929, Father Bermingham gathered his small flock into two rooms of his house until a church could be provided. This church-home was dedicated to St. Edward by Bishop Hoban in October of 1930.

Father Emmett W. Murphy (1933-1973) was appointed pastor in 1933. These early years at St. Edward were incredibly hard. They were Depression years, and Rockford area industries were especially hard hit. Catholics in the parish were barely able to survive, let alone support a new church.

The Dominican sisters from St. James helped Father Murphy with catechism instructions for the school children. The first church was built in 1941 and it opened for Masses on Easter Sunday in 1942.

After the new church was completed in 1942, work began on the original church to convert it into

◆ **The first St. Edward Church.**

a school with residence for the sisters upstairs. Three classrooms were made available and three Dominican sisters from Adrian, Michigan, opened the school in September 1942. Two classrooms were added the following year and two new sisters from Adrian were also added to the staff.

The Second World War brought the reactivation of Camp Grant, and the area around St. Edward grew rapidly, but with a more or less transient population.

In 1946, another expansion of the school proved necessary. A surplus building was purchased from Camp Grant and remodeled into a seven-room school.

◆ **Bishop Boylan blessing the cornerstone for St. Edward School, 1951.**

On June 15, 1971, Bishop O'Neill appointed Father James J. Murphy (1971-1973), a nephew of Father Emmett Murphy, to be co-Pastor of St. Edward.

In December of 1972, Father Emmett Murphy was taken seriously ill. On Palm Sunday, 1973, he returned to St. Edward, attended Mass and gave his final homily to the

◆ **Father James Murphy.**

people whom he had served for 40 years. A week later, April 22, 1973, Easter Sunday, he died. Father James Murphy (1973-1996) then became the third pastor of St. Edward, beginning 23 years of service.

During the pastorate of Father James Murphy, the parish began a television ministry in 1974. It evolved into a weekly taped show. For its mass media evangelization efforts, the parish received the Joe Baisch Award from the diocese's St Francis de Sales Society in 1992. The ministry had to be discontinued in 1995 due to Father Murphy's illness.

Bishop Arthur J. O'Neill dedicated a new parish community center at St. Edward on September 23, 1984. The center contains a large meeting room, parish education offices and a lobby, which is attached to the church.

The old school was used for a convent. In 1951, work was started on a new school building which housed 10 classrooms, a gym, dressing and shower rooms, library, infirmary, office, social hall, kitchens and store room. A new convent with accommodations for 12 sisters was completed during 1958.

The parish continued to grow and expand and by 1968 it was evident that a new and larger church would be needed. Plans were made for the new church, which was completed in 1969.

In June 1969, the Adrian Domincan Sisters left St. Edward School, but in September 1969, the School Sisters of St. Francis arrived to staff the school. Under their direction the school was renovated and carpeted, and academic innovations were introduced.

During the pastorate of Monsignor Raymond J. Wahl (1996-2005), a youth center was built and dedicated on March 2, 1997, by Bishop Thomas G. Doran. Of the 57,000 square feet in the center, 35,000 are contained in a dividable gathering room.

The first Mass in the new church was celebrated in mid-September 1969. Through the generosity and hard work of the parishioners, the new $420,000 church was debt-free. Bishop Arthur J. O'Neill came to St. Edward Parish on October 1, 1972, to formally dedicate the new church building.

◆ **Father Emmett Murphy.**

The structure also contains a conference room, Youth Religious Education office, snack and storage area and basement storage room.

The parish celebrated its 75th anniversary on October 17, 2004.

A well attended Spanish Mass was begun in 2005.

As of March 2007, Father Michael G. Black is pastor. There are approximately 1,300 families currently registered at St. Edward Parish.

St. James Parish

◆ **St. James Church and rectory, 1886.**

St. James Church is not only the oldest church in the city of Rockford, but also the mother church of many new parishes organized after the establishment of the Diocese of Rockford in 1908.

Originally, the area was part of the Hartland parish. Father Patrick A. McMahon, made first pastor there in 1844, had charge of the entire area and it is known that he visited, with some degree of regularity, Rockford and Marengo.

On June 7, 1853, Bishop James O. Van de Velde visited Rockford to bless the new church of St. James, built on the site of the present St. James Rectory at the corner of North Second and Prairie Streets. Father John A. Hampston (1851-1854) had been pastor at Rockford almost two years before the church was built. In 1855, during the pastorate of Father William Lambert (1855-1858), the first St. James School was opened in the one-room building which served as church and school; it was staffed by lay teachers.

In 1861, the foundation was laid for the present St. James Church while Father John P. Donelan (1860-1866) was pastor. Father Jeremiah S. O'Neill (1866-1876) was the next pastor at St. James. He completed the building of the church, which was dedicated September 29, 1867, the cornerstone having been laid the previous April 28.

He bought property at the corner of North Second and Lafayette Streets and used the residence there as his rectory.

Father Thaddeus J. Butler (1876-1885) succeeded Father O'Neill on March 8, 1876, and was assisted by his brother, Father Thomas Butler. Since St. James was the only parish in the growing city, both priests were kept quite busy. Father Thaddeus Butler built the front part of the present rectory and closed the old school.

After nine years at St. James, Father Thaddeus Butler was transferred. On the eve of being made Bishop of Concordia, Kansas, he died in July 1897.

In 1885, Father James J. Flaherty (1885-1907) was appointed pastor and built a new school building. The cornerstone was laid on August 30, 1891, and the building was dedicated a few months later. Father Flaherty also enlarged the rectory.

◆ **First Communicant, Josephine Bardelli, 1906.**

Father Thomas Finn (1907-1920) was appointed pastor in 1907. In the following year, the Diocese of Rockford was separated from Chicago. Anticipating that St. James would be chosen as the cathedral, Father Finn worked hard to renovate the building in time; as it happened the church was made a pro-cathedral.

After Father Joseph T. Healey (1946-1950) was appointed Administrator in 1946, he undertook a program of remodeling. A kitchen was provided in the church basement, then the entire basement was excavated for use as a hall. The church was redecorated and marble altars installed. Extensive repairs were made in the convent, rectory and school.

Monsignor Leo M. Keenan (1950-1960) came in July 1950 and remained as pastor until January 4, 1960. Plans were soon made to extend the front of the church to the sidewalk. New pews and ceramic

◆ **Monsignor John McGuire with the altar boys of St. James, 1934.**

Stations of the Cross were the final touches to the program of redecoration which was completed by Easter of 1953.

◆ **St. James Church.**

On the evening of February 12, 1958, Father William H. Regnier, assistant priest at St. James, discovered a fire in the basement of the church. Before it was extinguished, extensive damage was done throughout the church. A program of repair and redecoration was begun immediately. Later in the year, the rectory underwent renovation. The porch was removed and the exterior of the building was faced with stone.

Father Herman A. Meilinger (1960-1964) announced a long-awaited, two-fold building program which would include a 12- to 16-room school and gymnasium, which would be used temporarily as a church. A new convent for the Dominican sisters teaching at St. James School was completed in August 1963, but the school was not opened for a few more years.

After becoming pastor in 1964, Father Norbert M. Richter (1964-1986) supervised the construction of the 12-room school and gym, which was completed in January 1968. In March 1968, the old St. James School, constructed in 1891, was torn down.

In 1973, St. James Church interior was repainted and carpeted and new drapes were hung behind the altar in the sanctuary.

◆ **Father Norbert Richter.**

A major renovation to the interior of the church took place during the pastorate of Father (later Monsignor) David D. Kagan (1990-1994) in 1992. A new altar, ambo and baptismal font were reconstructed from the existing marble, preserving the formal character of the church. A blessing and rededication took place on October 25, 1992, also commemorating the 125th anniversary of the church's original dedication. Bishop Arthur J. O'Neill, who was ordained a priest at St. James Church, presided.

Two building projects were completed in 2002, during the pastorate of Father David E. Beauvais (1994-2006). An addition to the school included two floors for religious education rooms, a meeting room and a social hall, and a new basement with music, multi-purpose room and youth rooms. The church's remodeling project featured new restrooms and an elevator, making the church, rectory and Richter Hall all accessible to the handicapped. On October 6, 2002, a rededication was celebrated by Bishop Thomas G. Doran, who was a member of St. James Parish and graduated from the parish school in 1950.

In 2003, Rockford's oldest parish marked the 150th anniversary of its church.

As of March 2007, Father Dean E. Russell is pastor. There are approximately 900 families currently registered at St. James Parish.

◆ **St. James Church interior.**

ST. MARY ORATORY

St. Mary Parish in Rockford dates from the middle of May 1885, when Father Edward A. Murphy (1885-1889) came to Rockford as assistant to the newly appointed pastor of St. James, Father James J. Flaherty.

He was sent by the Archbishop of Chicago for the purpose of organizing a parish on the west side of the Rock River, but no announcement was made of this fact until the property at the corner of South Winnebago and Elm Streets had been purchased from P. R. Chandler by Archbishop Patrick A. Feehan of Chicago.

On Sunday, July 19th, 1885, Father Murphy called a meeting of the men of the congregation and proposed to hold services on the west side of the river and to rent a hall to be used temporarily as a church. This proposal was met with great enthusiasm and when pledges were asked for, Lawrence Byrne at once headed the list with $500. Two-thousand dollars was pledged within a few minutes and Father Murphy lost no time in making the arrangements at the "Rink," a hall on North Wyman Street, and for six months Mass was celebrated there every Sunday.

Plans were drawn up and construction began immediately on a church. Mass was first said in the unfinished, unplastered basement, on December 6, 1885.

The cornerstone was laid by Archbishop Feehan, on July 11, 1886. The archbishop and priests, preceded by the Forest City Band, arrived in carriages and were followed by over one-hundred of the Ancient Order of Hibernians in full regalia. The mayor and other civic dignitaries were on the platform. The archbishop returned on October 16, 1887, to dedicate the completed church.

St. Mary's parochial school was opened by Father Murphy in September of 1888, in four improvised rooms in the

◆ **St. Mary graduating class, 1910.**

basement of the church. Dominican Sisters from Sinsinawa taught at that time. In 1906, Dominican Sisters of Blauvelt, New York took over, and they were succeeded in 1912 by the Sisters of Loretto.

The third pastor, Father Patrick A. McMahon (1892-1919) came in May of 1892 and remained for twenty-seven years. During his pastorate, the property adjoining the church property on Elm Street was purchased for a convent.

A new school was also built under his direction. In June 1913, he bought property at the corner of Elm and West Streets for a new convent, and proceeded to build a rectory at the site of the old convent. In addition to this large building program, Father McMahon liquidated a parish debt of $30,000 before his death on April 14, 1919.

Father Joseph M. Lonergan (1925-1929) built the Lourdes Grotto and the Shrine of the Little Flower. The grotto contains an altar and two shrines, one to St. Bernadette of Lourdes and another to St. Theresa.

In July of 1933, Bishop Edward F. Hoban placed St. Mary, together with St. Thomas High School, in the charge of

◆ **Father Edward Connolly with the boys of St. Mary School, in the 1920's.**

◆ **St. Mary Church arson fire, February 12, 1962.**

the Augustinian Fathers. The new pastor appointed was Father Cornelius Ford, O.S.A (1933-1939).

In those first years, the priests who taught at St. Thomas High School lived in the rectory, but as this made the living quarters crowded, the teaching fathers moved to remodeled classrooms in the high school building for the next twenty-nine years.

On February 12, 1962, fire destroyed the interior of the church. Through the efficiency of the Rockford Fire Department, only slight damage was done to the beautiful stained glass windows.

Father Aloysius J. Tierney, O.S.A.(1961-1968), pastor, was faced with a tremendous task of cleaning up the debris, rebuilding the interior of the church and replacing the pews.

In June of 1968 the Sisters of Loretto, who had charge of the school, left. Arrangements were made with sisters in the Philippine Islands of the Augustinian Order to take over the convent and school. They remained until June, 1974, when they were recalled to their own country because of the shortage of sisters there. The school closed with their departure.

A former teacher at St. Thomas High School, Father Robert V. Lawrence, O.S.A. (1968-1979), returned to Rockford and was appointed pastor in August, 1968. Since that time extensive repairs have been made to the exterior of the church and the interior of the convent and school buildings. The interior of the church was redecorated in 1973. St. Mary's continues to be a gathering place, not only for parishioners, but also for downtown shoppers and business people.

On June 19, 1994, the grotto chapel opened again after renovations to add heat, which was much needed on cold winter days.

◆ **St. Mary Oratory interior.**

In 1997, Bishop Thomas G. Doran designated St. Mary's as a shrine and entrusted it to the care of the Institute of Christ the King Sovereign Priest's special apostolate, as a way to keep the church open to the needs of Rockford's downtown.

During the rectorship of Father Brian A. T. Bovee, Bishop Doran announced on August 15, 2002 the establishment of St. Mary Shrine as a public oratory. The designation makes the sacraments available to those who assemble there as a Latin Rite Faith Community.

As of March 2007 Father Brian A. T. Bovee, STL is rector. There are approximately 420 people currently in attendance at St. Mary Oratory.

◆ **Detail of ceiling above altar.**

◆ **St. Mary Oratory**

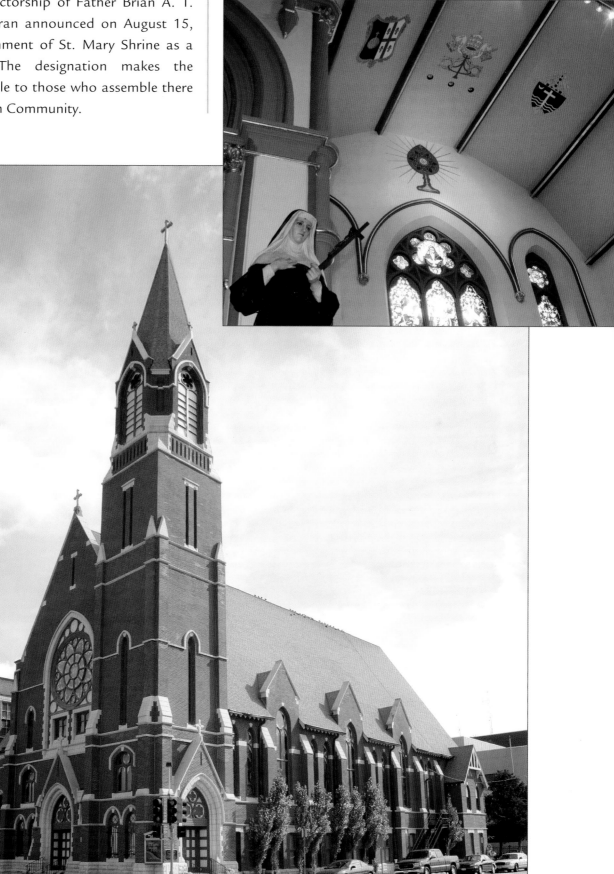

ST. PATRICK PARISH

In the summer of 1919, Bishop Peter J. Muldoon realized that the growing Catholic population in the west end of Rockford could no longer be ignored. He called together a group of laymen from that section of the city and laid before them his plan for the formation of a new parish. St. Patrick Parish had its beginning at this meeting held in the original St. Thomas High School.

Father Walter J. Scollin (1919-1927), who had just returned from his chaplaincy in the army, was appointed the first pastor late in August, 1919. The first parish Mass was offered on August 31, 1919, in the hall of St. Thomas High School, which served as a temporary church for the next 14-and-one-half years. This original St. Thomas High School was actually the old convent near the former Muldoon High School. The second St. Thomas High School, which was located at 921 West State Street, was not built until 1929.

Bishop Muldoon proceeded to purchase, at a cost of $13,500, four adjoining lots as a site for the new church, two on West State Street and two on Royal Avenue. The house situated on the second lot from the corner facing West State Street became the priest's rectory. Because of his generous donation of $1,000, James O'Brien was given the privilege of choosing a patron saint. He picked the name of St. Patrick to honor the memory of his father, Patrick O'Brien, one of the pioneer Catholics who traveled 14 miles every Sunday to attend Mass in Rockford.

Ground for the foundation of a new church was broken in May 1920. A building from Camp Grant was moved to the site of the first St. Patrick Church; from the beginning this was intended to be a temporary church. The church was completed in November 1920, and Father Scollin said the first Mass within the new St. Patrick Church on November 14, 1920. Bishop Muldoon officiated at the solemn dedication of the church on the Feast of St. Patrick, March 17, 1921.

◆ **Father Francis J. Keenan.**

Almost immediately after his appointment as pastor in May of 1927, Father Francis J. Keenan (1927-1944) saw the need of a parochial school. A new school opened on February 4, 1929, with a gymnasium and eight classrooms, six of which were put to use that first year. One hundred and forty pupils were enrolled that day to be taught by a faculty of Dominican Sisters from Sinsinawa Mound in Wisconsin.

Despite the hard times of the Depression, the parish continued to grow, and, with the determined efforts of the pastor and loyal parishioners, soon was able to take care of its financial obligations.

Father Laurence C. Prendergast (1944-1950) became pastor on October 19, 1944, and began the work of constructing a new church. Ten acres of ground were purchased for the new site on the northwest corner of School Street and North Johnston Avenue. Construction began on June 8, 1950.

Father Francis P. McNally (1950-1957) became the fourth pastor on October 20, 1950. Under his direction, the new church and rectory were completed at a cost of over $600,000. They were

◆ **The first St. Patrick Church on West State Street and Royal Avenue.**

◆ **Father Laurence Prendergast, assisted by Fathers Norbert Richter and Daniel Geoghegan, at the groundbreaking of the church.**

◆ **St. Patrick Church at the 1952 dedication.**

dedicated on May 20, 1952, by Bishop John J. Boylan. Samuel Cardinal Stritch gave the homily at the dedication.

On May 30, 1954, a parochial school was dedicated at the new site. It contained, in addition to eight classrooms, an assembly hall, office, infirmary, and music, boiler storage, mimeograph and four "multi-purpose" rooms. Before the building was used, it was evident that it would be inadequate, so rapid was the growth of the parish. A new convent was completed, large enough to house 22 sisters, before an addition to the school was begun. In the meantime, the school operated on a double shift, with the help of lay teachers.

Under the direction of Father John F. Regan (1957-1964), who was appointed pastor in December 1957, the eight-room school addition, which was started by Father McNally, was completed in the fall of 1958.

A new parish center was dedicated by Bishop Arthur J. O'Neill on November 25, 1990, during the pastorate of Father Michael J. Tierney (1982-1993). The center was in the former convent, which also housed the parish food pantry and clothes closet. Many volunteers helped keep the remodeling costs to a minimum.

After 66 years of schooling thousands of children, St. Patrick School, falling victim to higher costs and growing debt, closed on June 2, 1995. Father Ronald A. Jones (1994-1997) was pastor at the time of the closure.

St. Patrick Parish has held a Corned Beef and Cabbage Dinner every March for 74 years, serving more than 1,000 people annually.

As of March 2007, Father Brian A. Geary is pastor. There are approximately 400 families currently registered at St. Patrick Parish.

◆ **St. Patrick Church.**

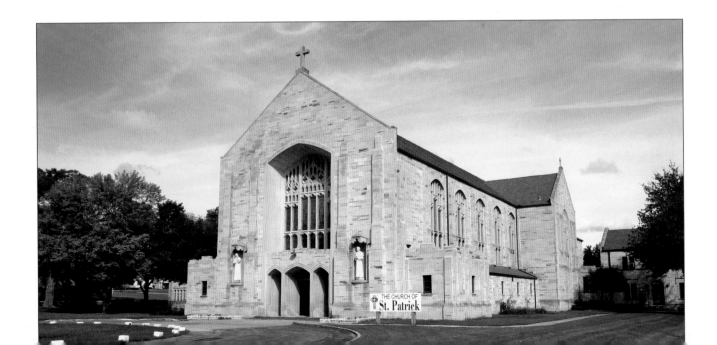

CATHEDRAL OF ST. PETER

◆ Bishop Lane at the groundbreaking of the current church.

◆ Father Frederick Connor with the First Communicants of 1925.

In the early days of Bishop Peter J. Muldoon's episcopacy, Rockford was in one of its periods of expansion. There was much building going on, particularly in the north end. Many of the Catholics living north of Auburn Street had a long distance to travel to St. Mary Church.

On June 4, 1915, property was bought in the Auburndale subdivision and a small frame chapel was built on it later that year. In December, the chapel was dedicated to St. William and was utilized as a mission for the north end of St. Mary Parish. Father John J. Flanagan (1915-1921) was appointed to take charge.

As time went on, the facilities became less and less adequate. But, as the center of the area's population had not moved out as far as the mission, a new location, slightly to the south was sought. Since lots at the summit of Council Hill (or Piety Hill), reputedly the highest spot in Rockford, were available, they were bought in the fall of 1920. Construction was begun in June of 1921 for a combination church and school building, fronting on Court Street.

The building was dedicated on February 19, 1922, by Bishop Muldoon. Father Flanagan, who, although he had not actually been their pastor, had been in charge of the congregation, gave the homily at the dedication Mass. On October 18, 1922, Father Frederick F. Connor (1921-1932) was appointed the first resident pastor of the new St. Peter Parish, within the same area as the St. William mission. Father Connor remained until February 1, 1932.

The parochial grade school, consisting of only two classrooms, opened that fall with 63 pupils registered. The Sisters of Loretto staffed the school. A convent was provided for them at 1229 North Court Street. This frame building was moved across the street in July, 1929, and a new convent was built.

◆ Father John Flanagan.

On February 1, 1932, Father Leo W. Binz (1932-1933) was appointed pastor. Since St. Peter Parish, like the rest of the diocese, had been hard hit by the Depression, Father Binz continued living at the Bishop's residence to conserve parish resources and the rectory was rented to a private family.

Father Binz was succeeded by Father William G. McMillan (1933-1967), who continued the practice initiated by Father Binz of living at the Bishop's house. This arrangement lasted until 1939, when he and his assistant moved into the parish rectory.

The enrollment in the school continued to grow to such a degree that by 1948 it was necessary to provide additional classroom space. The church was moved into the auditorium, and the second floor was converted into classrooms.

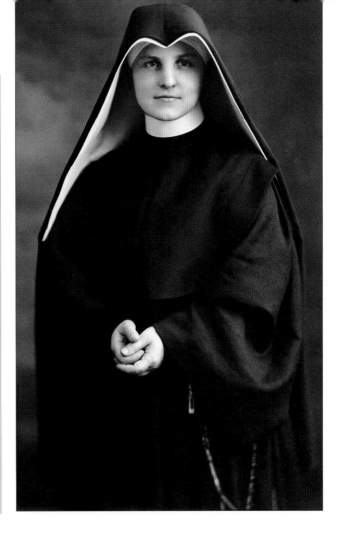

◆ **Sister Laurian, one of the first sisters to teach at St. Peter School.**

◆ **Cathedral of St. Peter.**

◆ **Father Binz and the graduating class of 1933.**

◆ **The covent chapel, 1930.**

As the parish continued to expand and grow, it became increasingly evident that no program of remodeling would suffice. Bishop John J. Boylan had obtained property in the northwest part of the parish, about ten acres from Rockton Avenue, between Fulton and Bell, east almost to Ridge Avenue. In October 1954, Bishop Raymond P. Hillinger authorized Monsignor McMillan to begin construction of a new school at this site, but the Bishop's illness forced a halt in the program. In April 1957, Bishop Loras T. Lane gave permission to resume construction on the school, and a convent to house the Sisters of Notre Dame. Late in 1957, the area was separated from St. Peter Parish and became an independent parish, St. Bernadette.

The problem of housing the mother parish still remained. Property was acquired on the east side of the 1200 block on Church Street. The houses occupying the site were razed and construction was begun on a new church and rectory there, and additional classrooms were constructed in the former church.

The cornerstone for the new church was blessed by Bishop Lane in August of 1958 and the church was dedicated on May 15, 1960. On January 9, 1967, Monsignor William McMillan retired and Monsignor Arthur J. O'Neill (1967-1968) was appointed pastor. He was ordained Bishop of Rockford on October 11, 1968.

On January 6, 1969, Bishop O'Neill appointed Monsignor Thomas S. Green (1969-1979) to succeed him as pastor of St. Peter.

On October 11, 1970, Bishop O'Neill designated St. Peter as the cathedral for the diocese. Monsignor Green was named the first rector of the new St. Peter Cathedral Parish.

During the spring and summer of 1974, Summer Street between Court and Church Street was closed off and the street, together with the existing parking lot, was enlarged and redesigned to provide additional parking space for the cathedral and Chancery Office.

◆ **Laying the cornerstone for the current St. Peter Church.**

◆ **Cathedral of St. Peter interior.**

The formal dedication of St. Peter Cathedral was October 11, 1978. The day was also the 10ᵗʰ anniversary of Bishop Arthur J. O'Neill's ordination as Bishop of Rockford.

Ground was broken for a new addition to the cathedral on June 19, 1983 with Bishop O'Neill and Father Thomas C. Brady (1979-1984), rector, officiating. The new parish activities center, which is attached to the cathedral, was dedicated on June 3, 1984 by Bishop O'Neill. The new center included a large fellowship hall, offices, a bride's room, meeting rooms and rest rooms. The lower level included a gymnasium, offices, meeting rooms, kitchen and rest rooms.

During Monsignor William H. Schwartz's term as rector, the new altar and sanctuary in St. Peter Cathedral were dedicated on September 29, 1998 by His Eminence Francis Cardinal George from the Chicago Archdiocese. The major renovation included moving the altar forward, removing front pews and replacing them with moveable chairs, replacing the back wall with clear glass and placing a large

baptismal font in the entrance vestibule. This huge project was made possible through the generosity of Mrs. Frances Deming in memory of her husband, Richard.

As of March 2007 Monsignor William H. Schwartz is rector. There are approximately 1200 families currently registered at the Cathedral of St. Peter.

St. Rita Parish

◆ **Mrs. Luke Burke stands in front of her home, where the first Masses were held.**

The first Catholics in the Cherry Valley area, southeast of Rockford, were served by the priests who attended Rockford and Belvidere. The first Mass celebrated in Cherry Valley was offered at the home of Thomas Steele, in 1855, by Father William Lambert, the Pastor of St. James Parish in Rockford.

It was during the pastorate of Father Jeremiah S. O'Neill that, in July 1864, the Rockford-Belvidere parish was divided. Father Patrick McGuire became the pastor at Belvidere with Cherry Valley as a mission.

◆ **The first St. Rita Church in Cherry Valley.**

In 1891, Father Thomas Smith, an assistant to Father McGuire at Belvidere, raised about $1,100 toward building a church in Cherry Valley. It proved difficult to secure a desirable piece of property with a clear title, so the project was dropped. The money was held for a few years, then turned over to the Belvidere parish.

While Father Thomas Finn was pastor at St. James Church in Rockford, St. Rita mission was turned over to him. Mass was offered once a month in Woodman Hall. This was in 1907. In the spring of 1914, property was deeded to Bishop Peter J. Muldoon by Mr. and Mrs. Garlock. On June 21, the cornerstone was laid and the first Mass was said in the new church on September 13, 1914. Bishop Muldoon dedicated the church on October 25, 1914. He came to Cherry Valley on an Interurban streetcar, where he was met by a band and many members of the clergy and laity. Together they marched from the center of the village to the church for the dedication.

◆ **Father Leo Binz.**

Priests from St. James Pro-Cathedral cared for Cherry Valley until July 19, 1929, when Bishop Edward F. Hoban appointed Father Leo W. Binz (1929-1932) pastor. On February 1, 1932, Father Charles A. Meehan was appointed pastor of St. Rita, but served only until September 21, 1932, when it was again placed under St. James Pro-Cathedral in Rockford.

On July 19, 1933, Father Charles H. Quinn (1933-1940) was appointed pastor of the parish, with residence at the Poor Clare Monastery in Rockford, where he acted as chaplain.

During the administration of Father Michael J. Shanahan (1957-1962), the interior and exterior of the church was renovated. The Thomas Healey

◆ St. Rita Church.

◆ The second St. Rita Church interior.

home, which was next door to the church, was purchased for a rectory. The Healeys were parents of Monsignor Joseph T. Healey, the first priest ordained from St. Rita.

Monsignor Raymond J. Wahl (1962-1970) was appointed pastor of St. Rita Parish on September 4, 1962. Monsignor Wahl opened a school in Cherry Valley for 4- and 5-year-old children. It was staffed by two sisters of Notre Dame de Namur. Due to the rapid growth of the area, it became necessary to look for more property for a larger church and school.

In 1965, the parish purchased 28 acres of land in Panorama Valley in Cherry Valley Township and built a 440-seat church, together with a four-room school.

In 1968, four additional classrooms and a gymnasium were added to St. Rita School, which taught children in kindergarten through sixth grade. Seventh grade was added 16 years later, and eighth grade the year after that.

A new church was dedicated in June 1983 by Bishop Arthur J. O'Neill, during the pastorate of Father Edward R. Hughes (1975-1987). The interior of the church is a horseshoe shape, with seating for 600-800 people arrayed on three sides of the altar. The narthex is large and is used for coffee and donuts after Mass. Off the narthex is a large room currently used as the pre-kindergarten classroom. The lower level has a chapel, offices, meeting and rest rooms.

A new statue of St. Rita was dedicated on May 22, 2000, the feast day of St. Rita of Cascia. The five-foot statue was placed in the sanctuary of the church.

For 55 years, since 1952, on the Fridays of Lent, St. Rita Parish has held a fish fry dinner.

As of March 2007, Father Gerald P. Kobbeman is pastor. There are approximately 1,500 families currently registered at St. Rita Parish.

◆ Monsignor Raymond Wahl joins the men of the Holy Name Society painting the parish hall.

St. Stanislaus Kostka Parish

One of the first challenges which concerned Bishop Peter J. Muldoon when he became the first Bishop of Rockford was that of caring for foreign-born Catholics, many of whom did not as yet understand or speak the language of their new land. As with other nationalities, so it was with the Polish.

Father Julius Grzezinski, ordained for the Diocese, came to Rockford late in 1909 to work among the Polish Catholics. For three months he worked here, gathering them together to attend a regular Sunday Mass in their own language at St. James Pro-Cathedral.

The Polish population gradually increased and by 1911 it became evident that soon they would need a church of their own. In September of that year, Bishop Muldoon purchased two lots at the corner of Buckbee and Magnolia Streets. The following January 12, he called a meeting of the Polish Catholics in the hall of St. James School, at which he told them of his plans for their parish. Ground was broken on April 6, 1912, for a stucco church, 32 feet by 65 feet; it was completed early in August.

Bishop Muldoon was able to secure the services of Father Julian A. Burzynski (1909-1927) of Chicago on June 6, 1912. Father Burzynski completed the organization of the parish and became its first pastor. On the Feast of the Assumption, the new church was dedicated by Bishop Muldoon. Three altars were donated by St. Patrick Parish, Amboy; the Catholic Women's League donated linens and Father Daniel A. Feeley, Pastor of St. Mary Parish, Durand, presented the organ. A house, located diagonally across Magnolia Street from the church, was purchased in the spring of 1913, for use as a rectory. A parochial school was built in 1923; classes were begun in September 1924.

Father Burzynski died after a short illness on November 15, 1927. Because of the scarcity of Polish clergy, Bishop Edward F. Hoban invited the Franciscan Conventual Fathers, of Buffalo, New York, to administer the parish. Father Felix Baran, O.F.M. Conv., at that time Pastor of St. Josaphat Basilica in Milwaukee, provided for the spiritual needs of the parish on Sundays and holy days of obligation, with the help of his assistant priests.

With substantial growth, the original church was becoming too small to serve the parish. Bishop Loras T. Lane gave permission for the construction of a new church and rectory for St. Stanislaus Kostka Parish on May 26, 1959.

In July 1960, permission was granted to raze the original church. On April 23, 1961, Bishop Loras T. Lane blessed the cornerstone of the new church, which was erected on the site of the old church. The rectory adjoins the church on the east.

The dedication of the new St. Stanislaus Kostka Church, held in conjunction with the observance of the Golden Jubilee of the parish, was celebrated on May 27, 1961. A Mass of Thanksgiving was celebrated by the Bishop Loras T. Lane, along with the pastor, Father Roman Malkowski, O.F.M. Conv. (1957-1963).

◆ **The first St. Stanislaus Kostka Church.**

◆ **The 1927 graduating class of Muldoon School, which was later renamed St. Stanislaus School.**

◆ **Janina Korab in the Pope John Paul II Cultural Center.**

In September 1973, St. Anthony, SS. Peter and Paul, and St. Stanislaus schools opened St. Francis Catholic Consolidated School. Due to declining enrollment, St. Francis School closed at the end of the school year in 1985.

Bishop Arthur J. O'Neill, along with Father John J. Mikula (1994-2005), Pastor, dedicated the new Pope John Paul II Cultural Center on August 19, 1990, at the parish. The center includes items showing Polish culture, as well as those which recall the establishment of the parish. Many parishioners donated items for the permanent display.

In August of 2005, after 74 years, care of St. Stanislaus transferred from the Conventual Franciscans of the St. Bonaventure Province, to the Conventual Franciscans of the St. Anthony of Padua and Blessed James of Strepa Province from Krakow, Poland. Father Piotr Sarnicki was installed as the first pastor from this province. He was accompanied by Brother Jan Pawlik, who is in residence at the parish.

The parish is known for its Polish Fest, which started in 1981 and has been held every August for over 25 years.

As of March 2007, Father Piotr Sarnicki, OFM Conv., is pastor. There are approximately 350 families currently registered at St. Stanislaus Kostka Parish.

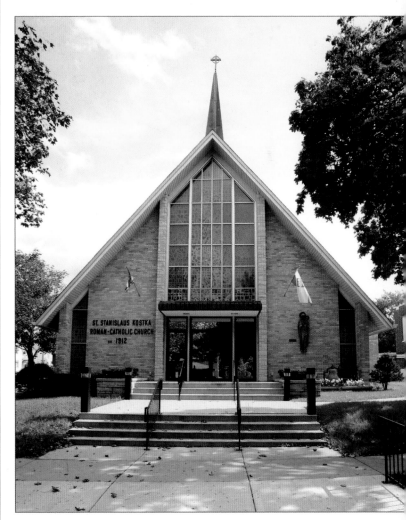

◆ **St. Stanislaus Kostka Church.**

◆ **Polish Fest 2004.**

SS. Peter and Paul Parish

◆ **Father Peter Williamovicz with parishioners, 1924.**

There had been, for a few years, a growing colony of Lithuanian Catholics in the southwest end of Rockford by the time the Diocese was established in 1908. Bishop Peter J. Muldoon, in an effort to look out for their spiritual welfare, made temporary arrangements with Father Thomas Finn, rector of St. James Pro-Cathedral, to have a special Sunday Mass designated for them.

In 1911, the Bishop was able to secure for the Diocese the services of Father John Malinauskas (1911-1912), a Lithuanian priest. He was appointed the first pastor of the Lithuanian parish. Property was purchased at the corner of South West Street and Lincoln Avenue. A frame church was constructed there and was dedicated on July 2, 1911. Bishop Muldoon presided, Father Finn said the Mass and Father Malinauskas gave the homily. A rectory was purchased on April 20, 1912.

In 1928, Father V. Kulikauskas, M.I.C. (1928-1934), of the Marian Fathers of Hinsdale, Illinois, was appointed pastor. The present church and school were built under his direction in 1929. The school opened that year staffed by the Sisters of St. Casimir, of Chicago. Father M. Svarlis was pastor from 1934 to 1937, when the Augustinian Fathers took over for a period.

In 1947, the parish was again placed under the care of the diocesan priests, with Father Joseph J. Reikas (1947-1966) being appointed the pastor. During Father Reikas's pastorate, he worked very hard at retiring the parish debt.

In 1965, Father Reikas completely renovated the church, bringing it up to the standards of the Second Vatican Council. New stained glass windows were installed, the church was air-conditioned, carpeted, repainted, and the sanctuary renovated. Before Father Reikas was transferred, the renovation debt was completely paid off.

◆ **The first SS. Peter & Paul Church.**

◆ **The first graduating class.**

On June 20, 1966, Father Bruno E. Daukas (1966-1972) was appointed by Bishop Loras T. Lane to succeed Father Reikas. During Father Daukas' administration, the renovation process was completed by remodeling the parish hall, the convent and the priest's living quarters which are built onto the church. This work was paid off before Father Daukas was transferred in February 1972.

In August 1985, the Office of Black Catholic Ministry was established at SS. Peter and Paul Parish by Bishop Arthur J. O'Neill. The parish was designated the home parish (hogar) for all Spanish-speaking people of the Rockford area by Bishop O'Neill in May 1992.

During the pastorate of Father Timothy R. Piasecki (1997-2005) the church interior was renovated. Major changes included moving the altar to a more central location, creating a Blessed Sacrament chapel, and installing a new hardwood floor.

In the fall of 2006, renovations were done to the interior of the church during the administration of Father Ricardo F. Hernandez. Included were a new altar, confessional, baptismal font and murals.

Many annual events are held at the parish, including the Feast of Our Lady of Guadalupe celebration, Las Posadas, May crowning and a Mother's Day celebration.

As of March 2007, Father Ricardo Hernandez is parochial administrator. There are approximately 500 families currently registered at SS. Peter and Paul Parish.

◆ **SS. Peter & Paul Church interior and exterior.**

CHURCH OF THE HOLY SPIRIT PARISH

The Church of the Holy Spirit was erected by decree of Bishop Arthur J. O'Neill on August 28, 1980. The parish began formation when a group of Catholic families began a parent-child catechetical program in 1977. In 1979, the group purchased a former church building in Roscoe and designated it the Faith Community of Roscoe. Father Melvin Vlasz, a faculty member at Boylan Central Catholic High School in Rockford, with the approval of Bishop O'Neill, became the chaplain for the group shortly after its formation.

When the parish was formed in 1980, it was put under the jurisdiction of the pastor of South Beloit. The parish boundaries are the legal boundaries of Roscoe Township. People in the township can continue to attend in South Beloit or join the Church of the Holy Spirit in Roscoe.

◆ **Church of the Holy Spirit.**

On November 26, 1995, during the pastorate of Monsignor Thomas C. Brady (1989-2004), the Church of the Holy Spirit parishioners came together on the Feast of Christ the King to celebrate the installation of their first tabernacle. Many parishioners provided hands-on contributions; others gave of their treasure to help pay for the tabernacle, sanctuary lamp, monstrance, flower stand, linens, celebrant's stole, new chairs, plaster and paint.

Members of St. Peter Parish in South Beloit and Church of the Holy Spirit Parish in Roscoe were surveyed in August 2002 to see if it was feasible for the parishes to build a new church on Hononegah Road near its intersection with Illinois Route 251. Around 1995, the Rockford Diocese purchased a 15-acre parcel for possible future expansion. Monsignor Brady was pastor when this survey was done.

On September 24, 2005, a 25th anniversary Mass was celebrated.

As of March 2007, Father Jerome P. Koutnik is parochial administrator. There are approximately 100 families currently registered at Church of the Holy Spirit Parish.

◆ **First Communicants in the 1980s.**

◆ **Church of the Holy Spirit interior.**

ST. JOHN NEUMANN PARISH

◆ **Bishop O'Neill and Father Daniel Hermes at the groundbreaking.**

◆ **Bishop O'Neill celebrates Mass at the dedication of the first church.**

In the summer of 1977, the Diocese of Rockford accepted a donation of 10 acres of land for the construction of a new parish to serve the needs of a growing Catholic community on the east side of St. Charles. Gertrude and Maurice Regole, the donors of the land, requested that the new parish be named after a saint with the name of John, to honor their deceased son. On June 19, 1977, John Neumann, fourth Bishop of Philadelphia, was canonized a saint. Bishop Arthur J. O'Neill took advantage of the occasion to create the parish of St. John Neumann on the very same day.

Father Daniel J. Hermes (1977-1989) was appointed the first pastor of the new parish. Speaking at all Masses at St. Patrick Church in St. Charles in July 1977, Father Hermes invited all of those living on the east side of St. Charles to join him at the Ramada Inn (currently the Holiday Inn Express) to celebrate Mass. Father Hermes formed a building committee and a fund-raising campaign was organized that involved dozens of parish volunteers who visited families asking for financial pledges.

A groundbreaking ceremony was held in June 1978 and the cornerstone of the new church building was laid in July 1979. On December 9, 1979, Bishop Arthur J. O'Neill dedicated the new church while presiding at the first Mass there. Concelebrating with Bishop O'Neill were Bishop John Paul of LaCrosse, Wisconsin, and Father Hermes. Strong ties with St. Patrick Parish remained and both parishes have shared the school facilities at St. Patrick School since 1977.

◆ **Blessed Sacrament chapel**

On August 29, 1987, a groundbreaking ceremony, led by Bishop Arthur J. O'Neill, was held to begin building a family center. A wing of the church, it included a family center, classrooms, offices and meeting rooms. The center was dedicated by Bishop O'Neill on October 2, 1989. The Mass was concelebrated with Father Hermes.

During the 1990s, the parish continued to grow and it became apparent that a larger church was needed. On May 7, 2000, during the pastorate of Monsignor Robert Hoffman, a groundbreaking ceremony was held, led by Bishop Thomas G. Doran. On February 10, 2002, Bishop Doran dedicated the new 1,500-seat St. John Neumann Church, chapels and renovated offices and meeting areas.

As of March 2007, Monsignor Robert B. Hoffman is pastor. There are approximately 3,200 families currently registered at St. John Neumann Parish.

◆ **St. John Neumann Church interior at the dedication.**

◆ **St. John Neumann Church.**

St. Patrick Parish

From reports of old Catholic settlers in Kane County, as recorded by R. Waite Joslyn and Frank W. Joslyn in a 1908 Kane County History, Father Maurice de St. Palais was the first priest to visit the Kane County area and say Mass in Elgin, and probably in St. Charles, in 1837.

Before St. Patrick Parish was established in 1851, missionary priests offered Mass in pioneer homes. Father John Guiguen and Father Dupontavice were among the priests who would come on horseback and by wagon from Chicago and Joliet to visit the Catholics in the Fox River Valley once every four months to say Mass and administer the sacraments.

In the 1840s, Catholics in the St. Charles area usually attended Mass near what is now Gilberts. Later, they were attended by Father William Feely, appointed pastor of St. Mary Parish in Elgin in 1848. It was Father Feely who began the construction of the St. Charles church. However, he completed only the exterior of the church. The records are not clear as to who actually completed the interior of the church.

On July 9, 1851, Chicago Bishop James O. Van de Velde visited St. Charles to dedicate the newly finished St. Patrick Church.

Bishop Van de Velde divided St. Patrick Parish from St. Mary Parish in Elgin in 1853. It was at this time that Father Patrick O'Dwyer (1853-1860) was appointed from Chicago as the first resident pastor of St. Patrick. The baptismal registers from St. Patrick Parish give proof that Father O'Dwyer was serving the people of St. Patrick as far back as December 5, 1852.

At this time the parish of St. Patrick's included Elburn, West Chicago, and Geneva as missions. The people in the Batavia area also came to St. Patrick to fulfill their religious obligations until Father O'Dwyer purchased property in Batavia and Holy Cross Parish became a mission church of St. Patrick, sometime during the years of 1855 and 1860. People from Elburn continued to come to St. Patrick Parish until St. Gall's was established

◆ **The first St. Patrick Church, circa 1902.**

officially as a parish in 1872. The people in Geneva continued to attend either the church in St. Charles or the Holy Cross Church in Batavia until Bishop Peter J. Muldoon, the first Bishop of Rockford, established St. Peter Parish in Geneva in 1912.

◆ **St. Patrick Church.**

◆ **Father Maurice Stack with St. Patrick's altar boys, 1902.**

A Dominican priest, Father Michael Prendergast, O.P. (1870-1875), took up his duties as pastor. During his time as pastor he saw a hopeful future for the growth of Batavia and purchased land for the site of a future parish in Batavia. It was at this time that he left St. Charles and went to Batavia to take up residence. From the early record, St. Patrick was treated as a mission of the Batavia church at this time. During the pastorates of the priests who succeeded Father Prendergast, it is believed that they resided in Batavia while caring for the parishioners at St. Patrick.

In June of 1883, Father Ambrose J. Goulet (1883-1886) made St. Patrick an independent parish again when he took up residence as pastor.

While he was pastor, Father Timothy Ryan (1905-1909) made many improvements in the church property and redecorated the interior of the church.

In May of 1909, Father Robert J. Carse (1909-1950) began his 41-year pastorate of the parish in St. Charles. Father Carse began the construction of the present church in 1911 and it was completed in 1912. On June 16, 1912, Bishop Peter J. Muldoon dedicated the new church. The rectory was also built at this time.

St. Patrick School was built in 1929, mainly with the donations of Mrs. George H. Rempe, as a memorial to her late husband. The school was staffed by the Adrian Dominican Sisters.

During Father Thomas L. Walsh's pastorate (1950-1956), the church, rectory, and convent were completely redecorated.

On St. Patrick's Day, March 17, 1959, Father Walter J. Ryan (1957-1969) broke ground for an addition to the school, and on March 17, 1960, Bishop Loras T. Lane dedicated the addition

In 1970, the school, rectory, and convent were renovated and in 1975 the church was completely remodeled.

In 1977, St. Patrick Parish was divided into two parishes, and St. John Neuman Parish was established on the east side of St. Charles.

Thirty acres of land were purchased on Crane Road in 1987 to accommodate a new church for St. Patrick Parish. On December 8, 1991, Bishop Arthur J. O'Neill dedicated the new St. Patrick Mission Church. The 36,000-square-foot, six-story church reflects the growth of Catholic families in the St. Charles area. The new church seats 1,200 people and a 15,000-square-foot multi-purpose room is attached to it. In January 1993, the multi-purpose room was renamed the

◆ **Father Robert Carse.**

Father Thomas J. Dempsey Hall in the pastor's honor.

Mass on January 1, 2001, offered by the pastor, Father Joseph B. Linster, celebrated the official kick-off of the sesquicentennial of St. Patrick Parish called "Celebrate 150!"

For more than 40 years, the parish has held the Shamrock Shuffle to celebrate St. Patrick's Day.

As of March 2007, Monsignor Joseph B. Linster is pastor. There are approximately 4,500 families currently registered at St .Patrick Parish.

◆ **St. Patrick Church, Crane Road site.**

St. Paul the Apostle Parish

◆ **The first St. Paul the Apostle Church.**

The Catholic parish in Sandwich came close to being organized in the mid-1880's, but the event wasn't actually to occur until 1910, shortly after the Diocese of Rockford was created in 1908. It also was to be another 15 years before the first resident pastor arrived.

Early Catholics in the Sandwich area, located in the southeast corner of DeKalb County, had been attending Mass a short distance to the west in Somonauk. St. John the Baptist Parish had been formed in Somonauk in the mid-1860's.

The region's growing population caused St. John's second pastor, Father Lawrence A. Ehrhard, to institute a building program. St. Mary Church was built in 1884 at Plano, east of Sandwich in Kendall County, and St. Patrick at Bristol, also Kendall County, in 1885.

Plans were also made for a church in Sandwich, but they were abandoned. The faithful in Sandwich continued to attend St. John the Baptist Church in Somonauk.

Father Charles F. Mertens, the fifth pastor at Somonauk, moved to provide Sandwich residents with a church of their own in 1910. He purchased the Sandwich Presbyterian Church, remodeled it, and furnished it with the help of his Somonauk congregation. It was dedicated to St. Paul the Apostle, with the first Mass being celebrated Easter Sunday, 1911.

Father Mertens attended the Sandwich parish on a regular basis until his transfer in 1915.

St. Paul Parish was then attached to St. Mary in Plano, where Father James W. Friedrich had just taken over as pastor. That arrangement was to continue until Sandwich obtained its first resident pastor, Father Bernard L. Heffernan (1925-1928), in 1925. Father Heffernan took up residence in a Sandwich hotel and ordered work started on a rectory in November, 1925. The building was completed in June, 1926.

In July, 1932, the parish was once again attached as a mission to Plano, until the arrival of Father Francis P. Heckinger in December (1933-1935).

Major renovations were conducted during the pastorate of Father John P. Crotty (1936-1938).

Father Charles K. McCarren (1957-1965) became pastor in 1957 and, in 1959, bought ten acres of land a mile and a half north of Sandwich. There he established a parish cemetery. It was also during 1959 that Father McCarren, with an eye for the future growth of the parish, purchased another ten acres in the northwest section of the town for future development of the parish.

◆ **Father Charles F. Mertens.**

In October of 1975, during the pastorate of Father Thomas P. Kane (1965-1983), groundbreaking ceremonies were held for a St. Paul Parish Center. The new parish center housed a much needed parish hall, kitchen and eight religious education classrooms.

An early fundraiser that continues today was the establishment of a food concession at the Sandwich Fair by Father McCarren. In 1959, the food stand began serving pancakes and sausage out of a tent with dirt floors. A permanent building with a concrete floor and screen doors eventually replaced the tent. Other

◆ **Father Thomas Kane.**

items, such as barbeque, were added to the menu over the last 47 years. It takes many parishioners to staff the four-hour shifts during the seven days of the fair. Proceeds from the yearly event are used to fund two $500 scholarships. The rest is used wherever needed in the parish.

In 2005, during the pastorate of Father John T. Heraty, committees were formed to work on plans for a new church.

As of March 2007 the pastor is Father John T. Heraty. There are approximately 500 families currently registered at St. Paul Parish.

◆ **St. Paul the Apostle Church.**

St. John the Baptist Parish

The first records kept at St. John the Baptist date from 1884, when Father Francis J. Antl (1884-1926) became pastor. Father Antl reports in his diary that the first priest to visit Savanna, according to the memory of the settlers still alive, was a Father Smith, who visited a few Catholic families in 1862.

From about 1870 to 1873, Father Peter J. Gormley attended Savanna as a mission of Fulton, where he was pastor. Father Gormley purchased the original public school building at the corner of Third Street and Van Buren, which was used as a church until 1879.

In 1880, the first church building was sold and another hall, known as the "sweatbox," was purchased. In the same year Father George Ratz was appointed the first resident pastor, a position he held for three-and-a-half years. He built a rectory next to the church and bought four acres of land for a cemetery in the Chestnut Park area outside the town, next to the city cemetery.

Father Francis J. Antl was appointed pastor May 24, 1884. There is a verbal tradition that Father Antl was sent to Savanna to die, having been operated on shortly before and given six months to

live. Die in Savanna he did, but 42 years later! When he arrived he found a battered missal and a debt of $1,000—no chalice, no vestments and almost no congregation. People were grossly negligent, with few exceptions, in the practice of their religion, and the area was fanatic in its anti-Catholic feeling. Father Antl reports that in the early days children followed him on the streets hurling abusive language, and even a few rocks, as he passed along.

◆ **Father Francis Antl.**

His first official act was to buy a bell, for which he had no belfry, for $500. Evidently this outwardly foolish act of faith impressed the congregation, for two months later a mission was held and 120 Catholics received the Sacraments. From the outset it was certain that St. John the Baptist had no ordinary pastor.

In November 1884, a school was erected, and in 1886, enlarged. In 1887 a gallery was added to the church to accommodate the increasing crowds. Five Sisters of Providence were engaged to teach and a convent was provided for them. Although in 1887 the income was not sufficient to support the pastor, the church and school were decorated. With more of his own money, Father Antl sponsored immigrant families from his native Bohemia and bolstered the Catholic blood in his parish.

In 1896, the property at the corner of Chicago Avenue and Fifth Street was purchased, as Father Antl realized the community would grow toward the site. Work on a new brick church, the present structure, began immediately. The cornerstone was laid August 2, 1896; the church was opened with a

◆ **The first St. John the Baptist Church.**

◆ **St. John the Baptist Church in 1926, prepared for the funeral of Father Antl.**

solemn Mass August 27, 1899. A rectory was built the same year, as was a three-story school. In 1903, the Franciscan Sisters of Milwaukee took over the parish school.

By 1904, Father Antl had buildings valued at better than $25,000 in a parish which could barely support him. But he continued to expand and improve, redecorating, adding statuary and art work, slating the roof, not stinting anywhere, even ordering a Baptismal font of Carrara marble.

By 1910, the financial situation was sufficiently bright for Father Antl to make a donation of $1,000 to the diocesan orphanage. In the same year, he acquired property upon which the rectory was erected in 1917. In 1923, the school, which eventually closed in 1968, was built at a cost of more than $60,000.

In 1914, the pastor of St. John the Baptist was also charged with operating the mission church of St. Peter in Thomson. Father Antl built the church there. Shortly afterwards it was transferred to the parish at Fulton.

The years, the struggle, and the ill health took their toll on Father Antl. One of his final purchases was a pipe organ which was not completely installed at the time of his death, May 8, 1926.

For Father Antl's funeral, all business places in Savanna closed, and nearly the entire population walked behind his body from the church to the cemetery, a distance of better than two miles.

Father William M. McGuire (1926-1928), purchased the convent on Fourth Street, which adjoins the playground and the rear of the rectory lot. He also had all the parish property, including the cemetery, surveyed and, in addition, had the sanctuary of the church decorated.

In November 1928, the new pastor, Father John R. Quigley (1928-1938), remodeled the rectory and the convent and made extensive repairs on the organ. During the Depression years, Savanna was extremely hard hit and consequently the parish suffered financially.

Father Edward A. O'Brien (1939-1944) was appointed pastor in January 1939. Although these

◆ **Parish center.**

were extremely difficult years, Father O'Brien was successful in reducing the parish debt.

Bishop John J. Boylan appointed Father Walter J. Ryan (1944-1952) as pastor in 1944. Although the war had pulled much of the rest of the country out of the depression, Savanna was still on hard times. Father Ryan, nevertheless, in addition to completely redecorating the church, making improvements in the other buildings, and installing new heating plants in the church and rectory, was able to eliminate the parish debt and improve parish finances.

Father Edward J. McIsaac (1952-1963) came as pastor to Savanna in September 1952. He initiated an extensive program of repairs in the school and rectory. A heating plant to supply both school and church was installed and the convent was redecorated. In the fall of 1957, a campaign was launched to raise funds for

remodeling and redecorating all the parish buildings. This work was completed in time for the celebration of the Diocesan Jubilee in 1958.

The church of SS. John and Catherine in Mount Carroll was operated as a mission of Savanna from 1929 to 1972. In 1972, SS. John and Catherine Mission was raised to the status of a parish.

In October 1966, Bishop Loras T. Lane assigned Father Henry L. Weckerle (1966-1986) to St. John the Baptist Parish as pastor. Two years later, in June 1968, the parish had to close the doors of its parochial school; the parish could not keep pace with the rising cost of education. St. John the Baptist Parochial School became St. John's Center and was used to accommodate the religious education program for the parish.

During the pastorate of Father Joseph F. Jarmoluk (1990-1997), a new St. John the Baptist Parish Center was built. The dedication and blessing took place on August 25, 1996, with Bishop Thomas G. Doran the main celebrant.

As of March 2007, Father Dennis D. Atto is parochial administrator. There are approximately 250 families currently registered at St. John the Baptist Parish.

◆ **The Catholic Women of St. John the Baptist Club.**

◆ **St. John the Baptist Church, interior and exterior.**

HOLY TRINITY PARISH

Holy Trinity in Scales Mound was organized in 1853. Mass was celebrated in private homes, one being the log home of Henry Singer on Cording Road. Mr. Singer donated eight acres of land off Stagecoach Trail to be used as a cemetery.

Early Catholics in the Scales Mound area were attended from the nearby town of Galena and by missionaries from Freeport who went up to the region after services in Shannon. One of these missionaries, Father Peter Corcoran, supervised the completion of the brick church at Scales Mound in 1864.

Holy Trinity Church had been constructed in 1864, but there is some doubt that it was built at that time. Some historians of Jo Daviess County claim the building had started out as a store,

◆ **Holy Trinity Church.**

◆ **The first Holy Trinity Church.**

but this story was always refuted by Father William M. McGuire. In any case, the original building proved inadequate within a short time and an addition was constructed in 1874.

In 1914, Father William M. McGuire (1914-1918) was made pastor of St. Joseph in Apple River and of Holy Trinity in Scales Mound. From then until 1983, the pastor of St. Joseph was also pastor of Holy Trinity.

The church was enlarged once again during the pastorate of Father Russell J. Guccione (1933-1940).

The cast bell, still in use at Holy Trinity, was originally installed at the Irish mission church at Vinegar Hill, north of Galena, in 1835. When Holy Trinity was renovated in the mid-1930s, the bell was transported to Scales Mound and installed there.

In 1978, Apple Canyon Lake was developed and, a few years later, The Galena Territory. During the summer months, the church was filled to capacity.

Father Daniel D. Tranel was appointed pastor of both St. Mary's Parish in Galena and of Holy Trinity Parish in Scales Mound in

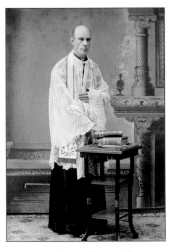

◆ **Father William Bally, pastor 1864-1887.**

◆ **Father Ronald Conro.**

1983. In 1985, under his pastorate, another addition was made to the church, along with a basement, which has rest rooms and a kitchen. The church also was made accessible to the handicapped.

In 1988, Father Ronald J. Conro (1988-1999) was appointed pastor of St. Mary, Elizabeth and of Holy Trinity Parish. During Father Conro's pastorate, the church was remodeled in 1993.

A Clavinova was purchased and the choir was moved from the loft to near the sanctuary in 2002 while Father Michael A. Librandi (1999-2002) was pastor.

During the pastorate of Father Christopher J. Kuhn, the church was renovated in 2006.

As of March 2007, Father Christopher J. Kuhn is pastor. There are approximately 125 families currently registered at Holy Trinity Parish.

◆ **Holy Trinity Church interior.**

St. Wendelin Parish

During the years preceding 1870, the Catholic pioneers of this vicinity used to assemble at the home of Dionysius Bear to assist at Mass whenever a missionary came along. Father Ignatius Baluff, Pastor of St. Joseph, Freeport, was the first priest whose visits here are recorded. Shannon was not, as its name might lead one to think, an Irish settlement; most of the early settlers in Shannon were German. The town is named after William Shannon, a prominent early resident, who was instrumental in platting the town site in 1860.

St. Wendelin Parish dates its beginning to 1870, the year that area Catholics bought an old Presbyterian church and renovated it for their own use.

After 1870, until the first resident pastor was appointed in 1876, services were provided more regularly, primarily by Fathers Francis X. Nighe and Peter Corcoran. Father Nighe had been a pastor in Fulton and had attended the congregation at Savanna. Father Corcoran was a missionary working

◆ **St. Wendelin Church.**

out of Freeport and Galena. The first resident pastor for St. Wendelin, Father Adrian von Steinberg (1876-1879), came to Shannon on April 9, 1876. Services were still being held in the renovated church.

Father Anthony B. Buetter (1881-1913) began 32 years of pastoral service in Shannon on August 15, 1881. Father Buetter's era saw the construction of two churches in Shannon, the purchase of a rectory, the start of a cemetery and, of course, the start of the Mount Carroll parish.

In just over a decade, the original church building proved inadequate and Father Buetter began planning for a new church. This was completed in 1884 and dedicated the same year by Archbishop Patrick A. Feehan of Chicago.

On October 9, 1905, the congregation's second church was destroyed by fire. Plans for another new church were under way immediately.

In August 1906, the present church structure was completed and used for the first time. The building was dedicated October 22, 1907, by the Most Reverend James E. Quigley, the new Archbishop of Chicago.

With the retirement of Father John M. Clifford (1916-1929), Bishop Edward F. Hoban attached the parish to St. Mary Parish, Polo. In 1945, St. Wendelin was transferred to St. Catherine Parish, Freeport. It wasn't until 1948 that St. Wendelin regained the status of a parish when Bishop John J. Boylan appointed Father Peter A. Watgen (1948-1969) to the parish.

In 1959, Father Watgen, added a basement to the building, which provided a hall and kitchen facilities.

Due to Father Watgen's failing health St. Wendelin's was attended from Rockford from 1966 to 1972. During this time the church underwent a large renovation program and the newly renovated church was blessed by Bishop Arthur J. O'Neill on March 16, 1969.

◆ **St. Wendelin Church interior.**

Father William P. Collins (1970-1972) was appointed pastor on June 3, 1970, and during his pastorate the construction of the parish's education wing, attached to the west end of the church, was completed in time for the parish's centennial celebration. It was dedicated as part of the celebration in October 1970.

A new rectory was built in 1984 and dedicated on November 3, 1984, during the pastorate of Father David E. Beauvais (1983-1987).

On October 22, 2006, a Mass celebrating the 100th anniversary of the church was held with Father Michael J. Bolger officiating. A new painting of St. Wendelin was blessed at the celebration and then hung in the church. The new painting is a copy of one that disappeared from the church in the 1960s.

St. Wendelin has three long-standing parish events. A Mother-Daughter luncheon, held in May every year since 1955. A ham dinner, held annually in October, was begun in 1961. A February Father-Son luncheon has been held every year since 1965.

As of March 2007, Father Michael J. Bolger is parochial administrator. There are approximately 200 families currently registered at St. Wendelin Parish.

◆ **Father Peter Watgen.**

St. John the Baptist Parish

In 1837, a mail route was established from Chicago to John Dixon's residence on the Rock River, and this route crossed the southern end of DeKalb County. A log hut was built for a station at the crossing of Somonauk Creek and given the name of Somonauk. The early traveling missionaries made it a regular stopping place. When, in 1853, the railroad was built through this region, a village sprang up, into which moved several Catholic families.

The first Catholic household in the parish was that of Francis and Nancy Riley Devine. They arrived from New York State in 1837, just two years after the arrival of the first Catholic in the area, the wife of Stephen Sherman. The Shermans were Catholics who immigrated to Somonauk from Alsace Lorraine. Most of the pioneers of Somonauk were from Alsace Lorraine. Among other early Catholic settlers in Somonauk, besides the French, were the Germans and some Irish families.

Mass was offered in the town's hotel or in pioneer homes at irregular intervals until 1863 when Catholics purchased Turner Hall for use as a church. It was moved across LaSalle Street to the present parish property at LaSalle and Depot Streets.

An unusual aspect of the Somonauk parish is the role that order priests have played in its development and current history. The parish organization began with the assistance of a Jesuit and was served for many years by priests of the Norbertine Order.

Parish records date to 1865, with the earliest ones being signed by Father Dominic Niederkorn, S. J., who attended the area from Chicago.

Turner Hall did not last long as a church. It was quickly inadequate for the size of the congregation and was replaced with a $6,000 frame building and given the name of St. John the Baptist. The second church didn't last long either, for in May, 1868, this building was destroyed by fire. Immediate plans were made for the building of a brick church when a resident

◆ **Father Dominic Niederkorn.**

pastor was sent to Somonauk. The first resident pastor was Father Casper J. Huth (1869-1884), who arrived February 14, 1869. The parish then included part of DeKalb County, Kane County and the

◆ **Parish gathering, circa 1890.**

◆ **The first St. John the Baptist Church, 1914.**

◆ **St. John the Baptist Church interior, circa 1930.**

northeastern part of LaSalle County. Missions were regularly attended in Plano and Bristol, and stations in Leland and Shabbona Grove.

During the fifteen years of his pastorate, Father Huth set about building and completing the church. Father Lawrence A. Ehrhard (1884-1903) became pastor in 1884 and built churches in Plano and Bristol.

Father Peter J. Weber (1906-1910) built a rectory that was used until a new one was constructed in 1975.

Father Cornelius Kirkfleet, O.Praem. (1928-1947), became pastor of St. John the Baptist on July 26, 1928. His first step was to remodel the church completely. In 1935, he purchased the site of a burned-out store in the business section of town. Under the direction of a contractor, a group of men, Catholic and non-Catholic, built a social hall. This he named Feehan Hall, after Archbishop Feehan of Chicago. The hall was paid for out of community funds and was regarded as a community hall, although it belonged to the parish and was used primarily as a parish hall. Similarly, tennis courts were built on two lots near the church for the use of the community, although they were property of the church.

In July, 1953, Father Maurice J. Windt, O.Praem. (1953-1963) began a program of remodeling. He had the 2nd and 3rd floors of the rectory removed and had the church's ceiling redecorated.

On August 23, 1972, diocesan priests once again took charge of the parish with Father Michael J. Shanahan (1972-1974) being named the pastor. Under his administration, extensive remodeling, repairs and redecoration of the interior of the church were completed.

A rectory-administration building was completed in March of 1975, and the summer of 1975 saw extensive repairs made to the exterior of the church.

A new parish center was dedicated during the pastorate of Father Charles E. Sherman (1974-1996). The Mass of Thanksgiving was celebrated by Bishop Arthur J. O'Neill in October of 1980.

Under the supervision of Father Donald D. DeSalvo, pastor, the church was repaired and redecorated. A new baptistery was also added. The rite of rededication took place on August 17, 2003. Bishop Thomas G. Doran celebrated the Mass.

The parish continues to hold an annual Corned Beef and Cabbage Dinner which it has done for 69 years, since 1938.

As of March 2007 the parish administrator is Monsignor Glenn Nelson. There are approximately 500 families currently registered at St. John the Baptist Parish.

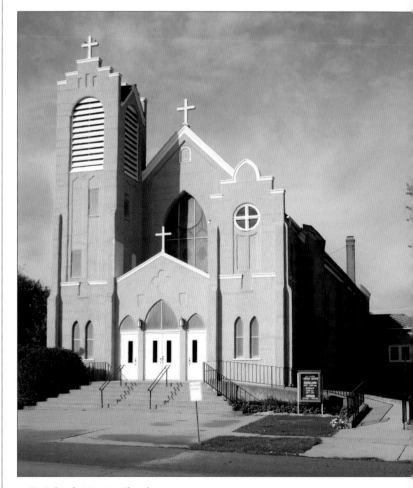

◆ **St. John the Baptist Church.**

◆ **Bishop Muldoon with the First Communicants at the first St. Peter Church, 1909.**

Shortly after his appointment to the newly established Diocese of Rockford, Bishop Peter J. Muldoon established St. Peter Parish in South Beloit. Residents of South Beloit had previously attended St. Thomas Church in Beloit, Wisconsin.

Father Bernard X. O'Reilly (1909-1911) was named the first pastor and he celebrated Mass in Kent Hall (later known as Mark Hall) until he built the first church of St. Peter. Mass was celebrated in it for the first time on the Feast of the Assumption, August 15, 1909. On January 30, 1910, the frame church was dedicated by Bishop Muldoon.

◆ **Father Martin J. McEvoy, pastor 1911-1915.**

Father James T. Donohue (1915-1928) was appointed pastor in 1915. He purchased land on the highest site in the city and ground was broken for the present church and rectory on October 24, 1924. The cornerstone for the church was laid on February 1, 1925, and on October 25, 1925, Bishop Muldoon came to St. Peter's to dedicate the church. The old building was sold and became the American Legion Hall.

Father Ronald L. French (1930-1940) was pastor during the Depression. Since the parish at that time was made up mostly of factory workers, the weakened economy took a heavy toll.

Father Edward J. McIsaac (1940-1952) became pastor in 1940. As a result of the war boom, prosperity returned to the workers and to the parish.

Father James F. Mulcaire (1952-1966) assumed the pastoral responsibilities in 1952. In 1955, he bought four acres of land on Elmwood Avenue to build a school, which was constructed in 1962 and officially opened for the 1963-1964 school term. The school first served students in first-through fourth-grade and was staffed by the Sisters of Notre Dame de Namur. Each succeeding year another grade was added until the school reached its capacity of eight grades.

Father James F. McGuire was appointed Administrator of the parish in January 1966, and in the spring of that year, construction of a new convent began. It was completed in February 1967 during the pastorate of Father Raymond M. Hettermann (1966-1974).

St. Peter Parish includes the city of South Beloit, along with a great deal of farm country and the towns of Rockton and Roscoe. In addition to

◆ **First Communicants, 1909.**

Masses at St. Peter, the parish's congregation was also served by a weekly Mass held at a chapel on the property of the Wagon Wheel Lodge in Rockton. This was discontinued in July 1974.

A rededication of the church was held on November 16, 1986, during the pastorate of Father Daniel B. Geoghegan (1983-1989). Bishop Arthur J. O'Neill was the celebrant. The extensive remodeling project included a new ceiling and replastered walls, a new altar, a remodeled sacristy, and new carpeting. Parishioners did much of the work, saving the parish thousands of dollars.

On September 15, 1996, Bishop Thomas G. Doran installed the Blessed Sacrament in the new Sacred Heart of Jesus and Immaculate Heart of Mary Perpetual Adoration Chapel. The chapel, which was built during the pastorate of Monsignor Thomas C. Brady (1989-2004), is set amid trees behind the church, and prayers are said there 24 hours a day, seven days a week.

As of March 2007, Father Jerome P. Koutnik is pastor. There are approximately 1,000 families currently registered at St. Peter Parish.

◆ **Adoration Chapel.**

◆ **St. Peter Church.**

ST. PETER PARISH

The tragic loss by fire of St. John the Baptist Church in Johnsburg in early 1900 provided the impetus for the establishment of St. Peter Parish in Spring Grove.

Prior to 1900, when the huge Johnsburg church was destroyed, German Catholics north of that McHenry County city were considered to be part of St. John the Baptist Parish. After the fire, a group of about 30 families, most in Spring Grove, met and agreed that a church at Spring Grove, situated about four-and-one-half miles north of Johnsburg, could be more convenient for them. A committee composed of Nicholas Freund, John Wagner, Martin Freund and William Carey called on Archbishop Patrick A. Feehan in Chicago and sought his permission to have their own parish. The Archbishop granted permission to start a parish providing the parishioners could find a priest willing to take over as pastor.

◆ **Father Clement Duerr, pastor 1900-1910.**

◆ **St. Peter School students, circa 1910.**

Father Clement Duerr (1900-1910), who was about to retire in 1900, agreed to organize the new Spring Grove congregation. He was to serve 10 years before finally retiring. Father Duerr's niece, Margaret Zugg of Chicago, would eventually donate 10 acres of land to the parish in 1942.

The year 1900 was also the year in which the Chicago, Milwaukee and St. Paul Railroad came through Spring Grove, with incorporation as a village following in two years. The Burton Township area had originally been known as Blivins Mills and had been settled back in the early 1840s.

St. Peter Church was constructed a year before Spring Grove became a village. On Candlemas Day, February 2, 1901, the church was dedicated. The rectory was built in the summer of 1902.

The first parish school was a wooden addition to the church. It was completed in 1905 and classes began with lay teachers. Later, in 1915, the Sisters of St. Francis became the teaching staff.

The next parish building project was a convent, completed in 1915 during the pastorate of Father William Dommermuth (1910-1919).

In May of 1919, Father Benno A. Hildebrand (1919-1926) took charge of the parish. His seven year period was marked by repairs to the church and school.

◆ **St. Peter Church.**

Father Anthony R. Schunicht (1926-1929) expanded the parish property with the purchase of two acres of land and a house situated immediately to the west of the church property. This house became the rectory.

On July 25, 1933, the long and industrious pastorate of Father John L. Daleiden (1933-1960) began. Father Daleiden served the people of St. Peter's until January 4, 1960.

On April 1, 1948, ground was broken for a new school and renovations on the church were started. A shrine to Our Lady of Fatima was dedicated in 1952. It was also during the years of Father Daleiden's pastorate that the remodeling of the rectory and convent was accomplished.

Father John J. Kilduff (1965-1988) arrived on June 18, 1965. He inaugurated the first of many improvements when he replaced an old coal-fired steam boiler with a modern gas-fired boiler, thus renovating the entire heating system of the building which served as church, school and parish hall. Another improvement was the installation of a modern kitchen in the parish hall, a project of the Christian Mothers and Holy Name Societies.

At that time, one lay teacher and three Missionary Sisters of the Immaculate Conception staffed the parish school, a four-classroom, eight–grade facility. Faced with an acute and growing shortage of teaching sisters, the order withdrew the sisters from Spring Grove in June 1967.

◆ **Father Charles Meehan with graduates, circa 1932.**

Father Kilduff lost no time in assembling an all-lay teaching staff. But enrollment in the once-flourishing school fell to about 90 pupils from a high of 200. Parents, parishioners and Father Kilduff discussed the matter, and the decision to close the school was made in October 1967.

In 1985, the church was completely renovated in the Georgian style. An estimated 88 people, both from the parish and the surrounding community, donated 5,000 hours of time and talent to complete the job two months ahead of schedule. Among many additions, the church was made accessible to the handicapped. A new statue of St. Peter was also installed. Bishop Arthur J. O'Neill rededicated the church on October 13, 1985. Concelebrating with Bishop O'Neill was Father Kilduff.

In 1990, a 15-ton boulder was placed at the entrance to the parish parking lot. A fitting symbol of the parish named in honor of the first head of the Church, Peter, it is inscribed "You are Rock and on this Rock I will build my Church."

During the pastorate of Father Andrew J. Plesa (1988-2001), a Mass for St. Peter Parish's centennial celebration took place on June 25, 2000, with Bishop Thomas G. Doran officiating. Bishop Doran also consecrated a new cemetery on the same day.

As of March 2007, Father Steven J. Lange is pastor. There are approximately 900 families currently registered at St. Peter Parish.

◆ **St. Peter School students, circa 1925.**

Sacred Heart Parish

Prior to 1870, the pioneer German Catholic families living in and around Sterling had no church of their own, but were often visited by German speaking priests from Freeport. Most of the early German families arrived about the time the Galena division of the Chicago-Northwestern railroad was being built in the year 1855.

In the year 1870, Father Peter Fisher, Vicar General of the Chicago Diocese at that time, appointed Father William Schamoni the first resident pastor for the Germans of Sterling. For a time, he offered Mass in the old Bressler hall, but soon began the construction of a little church and bought a small house to be used as his rectory. On Easter Sunday 1870, Mass was offered for the first time in the new church, which served the congregation until May 1, 1886.

On January 1, 1871, Father Schamoni (1870-1871) was appointed pastor and the parish in Oregon was made a mission of Sacred Heart Parish.

Father Ferdinand Allgayer became pastor in 1875 and remained until October 1876. During his pastorate two lots were purchased for the purpose of building a school and convent. His successor, Father Joseph Beinecke (1876-1881), arrived in December 1876 and saw to the building of the school and convent. The school was in operation until June 15, 1910, when it was closed because the small attendance did not warrant the expensive repairs necessary at that time.

During the pastorate of Father George M. Miller (1881-1885), the building of the second church was begun.

The next pastor, Father Hubert M. Fegers (1885-1914), remained in Sterling for nearly 30 years as pastor of the Sacred Heart Parish. His first work was to finish the church which was solemnly dedicated by Archbishop Patrick A. Feehan of Chicago on May 2, 1886. The church was then completely furnished and six years later, was debt free. Still under the pastorate of Father Fegers, the parish observed its Silver Jubilee in 1895.

When Father Michael B. Krug (1925-1955) came to Sterling as pastor (later monsignor), he came to a parish deeply in debt. Father Krug was instrumental in retiring the parish debt and in making many improvements in the building. The church was enlarged and redecorated and furnished with statues and art work to the extent that it was known as the "jewel box" of the Rockford Diocese.

In June 1964, Father Joseph D. Highland was appointed Administrator of the parish. During his tenure at the parish, a new Sacred Heart Church was planned across from Newman Central Catholic High School. The church was built on seven acres of land in the northwest part of the city.

◆ **The first Sacred Heart Church.**

◆ **Monsignor Michael B. Krug.**

◆ **Father John Schulte with the First Communicants, May 27, 1923.**

Father Highland served Sacred Heart Parish until July of 1970 when Bishop Arthur J. O'Neill announced a structural change that created an experimental team ministry in Sterling to serve both parishes, Sacred Heart and St. Mary. Father Everett

◆ **The interior of the second Sacred Heart Church.**

J. Hiller, at that time Pastor of St. Mary, was appointed as coordinator for both parishes with Father Philip Kennedy, Father Robert N. Sherry and Father Humberto C. Rodriguez, as members of the first ministry team.

Father Sherry and Father Kennedy came to live in the rectory on the site of the new church and on

September 26, 1971, the new Sacred Heart Church was dedicated by Bishop Arthur J. O'Neill.

The new parish is organized as a compound of buildings clustered around a church courtyard. The form of the buildings recalls the qualities of traditional Northern European construction, thus expressing the Germanic traditions of the parish. A free-standing bell tower near the church houses the bell donated to the parish in 1895 by Jacob Lauff. The bell had been preserved when the old church was demolished in 1970.

Large scale photographic murals, expressing traditional concepts of faith in contemporary terms, adorn the interior brick walls of the new church.

The church design won national honors from the Guild for Religious Architecture in May 1972.

In the fall of 1973, it was decided to discontinue the team ministry in Sterling and return to the traditional system of each parish having its own pastor. On October 1, 1973, Bishop O'Neill appointed Father Lawrence London (1973-1976) as Pastor of Sacred Heart and Father William P. Knott as Pastor of St. Mary's.

On June 5, 2005, Father Paul White, pastor since 1997, dedicated the parish's new handicapped-accessible entrance. Local businesses owned by parishioners, and other professionals, donated their skills, keeping construction costs to a minimum.

At the time of the dedication, Eugene and Rita Graff donated a life-sized statue of the Sacred Heart that had once stood in the original church on First Avenue. That church was demolished after a storm caused the steeple to collapse into the church. Many of the statues were sold at auction. The Graffs purchased the Sacred Heart statue and kept it safely stored in their barn for 33 years. They restored the statue and presented it as a gift to the parish in memory of Rita's parents, John and Bertha Minertz.

As of March 2007, Father Paul C. White is pastor. There are approximately 600 families currently registered at Sacred Heart Parish.

◆ **Sacred Heart Church interior and exterior.**

ST. MARY PARISH

The earliest Catholic settlers in Sterling were attended by priests from Dixon. As early as 1854, Father James Fitzgerald, the resident pastor in Dixon, came to St. Mary's, known then as St. Patrick's. He was succeeded two years later by Father Thomas Kennedy, who celebrated Mass in Sterling three or four times a year. A Captain Lyons donated a log cabin in the east end of town; this served as a place for the celebration of Mass. Later, a larger building, Crandall Hall, was used as a place of worship until the first church was built.

◆ **The first St. Mary Church, built in 1885.**

Father Michael Ford was appointed to Dixon in April 1859, with Sterling as a mission. As a result of this move, Sterling was regularly attended once a month for the next four years. Though Father Ford died in the fall of 1862, he would not immediately rest in peace, even though Catholics at both parishes professed a love of him. He was buried at Dixon, but Sterling Catholics came by night and removed his body to their cemetery. When the present Calvary Cemetery was bought, his body was moved to it, where it remains.

Father William Herbert came to Sterling in the 1860s, and directed the building of a small frame church and house, but the congregation was dissatisfied with their location.

Father John Daly (1863-1876) was appointed by Bishop James Duggan of Chicago as the first resident pastor of Sterling in June 1863. In 1865, Father Daly began the building of a new brick church and rectory. The old rectory was used as a school that became known as St. Anne's Academy.

In 1870, the German Catholics of Sterling were given a pastor of their own, Father William Schamoni, when Sacred Heart Parish was formed.

In 1876, the parish, through litigation, lost its property and it was necessary for Bishop Thomas Foley to purchase the old Presbyterian church. Father Patrick A. McMahon (1889-1892) became pastor in 1889. During his time as pastor, the present Calvary Cemetery was purchased.

In October 1893, Father James J. Bennett (1893-1909), became pastor. During his pastorate the old Presbyterian church was sold to the public school system and the present church and rectory were built in 1898. It was also at this time that the parish name was changed from St. Patrick to St. Mary. Father Andrew J. Burns (1909-1957) (later to be Monsignor Burns) was appointed pastor of St. Mary Parish in Sterling on June 1, 1909. This was the beginning of his nearly half a century of service to the people of Sterling. The parochial school, which served both parishes in Sterling, was built at a cost of $70,000 and was debt free when it was dedicated by Bishop Peter J. Muldoon in 1913.

◆ **First Communicant, Margaret Weber, 1910.**

◆ **Construction of the current St. Mary Church, 1897.**

The Community High School was built in 1922 at a cost of $140,000 and dedicated in 1923 by Bishop Muldoon.

The old convent soon proved too small. Another story was added to provide rooms for more sisters. What is known as the "Little University" was later acquired. This is a former private residence which was remodeled to house three classrooms for first-graders and a health office.

On October 27, 1952, the Newman Center, now called the Parish Center, was dedicated. At the time of the dedication of the Newman Center, the name of the Community High School was changed to Newman High School in honor of John Henry Cardinal Newman.

On July 12, 1957, Bishop Loras T. Lane appointed Father Thomas S. Green (1957-1969) as pastor of St. Mary Parish. On January 17, 1958, Bishop Lane announced plans for a new Newman Central High School to serve the Sterling area of the diocese. When it opened its doors in September 1959, the old high school building became part of the St. Mary grade school complex.

After becoming pastor in 1969, Father Everett Hiller (1969-1973) had the church completely renovated. It was also during Father Hiller's administration that a team ministry served both St. Mary and Sacred Heart Parishes in Sterling.

The team ministry was discontinued when Bishop O'Neill appointed Father William P. Knott (1973-1980) as Pastor of St. Mary's on October 1, 1973. Among the improvements during Father Knott's appointment was the addition of air-conditioning to the church.

During the pastorate of Father Geoffrey D. Wirth (1980-1985), a new parish center was dedicated by Bishop Arthur J. O'Neill on May 13, 1984. The 15,000-square-foot brick building is all ground level. The heart of the center is the chapel which seats 60 people. The auditorium seats 500 and can accommodate 400 tables.

Father Thomas E. Bales (1987-2001), who became pastor in 1987, renovated the interior of the church soon after his arrival. He also dedicated a children's memorial to unborn babies on All Souls Day, November 2, 1991, at Calvary Cemetery.

Bishop Thomas G. Doran and Father Bales dedicated a new 44,000-square-foot school on September 4, 1997. The school serves kindergarten through eighth-grade students from St. Mary and Sacred Heart Parishes in Sterling, and middle school students from St. Andrew Parish in Rock Falls.

As of March 2007, Father Donald M. Ahles is pastor. There are approximately 1,200 families currently registered at St. Mary Parish.

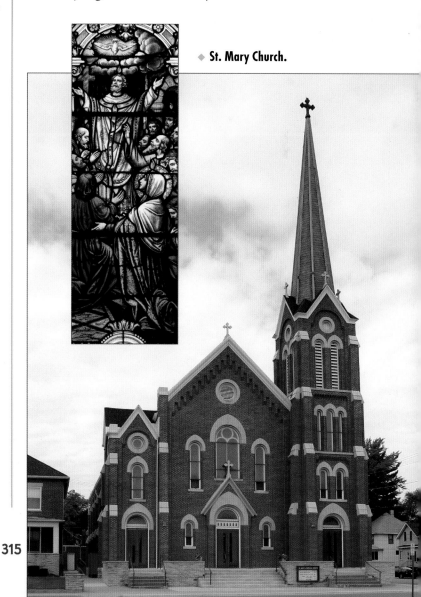

◆ **St. Mary Church.**

◆ **1905 parish picnic.**

HOLY CROSS PARISH

◆ **Holy Cross Church.**

Some members of today's Holy Cross Parish in Stockton are descendents of the pioneers who established a parish in New Dublin in the late 1830s and early 1840s.

New Dublin, located in Erin Township, Stephenson County, actually had a log church in 1836, but area Catholics were served by the irregular visits of missionaries until 1843. Father Francis Derevin (Derwin), assigned there by Bishop Joseph Rosati of St. Louis in 1843, was the first resident priest for the community.

In 1846, three years after all of Illinois came under the jurisdiction of the newly-created Chicago Diocese, Father John Cavanaugh became pastor of New Dublin's St. Mary of the Mound Church.

Gradually, the children of many New Dublin settlers moved westward into the Pleasant Valley section of Jo Daviess County. They built a church and established the Plum River mission parish of St. Patrick. Many of the following generations also migrated, this time north to a cattle and produce shipping center they called Stocktown, which, of course, officially became Stockton.

Early Catholic settlers of the Stockton area attended Mass at New Dublin and Plum River, both of which had become mission parishes. They also attended church at Elizabeth, where a church had existed since 1855; at Lena, where a church was built in 1870; or at Apple River, where Father Peter Corcoran of Shannon had erected a church in 1863.

◆ **The first Holy Cross Church, 1924.**

◆ **Holy Cross Church interior, circa 1950.**

Railroad construction continued to bring new immigrants, and by the early 1890s it was obvious that a church in Stockton itself was a necessity. Following an organizational meeting in 1892, Stockton Catholics purchased property on March 16, 1892, from the estate of Enoch Hawes. Construction on the site at Hudson and Benton Streets began immediately.

The first Mass was celebrated by Father Emmerich Weber, who was Pastor of St. Mary in Elizabeth from 1891 to 1903.

Archbishop Patrick A. Feehan of Chicago established Stockton as a parish in 1893 and gave it the name of Holy Cross, and assigned its first resident pastor, Father Francis J. Hartman (1893-1896). Father Hartman acquired St. Patrick Church in Plum River as a mission and supervised the construction of a rectory during his first year in Stockton.

During Father Stephen Wolfgarten's time (1902-1908), a school was built and placed under the care of the School Sisters of St. Francis.

Construction continued under Father Alfred A. Heinzler (1908-1923), with the completion of a rectory on East Benton Street. Father Heinzler was planning a new church when he was transferred.

A new parish school was built for the Stockton parish during the term of Father Joseph W. Rojemann (1936-1945).

During the term of Father C. Alfred Dietsch (1945 to 1959), an addition to the school was completed.

A new church was completed under the supervision of Father Clarence J. Thennes (1959-1981),

◆ **Holy Cross Church interior.**

pastor. The windows in the church were made by Father Thennes, whose hobby was polishing stones. He arranged the polished stones in the form of crosses and inlaid them in clear plastic. Some memorials from the old church were transferred to the new church. Bishop Arthur J. O'Neill was the main celebrant of the Mass of Dedication on October 28, 1979.

◆ **Father Clarence Thennes.**

The old church building was razed in October 1980, and Holy Cross School was closed in 1984, after 82 years of existence.

When the new church was built in 1979, bricks were bought at the same time for a parish center. Those bricks were in storage for 22 years until the center was built during the pastorate of Father Robert W. Jones (1998-2001). The old bricks helped the new center better match the church. The 7,200-square-foot facility was dedicated by Bishop Thomas G. Doran on June 24, 2001.

The Most Reverend Leo W. Binz, D.D., former Archbishop of the St. Paul Diocese, is a native son of Holy Cross parish in Stockton.

As of March 2007, Father Dean M. Smith is pastor. There are approximately 250 families currently registered at Holy Cross Parish.

OUR LADY OF PERPETUAL HELP PARISH

The roots of Our Lady of Perpetual Help Parish in Sublette go back to the church at Perkin's Grove, a few miles southwest of Sublette, which was one of the pioneer parishes of Lee County.

Sublette got its first church in 1867, while the Perkin's Grove church was completed in 1853. Mass had been celebrated in Perkin's Grove as early as 1846.

In 1860, a rectory was built and Perkin's Grove received its first resident pastor, Father M. J. Clarke. A school was erected in the same year that Sublette received permission to build a church, 1866, but a fire in 1870 destroyed the school, rectory and teachers' house on Christmas Day.

During this time, the village began to disintegrate, separating into the communities of Sublette, West Brooklyn and East Maytown. The fire in 1870 dealt the blow from which the Perkin's Grove church never recovered. The chapel at Perkin's Grove was later reopened as a mission of Sublette and Mass was celebrated several times a year there as late as 1938 by Father Joseph J. Weitekamp.

Father Anthony B. Buetter (1870-1876) was the first resident pastor at Sublette. He purchased a rectory and later built an addition; it served the parish until 1919. Father Buetter also decorated the three-year-old church which would serve the parish until 1905.

Father Francis Schreiber (1876-1877) succeeded Father Buetter. In the few months he was pastor, he paid off the church debt, collected money for an altar, installed new windows in the church, partially furnished the house, constructed a gallery

◆ **Flag pole dedication, circa 1928.**

inside the church and built and paid for the first Sublette parochial school, which was served by the Sisters of St. Francis.

Father Joseph Rempe (1897-1902), began making plans for a new church. Father C. Tasche (1902-1904) became pastor in 1902. It was under his direction that the present church, planned by Father Rempe, was constructed in 1905. Shortly after his arrival in Sublette, the convent burned down and the Sisters of St. Francis who had been in charge of the school left.

The next pastor, Father Henry J. Hauser (1905-1906), was the first priest to celebrate Mass in the new church. He was succeeded by Father Charles F. Mertens (1906-1908), the last pastor assigned from the Chicago Archdiocese. Father Mertens reduced the parish debt in half; and due to a sizeable donation, was able to decorate the church quite suitably.

◆ **Father Bernard Schuette with the school students, 1890.**

At the creation of the Rockford Diocese, Bishop Peter J. Muldoon appointed Father Henry A. Hagen (1909-1913) as Sublette's pastor. Father Hagen built a new convent, brought back the School Sisters of St. Francis, and remodeled the rectory during his five-year stay.

During Father Magnus A. Schumacher's pastorate (1913-1923), the old frame school was sold in 1914 and a brick school and a rectory were built. By 1917, the debt was liquidated. In 1921, the convent was moved and brick-veneered.

Father Joseph J. Weitekamp (1926-1940) began his pastorate on June 10, 1926. In spite of the Depression, new flooring was laid throughout the church and the stained glass window of Our Lady of Perpetual Help was installed in the vestibule.

◆ **Our Lady of Perpetual Help Church interior.**

Father Edward J. Lehman (1940-1960) came to Sublette on May 22, 1940. Under his direction the church was redecorated for the Golden Jubilee year of 1952.

In 1957, the former public school property adjoining the parish was purchased, and three acres of land were added to the cemetery.

Near the end of Father Lehman's pastorate, an extensive remodeling program was begun on St. Mary School, which was completed during Father Bertram C. Jaeger's pastorate (1960).

◆ **Father Edward Lehman.**

Father Philip Bajo (1966-1986) came to Sublette in 1966. In 1967, the school was closed due to a lack of funds and the shortage of religious sisters. The entire church was extensively renovated under Father Bajo's administration. The altar was moved down into the seating area to provide a three-sided effect.

On December 11, 2004, during the pastorate of Father Edward R. Hughes, Bishop Thomas G. Doran celebrated Mass to mark the completion of the new parish center. The Bishop then blessed the building which features a banquet hall that seats about 400 people, a kitchen and four classrooms for religious education.

As of March 2007, Father Edward R. Hughes is pastor. There are approximately 175 families currently registered at Our Lady of Perpetual Help Parish.

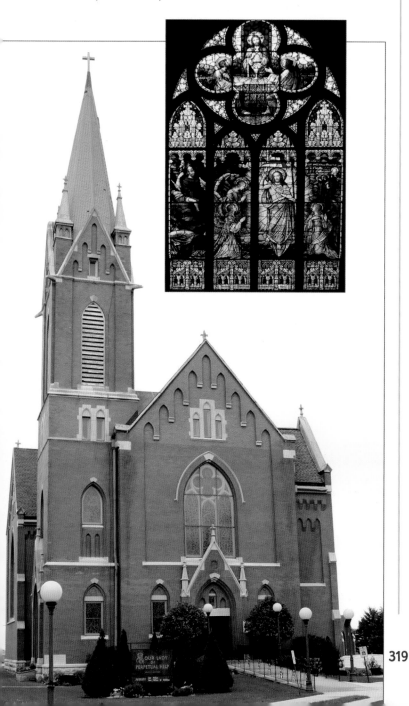

◆ **Our Lady of Perpetual Help Church.**

St. Mary Parish

Early pastors of St. Patrick Parish in St. Charles began regular services in Sycamore, usually celebrating Mass in the courthouse. In 1862, the Sycamore congregation was given mission status and placed in the care of St. Mary Parish, located just south in DeKalb.

Father John B. Murray, who had become DeKalb's first resident pastor in 1861, supervised the construction of Sycamore's first Catholic church in 1862. The church was intended to last 40 years, but the mission parish arrangement was only to extend to 1885.

In that year of 1885, Father Patrick A. Egan (1885-1887) was appointed to organize the parish and become its first resident pastor. During the first year of his two-year stay, Father Egan also built a rectory on the parish property on Waterman Street.

The only building program carried on during the service of Father Michael J. Foley, 1889-1892, was when the Mt. Carmel Cemetery was expanded and improved.

Major construction projects were undertaken during the terms of Father William J. Meehan (1899-1903) and Father Sylvester J. O'Hara (1909-1922). Father Meehan had a new church built in 1902, at a cost of $22,000 and Father O'Hara made improvements to the church building, as well as supervising the construction of a mission church, St. Michael, at Clare, Illinois.

The Sycamore connection with Clare, located about seven miles west of Sycamore, began during 1897, when Father J. F. Feeley (1896-1899) started catechism classes in the town. The church erected by Father O'Hara was dedicated by Bishop Peter J. Muldoon in June of 1913.

The mission church of St. Michael at Clare was closed in the early 1930's.

Father Desire D. Miller (1922-1927) became the pastor of St. Mary Parish in 1922. During his five years of service, a school was constructed next to the church. The school was designed by Mr. Wybe Van der Meer, a well-known architect who designed many churches and schools in the Rockford Diocese and the Chicago Archdiocese.

The purchase of a house by the next pastor, Father Peter S. Masterson (1927-1945), brought about several changes in the parish. The new house, located next to the church, was converted into a rectory. The school sisters moved into the former rectory, and the old convent was sold.

A complete redecoration of St. Mary Church was almost finished when Father Masterson died on December 5, 1945.

The long pastorate of Father Masterson was followed by one of almost equal length by Father Clement W. Caine (1945-1962). By the Diocese's Golden Jubilee Year, 1958, St. Mary Parish had nearly doubled in size and had paid off its debt.

Plans were well underway for an addition to the school and another remodeling of the church. More property was purchased for a playground site, an apartment house was purchased as a convent, and two acres were added to the cemetery.

Following Father Caine's retirement late in 1962, Father Michael J. Shanahan (1962-1969) was appointed St. Mary's pastor. Father Shanahan, greatly aided by a quarter of a million dollar donation from Miss Nellie

♦ **Bishop Lane with Mrs. Joseph Smith, the woman of the year in 1967.**

Murphy, expanded the redecoration plans of Father Caine and the result was one of the diocese's most beautiful church interiors.

Father Shanahan also extended the parish property to include a lot next to the rectory and a house next to that for use as a convent. The apartment building, originally intended as a convent, was sold to the city.

In 1991-1992, the church building was renovated during the pastorate of Father Frank J. Timar, MSC. New property was also purchased during this time for expansion needs of the future.

On July 21, 2002, the dedication ceremony culminated many years of planning for a new parish center. Father Timar welcomed Bishop Thomas G. Doran who blessed the new St. Mary Parish Center. The hall portion of the building seats 400 people at round tables. The rest of the building houses two meeting rooms, a conference room, and four staff offices in its almost 12,000 square feet.

◆ **Father William Regnier, pastor 1974-1988.**

◆ **Tabernacle at the side altar.**

The year 2002 also marked the 100-year anniversary of the St. Mary Church building. A parish history in the form of old stories and photographs is on permanent display in the parish center.

As of March 2007 Father Frank J. Timar is the pastor. There are approximately 1200 families currently registered at St. Mary Parish.

◆ **St. Mary Church exterior and interior.**

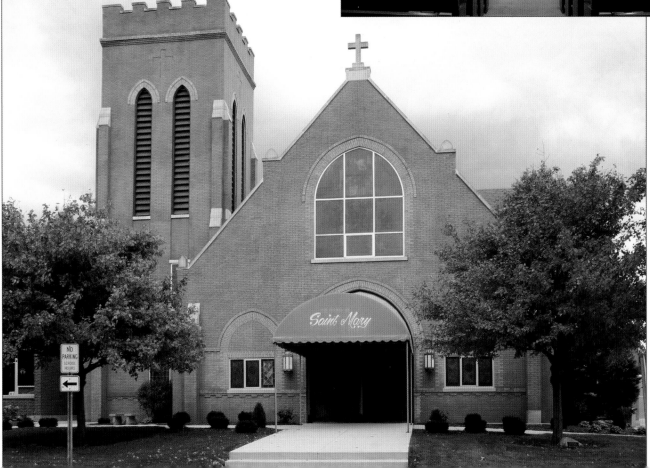

St. Mary Parish

Prior to the early 1860s, the few Catholics living in the Tampico area were dependent on missionaries for irregular annual visits. In 1863, Father John Daly became the first resident pastor at Sterling, and Tampico was placed under his care.

Father Daly served a wide area that also included Morrison, Savanna, Fulton, Albany, Genessee Grove and Prophetstown. He was, therefore, only able to visit Tampico about three times a year. He traveled the area on horseback, sometimes stopping for services at the Hutten Schoolhouse, within the boundaries of the present Tampico parish, nine miles southwest of Sterling and about midway between Prophetstown and Tampico. This arrangement continued for about seven years.

Tampico's location in the southwest portion of Whiteside County was close to several parishes that later would become part of the Peoria Diocese, and those parishes were vital to the early development of St. Mary Parish in Tampico.

In the first half of the 1870s, St. Mary's was attended from Sheffield, Illinois, presently within the Diocese of Peoria, under the pastorate of Father Hugh McShane.

In 1875, the Parish of St. Mary was attached as a mission to the parish at Ohio, Illinois, now also in the Peoria Diocese. Father Peter J. Gormley, pastor there, built the first church at Tampico. It served the parish for 25 years.

The first resident pastor of St. Mary, Father Richard H. McGuire (1879-1885), was appointed in 1879.

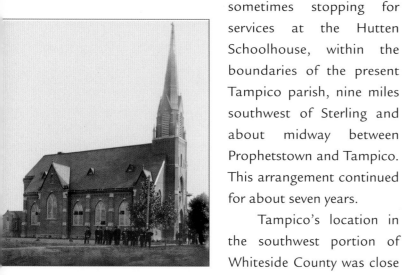

◆ **Dedication of St. Mary Church, September 8, 1904.**

◆ **St. Mary Church interior, circa 1904.**

The major acquisition during his six-year term was land for a parish cemetery.

In 1895, Father Peter J. Weber (1895-1906) began a pastorate that was highlighted by several building projects. In 1895, Father Weber built the first rectory. In 1902, he began the construction of the present Gothic church. Bishop Peter J. Muldoon dedicated this church on September 8, 1904. Built at a cost of $30,000, the entire debt was liquidated by 1920.

Father Leon X. DuFour (1906-1928) became the Pastor of St. Mary in 1906 and served the Tampico parish for nearly 23 years. He was succeeded by Father Joseph P. Lynch (1928-1930), who replaced the old rectory with the present one for $12,000.

Father Thomas O. Maguire (1930-1946) became pastor in 1930. The Depression kept him from realizing his program of building a parish hall.

Father Ambrose M. Weitekamp (1946-1966), who had been an assistant under Father DuFour, returned as pastor in 1946. The church and rectory were completely redecorated, and when this was paid for, a parish school and hall were contemplated in the fall of 1952. Since at that time there were only about 75 children of school

◆ **Father L.X. DuFour.**

◆ **Our Lady of Fatima display.**

age, it was decided to build a hall that could be suitably used for catechism classes as well as for social functions.

This building was completed in January 1954, and dedicated by Bishop Raymond P. Hillinger on Mother's Day, May 9, 1954.

On May 15, 1955, Father Weitekamp blessed an outdoor shrine in honor of Our Lady of Fatima. This was donated by William Burden, in memory of his wife Margaret.

In the early 1960s, Father Weitekamp again completely redecorated the interior of the church in time for the celebration of his 40th anniversary of Ordination.

Father Robert P. Donavan (1966-1970) was appointed as pastor on July 19, 1966. During his tenure at the parish, he carpeted the church and, at the direction of Bishop Loras T. Lane, removed the communion railing.

Father Eugene D. Parker (1970-1983) was appointed pastor on March 5, 1970. In 1973, additional parking space was provided north of the church. In June of 1974, a severe windstorm hit Tampico, severely damaging the rectory and church. At that time, the church and rectory were repaired and some redecorating begun in both buildings. In December 1974, new Schulmerich Carillon bells were installed due to the generosity of Mrs. Robert B. Adams and Mrs. Neil Hamblock in memory of their late husbands.

Between 1987 and 1990, a renovation project was undertaken. Among other improvements, the stations and all the statues were repainted, the original pipe organ was repaired and restored, and the church was made accessible to the handicapped. The projects were paid for by parishioners who adopted a particular project and paid for it in memory of a loved one.

A special event at St. Mary Parish is Cemetery Sunday. Held for over 60 years, parishioners, relatives and friends have gathered in May for a special tribute to their deceased loved ones in the parish cemetery north of the church. Following Mass, the rosary is said while the group processes from the church to the cemetery. The event concludes with a breakfast in the parish hall.

As of March 2007, Monsignor Thomas L. Dzielak is parochial administrator. There are approximately 100 families currently registered at St. Mary Parish.

◆ **St. Mary Church interior and exterior.**

SS. Peter and Paul Parish

SS. Peter and Paul Parish in Virgil dates its history as an independent parish to the formation of the Rockford Diocese, but its beginning actually came some 30 years before when it was organized as a joint parish with St. Mary, Maple Park, in 1879.

Catholics in Maple Park, or Lodi as it was then known, had formed a parish in 1853, under the pastorship of Father Patrick O'Dwyer of St. Charles.

The first Catholics in the Virgil area, starting with the family of Nicholaus Keifer in 1861, attended the church in the community to the south. Eventually, their numbers increased to the point that a church of their own was desired.

A small committee traveled to Chicago in 1879, and obtained permission to build a church in Virgil. A frame structure was constructed that same year.

For the next three decades, the Virgil parish was almost a mission of St. Mary in Maple Park, existing as a dual parish under the pastor living in Maple Park.

SS. Peter and Paul was organized during the pastorate of Father Paul Halbmeier (1879-1883). It

◆ **Bishop Muldoon laying the cornerstone, June 6, 1909.**

was during this time that the first school was built next to the original church near the cemetery on the south end of the town.

The formation of an individual parish in Virgil was also the result of a committee's work. After the Rockford Diocese was created in 1908, another group met with Bishop Peter J. Muldoon and obtained a resident pastor for SS. Peter and Paul.

◆ **SS. Peter & Paul Church.**

In April, 1909, Father Charles S. Nix (1909-1921) arrived to take over the Virgil congregation. Due to the growth of the area, Father Nix's first task was to build a new church.

The route of the Great Western Railroad had come through Virgil at a point about two miles north of the original church, and the present church was built on a site just south of Illinois Route 64, closer to what was in use as a railroad station. The cornerstone for the new church was laid on June 6, 1909. Bishop Muldoon dedicated the church and a newly constructed rectory on November 4, 1909.

SS. Peter and Paul parishioners moved the original school building to the new site and used it until 1913, when another building program resulted in a structure that was used as a school, parish hall and residence for the Sisters of the Third Order of St. Francis. Father Edward Berthold (1921-1927) succeeded Father Nix as pastor in 1921.

◆ **SS. Peter & Paul School sisters.**

The parish's third school building was constructed in 1953 on the site of the second, just south of the rectory. A decrease in enrollment, combined with a shortage of teaching sisters, brought about the closing of the school in 1971.

The $120,000 school building program in 1953 had been accomplished under the pastorate of Father Ivon A. Esser (1935-1967). His years of service to the people of SS. Peter and Paul were marred by a fire in February 1942, which destroyed the sacristy, a tragedy that was heightened by the fact that the church had been completely remodeled the previous year.

During the pastorate of Father Michael A. Librandi (1984-1989), the school was used as the Center for Diocesan Youth Ministry. The rectory was also remodeled during this time.

On November 4, 1984, Bishop Arthur J. O'Neill, offered Mass to celebrate the 75th anniversary of the parish.

In the summer of 1991, under the supervision of Father Thomas W. Neville (1989-1998), the church was remodeled.

Another remodeling was completed in December 2006 during the pastorate of Father Les Suberi Echevia.

The parish remains in a strong, healthy state. The church is the only church in Virgil, a farm community that is about 95 per cent Catholic.

As of March 2007, Father Les Suberi Echevia is pastor. There are approximately 200 families currently registered at SS. Peter and Paul Parish.

◆ **SS. Peter & Paul Church, 1946.**

◆ **Father Ivon Esser on the 25th anniversary of his ordination, April 24, 1959.**

ST. MARY PARISH

◆ **St Mary Church, circa 1905.**

◆ **Bishop Muldoon laying the cornerstone.**

The first Mass was offered in Walton in October 1903. Before that, Catholics in Marion Township attended churches in the surrounding communities of Dixon, Amboy and Harmon. Father Joseph S. Gallagher, pastor in Amboy, celebrated the first Mass in a frame structure which had been provided on a two-acre plot of land. At that time, Walton was made a mission of Amboy and Mass was said regularly each week.

Father Thomas J. Cullen became pastor at Amboy in 1910 and devoted much of his time and energy to directing the mission parish. During his pastorate, construction began on a new church and a rectory. The brick church was dedicated by Bishop Peter J. Muldoon on August 19, 1913. A month later, the first resident pastor, Father Charles F. Conley (1913-1924), was appointed and St. Mary became an independent parish. The rectory had been completed and furnished and the old church remodeled into a hall. Father Conley managed to retire the parish debt and to acquire

two and one half acres of land for a future cemetery. The property was soon afterwards equipped for a parish recreational center.

Father Conley remained in Walton until 1924 when he was succeeded by Father Thomas G. Flynn (1924-1928); Father Joseph A. Driscoll (1929-1933); and Father Walter J. Ryan (1933-1936). During Father Driscoll's and Father Ryan's pastorates, the Depression severely affected the finances of the little parish.

In 1942, during the pastorate of Father Daniel R. Daley (1938-1948), the United States government took over one-fourth of Marion Township for a war plant. About a third of the parish was lost when families whose land had been appropriated were forced to move. After the war, some of the land was bought back, but the homes and barns had been destroyed and the land is used largely for crops.

◆ **Father Joseph Gallagher, pastor 1903-1910.**

◆ **St. Mary Church Hall, 1914.**

In July 1967, St. Mary Parish began being administered by the Pastor of St. Flannen Parish in Harmon, Father James F. Lafferty (1967-1978). It continues to be served by the pastor of St. Flannen Parish.

As of March 2007, Father Carl E. Beekman is parochial administrator. There are approximately 60 families currently registered at St. Mary Parish.

◆ **St. Mary Church interior and exterior.**

St. Ann Parish

Catholic services were first celebrated in Warren at the home of an early settler, William Moran, in the late 1850s. The two priests most often mentioned in connection with that beginning were Father Thomas McLaughlin and Father Thomas O'Gara, who was Pastor of St. Mary Parish, Freeport, from 1859 to 1866.

From 1870 to 1879, Father Joseph Kindekens, pastor in Apple River, began monthly visits to Warren and supervised the construction of Warren's first church. Started in 1876, the building was completed after Father Michael Zara became pastor at Apple River in 1878. For almost 40 years, pastors from Apple River served the Warren church.

◆ **Father Peter Masterson.**

In 1914, Warren was made a separate parish and the first resident pastor at St. Ann, Father Peter S. Masterson (1914-1927), was appointed on July 18, 1914. He purchased a house east of Beebe Street on Railroad Street and renovated it for use as a rectory. He also purchased five acres of land for a

◆ **Grotto of the Blessed Virgin Mary.**

cemetery and the lot next to the rectory (across the street from the original church) for the site of a badly needed larger church. Work on the new structure, still in use, was started in 1923 and completed the following year.

When the second church was finished, the original building was sold to A. H. Burrows (for a time, mayor in Warren), and moved to a farm north of town. A private residence now occupies the original site.

During the pastorate of Father John E. Reuland (1963-1967), a major program of renovation of the church, rectory and hall was undertaken.

Following Father Reuland's term, Father Herman A. Porter (1967-1968) attended the parish on a visiting basis from Rockford and saved an appreciable reserve for continued remodeling.

In 1968, Father John P. Dolan (1968-1977) was appointed pastor. Under his supervision, the church was completely remodeled and much work was done on the outside of the parish buildings, as well as on the parish grounds.

During the pastorate of Father William A. Budden (1977-1984), the stained glass windows were repaired and weatherproofed, and new Stations of the Cross were installed.

◆ **The old St. Ann Church.**

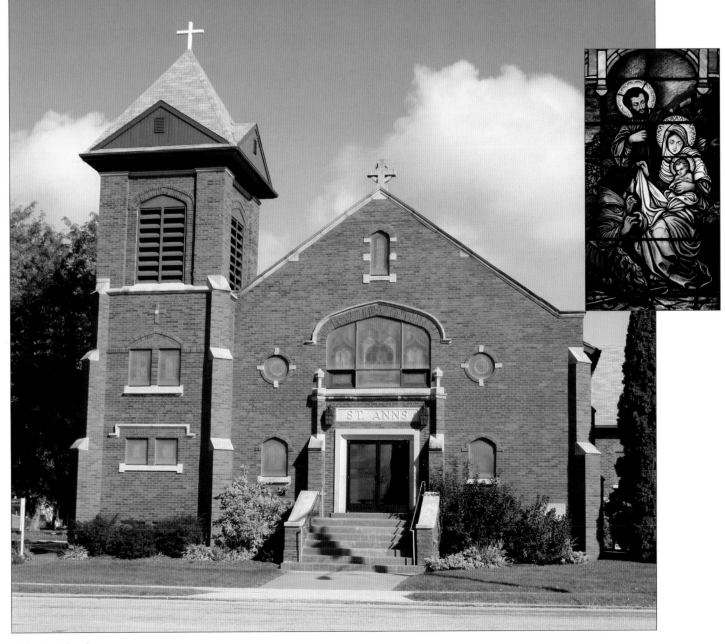

◆ **St. Ann Church.**

Father Everett J. Hiller (1985-2000), Pastor of St. Ann Parish, blessed a parish addition on November 12, 1995. Features of the addition include an enlarged sacristy, which allows room for daily Masses, and a class and meeting room, an elevator, rest rooms, and a double garage.

Returning in spring of 2001 from his homeland of Poland, Father Miroslaw A. Reikowski (2000-2002) brought back a three-foot tall statue of the Blessed Virgin Mary. Sponsorship from both St. Ann Parish in Warren and St. Joseph Parish in Apple River, allowed a grotto to be built. It occupies a small area on the east side of St. Ann Church. On September 30, 2001, Bishop Thomas G. Doran blessed the site.

Father Reikowski also had the rectory completely remodeled, and a Mary Chapel placed in an alcove of the church. The cemetery had a beautification project which included adding the Stations of the Cross.

As of March 2007, Father Brian D. Grady is parochial administrator. There are approximately 100 families currently registered at St. Ann Parish.

◆ **Father Everett Hiller.**

St. Mary Parish

The first Mass celebrated in the West Brooklyn area came several years before the town itself was laid out and was some 20 years before the first resident pastor arrived.

The first settlers in the region were predominately French, who had come about 1865, from Portsmouth, Ohio. They were joined by some of the German farmers from around Sublette, and the early German pastors from Perkin's Grove looked after their spiritual welfare. Each year at Easter, a French priest from Aurora would come out to hear the confessions of his countrymen. The first Mass celebrated in the area was said at the farm house of Modest Gehant, located about a mile north of what was to become the town site. The visiting priest traveled to the area from Perkin's Grove, a parish about four miles southwest of Sublette.

Perkin's Grove received its first resident pastor in 1860. In 1847, the first church was constructed, southwest of Perkin's Grove, near Maytown. In 1866 a church was built in Sublette.

Gehant and a brother, Laurent, had been among the early settlers of the West Brooklyn region in the mid-1860s. Another brother, Claude Gehant, arrived a bit later from their home region of Alsace-Lorraine in France. Other early settlers of German heritage had come from Ohio and from the Perkin's Grove area.

Damas L. Harris, Reuben N. Woods, and P. Johnson, three area residents, laid out the town in August 1872, and named it after its location in the western part of Brooklyn Township. Catholics in and around the town were considered to be part of the Perkin's Grove parish, in spite of the fact that a fire in 1870 had destroyed the Perkin's Grove church and forced the center of operations to Sublette. The Perkin's Grove parish never fully recovered, and Sublette became the home parish in 1877.

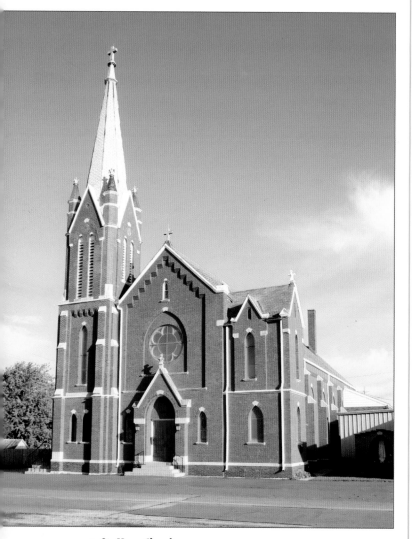

◆ **St. Mary Church.**

◆ **Procession to the cemetery after Confirmation, 1907.**

In 1877, West Brooklyn Catholics sent two men, Albert Bieschke and Adam Mayer, to Chicago to obtain official permission from Archbishop Patrick A. Feehan for the church at West Brooklyn to be attached as a mission. By that time, there was a small frame church in West Brooklyn and Mass was celebrated once a month.

Until the arrival of Father A. Leising (1889-1907) as the first resident pastor, West Brooklyn was visited once a month by Sublette pastors.

Father Leising began the construction of a brick veneer church in the mid-1890s. The original frame church was moved to the east side of the property, next to a site for a rectory. The new church was completed in 1902.

In the early 1900s, Maytown was a mission of West Brooklyn, in spite of the fact that the Sublette parish was between West Brooklyn and Maytown. On one Sunday a month, Catholics in West Brooklyn would pack picnic lunches and travel to Maytown for a day's outing.

◆ **Father A. Leising.**

Father Leising finished a rectory before leaving the parish in 1907. He was succeeded by Father Edward Berthold (1907-1912), during whose pastorate a fire destroyed the church. After the fire, Father Berthold immediately started construction on the present church. He was transferred in 1912 and was succeeded by Father Michael B. Krug (1912-1923), who paid the remaining debt on the church, furnished it, improved the cemetery and built a parochial school.

Father Charles H. Quinn (1923-1929) became pastor in August 1923. During the six years he was in charge, improvements were made in the existing facilities.

It was under Father Lawrence London (1967-1973) that many parish improvements were made. The interior of the church underwent major redecoration from 1968 to 1970. The walls were repainted, the church was carpeted, and modern dark wood altar furnishings were installed in the sanctuary.

The school, which was closed in 1968, is now used for parish meetings and for religious education classes.

Another change was the removal of the old rectory in 1971, while the convent, a ranch-type house north of the church, was renovated for use as a rectory.

During the pastorate of Father Louis J. Pesut (1973-1986), a parish hall was built between 1982 and 1983.

As of March 2007, Father Edward R. Hughes is pastor. There are approximately 100 families currently registered at St. Mary Parish.

◆ **Fr. Russell Guccione with the St. Mary graduating class, 1942.**

CHRIST THE KING PARISH

Before 1928, there was no Wonder Lake. During that year a group of Chicago businessmen purchased as much farmland along Nippersink Creek in McHenry County as was possible. A dam (long since condemned) was built at the north end of the creek, thereby flooding a large, marshy spring-fed area to the south, forming what is now known as Wonder Lake. For a few years, land was sold only to a small number of people and not many cabins were built on this largest privately-owned lake in the state of Illinois.

Then during the Depression in the 1930s, many poor families bought modest cabins along the lake. Such purchases were, in many cases, a last resort, since most of them worked, if they had jobs, in Chicago, 60 miles away.

The 1940s saw a rapid growth in population—largely summer residents of modest means. The 1950s saw an even greater increase, with one significant difference: the number of summer residents began to decline and the number of permanent residents increased.

Catholics moving into the Wonder Lake region attended Mass in the city of McHenry, mainly at St. Patrick Church. In 1947, Bishop John J. Boylan appointed Father James A. Vanderpool to be Administrator of St. Patrick, with the intent of having Father Vanderpool investigate the religious outlook of a possible parish at Wonder Lake.

This investigation and concern for Wonder Lake resulted from the long-standing interest of Monsignor Charles S. Nix, Pastor at St. Mary in McHenry from 1921 until his death in 1960.

The family census taken by Father Vanderpool did not indicate any great need for a Wonder Lake parish, since it revealed only 17 families attending services in McHenry.

Nevertheless, arrangements were made to rent space in Harrison public school for the celebration of Mass. More than 600 persons jammed into the small school for the two Masses that first Sunday. It was obvious on that first day that a church was needed for the new congregation.

McHenry Catholics again and again came to the aid of the Wonder Lake area. In July 1947, a carnival was sponsored by St. Mary Parish to aid the Wonder Lake building fund. The fund was further supplemented by a Labor Day festival, and work began shortly after on the first Christ the King Church.

The first church was, in fact, a basement constructed on property donated by the Wonder Lake developers, headed by E. R. Jacobson. The basement was completed in July 1947. A roof was put on it, and that structure, complete with a vital

◆ **Father James Vanderpool with First Communicants.**

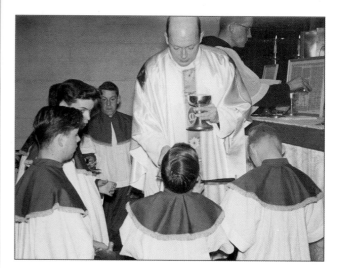

◆ **Holy Week, 1956.**

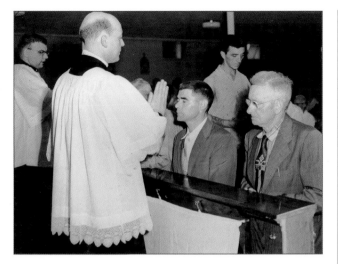

◆ **Pledge Drive Blessing, 1957.**

coal stove, was to serve the parish for the next 10 years.

In May 1948, Father Edward C. Coakley (1948-1949) was appointed Pastor of St. Patrick. Father Coakley assumed charge over the mission at Wonder Lake until August 25, 1949, when Bishop John J. Boylan raised Christ the King from the status of a mission to that of an independent parish and appointed Father Vanderpool as Administrator. A house was rented for a few months until a temporary rectory was purchased in 1950.

The parish bought a 24-acre tract several miles north of the original church in 1954. A cemetery, part of the new property, was consecrated in February 1955, by Bishop Raymond P. Hillinger. Enough funds had been raised by the summer of 1957 for permission to be granted for the construction of a new church, school and rectory

complex. On August 13, 1957, Father Vanderpool (1957-1967) was appointed pastor.

The new Christ the King Church was dedicated on October 26, 1958, by Bishop Loras T. Lane. The old structure was sold.

Father Vanderpool was succeeded by Father Eugene D. Parker (1967-1969) in June 1967.

The school was never opened because of a lack of religious teachers to staff it.

In 2000, under the pastorate of Father Dorrance E. Tranel, air conditioning was added to the church. During the administration of Father Steven M. Sabo, in 2006, improvements were made to the parish cemetery, including new fencing.

As of March 2007, Father Steven M. Sabo is parochial administrator. There are approximately 500 families currently registered at Christ the King Parish.

◆ **Christ the King Church interior and exterior.**

Resurrection Parish

Resurrection Parish was founded in October 1978, with Father Michael E. Mas, C.R. (1978-1981), named the first pastor. Parishioners met at Resurrection Center, a retreat facility run by the Congregation of the Resurrection, outside of Woodstock, Illinois, at 2710 South Country Club Road. They met at the center until 1995 when they moved into their new church.

On March 13, 1994, Bishop Arthur J. O'Neill and Father Eugene Majewski, C.R. (1990-1999), pastor, held a groundbreaking ceremony to build a new church for the parish. On June 30, 1995 Bishop Thomas G. Doran dedicated the new church.

The worship space is entered from the north, past the baptistery to symbolize entry into Christian life. At the south wall is a figure of the risen Christ, one hand raised to heaven, the other lowered to assist others. The statue's eyes are focused on the altar in the center of the nave to remind all that the Risen Christ is now experienced in the Eucharistic gathering of the faithful. The new building houses the church sanctuary, eight classrooms, parish offices, a meeting room, an adaptable center court for gatherings, and the Blessed Sacrament chapel.

The Resurrection Parish is situated on 10 acres of land adjacent to Resurrection Retreat Center. Clear glass windows and doors bring the beauty of the surrounding wooded acres inside. The tallest point of the worship space faces east toward the rising sun, a symbol of the Resurrection.

As of March 2007, Father Paul Sims, C.R., is Administrator. There are approximately 200 families currently registered at Resurrection Parish.

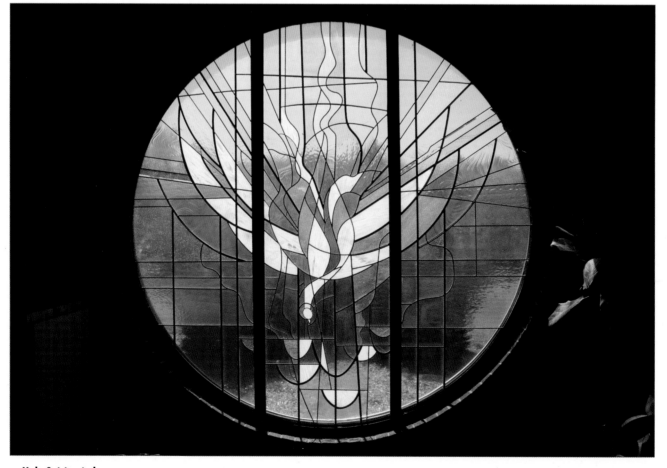

◆ **Holy Spirit window.**

◆ **Resurrection Parish interior.**

◆ **Resurrection Parish.**

St. Mary Parish

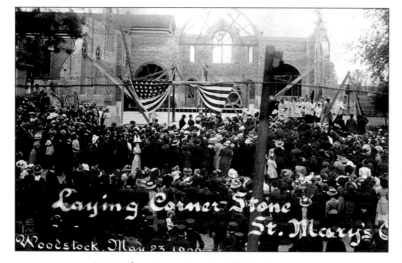

◆ **Laying the cornerstone, circa 1909.**

◆ **1921 cast of class play.**

Woodstock is an old Catholic community dating back to the time of Donnelley's Settlement and Little Port (which became Waukegan) in the early 1840s. It is known that Bishop Simon Brute of Vincennes traveled through the neighborhood, as did Fathers John St. Cyr and John Guiguen. Aside from the traveling missionaries, Woodstock was first attended from Hartland.

According to anecdote, Father Hugh T. Brady, who was pastor at Hartland from May 10, 1850 until 1853, was transferred to Woodstock in 1853. Father Bernard O'Hara is listed by Father Cornelius Kirkfleet, O.Praem., as the first resident pastor, coming in 1855.

The next definite date available is the pastorate of Father John Carroll from 1870 to 1877. Preceding him was Father Patrick Riordan, who later became Archbishop of San Francisco.

During the pastorate of Father Thomas F. Leydon (1877-1885), the church was enlarged. At this time, Crystal Lake and Barrington were attended from Woodstock.

Father James J. Clancy (1885-1895) attended the above missions. The large bell which hung in the old St. Mary Church was placed there by Father Clancy.

In June 1905, Father Michael S. Gilmartin (1905-1909) was appointed pastor. Father Gilmartin built a new rectory, acquired additional ground for a cemetery and raised about $30,000 toward a new church.

Work had already begun on the church when Father Gilmartin was transferred to Chicago, and the Diocese of Rockford was separated from the Chicago Archdiocese. Father David J. Conway (1909-1929) was appointed by Bishop Peter J. Muldoon to succeed him.

Bishop Muldoon placed the cornerstone on May 23, 1909, and building proceeded under Father Conway's direction. On Passion Sunday, 1910, the new Church of St. Mary was dedicated. Three years later, the entire cost of $60,000 was paid.

In March 1916, the old church was torn down. The site, along with an adjoining lot which had been purchased two years earlier, would be used for a parochial school. The school opened January 1, 1917, with six Sisters of the Holy Cross serving as the faculty. The high school began in 1923 with a single classroom in the grade school building, and with 22 freshmen. The later expansion of the high school required moving the sisters out of the rooms they had been occupying in the school building. In 1925, the Dacy home was purchased and remodeled as a convent for the sisters. The gymnasium was built in 1929.

During Father Joseph M. Egan's pastorate (1934-1968), the increased enrollment in the schools called for the separation of the grade school from the high school. In January 1951, the new St. Mary High School building was opened. In the fall of 1959, Marian

◆ **St. Mary Church, circa 1930.**

Central High School was opened in Woodstock and the St. Mary High School building was converted into classrooms for the parish junior high school.

A new rectory was built in 1964, with the entire cost paid for through a donation from Mrs. Audrey Berdeau in memory of her mother, Mrs. Elizabeth Glennon Quinn.

Father William H. Regnier (1970-1973) became pastor in 1970 and had the sanctuary remodeled in keeping with changes adopted during the Second Vatican Council.

Under the pastorate of Father John W. Cahill (1983-1989), the church was air-conditioned and under the pastorate of Monsignor Alphonsus F. Harte (1989-1997), the school expanded to various buildings.

Father James W. McLoughlin succeeded Monsignor Harte as pastor on November 11, 1997. The new St. Joseph Center was dedicated on November 5, 2000 by Bishop Thomas G. Doran. The center is 13,000 square feet, and is connected to both the church and the parish office building. The two floors and basement are all connected by an elevator, which makes the church accessible to the handicapped.

Plans were then begun for extensive renovating and restoring of the aging church and school buildings. Much of the labor came from parishioners. Upon completion, Bishop Thomas G. Doran blessed the improvements and anointed the new altar on June 27, 2004. The Woodstock Historical Society has declared the church a historical site and provided a plaque for the parish.

St. Mary Parish, during the term of Father McLoughlin, who was elevated to Monsignor on January 24, 2003, celebrated its sesquicentennial anniversary in 2003.

As of March 2007, Monsignor James W. McLoughlin is pastor. There are approximately 2,000 families currently registered at St. Mary Parish.

◆ **St. Mary Church interior and exterior.**

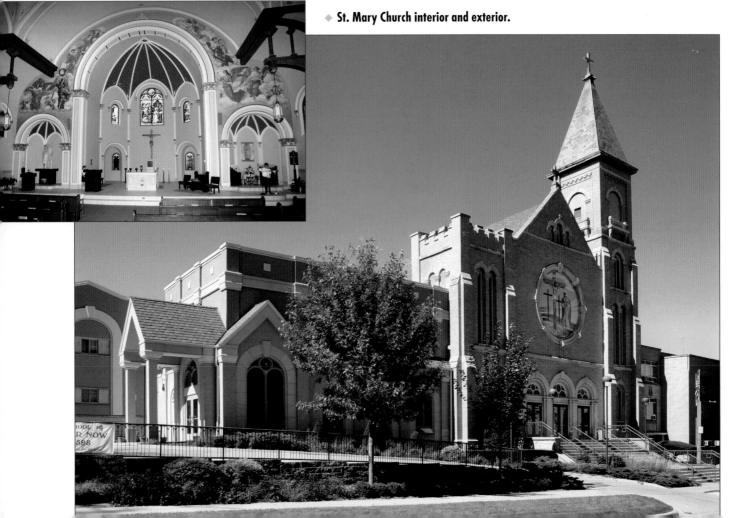

Former Parishes and Missions

◆ The funeral of Mrs. McGowan, from St. Michael Mission, Maytown, circa 1900.

◆ **St. Mary Church.**

For many years the church of St. Mary, in Ashton, was a mission of Rochelle. Catholics there had purchased property for a church as far back as 1867.

For a while they were served by priests from Dixon, then by priests from Oregon and later by priests from Rochelle. Father Peter J. Gormley, while pastor at Rochelle, built the Ashton church in 1869; it was dedicated by Bishop Thomas Foley of Chicago in 1870.

The Catholic congregation dwindled to a mere eight families by the time of the first diocesan history, 1924. The mission was finally closed in 1926.

◆ **Father Lawrence J. Cunningham with the First Communicants in 1896.**

About 1897 Father J. F. Feeley, pastor of Sycamore started a catechism class in Clare and occasionally offered Mass there.

This pastoral service was continued by his successors, Father William J. Meehan, Father J. J. Mullaly and Father Sylvester O'Hara. It was under Father O'Hara's pastorate that a church, costing about $3,000 was erected at Clare.

Bishop Peter J. Muldoon solemnly dedicated the church and placed it under the patronage of St. Michael on June 10, 1913. By 1924 only 20 families belonged to this mission. The mission was discontinued in the early 1930s and the building later sold.

◆ **St. Michael Church interior.**

◆ **St. Michael Church, 1913.**

The history of St. Patrick Mission Church at Coffey's Corners is tightly bound with the history of St. Patrick Church, Albany.

Please see the entry under the Albany parish for more information about the Coffey's Corners mission.

◆ **St. Patrick Mission of Docia, 1927.**

The first Mass in Davis Junction was celebrated in the town hall by Father John J. Flanagan on December 31, 1913. The first church was erected in the spring of 1914. Elizabeth Finkler, of Chicago, gave one thousand dollars toward the building fund and the building was named St. Peter in memory of her father. The church was dedicated on June 21, 1914, by Bishop Peter J. Muldoon. The choir of St. James, Rockford, was present and the services were described as being very impressive.

For two years St. Peter's mission was attended from St. James Pro-Cathedral. It was then made a mission of St. Catherine's, Genoa, but in 1922 it was attached to St. Patrick, Rockford. On March 7, 1954, when Bishop Raymond P. Hillinger appointed Father Paul E. Kunkel as pastor of St. Mary, Byron, Davis Junction was transferred to the jurisdiction of that parish. In December 1966 Bishop Loras T. Lane assigned Father Edward S. Wright to be pastor of St. Mary and the St. Peter Mission in Davis Junction. Soon afterwards Bishop Lane decided to close the mission church and this was done in September 1969.

◆ **St. Peter Mission Church.**

In 1875 St. Mary Church was built about five and one-half miles from St. Patrick, Maytown, by early German settlers. Before ever a priest came to officiate, tradition states that devotional services were held regularly every Sunday by the parishioners themselves. One year later Mass was offered in East Maytown for the first time by a priest from Mendota, Father Wagner. Eventually priests from Maytown attended the mission church at East Maytown. Later it was attended by priests from Sublette and West Brooklyn.

Father Ivon A. Esser (1928-1930) had the church decorated and Father J. Urban Halbmaier (1931-1943) had a new furnace installed. Under the direction of Father John T. Smith (1943-1949), a new basement was excavated, new stained glass windows, confessional, electric lights and other improvements were provided. An organ was purchased in 1953, during the pastorate of Father Clement P. Petit (1951-1957).

St. Mary Mission Church closed in 1975, 100 years after the church was built.

◆ **St. Mary Mission Church interior.**

◆ **St. Mary Mission Church.**

FORRESTON

The mission at Forreston is first mentioned in the 1924 diocesan history. The author, Father Cornelius J. Kirkfleet, O. Praem, noted that on November 28, 1894, Archbishop Patrick A. Feehan of Chicago appointed Father John J. McCann to the missions of Oregon, Polo and Forreston. It was known that Catholics lived in the area since the late 1840's or early 1850's, when men from Ireland came to the region around Polo to build the railroad. On Sundays these men would take a handcar and go to Dixon, bringing back a priest to say Mass. Another handcar would come down from Forreston and take the priest on from there to say Mass.

Not much else is known about the mission at Forreston. It is likely that it did not have a formal name but may have been referred to simply as the "Forreston mission." There is no evidence in previous diocesan histories that a church or chapel was ever built in Forreston; perhaps Mass was celebrated in a public hall. It is also not known when the mission closed.

No photos for this church were located

◆ The parishioners of St. John Nepomucene, 1893.

In 1860, about 18 immigrant families of Czech ancestry settled in McHenry County around Algonquin, Fox River Grove and Cary. In 1867 land was purchased between Algonquin and Fox River Grove for a church and cemetery. The church, named after the patron saint of Bohemia, was completed in 1873.

Since the parishioners were so few in number, once a year a priest came from Chicago by train to Barrington, and by horse and wagon to the church. In 1892, the number of visits was increased to two. As the parish grew in numbers, a priest began to come every three months and finally once a month to tend to the spiritual welfare of the people. Each family would take a turn in giving him room and board and paying for his transportation.

The hope was that the Bishop would appoint a resident pastor and establish the parish of St. John Nepomucene in Fox River Grove. The local congregation never did acquire a resident pastor, and parishes were formed at nearby population centers. The nearest parish was SS. Peter and Paul, Cary, which was organized in 1911. Father Joseph M. Lonergan saw to it that Mass continued to be celebrated at St. John Nepomucene once a month.

These monthly Masses were stopped about 1915, when a mission church was established at Algonquin. Priests from Cary and Algonquin held services once a year on Cemetery Sunday in the spring. Mass is now celebrated at St. John Nepomucene once a year, on Labor Day, by a priest from SS. Peter and Paul, Cary.

The chapel and its cemetery are owned by the St. John Nepomucene Catholic Cemetery Association, making it the only privately-owned Catholic chapel and cemetery in the Rockford Diocese.

◆ St. John Nepomucene as it looks today.

The Catholic Instruction League, begun in Freeport in 1917, had been organized to provide instruction for Catholic children not attending parochial schools. The number of children served proved to be greater than had been expected, and the CIL demonstrated the need for new parishes. Bishop Peter J. Muldoon consequently appointed Father William G. McMillan, spiritual director of the organization, to lay the foundation for the needed parishes.

In April 1919, the former Congregational church on East Stephenson Street was purchased and remodeled. It was possible for Father McMillan to offer the first Mass there on July 7, 1919. Further changes were made in the building, and on May 16, 1920, Bishop Muldoon dedicated it to St. Catherine, in memory of a generous benefactor.

In November 1921, Father McMillan was commissioned to organize St. Thomas Aquinas Parish. St. Catherine was then placed in the care of Father Laurence C. Prendergast, chaplain of St. Francis Hospital.

Under the pastorate of Father Philip Kennedy (1938-1945, 1948-1954), extensive repairs at the church were initiated, among them a new floor and a new roof. Father Kennedy, who was Superintendent of St. Vincent Home and St. Joseph Home when appointed as pastor, kept his residence at St. Vincent Home.

The last pastor of St. Catherine was Father Charles K. McCarren (1982-1991). The parish was closed on October 20, 1991. At the time of the closing 25 families were registered.

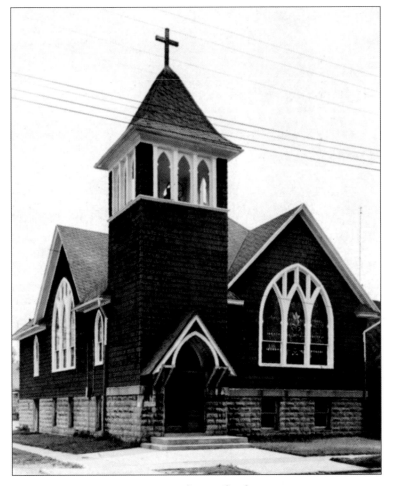

◆ **St. Catherine Church.**

KIRKLAND

Prior to 1912 Father Casper J. Huth came from Hampshire occasionally and offered Mass at the home of Patrick Smith. From 1912 to 1916 the Mystic Workers hall was used as a temporary chapel. In 1916 a new chapel was built in Kirkland and solemnly dedicated to St. Peter by Bishop Peter J. Muldoon. St. Peter was chosen the patron of the church because a generous donor, whose father's name was Peter, gave the first gift of $1,000.

Father Thomas J. O'Brien, pastor of St. Catherine, Genoa, celebrated Mass twice a month for the Kirkland Catholics. By 1924 about 24 families belonged to the mission. By about 1926, however, most of these families moved away and the mission chapel was closed with the permission of Bishop Boylan.

No photos for this church were located

MAYTOWN (SANDY HILL)

On April 28, 1840, Mass was celebrated in the township of May for the first time, by Father Parody, a Vincentian, in the log cabin home of William Dolan. For the next seven years Mass was offered in this house on those infrequent occasions when a priest passed through. This was wilderness at the time, with wolves and bears prowling the prairies and woods. Neither Amboy nor Dixon existed at the time and old records sometimes referred to the locality as "Palestine Grove."

Catholics came from as far as twenty-five miles away to hear Mass, bringing food for themselves and their animals, camping in the Dolan yard on Saturday nights. Many young people were married and babies baptized in this pioneer home. This location was close to the ruins of the old St. Michael Church, in an area popularly known as Sandy Hill. It was three miles east of the present St. Patrick Church, Maytown.

The first church, a log church, was built in 1847 by a congregation of about 20 families. There is a tradition that William Dolan walked to Dixon carrying a pail of butter, donated by Catholic families, which he exchanged for the nails used in building the church. Eight years later a brick church was erected and, for years, attended at regular intervals from LaSalle and Ottawa by Vincentian Fathers. About 1860, when Amboy built a parish church of its own, St. Michael became a mission church and was attended by the Amboy priest.

The area continued to grow with the influx of Irish settlers; by 1870, the 60 families proved too large a congregation for the tiny St. Michael mission. Since most of the new families were moving in west of the church, a new site was contemplated. Father Francis A. Keenan, pastor at Amboy, purchased six acres in 1875, and in 1876, a $6,000 frame church was built and put under the patronage of St. Patrick. The old church of St. Michael was not yet abandoned, however; in 1883, in fact, an addition was built. In 1893, bowing to the inevitable, it was abandoned as a parish church. In 1923, the walls were torn down, and a new front was appended to the old sacristy, making a cemetery chapel as a memorial to the pioneer Catholics of the parish.

An interesting sidebar to the history of St. Michael Mission, Sandy Hill, is the story of the Maytown Academy. By the time of the first diocesan history in 1924, there was no longer a trace left of the old Academy and not even any scholastic records. Father Cornelius J. Kirkfleet, O. Praem, author of the first history, found an account of the Academy in the "History of Lee County," by Frank Stevens. It states that Patrick Reily, a hardworking and frugal man left 120 acres of land to be held in trust for the purpose of constructing an Academy in Maytown.

The Academy was located on the old Peoria Stage Road, eight miles south from Amboy, and accepted young ladies as boarders. It was dedicated in September 1880. Six Benedictine Sisters taught standard academic courses, as well as music, drawing, French and German. After about ten years of success, attendance fell off until it was considered best to abandon it. In 1895 the property was sold and the old academy was torn down.

◆ **The cemetery association, 1934.**

The New Dublin settlement took in about four square miles of territory, several miles north of the present Pearl City. It was largely settled by Irish farmers who came from the immediate vicinity of Dublin about 1835. The first Catholic church built in Stephenson County, St. Mary of the Mound, was a log church constructed by the New Dublin settlers in 1836. The parishioners of St. Patrick Church, Irish Grove, however, disputed this claim and stated that their church was built earlier.

In 1843, Father Francis Derevin (Derwin) was appointed resident pastor of New Dublin by the Bishop of St. Louis. His parish extended over the counties of Stephenson, Lee, Ogle and Winnebago. In 1844 Bishop William Quarter of Chicago was given jurisdiction over all Illinois and in 1846 he appointed Father James Cavanaugh as pastor of New Dublin and the missions in its vicinity. Father Cavanaugh replaced the log church with a larger building which also contained housing for the pastor. This church was destroyed by fire in 1855, and replaced by the third structure.

In the mid-1860's, priests from New Dublin attended Lena, Plum River, Apple River and Warren. After 1869 no more mention is made in historical accounts of either Apple River or Warren as missions of Dublin.

The last resident pastor of St. Mary of the Mound was Father John J. Kilkenney, who was transferred in 1890. After that New Dublin became a mission attended from St. Joseph Parish, Lena. The New Dublin church, in very poor condition, was abandoned in 1936. There is still a cemetery at the site of the church comprising five acres of ground, and Father Francis O'Connor is buried there.

The death of Father O'Connor in 1877 provoked newspaper headlines in the Freeport Daily Bulletin on three dates in December 1877. When Father O'Connor did not show up for Sunday Mass, parishioners looked for him and found him dead in the rectory. Rumors of foul play circulated and his brother, who had been visiting from California, was arrested for murder. Though the brothers did have a physical altercation, the grand jury reported that the fight could not have caused the priest's death since it took place three days earlier. The Freeport paper reported, "This verdict should put a quietus on all gossip in regard to that sad affair."

◆ **St. Mary of the Mound Church.**

Germans settled in Sublette Township in the 1840's and looked for opportunities to worship God in their new land. When a priest was available, Mass was held in the Bartholomaeus Theiss home, at other homes, and even in the Lindstrom Hotel in Sublette. Mr. Theiss had been one of Napoleon's personal bodyguards and moved to the United States in 1846 with his wife and six children to escape the wars of Europe.

The first church was constructed by 1850, with Mr. Theiss' son-in-law, Paul Lindstrom, doing most of the construction. All interior woodwork, including the altar, was done by him with just an ordinary pocketknife. This church was called simply the Perkins Grove Catholic Church or the Theiss Church. It was located one mile west and three miles south of Sublette. Later a school and cemetery were added.

For the next decade itinerant missionaries cared for the spiritual needs of Catholics in the vicinity. Beginning in 1860, however, several divisions occurred in the Perkins Grove Church. This was chiefly because Perkins Grove had never developed along the lines of a town, while whole new villages mushroomed along the newly constructed Illinois Central Railroad that ran from Mendota through Amboy and Dixon to Freeport.

The village of Sublette was the first area to break off from the Perkins Grove Church. A rectory was built there in 1860 and Catholics no longer had to depend upon itinerant missionaries. Father M.J. Clarke became the first priest to reside there. Between 1870 and 1880, West Brooklyn and East Maytown formed parishes and also split from the Perkins Grove Church.

When Our Lady of Perpetual Help Church, Sublette, was built in 1867, the Perkins Grove Church lost its pastor, Father William Goebbels, and became a mission for a few years. Later the church was attended only on special occasions.

There are no known records of the baptisms, marriages and burials at Perkins Grove. The absence of these can be accounted for since the missionaries usually took them back to their headquarters. It is not known whether any Bishop had ever set foot inside the Perkins Grove Church or ever admitted that this edifice was under his authority.

Today the church cemetery is generally known as the Theiss cemetery, and is the burial place for Bartholomaeus Theiss.

◆ **Perkin's Grove Church.**

◆ **Parishioners gathered around the second church, 1906.**

In 1846, three years after all of Illinois came under the jurisdiction of the newly-created Chicago Diocese, Father John Cavanaugh became pastor of the New Dublin Parish, St. Mary of the Mound. Gradually the children of many New Dublin settlers moved westward into the Pleasant Valley section of Jo Daviess County, which included the Plum River area.

Prior to 1872, various priests of surrounding towns attended the Catholic families of the Plum River district. The pastors from Apple River, Galena, and New Dublin generally offered Mass in some private home of a parishioner. When Father D. J. Cogan became pastor of New Dublin in 1872 the building of the first church here was undertaken and it was finished in the time of Father Thomas F. Mangan (1874-1877).

In 1893, Plum River was attached to Stockton as a mission with Father T. J. Hartmann, as pastor. In 1906 the old church was destroyed by fire and another church erected by Father Stephen Wolfgarten. Since then Father Alfred A. Heinzler was in charge of the mission for 15 years. Apparently the last pastor was Father Nicholas J. Berg, who began his pastorate around 1924. The mission probably was closed in the mid-to-late 1920s, though none of the previous three diocesan histories record the exact date.

◆ **St. Patrick Church interior, 1923.**

The spiritual condition of the Catholics living in Rockford north of Auburn Street and between the Rock River and the western prairie had been a matter of grave concern to Bishop Peter J. Muldoon for several years before a way was found to bring religious services within easy reach of them. While St. Mary Church was relatively close, it had become increasingly difficult for the priests of the parish to cover the large expanse of territory within its boundaries.

On June 4, 1915, Bishop Muldoon purchased six lots in the Auburndale Subdivision to serve as a site for a mission church for the north end of St. Mary's parish. A small beautiful building was erected at a cost of $2,100, and dedicated in honor of St. William on December 12, 1915, by Bishop Muldoon. The new church was named in memory of William Hayes of St. James' Pro-Cathedral parish. His mother gave a donation of $1,000 to Bishop Muldoon in memory of her son, and the Bishop decided to use this money to make the first beginning of the north-end parish.

From the very beginning two Dominican Sisters from St. Thomas High School had charge of the Catechism classes at St. William on Sunday mornings. These sisters continued this work until the establishment of St. Peter Parish.

◆ **St. William Mission Church.**

As time went on the accommodations at St. William became less adequate. It was the gradual accentuation of this condition that prompted Bishop Muldoon to plan for a new and larger church. Since the area's population had not moved out as far as St. William, a new location, slightly to the south, was sought.

Construction began in June 1921, for St. Peter Parish. The new church was dedicated on February 19, 1922. Around this time the status of St. William changed from being a mission of St. Mary to being a mission of St. Peter. By the 1950's its status had changed again, from a mission to a chapel.

In October 1957, the pastor of St. Peter Parish announced to his parishioners that the parish's northwest section had been separated and that a new parish was being established there. A new parochial school had recently been completed at Rockton and Bell Avenues, and this school was to be on the site of the newly established St. Bernadette Parish.

St. William chapel was not used after the formal organization of St. Bernadette parish on November 17, 1957. St. William was located at 2827 Ridgeway, at the corner of Ridgeway and Greenshaw. After it closed it was renovated to be a residence.

◆ **St. William Mission Church interior.**

Before 1870 the Catholics of Seward were attended from Rockford and Mass was offered in the different homes of the parishioners. Generally the people went to St. James in Rockford, a considerable journey. The trips were usually made on hand-cars over the Chicago & Union Railroad, which had been extended from East Rockford to Freeport in 1853.

The church of St. Thomas of Canterbury, Seward was built in 1870-1871. The church property was donated by Squire Lawrence McDonald, who later became a member of the state legislature. Mr. McDonald not only donated the land, but also collected the necessary funds for the building of the church.

In February 1872, Father Peter Birch (1872-1875) became pastor of St. Mary Church, Pecatonica, and was also given charge of the mission of Seward. Since this time the Seward mission was attended from Pecatonica and the history of both are quite similar. In 1910, however, during the pastorate of Father Hercules E. Ouimet (1909-1918), the mission church was remodeled at a cost of about $5,000.

The Seward mission was abandoned in November, 1954. The last pastor was Father Eugene C. Baumhofer.

◆ **St. Thomas of Canterbury Church.**

THOMSON

◆ **St. Peter Mission Church.**

The St. Peter Mission was organized and the first church built by Father Francis J. Antl, of Savanna, in 1914. The church was dedicated by Bishop Peter J. Muldoon on November 25, 1914. The mission was located about 10 miles north of Fulton.

When St. Peter Mission first opened in 1914, the pastor of St. John the Baptist, Savanna, was given responsibility for operating it. Shortly afterwards it was transferred to the pastor of Immaculate Conception, Fulton. The mission church at Thomson was closed in 1949.

TWIN GROVE

Records show that about 12 Catholic families came to America from Germany in the mid-1860's and settled in Twin Grove, an area about two miles west of the town of Lee. They were men and women of great faith, and in spite of meager means, they succeeded with great difficulty in building a stone church, which was completed in 1867. The stone used was hauled many long miles from the quarry in horse-drawn wagons.

In its early years the Catholics at St. Mary Mission were dependent for religious services upon itinerant missionaries, most of whom where Redemptorists. Typical of early priests was Father Anthony B. Buetter, who served the mission between 1870 and 1876. He attended Sublette two Sundays in the month, gave one Sunday to Perkins Grove and one to Twin Grove. Around 1898 the mission was regularly visited by Father John F. Schmitt, pastor of St. Joseph Parish, Aurora.

When St. James, Lee, became an independent parish in 1906 Twin Grove was attached to it as a regular mission and had Mass on t h e second Sunday of every month. During the pastorate of Father William P. Quinlisk (1912-1924) the mission church had to be abandoned, having been condemned by the State Board of Health as being in a dangerous condition. This closing likely took place in 1914.

◆ **St. Mary Mission Church.**

Vinegar Hill was a distinctly Irish community, located about seven miles north of Galena. The township was named Vinegar Hill after the Irish Vinegar Hill at Enniscorthy, County Wexford, Ireland, by John Furlong, who was the first white settler in the area in 1820.

Most adult men in this community worked in the nearby lead mines. Prior to the establishment of St. Michael Parish, Galena, in 1832, visiting missionaries made Vinegar Hill one of their regular stops. Mass was celebrated in Mr. Furlong's house as early as 1824. In 1828 Father Francis Vincent Badin, a brother of Father Stephen Theodore Badin, the first priest ordained in the United States, stopped here and on October 28 married John Furlong to Ann Carroll.

A church was built in 1843. Records show that in 1847 Father James McAuley was pastor, the first and only resident pastor. Much of the time he lived in Galena. The Dominican Fathers who had a school for boys at Sinsinawa were in charge from 1855 to 1866, at which time the school closed, and Vinegar Hill again was attended from of St. Michael Parish. From 1869 to 1886 it was attended from East Dubuque, then it reverted to St. Michael until 1900. The church was abandoned in 1900 and torn down soon after. All that remains at the site is the Vinegar Hill cemetery.

The original cast bell from St. Mary Mission Church was transported to Holy Trinity Church, Scales Mound, and installed there when the church was renovated in the mid-1930's. This bell is still in use and carries with it the spirit of the Irish community at Vinegar Hill.

◆ **St. Mary Mission Church.**

Appendix

OFFICIALS OF THE ROCKFORD DIOCESE

Vicars General

Monsignor James J. Bennett	1908-1922
Monsignor Clemens Kalvelage	1922-1929
Monsignor Andrew J. Burns	1929-1942; 1943-1957
Monsignor Louis J. Franey	1957-1987
Monsignor Thomas C. Brady	1987-1994; 1994-
Monsignor David D. Kagan	1995-
Monsignor Glenn L. Nelson	2002-

Chancellors

Father Thomas Finn	1908-1920
Father Frederick J. Connor	1921-1929
Father Leo Binz	1929-1932
Father Francis Conron	1932-1943
Father Louis J. Franey	1943-1957
Father Raymond J. Wahl	1957-1969
Father Thomas G. Doran	1969-1986
Father Charles W. McNamee	1986-1999
Monsignor David D. Kagan	1999-2000
Father Glenn L. Nelson	2000-

Officialis

Father Francis Conron	1932-1943
Father Louis J. Franey	1943-1957
Father Raymond J. Wahl	1957-1965
Father J. Francis Moroney	1965-1966
Father David Rock	1966-1969
Monsignor Raymond J. Wahl	1969-1976
Father Thomas G. Doran	1976-1984
Monsignor Raymond J. Wahl	1984-1985
Father David D. Kagan	1985-2005
Father Michael Kurz	2005-

According to the First Diocesan Synod [1916] the office of Judge of Matrimonial Causes was vacant and to be determined. It was the practice of that time that either the Diocesan Bishop or his Vicar General would actually judge the few matrimonial cases presented. With the promulgation of the Code of Canon Law the separate office of Officialis developed more fully so that the Diocese of Rockford's records show that by early in the Episcopate of Bishop Hoban, the then Father Francis Conron was named Officialis and Chancellor. The office of Secretary of the Matrimonial Curia was filled as a rule by the Vice-Chancellor, Father John J. Flanagan from 1910-1921. Father Frederick Connor served as the next Secretary for the period of time he served as Chancellor, 1921-1929, as did Father Leo Binz during his tenure as Chancellor, 1929-1932.

1784: Father John Carroll appointed by the Holy See to be the superior of Catholic missions in America.

1789: Pope Pius VI erects the Diocese of Baltimore and names Father John Carroll its first bishop.

1790: Father John Carroll consecrated in England as first Bishop of Baltimore.

1791: French Sulpicians open first seminary in the United States, St. Mary Seminary, Baltimore; Georgetown Academy begins classes.

1793: Holy See erects the Diocese of Louisiana and the Two Floridas.

1808: Baltimore raised to a Metropolitan See; Dioceses of Bardstown, Kentucky, Boston, New York and Philadelphia created as suffragan sees.

1809: Mother Elizabeth Ann Seton founds first American religious order of women, the Sisters of Charity, at Emmitsburg, Maryland.

1814: Opening of St. Joseph's Orphanage, Philadelphia, the first Catholic asylum for children in the United States.

1822: Bishop John England, first Bishop of Charleston, South Carolina, founds first Catholic newspaper in the United States - *United States Catholic Miscellany*.

1828: First Catholic hospital west of the Mississippi River opened in St. Louis, staffed by Mother Seton's Sisters of Charity.

1829: American bishops gather for the First Provincial Council of Baltimore.

1834: Diocese of Vincennes, Indiana, created by Pope Gregory XVI.

1843: Diocese of Chicago erected from the Diocese of Vincennes, Indiana.

1844: Orestes A. Brownson converts to Catholicism.

1845: Isaac T. Hecker converts to Catholicism; founding of first American conference of the St. Vincent de Paul Society at the Cathedral Parish in St. Louis; beginning of the potato famine in Ireland.

1846: Pope Pius IX elected Supreme Pontiff.

1848: Diplomatic relations established between the Papal States and the United States of America.

1850: Holy See creates three more Ecclesiastical Provinces with archbishops in Cincinnati, New Orleans and New York.

1852: First Plenary Council of Baltimore.

1853: Diocese of Springfield in Illinois erected (first at Quincy, then Alton).

1854: Pope Pius IX defines infallibly the dogma of the Immaculate Conception of the Blessed Virgin Mary.

1857: Opening of American College (major seminary) at Louvain, Belgium.

1858: Founding of Paulist Fathers by Isaac Hecker as first American religious order of men.

1859: Opening of The North American College (major seminary) in Rome, Italy.

1866: Second Plenary Council of Baltimore.

1869: Forty-nine American bishops attend the First Ecumenical Council of the Vatican.

1875: John McClosky, Archbishop of New York, becomes first American Cardinal.

1877: Diocese of Peoria, Illinois erected.

1878: Pope Pius IX dies and Pope Leo XIII elected Supreme Pontiff.

1880: Chicago elevated to the rank of Archdiocese by the Holy See.

1884: Third Plenary Council of Baltimore

1886: James Gibbons, Archbishop of Baltimore, named second American Cardinal.

1887: Diocese of Belleville, Illinois, erected.

1889: The Catholic University of America opens; centennial of the American hierarchy.

1891: Mother Katharine Drexel founds Sisters of the Blessed Sacrament to work among the Negroes and Indians in the United States.

1893: Apostolic Delegation established in Washington, D.C.

1900: Pope Leo XIII proclaims the Holy Year.

1903: Pope Leo XIII dies; Pope Pius X elected Supreme Pontiff.

1904: Founding of the National Catholic Education Association.

1905: The Catholic Church Extension Society founded for the home missions.

1908: June - Catholic Church in the United States removed from the jurisdiction of the Congregation de *Propaganda Fide* as it is no longer considered mission territory by the Holy See.

1908: September 23 - The Diocese of Rockford, Illinois, erected.

1911: Catholic Foreign Mission Society of America (Maryknoll) established.

1914: Pope Pius X dies; Pope Benedict XV elected Supreme Pontiff.

1917: National Catholic War Council established by Catholic Bishops of the United States.

1922: Pope Benedict XV dies and Pope Pius XI elected Supreme Pontiff; the Holy See grants final approval to the creation of the National Catholic Welfare Conference by the Catholic Bishops of the United States.

1924: Archbishop Mundelein made a Cardinal and is the first Cardinal Archbishop of Chicago.

1925: Pope Pius XI proclaims the Holy Year.

1926: 28th International Eucharistic Congress held in Chicago.

1928: Alfred E. Smith, Catholic governor of New York and first Catholic presidential candidate, defeated by Herbert C. Hoover.

1939: Sesquicentennial of the American hierarchy; Pope Pius XI dies and Pope Pius XII elected Supreme Pontiff.

1946: Mother Cabrini canonized by Pope Pius XII, first American citizen, feast is November 13.

1948: Diocese of Joliet, Illinois, erected.

1950: Pope Pius XII defines infallibly the dogma of the Assumption of the Blessed Virgin Mary; he proclaims the Holy Year.

1954: Pope Pius XII canonizes Pope St. Pius X, founder of the Diocese of Rockford.

1955: Death of Mother Katherine Drexel.

1956: Holy See erects three dioceses in United States, total number now 134 dioceses.

1958: Pope Pius XII dies and Pope John XXIII elected Supreme Pontiff; Samuel Cardinal Stritch, Archbishop of Chicago, named Pro-Prefect of the Congregation de *Propaganda Fide*, and he dies on May 27, 1958.

1959: Catholics become the largest religious group in the U.S. Congress with 12 senators and 91 representatives.

1959: Pope John XXIII announces the Second Vatican Council.

1960: John F. Kennedy is first Catholic to be elected President of the United States.

1962: Pope John XXIII opens the Second Ecumenical Council of the Vatican with almost 200 American bishops attending.

1963: Pope John XXIII dies and Pope Paul VI elected Supreme Pontiff; Mother Seton beatified; Bishop John Neumann, C.SS.R., fourth Bishop of Philadelphia beatified; John F. Kennedy assassinated in Dallas, Texas.

1965: Visit of Pope Paul VI to the United Nations; close of the Second Ecumenical Council of the Vatican.

1966: National Conference of Catholic Bishops established and John F. Deardon, Archbishop of Detroit, elected its first president; National Catholic Welfare Conference replaced by the United States Catholic Conference.

1968: Pope Paul VI issues the landmark Encyclical *Humanae Vitae*.

1973: U.S. Supreme Court decision *Roe v. Wade* legalizes abortion in the United States.

1975: Pope Paul VI proclaims the Holy Year; Mother Seton canonized by Pope Paul VI, first American-born saint, feast is January 4.

1977: Bishop John Neumann, C.SS.R., canonized by Pope Paul VI, first American male saint, feast is January 5.

1978: Pope Paul VI dies; Albino Luciani elected Supreme Pontiff and takes the name John Paul I and he dies 33 days later;

1978: October 16, Karol Wojtyla elected Supreme Pontiff and takes the name John Paul II, the first Pole elected Pope and the first non-Italian elected Pope since Adrian VI (1522-1523) and youngest Pope since Pope Pius IX (1846-1878).

1979: Pope John Paul II makes his third pastoral visit outside Italy to Ireland, the United Nations and the United States (September 29-October 7).

1980: Pope John Paul II receives the President of the United States, Jimmy Carter and his entourage at the Vatican; beatification of Kateri Tekawitha, first Native-American beatified, memorial is July 14.

1981: Pope John Paul II visits Guam (USA) and Anchorage, Alaska during his ninth foreign pastoral visit.

1981: May 13, Turkish terrorist Mehmet Ali Agca attempts to assassinate Pope John Paul II at the end of his general audience in St. Peter's Square.

1982: Pope John Paul II meets for the first time the President of the United States, Ronald Reagan and his entourage at the Vatican; November 26, the Pope announces the Holy Year of Redemption from Lent, 1983 to Easter, 1984.

1983: Pope John Paul II promulgates the Revised Code of Canon Law and becomes effective on First Sunday of Advent, 1983; March 25, Pope opens the Holy Year of Redemption which continues until April, 1984.

1984: Full diplomatic relations at the level of apostolic nunciature and embassy established between the Holy See and the United States of America.

1985: First World Youth Day gathering in Rome, March 30-31.

1986: Publication by the Holy See of a revised Manual of Indulgences.

1987: June 6, official visit of the President of the United States, Ronald Reagan to the Vatican; solemn opening of the Marian Year, June 7, 1987 to August 15, 1988; September 10-21, Pope visits the United States and Canada.

1988: July 2, Apostolic Letter *Ecclesia Dei;* September 30, Apostolic Letter *Mulieris Dignitatem;* December 30, Apostolic Exhortation *Christifideles Laici;* Father Junipero Serra beatified, memorial July 1.

1989: March 8-11, Pope and members of Roman Curia meet with the metropolitan archbishops of the United States of America on the theme: "Evangelization in the Context of the Culture and Society of the United States with particular emphasis on the Role of the Bishop as Teacher of the Faith;" May 27, Pope receives the President of the United States, George H.W. Bush and his entourage.

1991: Encyclical *Centesimus Annus* commemorating 100 years of Papal social teaching.

1992: Pope John Paul II institutes World Day for the Sick to be celebrated annually on February 11; November 16, Apostolic Constitution *Fidei Depositum* is made public and the *Catechism of the Catholic Church* is presented in the official French edition.

1993: Encyclical *Veritatis Splendor* is presented; World Youth Day is celebrated in Denver and Pope John Paul II visits; December 26, opening of the International Year of the Family of the Catholic Church.

1994: Pope John Paul II receives the President of the United States of America, William J. Clinton and his entourage; publication of Pope John Paul II's book *Crossing the Threshold of Hope* in 31 languages and in 35 countries; Apostolic Letter *Tertio Millennio Adveniente* on the beginning of the third millennium and preparation for the Jubilee of the Year 2000.

1995: Encyclical *Evangelium Vitae - The Gospel of Life;* July 17, the theme for the Jubilee 2000 announced: "Jesus Christ - The Same Yesterday, Today, Always"; Father Damien of Molokai beatified, memorial is May 10; October, Pope John Paul II visits the United States.

1996: November 1, 50th Anniversary of Pope John Paul II's ordination to the priesthood.

1997: Debut of the official Vatican website; Pope John Paul II proclaims St. Therese of Lisieux a Doctor of the Church; Pope inaugurates the Synod for America at the Vatican.

1998: Pope John Paul II visits Cuba.

1999: Pope John Paul II visits St. Louis, Missouri; Pope dispenses with the five-year waiting period and gives permission to start the cause of beatification for Mother Teresa of Calcutta; a new Manual of Indulgences published; December 24, Pope John Paul II opens the Holy Door at St. Peter Basilica, beginning the Jubilee Year of 2000.

2000: Pope John Paul II makes a pilgrimage to the Holy Land; presentation of the third secret of Fatima; proclamation of St. Thomas More the patron of statesmen and politicians; canonization of Mother Katherine Drexel, feast is March 3; beatification of Abbot Columba Marmion.

2001: January 6, conclusion of the Jubilee Year 2000 and publication of the Apostolic Letter *Novo Millennio Ineunte*; Pope John Paul II invites all Catholics to fast on December 14 in response to the September 11 terrorist attacks.

2002: Third edition of the Roman Missal presented; Pope John Paul II receives in audience the President of the United States, George W. Bush and his entourage; Apostolic Letter on the Rosary and the Pope adds the new Luminous Mysteries, declares October, 2002 to October 2003, the Year of the Rosary.

2003: Release of "Doctrinal Note on the Participation of Catholics in Political Life"; March 5, Cardinal Pio Laghi, the Pope's special envoy, meets with President George W. Bush to deliver a message from the Pope regarding the impending war with Iraq; the Encyclical *Ecclesia de Eucharistia* is published; October 16, the Silver Anniversary of the election of Pope John Paul II as Supreme Pontiff on October 16, 1978.

2005: April 2, 2005, Pope John Paul II dies on the Vigil of Divine Mercy, a feast dear to him and the entire Roman Catholic Church;
April 8, 2005, Joseph Cardinal Ratzinger, Dean of the College of Cardinals, celebrates the Funeral Mass for Pope John Paul II, who was buried in the Crypt of the Popes in the Basilica of Saint Peter; April 19, 2005, Joseph Cardinal Ratzinger is elected the 264th successor to St. Peter and takes to himself the name Benedict XVI;

Benedict XVI participates in World Youth Day in Germany during August;

Pope Benedict XVI issues the first encyclical of his pontificate, *Deus Caritas Est*.

2006: Pope Benedict XVI makes a pastoral visit to Turkey to seek to improve relations with the Orthodox and Muslims.

APPENDIX C

BISHOPS IN THE STATE OF ILLINOIS
AT THE TIME OF EACH BISHOP OF THE ROCKFORD DIOCESE

The Most Reverend Peter James Muldoon, D.D.
1908 - 1927

Chicago - The Most Reverend James E. Quigley - 1903-1915
- His Eminence, George Cardinal Mundelein - 1916-1939

Springfield - The Most Reverend James Ryan, D.D. - 1888-1923
- The Most Reverend James Griffin, D.D. - 1924-1948

Peoria - The Most Reverend John L. Spalding, D.D. - 1877-1908
- The Most Reverend Edmund M. Dunne, D.D. - 1909-1929

Belleville - The Most Reverend John Janssen, D.D. - 1888-1913
- The Most Reverend Henry J. Althoff, D.D. - 1914-1947

The Most Reverend Edward Francis Hoban, D.D.
1928 - 1942

Chicago - His Eminence, George Cardinal Mundelein - 1916-1939
- His Eminence, Samuel Cardinal Stritch - 1940-1958

Springfield - The Most Reverend James Griffin, D.D. - 1924-1948

Peoria - The Most Reverend Edmund M. Dunne, D.D. - 1909-1929
- The Most Reverend Joseph H. Schlarmann, D.D. - 1930-1951

Belleville - The Most Reverend Henry J. Althoff, D.D. - 1914-1947

The Most Reverend John Joseph Boylan, D.D.
1943 - 1953

Chicago - His Eminence, Samuel Cardinal Stritch - 1940-1958

Springfield - The Most Reverend James Griffin, D.D. - 1924-1948
- The Most Reverend William O'Connor, D.D. - 1948-1975

Peoria - The Most Reverend Joseph H. Schlarmann, D.D. - 1930-1951
- The Most Reverend William E. Cousins, D.D. - 1952-1958

Belleville - The Most Reverend Henry J. Althoff, D.D. - 1914-1947
- The Most Reverend Albert R. Zuroweste, D.D. - 1948-1976

Joliet - The Most Reverend Martin D. McNamara, D.D. - 1949-1966

The Most Reverend Raymond Peter Hillinger, D.D.
1954 - 1956

Chicago - His Eminence, Samuel Cardinal Stritch - 1940-1958

Springfield - The Most Reverend William O'Connor - 1948-1975

Peoria - The Most Reverend William E. Cousins, D.D. - 1952-1958

Belleville - The Most Reverend Albert R. Zuroweste, D.D. - 1948-1976

Joliet - The Most Reverend Martin D. McNamara, D.D. - 1949-1966

The Right Reverend Donald Martin Carroll, D.D.
June 27, 1956 to September 25, 1956

The Most Reverend Loras Thomas Lane, D.D.
1956 - 1968

Chicago - His Eminence, Samuel Cardinal Stritch - 1940-1958
- His Eminence, Albert Cardinal Meyer - 1959-1965
- His Eminence, John Cardinal Cody - 1965-1982

Springfield - The Most Reverend William O'Connor, D.D. - 1948-1975

Peoria - The Most Reverend William E. Cousins, D.D. - 1952-1958
- The Most Reverend John B. Franz, D.D. - 1959-1970

Belleville - The Most Reverend Albert R. Zuroweste, D.D. - 1948-1976

Joliet - The Most Reverend Martin D. McNamara, D.D. - 1949-1966
- The Most Reverend Romeo Blanchette, D.D. - 1966-1979

The Most Reverend Arthur Joseph O'Neill, D.D.
1968 - 1994

Chicago - His Eminence, John Cardinal Cody - 1965-1982
- His Eminence, Joseph Cardinal Bernardin - 1982-1996

Springfield - The Most Reverend William O'Connor, D.D. - 1948-1975
- The Most Reverend Joseph McNicholas, D.D. - 1975-1983
- The Most Reverend Daniel Ryan, D.D. - 1983-1999

Peoria - The Most Reverend Joseph B. Franz, D.D. - 1959-1970
- The Most Reverend Edward W. O'Rourke, D.D. - 1971-1990
- The Most Reverend John J. Myers, D.D. - 1990-2001

Belleville - The Most Reverend Albert R. Zuroweste, D.D. - 1948-1976
- The Most Reverend William M. Cosgrove, D.D. - 1976-1981
- The Most Reverend John N. Wurm, D.D. - 1981-1984
- The Most Reverend James P. Keleher, D.D. - 1984-1993
- The Most Reverend Wilton D. Gregory, D.D. - 1994-2005

Joliet - The Most Reverend Romeo Blanchette, D.D. - 1966-1979
- The Most Reverend Joseph L. Imesch, D.D. - 1979-2006

The Most Reverend Thomas George Doran, D.D.
1994 - present

Chicago - His Eminence, Joseph Cardinal Bernardin - 1982-1996
- His Eminence, Francis Cardinal George, OMI - 1997-present

Springfield - The Most Reverend Daniel Ryan, D.D. - 1983-1999
- The Most Reverend George J. Lucas, D.D. - 1999-present

Peoria - The Most Reverend John J. Myers, D.D. - 1990-2001
- The Reverend Daniel R. Jenky, C.S.C., D.D. - 2002-present

Belleville - The Most Reverend Wilton D. Gregory, D.D. - 1994-2005
- The Most Reverend Edward K. Braxton, D.D. - 2005-present

Joliet - The Most Reverend Joseph L. Imesch, D.D. - 1979-2006
- The Most Reverend J. Peter Sartain, D.D. - 2006-present